THE UPPER TANANA DENE

THE UPPER TANANA DENE

PEOPLE OF THIS LAND

William E. Simeone

UNIVERSITY OF ALASKA PRESS
Fairbanks

Published by University of Alaska Press
An imprint of University Press of Colorado
1624 Market Street, Suite 226
PMB 39883
Denver, Colorado 80202-1559

 The University Press of Colorado is a proud member of
Association of University Presses.

The University Press of Colorado is a cooperative publishing enterprise supported, in part, by Adams
State University, Colorado State University, Fort Lewis College, Metropolitan State University of Denver,
University of Alaska Fairbanks, University of Colorado, University of Denver, University of Northern
Colorado, University of Wyoming, Utah State University, and Western Colorado University.

∞ This paper meets the requirements of the ANSI/NISO Z39.48-1992 (Permanence of Paper).

ISBN: 978-1-64642-490-0 (hardcover)
ISBN: 978-1-64642-333-0 (paperback)
ISBN: 978-1-64642-334-7 (ebook)
https://doi.org/10.5876/9781646423347

Library of Congress Cataloging-in-Publication Data

Names: Simeone, William E., author.
Title: The upper Tanana Dene : people of this land / William Simeone.
Other titles: People of this land
Description: Fairbanks : University of Alaska Press, [2022] | Some interviews recorded
  and translated by linguist Olga Lovick with assistance from Avis and Roy Sam, Caleb
  Brucks, and Rosa Brewer. | Includes bibliographical references and index.
Identifiers: LCCN 2022015093 (print) | LCCN 2022015094 (ebook) | ISBN 9781646424900
  (hardcover) | ISBN 9781646423330 (paperback) | ISBN 9781646423347 (ebook)
Subjects: LCSH: Tanana Indians—Alaska—Tanana River Valley—Social life and customs. | Tanana
  Indians—Alaska—Tanacross Region—Social life and customs. | Tanana Indians—Alaska—Tanacross
  Region—Interviews. | Indian elders (Indigenous leaders)—Alaska—Tanacross Region—Interviews.
  | Tanana River Valley (Alaska)—Social life and customs. | Tanana River Valley (Alaska)—History. |
  Tanacross Region (Alaska)—Social life and customs. | Tanacross Region (Alaska)—History.
Classification: LCC E99.T187 S56 2022 (print) | LCC E99.T187 (ebook) | DDC 979.8004/972—dc23/eng/20220512
LC record available at https://lccn.loc.gov/2022015093
LC ebook record available at https://lccn.loc.gov/2022015094

Cover photograph of Chief Healy from the Jeany Healy collection UAF-2000-181-23.

*Royalties from this book will be paid to the Tanana Chiefs Conference in the name of Oscar and
Martha Isaac, Kenneth and Ellen Thomas, Julius and Rica Paul, Andrew and Maggie Isaac,
Annie Denny, Silas Solomon, Titus and Jessie David, and Walter and Lilly Northway.*

We don't have to give up our culture. We don't have to act like we a different person. No. High school, we gotta keep our culture. Our culture is more than everything and for the children and the future. Our kids goin' learn.
—Ellen Demit

CONTENTS

PREFACE

It has been fifty years since I first went to Tanacross. In that time, I have developed relationships that have affected every aspect of my life. Both of my daughters were partially raised in the village, and I went through a divorce while living in Tanacross and doing research for my PhD. I have written a couple of books and several articles on the people and their history, so the village has, in many respects, helped me in my career as an anthropologist. Finally, I have experienced the loss of many dear, dear friends. This book is an attempt to give something back to those who have been a large part of my life.

I come from a family of Italian immigrants on my father's side; on my mother's side were Anglos from Wales and Scandinavia. I grew up in a small Midwestern town knowing nothing about Native Americans except what I saw in the movies. My favorite was *Chief Crazy Horse* starring Victor Mature, another Italian immigrant. In 1968, my then-wife Carolyn and I drove to Alaska and, like so many others, were captivated by the land. The following year we joined VISTA and served in the Yup'ik village of St. Michael. In 1971, as a conscientious objector to the war in Vietnam, I was assigned to Tanacross to perform alternative service as a lay worker for the Episcopal Church. I served eighteen months before moving to Fairbanks to attend the University of Alaska. In 1975, we returned to the village and built a house, where we lived for several years before moving to Anchorage. While living in Anchorage, we made frequent trips back to the village for visits that lasted from several days to several months. In 1985, I returned to the village and stayed for two years while conducting research for my PhD.

For this book I have taken my lead from my dear friend Oscar Isaac of Tanacross. Just like his ancestors before him, Oscar lived life from the land, and he thought it important to know about the past. He did not want to go back to the old times, because life was hard and there were hard times. Yet he said people should know how the elders "survived in the world." Oscar thought it was especially important that young people know how to conduct themselves as human beings. Reflecting on the problems that have beset Native people over the last 200 years, Oscar thought "old-time people" were better; there were not as many bad people as there now. "What people today need to learn is how to be a good person, how to love, be kind and friendly." Oscar also wanted to emphasize "that old people [traditional Dene] knew about God."

There is a risk that the elders' knowledge will be lost. In interviews, they often expressed concern that many young Dene are living like White people and ignoring the traditions that made the elders disciplined and strong enough to withstand the rigors of living on the land. The old life was taxing and made demands on the body and soul. The struggle to survive and achieve some security placed a premium on knowledge, endurance, and constant effort. Today, modern conveniences have made life easier, but elders firmly believe their knowledge is vital to future generations if they are to survive.

ACKNOWLEDGMENTS

I am especially pleased to thank the many individuals who contributed to this volume and encouraged me over the years. First and foremost, my wife Colleen Tyrrell has been a pillar of support and constructive critic. Second are my parents, William and Jane Simeone. Together they provided an unbeatable combination of adventurism and conservatism that has propelled me through life. My father, a retired English professor, has acted as editor. Third are Martha and Oscar Isaac. Over the years they, like my parents, provided me with love and kindness that enabled me to thrive.

I also want to especially thank the people of Tanacross and the elders. These include Julius and Rica Paul, Bella Paul, Herbert Paul, Franklin and Marylou Paul, Kenneth and Ellen Thomas, Andrew and Maggie Isaac, Silas Solomon, Charlie James, Gaither and Bee Paul, David Paul, Gene Henry, Larry Jonathan, Alfred and Mildred Jonathan, Emma and Stephen Northway, Brittan and Dolly Johnathan, Rosalyn Isaac, Jerry Isaac, Lee Isaac, Marian Isaac, Howard Isaac, Edward Isaac, Jacob Isaac, Arlene Isaac, Cora Isaac, Sharon Henry, Salina and Joe Joseph, Laura Sanford, Isabel and Arthur John, Ellen Demit, Agnes Abraham, Annie and Tom Denny, Alice and Leonard Brean, Mary and Robert Charlie, Roy and Bob Jonathan, Betty and Roy Denny, and Kathy McClellan. I also want to acknowledge Tetlin elders Titus and Jessie David, Roy and Cora David, Shirley Jimerson, and Charlie David Sr. From Northway are Walter and Lilly Northway, Annie and Frank Sam, and Roy and Avis Sam. Roy and Avis, along with Sherry Demit-Barnes, Darlene Northway, and Rosa Lee Brewer collaborated with the linguist Olga Lovick (Sam, Demit-Barnes, and Northway 2021) to produce several narratives in this book. Two other contributors from Northway are Mary Tyone and Ada Gallen. I owe a special thanks to Olga for allowing me to use some of her translations in the book, and for answering my questions.

Others who contributed to this project are the two reviewers, Michael Koskey and Bill Schneider, whose comments were invaluable. Terry Haynes provided many of the photographs, and I want to express my appreciation for his generosity and friendship. Many thanks also go to Ken Pratt and Matt O'Leary of the Bureau of Indian Affairs, ANCSA office. Besides providing funding in support of the project, Ken has provided friendship and wonderful discussions about anthropology and life in general. Matt has always been there when I needed a map. I appreciate his unstinting generosity of time and skill. I also want to thank Bob Sattler of the Tanana Chiefs Conference for all his help and goodwill. Last, I must express my appreciation for the anthropologists who came before me: Robert McKennan, Frederica de Laguna, Catharine McClellan, Marie-Françoise Guédon, Ramon Vitt, Roger Pitts, and Norm Easton. Finally, I want to acknowledge three people who have been important in my development as an anthropologist: Jim VanStone, Harvey Feit, and Jim Kari.

(*opposite*) Photo-montage by Hal Gage.

ELDERS WHO CONTRIBUTED TO THIS BOOK

These are the elders who contributed directly to this book either in conversation, interview, or publication. In traditional culture it is appropriate to provide some background information about a person, so I have done so where possible.

Oscar Isaac was born in 1914, and his wife Martha in 1918. Oscar's father was Walter Isaac, son of the famous Chief Isaac, and his mother was Maggie Demit from Ketchumstuk. Martha Isaac's parents were Joe Joseph, originally from the village of Salchaket, and Salina Paul, whose father Old Paul was from the Goodpaster area. Martha and Oscar had several children, including Jerry, a noted leader who served as president of the Tanana Chiefs Conference and Alaska-area vice president for the National Congress of American Indians. While in college, Jerry wrote an article about the potlatch, which, in lightly edited form, is included in this book.

Oscar had several siblings, including Jessie, who was born in 1909 at Ketchumstuk and married Titus David of Tetlin. Titus, whose father was Chief David, was born in Tetlin the same year as Jessie. Their son Roy married Cora David, who was born in 1935 to Alfred and Lucy Adam and collaborated with Olga Lovick to produce *Teedlay t'inn naholndak niign: Stories of the Tetlin People*, some of which are included in this book. Another of Oscar's sisters married Gene Henry, from the upper Ahtna village of *Nataełde*, or Batzulnetas. Gene became my good friend and blossomed into a font

Figure 0.1. Martha and Oscar Isaac, 1987. Photo by William E. Simeone.

of knowledge, which he wanted to convey to future generations.

Julius Paul was born in 1911 and his brother David in 1887. Both were born in Mansfield to Old Paul and Julia, who herself was born either at Dihthâad or Mansfield in 1861. The Pauls were an influential family tightly connected to the Episcopal Church. David became the first Dene in Alaska to be ordained a deacon. In 1957 the Reverend David Paul published, in

Figure 0.2. Jessie David was born in 1909 to Maggie Demit and Walter Isaac of Ketchumstuk. Jessie is holding a tool for fleshing skins called *nahttäl* in the Upper Tanana language. Photo by Terry Haynes.

Figure 0.3. Titus David was born in 1908. His father was Chief David. Photo by Terry Haynes.

Figure 0.4. Cora David and her husband Roy.

Figure 0.5. Gene Henry. Photo by Terry Haynes.

Figure 0.6. Alfred and Lucy Adams. Alfred Adams was born in 1895 to Anna and Charlie Adams. Lucy was born in 1902 to Helen and Chief Luke. Photo by Terry Haynes.

Figure 0.7. Julius Paul, 1987. Photo by William E. Simeone.

Figure 0.9. The Paul family at Mansfield, circa 1930. From left to right: Salina, Ellen, Jessie, Dora, Laura, Martha, Old Paul, Julia, Silas, David, Bailey, and Gaither. Photo by E. A. McIntosh, William E. Simeone photo collection.

Figure 0.8. David Paul, circa 1930. Jeany Healy collection UAF-2000-181-186.

Figure 0.10. Andrew Isaac, 1980. Photo by Terry Haynes.

Figure 0.11. Maggie Isaac. Photo by Terry Haynes.

collaboration with Audrey Loftus, *According to Papa*, a group of stories he heard from his father, Old Paul, and his great-uncle. David's book was a companion to another collection of stories, *According to Mama*, told by Helen David Charlie, who was born on the Goodpaster River in the 1850s.

In the 1970s Maggie and Andrew Isaac lived in Dot Lake. Maggie, a distinguished bead artist, was born in 1907 at *Dechenh Ghajenįį'ah Denh*, or Long Cabin, to Old Walter and Bessie. Andrew was born in *Saages Cheeg*, or Ketchumstuk, in 1898 to Titus and Annie Isaac. Titus was a son of Chief Isaac. Andrew became a leading figure in the land claims movement that eventually led to the Alaska Native Claims Settlement Act (ANCSA) of 1971. He was also the first traditional chief of the Doyon region. In 1987 Yvonne Yarber and Curt Madison produced a series of publications about prominent Dene elders, including Andrew Isaac and Walter Northway. At the time of that interview Walter was a prominent leader among upper Tanana Dene. His father was Taaiy Ta', who later became known as Northway, after the steamboat captain who took a boat up the Chisana

River, and his mother was named Anna. Walter married Lilly John from Scottie Creek.

Two of Andrew Isaac's sisters were Laura Sanford and Isabel John. Laura was born in 1928 in Mansfield and was married to Walter Sanford of Chistochina. Laura made a significant contribution to the *Tanacross Learners' Dictionary* and the *Tanacross Phrase and Conversation Lessons*. Isabel was born in 1922 at Ketchumstuk, and she married Arthur John, who was from Tetlin. Both Laura and Isabel grew up living the hunting life.

Chief Isaac had two nephews, Big Frank and Old Paul, who followed him up the Tanana River. Big Frank married Jessie, the daughter of Chief John of Mentasta, and Old Paul married Julia, who was the sister of Sam Thomas, Jennie Luke, and Peter Thomas. Sam Thomas, who, like Chief Isaac, figures prominently in Tanacross history, was born in 1859 at Mansfield, or *Dihthâad*, and was a highly regarded spokesperson. He was also Annie Denny's father. His sister "Grandma Jennie," as she came to be known, was an expert bead sewer who married Henry Luke. A noted orator and hunter, Peter Thomas married Sarah, who was from the upper Ahtna

Figure 0.12. Lilly Northway, 1980. Photo by Terry Haynes.

Figure 0.13. Walter Northway, 1980. Photo by Terry Haynes.

Figure 0.14. Laura Sanford, 1980. Photo by Terry Haynes.

Figure 0.15. Isabel John at Tanacross potlatch, 1972. Photo by William E. Simeone.

Figure 0.16. Annie and Tom Denny Sr., 1977. Photo by Terry Haynes.

Figure 0.17. Ellen and Kenny Thomas Sr., 1971. Photo by William E. Simeone.

Figure 0.18. Steven Northway, 1980. Photo by Terry Haynes.

village of Batzulnetas, and they had a son named Kenneth who married Ellen, Martha Isaac's sister. Ellen worked for the Bureau of Indian Affairs and was noted for her beadwork but more importantly for her kindness and intuition. Kenny was a noted singer and dance leader, and the long-time crew chief of the Tanacross firefighters. Kenny and the anthropologist Craig Mishler collaborated on a book titled *Crow Is My Boss* in which Kenny recounts many details about his life and offers important insights into the twentieth-century transitions occurring in the upper Tanana region.

Ellen and Kenny had several children, including Mildred, who, in 1971, was the village health aide. She lived with Alfred Jonathan in a small two-room cabin that was a meeting place for young men who came to drink tea and gossip. (Mildred and Alfred became lifelong friends of mine, as did Alfred's brothers Larry and Brittan.) Their mother was Emma, who married John Jonathan. After John died, Emma married Steven Northway. Both Emma and Steven were noted craftspeople, and Steven was renowned as a composer and dance leader. He is the father of Avis Sam.

Two other Tanacross elders I must mention are Silas Solomon and Charlie James. Silas was born in 1904 at Saages Cheeg. His father was Solomon and his mother Annie James, who was the sister of Charlie James as well as sister of Kenneth Thomas's mother Sarah. Charlie James was born at Nataełde on the upper Copper River in about 1895 and married Liza Saul from Ketchumstuk. Both Silas and Charlie had considerable knowledge of upper Tanana history and culture.

Figure 0.19. Emma Jonathan, 1987. Photo by William E. Simeone.

Figure 0.20. Silas Solomon, 1987. Photo by William E. Simeone.

Figure 0.21. Charlie James, 1980. Photo by Terry Haynes.

Silas's daughter Irene Arnold Solomon has been instrumental in documenting the Tanacross language and, in conjunction with the Alaska Native Language Center and the Yukon Native Language Centre, produced *Tanacross Athabaskan Language Lessons* and *Dihthâad Xt'een Iin Aandĕeg'—The Mansfield People's Language: Tanacross Athabascan Phrases and Conversations.* She also contributed to the *Tanacross Learners' Dictionary.*

Margaret and Paul Kirsteatter made a substantial contribution to this book. Margaret's parents were Gus Jacob and Agnes Sam. Gus, also known as Jacob Hunter, was from Ketchumstuk, and, according to some people, a noted doctor. According to Lee Saylor, Gus was brother to Belle Abraham, David Solomon, Silas Solomon's father, and Charlie Demit. Agnes was from Healy Lake, her mother was Belle Sam whose second husband was Chief Sam. Paul Kirsteatter was a non-Native who came to

Figure 0.22. Jacob Hunter (a.k.a. Gus Jacob) and his wife Agnes at St. Timothy's Mission in 1913. Photo by C. Betticher, courtesy Episcopal Church Archives, Austin, Texas.

Figure 0.23. Ellen Demit, 1980. Photo by Terry Haynes.

Alaska during World War II and settled in Healy Lake. Paul's knowledge of Dene culture and history was extensive, and he corresponded with the anthropologist Robert McKennan to produce the narrative found in appendix A.

One other elder with connections to Healy Lake was Ellen Demit. Born in Chena in 1913, Ellen was adopted by Selene and Old Blind Jimmy of Healy Lake after her parents died. Ellen was a highly respected elder who made a substantial contribution to the documentation of Dene culture in the upper Tanana region. She worked closely with the anthropologist Don Callaway and Connie Miller-Friend to produce *Mendees Cheeg Naltsiin Keyh': An Oral History of the People of Healy Lake Village* (2001). A series of Ellen's narratives forms the centerpiece of this collection, supplemented by the accounts of other village residents, and provide detailed information not previously recorded about the history of Healy Lake.

Figure 0.24. Salina, Blind Jimmy, and Ellen Demit. Jeany Healy collection UAF-2000-181-9.

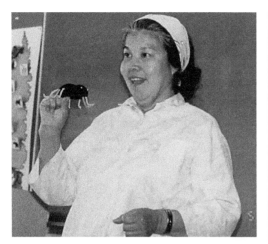

Figure 0.25. Avis Sam. Photo courtesy of Olga Lovick

The following elders worked with Olga Lovick to produce some of the narratives in this book, telling stories and helping to translate. I want to reiterate my appreciation for all their work. Their narratives and insights have made a substantial contribution to our knowledge of Dene history and culture.

Avis Sam was born in 1931 in the Ladue Hills to Steven and Edna Mark Northway. While she was growing up, her family followed a traditional lifestyle and moved around from place to place, harvesting the land's resources. Avis became interested in her language and went to Yukon College to become a language teacher. She graduated from Yukon College in 1990. Avis is deeply committed to passing on the traditional culture as well as the language.

Sherry Demit-Barnes was born 1935 in the old Northway village to Joe and Laura Northway Demit. Sherry said her father taught them not only subsistence skills but also traditional values.

Darlene Northway was born 1942 to Maggie Ann Northway and Andrew Bell John. Her dad passed away when she was only two years old, so she only knew him from stories; she had been his favorite and always wished she'd had more time with him. Darlene was married to Teddy Northway Sr. Maintaining the language

Figure 0.26. Darlene Northway. Photo courtesy of Olga Lovick

and culture was important to Darlene throughout her life. She worked for many years at the Tetlin National Wildlife Refuge and helped develop its representation of Northway culture.

Roy Sam, who worked on the translations with Olga, was born in old Northway village in 1933 to Frank Sam and Annie Sam. His grandfather was Chief Sam, who collaborated with the anthropologist Robert McKennan. Roy grew up in Northway and lived there all his life. He married Avis in 1956.

Rosa Lee Brewer also helped Olga with translations. She was born in 1948 in Northway to Peter and Mary Charlie. In the 1970s, Rosa took a class at the University of Alaska Fairbanks with the Reverend Paul Malinowski, where she learned to write her language. She has been working with the language ever since, translating stories and songs and writing them down. Along with her passion for translating hymns and kids' songs into her language, she also knows many traditional songs.

SOURCES OF WRITTEN INFORMATION

Interviews come from notes and recordings I made in the 1980s and interviews conducted in the 1960s by anthropologists Frederica de Laguna, Catharine McClellan, and Marie-Françoise Guédon. Additional interviews come from the translations of stories by elders from Tetlin and Northway recorded by linguist Olga Lovick with assistance from Avis and Roy Sam, Caleb Brucks, and Rosa Brewer. All spellings of Dene words follow the standard established by the Alaska Native Language Center at the University of Alaska Fairbanks. These translations are unique and add considerably to the story of Upper Tanana Dene culture and history. Additional sources of information include interviews conducted by Don Callaway and Connie Miller-Friend with people from Healy Lake, interviews with Andrew Isaac and Walter Northway conducted by Yvonne Yarber and Curt Madison, and interviews by Goldschmidt and Haas conducted in the 1940s. I collected contextual information from unpublished archival sources in the Alaska and Polar Regions Collections and Archives at the Rasmuson Library, University of Alaska Fairbanks: the Robert McKennan collection, the Mertie Baggen collection, and the John Hajdukovich collection. Published sources include regional histories and articles from the *Alaskan Churchman*, a periodical published by the Episcopal Church, and the newspaper *Tundra Times*.

https://doi.org/10.5876/9781646423347.c000c

THE UPPER TANANA DENE

Photo-montage by Hal Gage.

INTRODUCTION

Figure I.1. David Paul, Titus Isaac, Sam Abraham, and Peter Thomas, circa July 4, 1931, Tanacross. David Paul was married to Titus's daughter, Ena. Titus was married to Annie Esau. Peter Thomas was married to Sarah from Mentasta and was Kenneth Thomas Sr.'s father. Photo by E. A. McIntosh, William E. Simeone photo collection.

This book is about Northern Dene who live in the upper Tanana region of east-central Alaska. It is based largely on interviews with Dene elders born in the late nineteenth and early twentieth centuries. It is a link to their experiences, their lives, and their understanding of the world. It is also meant to be a primary source document for anyone trying to understand Dene heritage in the region, the significance of places, resources, and the cultural values that sustained a way of life.[1] Together, the elders' narratives reveal a unique and compelling perspective, offering a fascinating commentary on a way of life that is gone forever and their approach to continuity and change over the past 100 years. Through their stories, the elders unveil a sweep of history and events but also a detailed portrait of the people themselves.

---

1   I have to thank Bill Schneider for these words.

https://doi.org/10.5876/9781646423347.c000d

ARCHAEOLOGY

Archaeological evidence indicates people have occupied the Tanana River valley for at least 14,000 years (Potter, Holmes, and Yesner 2013; Smith 2022). Between 1,900 and 1,250 years ago, Mount Churchill, a volcano in the St. Elias Range on the border of Alaska and Yukon Territory, erupted, which may have been the impetus for the migration of the Dene ancestors of the Navajo and Apachean peoples into the American Southwest (Ives 2003). Since the last eruption about 1,200 years ago, the region's environment has been relatively stable. Archaeologists consider material dating to this time as Athabascan, representing the material culture of contemporary Dene ancestors.

LANGUAGE AND IDENTITY

Two languages, with several dialects, are spoken in the upper Tanana region: Upper Tanana (UT), spoken in the communities of Scottie Creek, Northway, and Tetlin, and Tanacross (T), spoken in Tanacross, Dot Lake, and Healy Lake. Anthropologists named the people Upper Tanana based on where they lived and their distinct Athabascan language. Upper Tanana Dene refer to themselves collectively as *dineh shyuh* (UT) or *dendeey shuh lin* (T). More specifically they are a "people of a certain place." For example, in the Tanacross language people from Ketchumstuk are called *Yaadóg Xt'een iin* or "inland area people," while those from Mansfield or Dihthâad are called *Dihthâad Xt'een iin*. Upper Tanana speakers refer collectively to people from Tanacross, Salcha, Chena, and Minto as *Ndaa'a tu' t'iinn*, indicating they come from downriver. Nabesna people are *Naabmiah niign ut'iin*, while people from the upper Chisana River are called *Ddhäł to t'iin*, or "among the mountains people." People from Northway are referred to as *K'ehtthîign ut'iin*, after their fish camp at K'ehtthiign, or "lake outlet," and Tetlin people are *Teedlay ut'iin*.

While the residents of contemporary villages have come to identify with their community, it is hard to talk about each community as a discrete or distinctive unit. Analysis of early census data (see appendix D) illustrates Robert McKennan's (1969) point that the upper Tanana bands formed interlocking social units rather than discrete entities. For example, the census shows the close connection between Upper Tanana, Tanacross, and Upper Ahtna. It also shows the movement between bands precipitated by the fur trade, mining development, and disease.

ENVIRONMENT AND CULTURE

The valley of the upper Tanana River is bounded on the south by the glaciated peaks of the Wrangell Mountains, the source of the Chisana and Nabesna Rivers. The northern periphery is formed by the vast rolling expanse of the Yukon-Tanana uplands that deliver the headwaters of the Fortymile and Ladue Rivers (see figure I.2). The region is bisected by the Tanana River, which emerges from the confluence of the Chisana and Nabesna Rivers. From there, the Tanana flows in a northwesterly direction fed by a series of smaller creeks and rivers, including Scottie, Gardiner, Mansfield, George, and Sand Creeks and the Tetlin, Tok, Robertson, Healy, and Johnson Rivers. Small lakes and wetlands are sprinkled across the flat plain of the upper Tanana valley and offer excellent habitat for wildlife and migratory birds. Except in the higher elevations of alpine tundra, the region is covered by forest dominated by white spruce and birch. In areas of permafrost, shallow rooted species such as black spruce prevail and stands of willow are common near streams. Plant life utilized by Dene include mosses, sedges, blueberries, bearberries, cranberries, rose hips, Labrador tea, wild potato or carrot, and wild celery.

The Fortymile, Nelchina, and Chisana caribou herds pass through the region on their annual migrations and were once the most

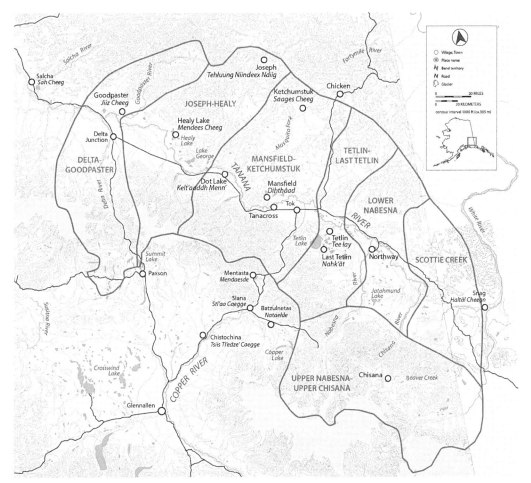

Figure I.2. The upper Tanana region showing historical and contemporary communities and the boundaries of traditional band territories. See appendix B for a description of band territories and village histories. Map by Matt O'Leary, adapted from McKennan (1981: 564).

important single source of food and material for clothing and tools. Dene elders say moose were scarce in the nineteenth century. Since then, the population has increased, and today moose are a major source of food in all upper Tanana communities. Dall sheep inhabit the higher elevations and were once extensively hunted for meat and their skins for clothing. Other animals include black and brown bears, snowshoe hare, beaver, muskrat, fox, lynx, wolf, and wolverine. Currently, no salmon runs reach the upper Tanana. Of major importance are various species of whitefish, northern pike, burbot, and grayling.

Dene life and culture are fundamentally tied to the environment, and most if not all the varied species of plants, animals, and fish have been integrated into upper Tanana culture and retain a social and spiritual relationship to the people. Dene people conceive of the world as a multidimensional space consisting of people, animals, plants, earth, water, and air. It is a landscape lived in and lived with. Dene elders born at the beginning of the twentieth century existed in and experienced a world very different from the one we live in today. Theirs was a world without capitalism or Christianity, towns, roads, grocery stores, electricity, running water, or television—a seemingly empty land. Everyone born before World War II was born away from hospitals, stores, and the eyes of White people. They all had considerable knowledge of country life.

In this world Dene created a life that embraced the stillness and the presence of powerful animals who, unlike humans, were contained unto themselves, had no need of anything outside of themselves, who could be seen and unseen, and could destroy humans. Humans knew animals were like them but more powerful because they were everything unto themselves. To survive, humans had to know animals, to feel them, to intuit them and absorb the animals' enduring traits of strength, speed, and agility.

Success depended on knowing what was įįjih (UT) or injih (T). Often translated as that which is forbidden or taboo, injih guided every detail of life, including hunting, the potlatch, washing one's face, and the use of language (Mishler 1986; Guédon 2005; Lovick 2020). It is įįjih, for example, to speak directly about animals. Instead, people must speak indirectly using euphemisms. For example, it is įįjih to say you are going hunting, or that you have killed a moose; instead, it is proper to refer to the moose indirectly. It is also injih to talk about oneself, which is seen as bragging and could lead to bad luck (Lovick 2020: 36–37). In knowing what is įįjih, humans learned to be attentive, cultivate awareness, maintain a proper attitude, and follow protocol.

In the Dene tradition everything is connected. Humans and nature are inseparable. All things are animate or have agency and possess a spirit. Human beings remain a part of nature and reciprocally obligated to animals not just because animals provide humans with food but as beings with a common origin and equivalent natures. Animals and humans participate in an enduring relationship governed by įįjih. The idea of the person extends to all living things. Animals are considered nonhuman

persons (see Hallowell 1960). Dene, for example, extend the term *grandfather* to both humans and grizzly bears. In the Upper Tanana language, the term for grandfather is *tsay* while the word for male bear is *neettsay* ("our grandfather"), which is considered a respectful term. Upper Tanana Dene do not make a distinction in the use of the term *grandfather*: it applies to both humans and nonhuman persons.

The important point here is that relationships matter. Human beings do not stand apart from the world but exist in a world of relatedness. It is human beings' relationship with the world that makes things happen. Whatever exists now, whatever success a person has, is the product of their relationship with the world. Knowledge is about learning, understanding, and participating through correct actions that sustain the web of life-giving relations of which the knower is part (Blaser 2018). In this respect every part of the Dene tradition is directed at living a balanced life in an unpredictable world in which human beings are completely dependent on the goodwill of powerful animals. This means living in harmony with all things, human and nonhuman. Elders point out it is essential to maintain approved standards of personal and social conduct because achieving a full life depends on one's own conduct as well as the conduct of others, whether human or animal. Humans have an obligation to act appropriately, whether dealing with other human beings or nonhuman persons. Sharing is a prime example of appropriate behavior. Sharing creates a balance or sense of proportion that must be maintained in all interpersonal relations and activities. Hoarding or any manifestation of greed is disapproved of. Sharing is of central importance, because without sharing no one can survive. Animals share their flesh so humans can survive; humans share with one another so they, too, can survive. But Dene were not simply altruistic; they share because not sharing can cause serious problems, including unrest and dissatisfaction or ultimately death if the person slighted decides to cause personal harm.

Margaret Kirsteatter talked about the importance of sharing when she talked about food and the necessity of saving everything in case of starvation. Margaret explained that when people experienced bad luck, others had an obligation to help them survive.

> Our old people used to tell us. People come through the country, if he is hungry, bad luck, they make the people survive [it]. Even old bone, put it away. And the marrow bone, moose foot. They dry. And some of these days people you know [have] bad luck, they come through the country visiting one another, you know, they survive it. So even still save those, too, right now. (Andrews and Huntington 1980: n.p.)

Up until the end of the nineteenth century, upper Tanana Dene lived in small, autonomous groups composed of closely related kin. Kinship affiliations were extensive, reaching beyond the immediate group and providing people with a network of relationships from which to seek assistance in time of need. Society was organized into moieties, or two halves, called Raven and Sea Gull. Each moiety was composed of several matrilineal clans. Moieties separate the different clans into opposites who intermarry, help one another during life crises, and support each other during potlatches. Approved marriages were between a man and woman of opposite clans. Descent was matrilineal, that is, a person traced their descent through their mother. A person was born into their mother's clan and remained a member of that clan their entire life. A person's clanmates were considered relatives, while people in other clans were considered nonrelatives, friends, sweethearts, and marriage partners.

As members of opposite moieties and clans, young people were instructed to share liberally with their friends and in-laws. As elder Fred John of Mentasta instructed, "Your friends, you should hold them up high. Leave your brothers and sisters alone" (Kari 1986: 38). In this regard sharing or gift-giving was an important part of clan reciprocity. To be a cohesive group, a functioning clan, members must acknowledge and honor those persons in the opposite clan, who, traditionally, were often the clan of their father. One of the most important ways of doing this was through the potlatch. The word *potlatch*, while widely used today, is derived from Native American trade jargon and was brought to Alaska by prospectors at the end of the nineteenth century. In the languages of the upper Tanana, the potlatch is *xtiitl* (T) or *tįįł* (UT) and applies to various formal occasions when one group hosts another, distributing gifts to the guests to mark important events, especially a change in a person's state of being as they progress from child to adult, from birth to death.

Sharing was also the obligation of rich men called *xáxkeh* (T) or *hàskeh* (UT), who were at the top of the social ladder and gained their station through their superior abilities in hunting, healing, generosity, oratory, and extensive knowledge of clan history and mythology. While wealth served to signify rank, a rich man's status was based on his generosity and ability to care for those less fortunate. In every instance, sharing connected Dene to the wider cosmos because sharing the meat, skins, and other products of the land pleased the spirits of the animals who were the source of all life. Sharing was a way of showing respect to those entities that gave their lives so humans could live, and it also ensured that animals would continue to give themselves to humans.

COLONIALISM

Under American colonialism, the world was transformed. Native people's beliefs were labeled as superstition, defined by the Cambridge Dictionary as "unjustified beliefs not supported by reason or scientific thinking." Injih became irrelevant. Humans became separated from the land and nature, and instead nature became grand, passive, and mechanical, the backdrop for human intentionality (Tsing 2015). The world was segregated into discrete, clear-cut categories. Nature was separated from culture and the natural from the supernatural. Elders like Darlene Northway lamented the loss of knowledge and the ignorance of young people today, saying they "live instead as White people" (Sam, Demit-Barnes, and Northway 2021: 226).

Colonization of Alaska began with the Russians in the eighteenth century, but because of their remote location, upper Tanana Dene were little affected. Russia ceded Alaska to the United States in 1867, and the new territory became a military district, but neither the army nor any other government agency paid much attention to interior Alaska until the discovery of gold in 1898 on the Klondike River in Yukon Territory, Canada. Intensive colonization followed. On one level, the gold rush changed everything: American colonialism, spearheaded by missionaries, traders, and government agents, sought to create a whole new world in which Dene either had to change or perish. Alaska became "White man's country," as Senator William Dillingham of Vermont put it (Dillingham 1904: 29). Dene became wards of the American government with no rights except those granted by the government. On another level, because the upper Tanana was isolated, there were no roads, and the Tanana River was difficult to navigate, Dene experienced minimal interference and retained almost complete control of their daily lives. It was not until the construction of the Alaska Highway in 1942 and influx of non-Native settlers after World War II that Dene felt the full impact of settler colonialism.

The process of colonizing Alaska was both overt and subtle. The fur trade, which influenced Dene long before they ever saw a White person, brought new goods, making their lives easier but also making Dene dependent on a system they had no control over. Trapping became a part of the Dene tradition and was integrated into the seasonal cycle. People altered their appearance, changing their hairstyles and clothing to mimic what they saw when attending rendezvous or visiting trading posts. In general, fur traders had little interest in changing Native people, preferring they stay on the land and trap. Missionaries, on the other hand, came with an expressed commitment to change Native life—not only to convert people to Christianity but recreate them in the missionaries' own image as settled, educated Christians. In this vision, life on the land, hunting and constantly moving with the seasons, was not an acceptable way of life. For their part, Dene accepted some of the missionaries' ideas and were willing to change to fit into the new world order, but they resisted other changes, for example, hiding traditional religious practices and outright rejecting the missionaries' insistence they give up the potlatch.

The construction of the Alaska Highway ended the isolation of the upper Tanana region and Alaska. After 1940, the pace of change accelerated, and Dene began losing control not only of the rate of change but their very lives. They became second-class citizens and learned a new kind of isolation in which they were largely ignored and left to fend for themselves in a changing world where they could no longer make a living from the land. Children were required to attend school, and many were sent away to boarding schools where they became estranged from the culture and language of those who stayed in the village. While life changed, people did not give up their attachment to the land or to their culture. The potlatch thrived. Land became the issue. Under the 1958 Statehood Act, the State of Alaska began to select lands, which put them at odds with Native elders such as Andrew Isaac. In countless interviews, Chief Andrew Isaac and others reiterated not only their attachment to the land but the necessity of keeping the land for future generations. For the elders, the land and the culture of the land was everything.

In 2021, upper Tanana Dene reside in five communities: the largest is Tetlin, with 120 people, followed by Tanacross (116), Northway (89), Dot Lake (41), and Healy Lake (23) (Alaska DCRA 2019; figure I.2). All except Healy Lake are accessible by a gravel road that leads to a cluster of single-family homes, a school, a church, and a community building where community feasts and potlatches are held. Few villages have a store. There is an elected government with president and village council. Members of extended families live close to one another, and most day-to-day activity takes place at this level. On certain occasions, the entire village functions as a unit, for example, to hold a potlatch or a spring carnival. Contemporary Dene, including those living outside the region, have a strong sense of identity with their communities and the surrounding landscape. While many aspects of the traditional social organization have disappeared, such as cross-cousin partnerships and clan-based marriage restrictions, there is still a strong emphasis on kinship and affiliation with family members. Traditionally defined relationships are still an important part of community life, and clans and clan membership still play a central role in upper Tanana social life.

The passage of the Alaska Native Claims Settlement Act (ANCSA) in December 1971 gave Alaska Native people some measure of self-determination, yet people still struggle to find something in modern American culture that will replace the all-engaging sense of purpose that life on the land provided. This is a big challenge. Now, in 2021, many young people—those in their thirties and forties—have left their villages to live in Fairbanks, Anchorage, or even out of state. They have jobs and families and still maintain close ties to the village. They hold language lessons and get together, often over the internet. They are building a new community. Their children will never know life in the country, and they may never know life in a village, but they are still Dene.

SOCIAL SCIENCE AMONG UPPER TANANA DENE

Robert McKennan came north in 1929 as a PhD student from Harvard University. He was the first anthropologist to spend time with Dene in east-central Alaska. Starting out in Chisana, where he met many relatives of people living today, he then attended a potlatch at Batzulnetas put on by Charlie Sanford, Katie John's father, and stayed at lower Nabesna, where he met Chief Sam, Follet Isaac, Walter Northway, and many other Dene before heading back to Harvard in the summer of 1930. In his monograph *The Upper Tanana Indians* (1959), McKennan describes various traits of upper Tanana culture along with a short history of the region. His aim was to document a fast-disappearing culture being rapidly transformed by Dene people's increasing contact with non-Natives.

When McKennan visited the region, Dene were deeply involved in the fur trade. During the Russian colonial period, they made trips down the Tanana River to trade at *Noochulo-ghoyet* at the confluence of the Tanana and Yukon Rivers. After Russia sold Alaska to the United States in 1867, Dene traveled over to the upper Yukon River to trade with Americans at Fort Reliance, Eagle, and Fortymile. By the time McKennan arrived, John Hajdukovich and other traders had firmly established themselves on the upper Tanana River and were supplying a steady stream of consumer goods.

The period between 1900 and the start of World War II in 1940 is richly documented by historian Michael Brown in his 1984 monograph *Indians, Traders, and Bureaucrats in the Upper Tanana District: A History of the Tetlin Reserve*, written for the Bureau of Land Management (BLM). Between 1910 and 1940, upper Tanana Dene were becoming accustomed to the presence of *nondlêed* (T) or *noodlee* (UT) (White people) in their homeland. They had to learn not only how to exist within a new world order where the US government claimed sovereignty over their homeland but how to deal with the idiosyncrasies of individual government agents, traders, and missionaries, all of whom had different agendas. For example, Upper Tanana Dene faced increasing pressure from White trappers and hunters, including wealthy trophy hunters brought into the region by the trader Hajdukovich. They also faced pressure from naturalists such as O. J. Murie, who were concerned Dene were killing too many caribou. Like most Western-trained scientists, Murie focused on the size of animal populations, believing that reducing the harvest was the way only way to maintain a healthy population. Dene viewed the situation differently. It was injih not to kill animals that presented themselves to be killed; the population was based not on how many animals were killed but killing them in a respectful manner. If animals were not killed, they would not reproduce themselves.

It was only after the war that anthropologists began to visit the region regularly. During a short trip in July 1946, Walter Goldschmidt and Theodore Haas documented "the present lands used and occupied by the native Athapascan Indians of the villages of Northway (Nabesna), Tanacross (Mansfield), and Tetlin (Tetling)" (Goldschmidt 1948). Their report contains a detailed examination of land ownership and use patterns, along with a description of conflicts between Dene and White trappers and hunters. In interviews with elders, such as Chief Walter Northway, Goldschmidt documented changes that many elders deplored, including the weakening bonds within communities and the older men's inability to control the behavior of the youth, which was essential for survival. In contrast Albert Heinrich (1957: 22), an anthropologist who worked primarily in Tetlin,

thought the social structure, while under stress, was "very much alive" and "barring some drastic, unforeseeable impetus toward acculturation, that, in gradually altering form, the 'old ways' will have considerable influence for quite some time to come."

In the summer of 1960, anthropologists Frederica de Laguna and Catharine McClellan made their first trip to the upper Tanana. McClellan was a student of de Laguna's who had begun a lifelong association with Tutchone in the Yukon Territory beginning in the 1940s. In 1954 she and de Laguna began working with Ahtna elders to document their traditional culture. Eight years later, in 1968, they were joined by another of de Laguna's students Marie-Françoise Guédon. Neither de Laguna nor McClellan ever published anything on upper Tanana culture (1960a), but they left copious notes as well as what they called "circumstances," or the setting. On their first day in Tanacross, for example, de Laguna wrote they were escorted around the village by Charlie James, who took them to Joe Joseph's house where they met Joe's wife Salina and her brother the Reverend David Paul. Later that day they met Annie Moses, and de Laguna took a photograph of Charlie holding a bear spear.

When de Laguna and McClellan arrived in 1960, much of the hunting culture was gone. Almost all the remote settlements had been abandoned as people relocated to live close to the Alaska Highway. They led relatively sedentary lives while working seasonal jobs, such as fighting forest fires in the summer. The highway offered Dene access to all parts of Alaska and brought influences from every direction of the country as tourists and new settlers flocked to the area. Christian missionaries made further inroads, and children attended school throughout much of the year. And alcohol had taken a toll to the point that some people, to get away from the drinking, had moved out of Tanacross and established the community of Dot Lake. At the same time, all the elders, and many of the older children, who had not been sent away, spoke their language, held traditional beliefs, and practiced the potlatch.

In 1968 de Laguna brought Guédon on a visit to Tetlin to introduce her to the community. Guédon returned to the village a year later and stayed to collect information for her dissertation, "People of Tetlin, Why Are You Singing" (Guédon 1974), which became a primary source of information on upper Tanana culture. While "almost completely settled," Guédon thought Upper Tanana Dene had "preserved" elements of their traditional culture and were involved in a culture revival based on what Dene were calling the "Indian way" (Guédon 1974: 19). Although she worked primarily in Tetlin, Guédon visited Tanacross and Northway, and in 2005 published *Le rêve et la forêt: Histories de chamanes nabesna*, about Dene shamanism.

Also in the 1960s, anthropologist Mertie Baggen began working with various elders from different communities on the middle and upper Tanana to document their traditional culture, but she was killed in an automobile accident before she could publish her findings. Mertie interviewed Myrtle Wright, who had served alongside her husband the Reverend Arthur Wright in Tanacross in the early 1920s. Mrs. Wright described a potlatch at Tanacross given by Big Frank and told Mertie that her husband had once written an article highly critical of the potlatch but later had a change of heart. Mertie's archival collection contains her fieldnotes and manuscript, which in 1974 were organized and summarized by Elizabeth Andrews into a paper called "A Partial Compilation of the Fieldnotes of Mertie Baggen, with an Emphasis on the Salchaket Band of the Middle Tanana." Eventually Elizabeth wrote her master's thesis "Salcha: An Athapaskan Band of the Tanana River and Its Culture" (1975), based in part on Baggen's notes.

In the early 1970s, Roger Pitts and Ramon Vitt, students from the University of Alaska Fairbanks, conducted research for their master's theses. In "The Changing Settlement Patterns and Housing Types of the Upper Tanana Indians," Pitts (1972) traced changes in Upper Tanana settlement patterns and housing types and described how fifty years of colonialism had profoundly affected the people as they shifted from an itinerant to more sedentary way of life. In "Hunting Practices of the Upper Tanana Athapaskans," Vitt (1971) set out to reconstruct the "hunting culture" and document subsequent changes that had occurred through 1970. He thought the traditional hunting culture had pretty much disappeared because fewer young men were active hunters, and reliance had grown on jobs and government support. He concluded that the Upper Tanana Athabascans had "abandoned their individuality and their independence for dependence on the non-native and his economic-based world and today they exist between two cultures, not really belonging to either one" (188).

Almost thirty years later, anthropologist Norm Easton (2001) wrote about the intergenerational differences between the younger and older generations of Dene, primarily along the Alaska-Canada border in the communities of Northway, Alaska, and Beaver Creek, Yukon Territory. According to Easton, the generation born prior to the mid-1950s had a culturally cohesive traditional upbringing with a lifelong participation in the hunting economy. Succeeding generations, on the other hand, are rooted in the non-Native system of schools and electronic media and are more reliant on wage labor or social assistance. In 2021 Easton published *An Ethnohistory of the Chisana River Basin*, which in many respects is a companion piece to this volume. In his conclusion, Easton (2021: 114) wrote that through the colonial process of separating people from the land there has been a "serious erosion of contemporary knowledge of the area's history, use and potential among many younger Dene," yet attachment to the land remains strong. He goes on to say that much of modern Dene culture, cloaked as it is in "homeboy fashions, the English language, use of automobiles and hip-hop music, is invisible to the casual outsider. Yet despite the changes it is still there and remains unalterably Dineh in nature" (114).

Starting in the early 1980s, the Alaska Department of Fish and Game's Division of Subsistence began research in many of the upper Tanana communities (Andersen and Jennings 2001; Case 1986; Halpin 1987; Koskey 2006, 2007; Marcotte 1989; Marcotte, Wheeler, and Alexander 1992; Martin 1983). The division's emphasis was on describing the subsistence economy of each community and quantifying the amount of wildlife resources consumed by residents. The question was, how much had outside influences, particularly the capitalist system and wage labor, altered traditional hunting and fishing activities and how much did animal, fish, and plant resources continue to add to local economies? Based on household surveys and analysis of quantitative data, the research found that, despite increased access to grocery stores, upper Tanana Dene continue to maintain a close connection to their homeland and harvest an abundance of wild foods, particularly moose, whitefish, and berries.

STRUCTURE OF THE BOOK

This book is composed of eleven chapters and four appendices. The first eight chapters, based on interviews with Dene elders from published and unpublished sources, are about traditional Dene culture as practiced from 1880 to 1940. During that time, Upper Tanana Dene went from living entirely from the land and moving with the seasons to living in permanent communities. The last three chapters are about the colonial processes that impinged on Dene, forcing them off the land and into the communities they occupy today. The four appendices include a description of Dene culture by Paul Kirsteatter; a description, with maps, of traditional band territories and the history of select Upper Tanana communities; a selection of documents relating to the fur trade; and census data.

The information presented in this book is drawn from both informant interviews conducted by the author and from other interviews conducted in different times by different interviewees. Interviews were conducted in both Dene and English, and those conducted in Dene were transcribed and then translated with the help of fluent Dene speakers. When interviewed, the elders often assumed a certain familiarity with local history and culture. For this reason, I have provided some contextual information from different sources, including the work of other anthropologists and historians. This information is intended to augment the context and chronology necessary to weave together the many Dene voices into a cohesive statement of their history. I have not edited the interviews except to add information for clarity. Words enclosed in square brackets were added by the interviewer, editor, or translator to provide additional information or clarification. While many of the elders were not completely fluent in English, their language has a distinctive rhythm and quality, and their facility with language is reflected in their emphatic statements. They knew what they wanted to say to their children, grandchildren, and future generations.

1 LIVING FROM THE LAND

A major concern for Dene was maintaining the goodwill of powerful animals that people needed to kill and eat to survive (Cruikshank 1990: 340). In both the Upper Tanana and Tanacross languages, the word for food, *shi'*, is also the word for meat. Animals were a constant preoccupation: people not only had to know animals' habits but had to be aware of them as unpredictable and powerful beings. For this reason, children were trained to persevere through hard times, to never waste anything, and to share. Dene elders said, "Always be prepared. Food should never be taken for granted, don't waste anything, save every part of the animal. Don't be careless; be aware of what you are doing and how you are thinking." As Minto elder Peter John said, "In the Indian way of life, you've got to understand the animals. Every meal came from the brush" (John 1996: 23).

In the "modern" Western view, nature and humans are separate. Created in God's image, humans have a soul and are cultural beings. Animals are simply instinctual. In the Dene tradition, humans and animals are equal beings. Everything in nature is considered sentient. Rocks, plants, and animals are not objects governed by instinct but social beings possessing power or a "spiritual potency," and protected by an elaborate system of taboos or rule called injih. Everything in nature, from animals to plants to stones to tools, has a degree of injih associated with it; if not treated with the proper consideration, the power or force inherent in these things can disrupt the balance between humans and nature, creating havoc. Humans must always be cognizant of the intersection between that which is seen and unseen.

In the Christian tradition, time begins with God's creation and ends with the last judgment. Earth is "provisional" or "preparatory" because the Christian's real home is in heaven with God the creator (Grant 1984: 24). In the Dene tradition, the souls of both humans and animals are constantly recycled so there is no notion of movement toward an end. Time is classified into two types, loosely termed "mythic time" and the human present. Mythic time is of a different order than the time in which we now live. In distant time, there was no distinction between animals and humans. Language was pure and free of distortion so that both humans and animals could speak directly to one another (Krupa 1999). Events that occurred in distant time are told in oral narratives that one Dene elder has called "the Bible of the Athabaskan people" (Attla 1990: ix). Some narratives are simply utilitarian, conveying specific kinds of information that show people how to protect their health and survive in an uncertain and difficult world; others are private knowledge, such as stories having to do with hunting magic, that are told only to certain people. Then there are epic narratives or mythic charters that explain how this world came to be and set out the nature of the relationship between human beings and the natural world.

In the Dene tradition Raven is the world maker and *Yamaagh Telch'eegh* is the transformer. As the creator, Raven is neither perfect

https://doi.org/10.5876/9781646423347.c001

Photo-montage by Hal Gage.

nor inscrutable but imperfect, full of trickery, and a great manipulator. It was Yamaagh Telch'eegh (T) or *Yamaagn Teeshyay* (UT)—literally "The One Who Goes Angrily Around the Edge of the Sky"—who created the current world order by transforming animals into the legitimate prey of human hunters (Cannon et al. 2020; Krupa 1999; Nelson 1983). In the distant time animals preyed on humans, could talk like humans, and could take human form. Yamaagh Telch'eegh established a new moral order in which humans became distinct beings but remained a part of nature and reciprocally obligated to animals. Animals and humans now exist in a covenant where animals sacrifice their bodies so humans can survive, but only on the condition that humans treat them with respect.

There are many stories about Yamaagn Teeshyay and his achievements. Traditionally, they were told during the long winter nights. Darlene Northway told several to Olga Lovick (Sam, Demit-Barnes, and Northway 2021), who recorded and translated them from the Upper Tanana language. In this story Darlene tells the story of how Yamaagn Teeshyay tamed eagles so they would not eat humans. Sherry Demit-Barnes was present when this story was told and helped with commentary.

Yamaagn Teeshyay eh Ch'ishyąą eh nahognnek
I talk about Yamaagn Teeshyay and Eagle

Yamaagn Teeshyaay huugn aahaał nts'ą̈
  nän' na'ehtsayh.
Yamaagn Teeshyaay is going around and
  making this world.

Huugn nän' k'it deltth'ii iin nuun iin dineey
  iin t'eey heldeel.
The ones who stay on the earth, animals,
  they eat people.

Ay natehtsiin xah hutaagn aahaał.
He is walking around [the earth] so he can
  fix them.

Hutaagn aahaał nts'ą̈ huts'ą̈ hǫǫheey.
He is going around and he is talking to
  them.

Huxah ni'ihaag tl'aan hudziit hǫǫheey.
He would come to them and teach them.

"Dąą' ch'a hutahnąy, dąą' ch'a hutahnąy, dąą'
  ch'a shyah hutah'aal."
"This is the way to live, this is the way to
  live, this is the way to make a home."

"Jah duugn ch'a nuhts'iikeey iin ichah'aal."
"This is the way you feed your kids."

Dineey iin ehnih nts'ą̈ hutah aahaał ay nts'ą̈.
He went around among them telling all the
  people that.

Yamaagn Teeshyaay hǫǫ' dį' nts'ą̈ t'eey
  Ch'ishyaan xah niniishyay eh t'eey hut'oh
  ha'aat da'ee'ąą yaa niniishyah.
As he was doing this Yaamaagn Teeshyaay
  went to [tell this to] the Eagle and he got
  to where their nest was sitting up high.

Hugaay łaakeey ishyiit deltth'ih.
Two chicks were sitting inside.

Yaa niniishyah.
He came to it.

"Sǫ' shinoljidn!"
"Don't be afraid of me!"

"Nełegn' uhłe' xah dihdį'," iyehnih.
"I'm doing this because I want to be your
  friend," he said.

Nashyign' it'oh shyiit uneh'ąy eh.
He is looking down in the nest.

Dineh heldeel tth'änh datneldok.
They eat people and it is stuffed with [human] bones.

Ay xah huts'ą̄' hǫǫheeyh.
And then he spoke to them.

"Nnąą, nnąą na'aadaał de' nts'ą̄ą̄' utaadįįł,"
    yehnih.
"When your mother returns, what is going
    to happen?" he [Yaamaagn Teeshyaay]
    said to them.

"Shnąą nanat-t'ah de' taałuut guuy nata-
    adeeh," nih.
"When my mother flies back a little hail will
    fall," he [the eaglet] said.

Ch'inłuut, le'e.
Hail, maybe.

"Shta' na'aadaał de' ch'inłuut de' natlüh
    dalthek," yehnih.
"When my father comes back it will hail
    lots," he said to him.

Yehnih.
He said to him.

Ay hǫǫ' yehnih, yeh naholndegn eh, yeh
    naholndegn eh.
He spoke thus to him, he was telling him
    and he was telling him.

Ay eh t'eey huugn chąą nadelthayh.
And then rain began to sprinkle.

"Oh, shnąą na'aadaał," yehnih.
"Oh, my mother is returning," he [the ea-
    glet] said to him.

"Hah'ogn, hah'ogn chindogn'įį'."
"Out there, I am going to hide out there."

"Sǫ' shaa nahǫlndegn!" yehnih.
"Don't tell her about me," he [Yaamaagn
    Teeshyaay] said to him.

"Sǫ' shaa nahǫlndegn!" yehnih.
"Don't tell her about me!" he said to him.

"Dootnųh'įį' de'," yehnih.
"Please keep it a secret," he [Yaamaagn
    Teeshyaay] said to him.

Hah'ogn nday chinel'įį.
He hid somewhere outside.

Ay eh t'eey dineh säk na'at-'aał tl'aan.
And she brought back a man's torso.

It'oh shyiit nts'ą̄' idehnąyh.
She threw it into the nest.

Ay eh t'eey ch'inłuut na'itdeeh.
And then hail began to fall.

Hunąą ninit'ak tl'aan staanett'ak.
Their mother flew up and away.

Huta' hǫǫ' ǫǫ ch'itl'aa' na'at-'ąą ch'itah du' ay
    tl'aan chih ishyiit xah idehnąy.
His father thus, is coming back with the
    lower body part and he threw it inside
    [the nest].

Ay ch'ale, "Dii ch'a aktsän?"
And then, "What do I smell?"

"Jah du' dii ch'a hunįįt'ay," dits'iiniin' ehnih.
"It is a strong smell," he said to his own
    child.

Ts'iiniin: "Naxat dii natįį'aagn ay t'eey
    įhtsänh dahnįh tah."
And the child: "Whatever you brought back,
    that is what you smell, you mean."

"Ay t'eey įhtsänh dadįįnih," yehnih.
"That is what you are smelling is what you
    mean," he said to him.

Ay nts'ą̄' t'eey.
And then.

[I know he Yamaagn Teeshyaay he killed one of them, I don't know which one.]

Yamaagn Teeshyaay yaa nii'inshyah.
Yaamaagn Teeshyaay went to him.

Huta' staanett'ay yaa nii'inshyah tl'aan shyi' ch'a naytiłeey.
When their father had flown off again [Yamaagn Teeshyaay] came back to them and threw the meat out.

"Dii sǫ' sǫ' jah sǫ' na'ųų'aal!"
"From now on don't eat this type of meat!"

"Dineey iin sǫ' aldeel," yehnih.
"Don't you guys eat humans," he said to them.

"K'ahdu' t'eey naa niitihdaał," yehnih.
"In a little while I will come back to you," he said to him.

Än staa'inshyah tl'aan.
He went away then.

Ishyiit nii'inshyah gah eh dimbee iin eh ii'eh tah huugn.
He came back there with rabbits and sheep and things like that.

Ts'iikeey iin xah niiynįlshyah tl'aan tl'oh shyiit dayiitehdeeł.
He brought them back to the children and he laid it out in the grass.

"<Jah> shyįį' ch'ah tah'aal jah ts'änh noo'."
"This is what you will eat from now on."

"Nahuugn dineey iin du' <<aldeel>>, ena', <k'at'eey hǫǫsǫǫ>," yeh<nih>.
"The other stuff, the people, they are no good [to eat]," he said to him.

<"Jah ts'änh noo dineh k'at'eey taldeel,'" hu'ehnih.>
From now on, you cannot eat people anymore, he said to them.
And that's where it ends.

"THEY KNOW US"

Dene elders say animals are dangerous, full of injih. If disrespected in any way, they can wreak havoc on people and make them starve. Animals know humans must kill them to survive. Killing is not offensive. What is offensive and forbidden, or įįjih, is taking an animal's life for no reason, wasting its flesh, killing it in a disrespectful manner, assuming a disrespectful familiarity, and letting an animal suffer.

No animal is insignificant. A woman from Tetlin explained how people should behave toward mice and muskrats, especially after taking their food cache. Small mammals such as mice and muskrats cache tender plant shoots and other vegetable matter to eat, and sometimes humans take them to eat. The woman's mother told her that these animals work hard for their food and must be compensated if you take their cache; otherwise they will take your food. The woman asked her mother how the animals would know, and the mother simply answered, "They know us."

> When you find ni'tsiil, muskrat food, you got to give a little piece of cloth. You got to give something to that rat. You got to pay for muskrat or mice food. Speak to them as to Indian: "This is for you, don't bother, this I give so you feel good."
>
> When I was a little girl I didn't know . . . I found mice cache. "Mom, I said, I find mice cache." My mom told me, that way: "You got to pay for it." I laughed: "How do they know us?" My mom told me, "They know us." My mom told me, "You got to pay for what you take. They do lots of hard work for that cache." "Mom," I said, "what if we don't pay?"

She said, "If you don't pay, they'll go inside our cache . . . and take our meat."

When I was small, I used to look for mice caches, rat caches too. Now, I don't like to bother those little animals. I feel sorry for them. . . . It's too cold. . . . I know how you feel when somebody takes your food. . . . I don't want them to starve. (Guédon 1974: 29)

Animals must never be abused or handled disrespectfully. Every precaution must be taken because the animal's spirit is vigilant and can wreak powerful revenge if its body is not handled respectfully. In this story, recorded and translated by Olga Lovick, Cora David (2017: 88–93) tells how a young girl sees some children playing with a baby crane, throwing it high in the air, abusing it. She tells her grandmother, who knows immediately that disaster will strike because of the children's behavior. She hears the mother crane singing and knows she is making "medicine" and that it will begin to snow. The mother crane's song brings so much snow, and the children are not prepared, so they starve to death.

Deeł xa nahogndak
I talk about cranes

Deeł
Cranes.
<<Ishyiit dą'>>ahnoo' tsw'ist'e' eł
At that time, an old lady

ts'exeh gaay eł dihisyįį' hihdeltth'ih.
and a little girl were staying out there all by themselves.

Ch'ithüh shyah shyiit
In a teepee

Ishyiit hutah hihdeltth'ii eł t'eey adog nts'ą́
ts'iijeey <<iin>>> shya'eh ą́ą,
they were sitting and the children up there were making a lot of noise,

hihdelxoh.
they were playing.

Ts'iiniin tinih' a' nts'ą́ "Adog ts'iikeey dii eł delxoo nįh'įh," ts'iiniin ehnih.
She sent the child out and "Look what the kids up there are playing with," she said to the child.

Ts'exeh gaay
The girl

Ishyiit nts' a' teeshyah.
went over there.

Deeł ugaay eł hihdelxoo hit'aatihiiyetthak adogn nt' eh.
They were playing with a baby crane, throwing it high up in the air.

Dahiiyihchik dgen' tay' t'aatihiiyehtthak.
They caught it and threw it up again.

Ts'exeh gaay dayihshił nts' ą́ di'eek t' aat yįhxał ha ditsoo nts'ą́nateltthat.
The girl caught the crane and threw it under her skin shawl and ran back to he grandmother.

<Ay eł> ditsoo: "Dii ch'a hiiyeh'ąy?"
And the grandmother: "What are they playing with?"

Ts'exeh gaay du': "Deeł gaay ch'ale hiiyeh' ąy!"
The girl: "They are playing with a baby crane!"

<Ay eł>
And

ts'ist'e:
the old lady:

"Tsat <łahtthag nts' ą'> nah'ogn nidnįįłeey!"
"Bring all the wood outside!"[1]

"Dii xa tihdiil?"
"Why should I do that?"

"Tahshyüü:: hukah.
"Because it is going to snow.

"Hihtałaa, dineey iin ts' iikeey iin <łahtthag
    nts'ą> hihtaałaa.
"They will die: the people, the children, they
    are all going to die.

"Łahtthag nts' ą' hihtaałaa."
"They are all going to die."

<<Nts'aa' utsoo yehnay niign dii>>tsexeh
    gaay tsat niidelshyeek, tsat niidelshyeek.
Just as her grandmother had told her, the
    girl brought in wood, brought in wood.

Ishyiit hihdelxoo iin du' k'at' eey nts' aa'
    t'eey hedąay.
The ones that had been playing didn't do
    anything.

Deeł hadogn sts'aakeenaat' ah nts' ą' jeh'ąą.
A crane was circling overhead and she was
    singing.[2]

Ay eł
And

utsoo': "Nahdog deeł sts' aakenaat' aa
    jeh'aan dįįtth'ak!
the grandmother: "You listen to that crane
    circling overhead and singing!
"K'a shyąą' nąy, tahshyüü.
"It doesn't say it for nothing, it's going to
    snow.

"Ay xa tnih."
"That's why she's singing."

Ay eł
And

ay eł t'eey ehshyüh ehshyüh ehshyüh nts'ą'
and then it snowed and snowed and
    snowed and

dinney iin nah' ogn deltth'ii iin
the people that had stayed outside

k'at' eey hushyi t'eey huułay nts' ą' <łaht-
    thag nts'ą'> hįįłaak łahtthag nts' ą' t'eey
    hįįłaak.
they had no food, they all died, all of them
    died.

<Łahtthag nts'ą'> ts'iikeey iin t'eey łahtthag
    nts'ą'nanįįłaak nts'ą'.
All the children died, all of them.

<Łahtthag nts'ą'> nahįįłaak nts'ą'.
All of them died.

< Łahtthag nts'ą' jahtthak!>
You all listen to the story!

Jah
This

Nts'aa'dihnay ay
what I've said

Uxa ts' ehuushya'xa ch'ale neehenay.
we become smart; that's why they tell us.

"Nah'ogn
"Out there

"ts'ugaay eł
"birds and

"diniign whatever nah'ogn

---

1   The woman is telling the girl to pile wood around the
base of the teepee to keep out the snow and insulate the
tent.
2   The crane is making medicine. Cora's mother knew the
crane's song, but Cora did not remember it.

"moose, whatever out there

"so' meh dalxoo," <neeninih>
  "don't play with it," they used to tell us.

Animals are sensitive to any slight. To avoid repercussions, Dene were required to follow a multitude of rules in their handling and processing of all animals, including fish. In this story Cora David (2017: 176–179) explains that menstruating women may not handle fish. She also explains that when fish are placed on a rack to dry, they must be positioned so their heads face downstream in the direction they came from, otherwise the fish will not return.

Łuugn dhakgaay dahdzał k'it dadhihdlah
I put fish on the fish rack for drying

Łuugn delgay tehłah tah
When the whitefish come,

ts'exeey iin
The girls

dishyįį' nahetdaagn iin k'at'eey
who are having their period may not

hiitthi' k'ii'etth'ii.
cut off their heads.

K'at'eey
Not

łuugn utaałeel hoo hedį de'.
there won't be any fish if they do that.

Adogn daats' ehłeeg tah chih
When we put them up [on the rack],
k'at'eey
not

ne'nts'ą' shyįį' datsaałaał utthi'
we may not put them so their heads face
  backward,

anno ts'ą' shyįį datsaałaał utthi'.
their heads have to face ahead. [the way
  they were swimming when caught]

Ay tah chih
And

k'at'eey keł natatdląą hendiik nane' nt'ą'
there will not be as many they say, backward

dahiiyehłeek tah.
when they put them up.

Utthi' ts'ą' ne' nts'ą' dadhahdlah de'
If you put them up so the sides of their
  heads face backward,

k'at'eey łuugn utaałeel.
there won't be any fish.

Utthi' ts'ąy noo nts'ą' dadhahdlah de' shyįį
Only if you put them up so the sides of their
  heads face ahead,

łuugn utaałeel heniik.
there will be lots of fish, they used to say.

Hugn t'eey ch'a k'a nuh'ah dįįnay nts'ą'.
Even those things they did not teach you
  guys.

Hugn t'eey k'a uk'e taatsuł' įį nahthan.
Even those things you don't want to do like
  them.

Hugn t'eey
Even those

hugn t'eey
Even those

haneehunehtanh
they taught us

uxa ts' ehuushya' xa ch'a needetnay.
so that we get smart by being told.
Hoo' shyįį' dihnih.
This much I said.

Another way to disrespect animals is to assume too much. It is injih to make explicit plans because that is considered bragging and could lead to reckless behavior. It also disregards the animal's autonomy and equality. In this regard it is injih to say "my moose" or "my rabbit," because humans do not own animals and it also suggests an unwillingness to share (Lovick 2020: 37, 330). As the Reverend David Paul said, it is bad luck or injih for a hunter to brag that he is going to kill a moose or to say that he will successfully cross a river.

> Don't brag . . . Boy say, "I kill moose today!" Man say "injih!" Don't say that. Say instead, "Maybe today, I see moose." Boy say "I cross river now." My grandfather say, "injih!" Maybe you fell in river, drown. You say that. Say, instead, "Maybe, I try cross river today." (Paul 1957b: 3)

Tanacross elder Oscar Isaac (Simeone 1987g) elaborated on injih and how it affects all relationships. He points out that injih exists in the mind, that both humans and animals can think of something bad and make it happen just with their thoughts. If a hunter wounds an animal, he will be afraid because he knows injih is in the animal. A wounded animal is injih and the hunter knows he will get bad luck, that something bad will occur if he does not take care of that animal. His belief in injih will make him scared.

When a hunter sees an animal and aims the gun at it, he must let the animal look away. Oscar said that if an animal sees you aim the gun and get ready to shoot, the animal will "return that happen," meaning the animal will cause the hunter to have bad luck. To avoid this, a hunter must avoid the animal's gaze. According to Oscar, animals, like humans, can

think about someone and with their minds they can "spear" or pierce them. Oscar said the mind is more powerful than the body; it can hurt oneself and others. That is why a person should not brag or talk about others. That is all injih because, as Oscar said, "what is in your mind will make things happen."

Oscar believed his parents had a good life because "they took care of injih," were aware of what they were doing and thinking. That is why traditional people or old-time people were good. Oscar said they were not "crazy around" or "laughing for other people." To make fun of someone is injih: if they do that, then "all the people's mind will hit you with mean." Oscar gave the example of a rich person ridiculing or making fun of a poor person, then the poor person's hate filling the rich man's mind and hurting him. They will exchange luck: all of the rich man's luck and success will transfer to the poor man. Not only will the poor person's hate fill the rich man but so will the hate of all the people who know that it is injih. For the Dene, success in hunting involves knowing what is įįjih, and that produces "luck" (teeshìh [UT] or ghałi' [T]). Without luck, a hunter cannot be successful. Luck is ephemeral: it can be taken away or negated, as when a hunter encounters a young girl in her menstrual cycle.

Oscar said he followed injih, but he breaks two rules: he laughs for other people, and he eats rabbit. But, he said, his laughter is to make friends, not to hurt people, to joke. Oscar said if you laugh at—that is, make fun of—a poor person, his mind will be unhappy and will put you in a "dirty place." If you share and are friendly, and then someone says something bad and you get angry and hate enters your mind, your mind will hurt that person. Oscar said it is worse than shooting them. Medicine men, according to Oscar, work with the mind and the eye. They love or care for no one. Oscar reiterated that if you follow injih, you will have a good life, not necessarily become rich but will get along. The "ordinary man" (i.e., irresponsible people) does not believe in injih and does not care for himself. Oscar said this is his interpretation, but it is not the "real way." This is not, Oscar said, the ultimate reality, only our explanation. Oscar finished by saying old people always kept busy: they gathered wood, did chores, tanned skin, never sat down like we do now. In other words, they focused on what they were doing and did not let their minds wander into dangerous realms of misunderstanding and chaos.

WORDS TO LIVE BY: CH'QQSI' (UT)/CH'UUSI' (T)

A successful hunter knows the habits of moose and how the animal will use the terrain, but a hunter can facilitate his success by tapping into the power of animals through incantations or words called *ch' qqsi'* (UT) or *ch'uusi'* (T). These are powerful words passed down from father to son that could help a person find and kill an animal, have incredible strength or endurance, entrance a young woman, or make sure everything a person gave away in a potlatch eventually came back to them. The Reverend David Paul compared these words to prayers asking for spiritual assistance before going out hunting and not being presumptuous.

> Today I go out somewhere. Give me moose or something. I go out like the spirits allow me and try to get moose. Don't say "I go out to get moose" but say "I want someone to help me get food for my family, give me something today for my family's food." (Vitt 1971: 120)

Walter Northway (1987: 40) said this about ch' qqsi':

> There are different kinds of words, Ch'oosii', meaning magic words, used for burns, hurts, walking, rain, animals, and bad luck. I know all of these words and used them. If they are not used right, they can be dangerous. I don't teach anyone these

things because they might be misused. Times have changed.

According to Andrew Isaac (Simeone 1987h), there are seven distinct words that a person can use to ensure their luck when hunting. Andrew's father, Titus Isaac, gave him these words late at night when no one else could hear.[3] When you are out by yourself on top of a high hill, you say the words clockwise, starting in the east and saying one word as you face each direction, another when you move a bit toward the west, then another when you move, until you have said all seven. Each word must be said precisely; because they are so powerful, they could hurt you if you make a mistake. You can feel physically bad, and Andrew attributed several elders' physical decline to the improper use of these words. After you have said these words, you can move in any direction and you will find game: "It will be there," Andrew said. He also said words associated with trapping are even stronger, and people can get very jealous of these words. Andrew said he could tell which person knew these words just by looking at them. You must judge what kind of people they are because they could be dangerous and misuse the power. These words sound different than regular words, he said; they "sound funny."

Oscar Isaac (Simeone 1987g) explained that ch'uusi' is more powerful than "medicine power," and there are various forms of ch'uusi'. *Nahten'uusi* are words that allow a man to kill a moose even at 60 degrees below zero, something that is very difficult to do. Having this power, a man must be acquainted with thunder. There is ch'uusi' for different animals such as wolf, bear, and wolverine. Wolverine ch'uusi' enables a man to walk thirty or forty miles on snowshoes; long walks don't bother a person with that power. Bear ch'uusi' is for packing heavy loads. Wolf ch'uusi' can be used for hunting or to make a crooked deal. There is also ch'uusi' connected with sex (*ch'et nindaag*).

---

3 Andrew did not tell me the words.

A person can commit murder with ch'uusi'. With ch'uusi', Oscar said, "you read it with your mind"—that is, you say the words in your head without saying them out loud.

Hunters said these words in private, and according to Oscar Isaac (Simeone 1987p), they were passed down and considered secret knowledge. If others overheard the words, they would not work. They only worked for those for whom they were intended. Oscar said that for these words to be effective, a hunter must know animals.

This kind of power only works if you believe it. Oscar said, for example, that if you encounter a medicine man on the trail and he tells you face-to-face that he is going to do something and you don't believe him, that will block his power. His mind cannot enter you. But if he says something and you don't hear him, he can hurt you; you cannot block his power. Since you don't know he wants to do something, and you don't block it, it will be easy for him to get into your body.

According to Oscar, ch'uusi' and medicine power are as real as the power of God; they exist out there. God made ch'uusi' and medicine so people would have something before Christianity or before modern medicine (Simeone 1987g).

Titus David of Tetlin explained how with magic words a person could have lots of money. He said Dene had special songs that, when sung after a potlatch, would ensure a person got back all of things they gave away.

> Indian had magic word. Got lots of money [if he had those words]. Got some kind of word for it [to acquire money]. Chief don't ever work, get lots of money [because he has those words]. My daddy knew two words. I too young, I missed it [Titus was not taught the words]. Different tribe [clan] used different words, Alts'ị'Dendeey and Dik'aagyu. Alts'ị'Dendeey got magic word best, they say. Use it once that's all. They got song over it, too. They sing by themselves,

nobody hear. [Sing in] evening, before bed. Not every night—when they have party [potlatch]. After the party go around the village, use that magic word. Stop at every door [sing it softly so no hears]. That means they get back everything [they gave away]. (de Laguna and Guédon 1968d)

Julius Paul (Simeone 1987a) said ch'uusi' is used to make a person an effective hunter by watching wolves and using their power to hunt.

> Some people use trick out of wolves to hunt. Wolves for hunting like this they use that kind [of word]. Also use it for potlatch; guy knows something about potlatch for money. This guy go around where they got stuff like blanket, like that, cut piece out of blanket and put it in their pocket then before they give away, that's what they doing with ch'uusi', kind of words they using in the mind to get that money back.

YOU ARE WHAT YOU EAT

Animals and humans live in different forms, but to survive humans must be like animals, absorbing their enduring traits of strength, speed, and agility. They can absorb these qualities by wearing amulets made from different animals. Pieces of certain animals were worn or sewn into children's clothing to impart the animal's strength or facility. A beaver shoulder blade strung across the chest meant the child would be strong, a hawk's claw would make a child swift to the prey, a bear claw meant they would not be afraid, and a weasel skin worn around the waist enabled them to walk on snow (McKennan 1959).

Another way to attain these virtues was to pay attention to what you eat. Cora David (2017: 172–176) tells which foods will make a child weak and lazy and which will make them strong and vigorous. She says that to be as agile and nimble as a baby caribou, children must eat baby caribou. They should not eat baby moose because at birth baby moose are awkward and considered lazy. She also says that putting wood shavings into a child's pocket will make them good with wood.

Hah' ogn nuun iin ay xa naak' udzuushya' xa
About how we become smart from the animals out there

Udzih ugaay
Baby caribou

ts' iikeey gay iin hii'eł natultthagn xa
so that small children run like them

ay xa huhiiyeh' aał
that's why they feed it to them.

Diniign du'
Moose though,

mbihoołeek tah ts' udetniik nts' ą' k' a xan
    tah niihaak nts' ą'.
when it is born it is lazy, and it barely gets
    up.

Natettluk k' e diign xa k' ay
It is weak the way it does things,

ay du' įįjih that ts' iikeey taa' aal.
and that's why it is forbidden that children
    eat it.

Tsa' du
Beaver though

ukelaagąy
its claws

dineey gay iin
little boys

gaan' k' it hiiyedlaak
they put them around their wrists

tsat huuttheel xa.
so they can chop wood.

Jign ntł' at <chih>
Blueberries and salmonberries

ay chih ts' iikeey k' a ihiitah' aal.
too they don't feed to children.

Hut' ay' utaakol, heniik
They will not be strong, they used to say,

shnąą iin.
our parents.

Huhoołįį noo
From the time they are born
that kind
that kind

hoo įįjih hihdiinih.
is forbidden, they say.

Ntł' aan du'
Lots

tsat hugn
firewood

tsat dihdoo
hollow wood

ay shyiit hugn
the kind

ch'elseek hii' ehnay hugn ay chih
what they call wood shavings

ts' iikeey t' ah hiidetł' aak ii' eh dutnay xa.
they put those in the kids' pockets so they
    are strong for wood[4]

Tsat hii eł ettheeł iłeek.
They like to cut lots of wood.

---

4   So they are strong enough to cut wood.

Hoo t' eey nuh' adetnay nts' ą'
You guys were not taught these things,

k' oht'iin naa' ahłįį k' ahdu'.
and that's the kind of people you are nowadays.

Hoo t' eey ch'a nee' adatnį' neexon' du.
That's the way we were taught, us.

Nts' aa'
The way

nts' aa' tsaat' eeł niign t' eey nee' ahdįįnih
   nts' ą'.
the way we should be in the future (when
   we grow up) we were taught.

Įįjih
Forbidden,

ay hoo shyįį' ts' iinįįthįį.
that's all we think about, forbidden.

Hoo shyįį' t' eey t' axoh.
   That's all.

Oscar Isaac (Simeone 1987b) said anyone, even teenage boys and girls, could eat dried fish, moose, or caribou. However young boys didn't eat moose head; to eat that, you had to be a hunter. Young boys who ate moose head would have bad luck. When he was young, Oscar's father split a moose's eyeball and rubbed the liquid all over his son's forearm to make him a good hunter. If a young man ate moose head soup and was not a good or able hunter, the moose would be able to see and hear him right away. In other words, a moose would sense the hunter through the organ (i.e., eye) the person ate. Also, young boys could not eat moose calf because that would cause them to become played out, or tired right away.

Larry Jonathan of Tanacross said:

Walking around in moose blood causes cramps. Moose liver, moose guts [women] don't eat them otherwise babies will be born with no hair. Eating a rabbit head will cause a baby to be a cry baby. Baby moose are only eaten by the elders, sort of a sacred, important food. Take care of moose fetus, [put it in the] proper place and cover. If mistreated [it] causes bad weather, blizzard or really cold temperatures. (Simeone 1987i)

It is important for people to be careful in the preparation of their food and to eat the right kinds of food for good health. Oscar Isaac said:

Lazy people who don't take proper care of their food won't have good food. People are then not satisfied for what they eat. Lazy people cannot live by animals, because it's important to take proper care of animals if one wants good food.

Some food should be sour, moose, fish and caribou. After you cut the meat off the bone you leave some meat on the ground until it begins to smell then you hang it up. You have to eat rotten food once in a while, cannot eat plain meat all of the time, because rotten meat is good for your health.

Oscar's father also told him:

Fish can be eaten rotten, red, but when the fish is in this condition you cannot cook it very long.

Oscar said:

You put it in a dishpan and lower it into the water to cook for five or ten minutes then put it on a plate.

The fish is good for your health, like medicine. People are supposed to eat this once or twice a month. People cannot drink the soup because it is too strong. (Simeone 1987j)

FOOD SHORTAGES AND STARVATION

Dene experienced periodic food shortages and starvation, especially in the late winter and spring or during extreme cold snaps when the temperature would plummet to 50 or 60 degrees below zero. Bessie Barnabas of Salcha remembered the last time people starved before White people came. It was very cold and there was no game. The people began to eat their babiche (rawhide) lines, and some had to be stopped from secretly cutting off strips of bear hides used as robes. Finally, the men caught a big pike in a lake near Dry Creek. They might have died if the men had not caught that fish.

Bessie's father showed her how to scrape spruce bark for food at such times. The scraping was eaten with lots of water to make everyone's stomach feel "just good." Bessie said the juice from the spruce bark is good medicine for the stomach. Eventually, some of the men from Salchaket went with Copper River John to Circle City on the Yukon River where they had relatives, and a White man gave them food there (Baggen n.d.a).

The following narrative illustrates just how hard survival could be in the old days. Andrew Isaac told this story about being hungry to Avis and Roy Sam (Sam, Demit-Barnes, and Northway 2021: 208–216). They use the word *dįįtsįį*, or hungry, instead of *ch'itth'än'*, or starving. Avis and Roy supplied additional information about Roy's father picking rosehips in winter and how his grandfather, Chief Sam, walked to Dawson on snowshoes to buy food. Avis Sam talks about how to make soup out of caribou feet and how the women looked for edible roots called *tsüh* (*Hedysarum alpinum*) to feed the hunters so they could keep up their strength. Nothing was wasted. Caribou feet and moose feet were cached for use in case of hard times. Even moose droppings were made into soup when there was nothing else to eat. In the spring, when food was scarce, old women snared snowbirds so they could have some meat. Fish were buried underground so they could ferment and be dug up in the winter.

Dineh iin hihdįįtsįį dą'
When people were hungry

Shtaay Andrew mǫǫsi' Tanacross dänh, no, Mansfield nee'eh naholnek dineh iin hihdįįtsįį.
My paternal uncle, Andrew [Isaac] was his name, from Tanacross, no, Mansfield, he told us how people used to be hungry.

Chiil gaay shyįį' t'eey hįįłįį ishyiit dänh.
They were just little boys back then.

Hi'elnayh unąą iin nts'ąą' hidąy xa hih-dįįtsįį:: t'axoh.
He remembered what his parents had done when they were starving.

Hah'ogn nuun t'eey kol.
There were no animals out there.

Ay eh that udzih udzih ke' hiiyehgąy.
And then they would dry caribou feet.

Chin shyiit t'eey eedlah.
They would keep it in the high cache.

Ay shyįį' t'eey ihelnay eh ishyiit hiixa nii'indeeł tl'aan hiiyehmbiah.
And finally, he remembered how they would go back for it and cook it.

Hiiyihmbiat ch'itth'eh hiitu' nadehtl'iit.[5]
The first time they boil it, they pour its water out.

Ay tl'aan tay' t'eey ch'ishyuuy tuu hiishyiit na'įįnäł tl'aan ay hitneexot.

---

5 Because the hooves are dried without skinning them first, they are furry and dirty.

And then again, they would put it in different water and would boil it.

Ay chih ay chih tthihiitehtl'iit tl'aan t'axoh.
And that also they would pour out and then.

Tuu tay' hiishyii na'įįnäl ay hitneexot.
Again, they would put it into water and boil it.

Ay du' t'axoh ay tuuthäl hetnąą.
That finally, that broth they would drink.

K'at'eey k'at'eey hǫǫsu' mihǫlnay de' t'eey "Atnaah de'," nih.
Even though it didn't taste good, "Drink it," he said.

"Ay ch'a huts'änh nuht'ayy' nootaltsay.'"
"From this your strength will come back."

Shtay naholnegn hǫǫ' nih.
My uncle who told that said so.

Dineh iin hihdįįtsįį::!
People were hungry!

Staahetdek ay t'oot'eey . . .
They would go hunting but

Staahetdek ay t'oot'eey tl'aan naxat ts'exeh iin, hutsǫǫ iin eh hu'aat iin hah'ogn tsüh kah shyüh t'aat t'eey huneh'įįk tl'aan.
They would go [hunting] but those women, their grandmothers and wives, they would look for edible roots under the snow.

Tsüh ndee nįįshyeey udih'aan de' naxat shyüh än hihtaathät tl'aan kon' hiik'it tdaak'aał.
If they found where edible roots grow, they would brush the snow aside and make a fire.

Ay tl'aan hǫǫ' hidį' tl'aan nashyugn' nän' na'alxįį eh tsüh hahdiłeek.
And they did that and down there the ground would thaw, and they would take out edible roots.

Ay du' k'at'eey diihii hiyi'aal nts'ą̈', hah'ogn dineh iin naxajelshyeegn iin xa hiineht-say nts'ą̈' dii gaay uhdiidlay hutl'aheh-chik.
And they don't eat that themselves, for the men who are hunting they gather it and what little they found they would give it to them.

Dineh iin naxajelshyeek k'at'eey ch'ihi'aal nts'ą̈' t'eey nah'ogn t'axoh nduugn ts'änh shyi' huuniiy?
The men who are hunting haven't eaten anything and out there, from where are they going to get (grab) meat?

Hihdįįtsįį!
They are hungry!

Hǫǫ' ch'a tsüh uuhdii'aagn.
That's why they find edible roots.

Ay tl'aan shta' du' hahdogn naxajelshyeek niign udzih and diniign huh.
And then my father, when he is hunting up there, caribou and moose.

Roy
Diniign ke'.
Moose feet.

Avis
Ay chih diniign ke' hǫǫ' hidįįk.
They also used to do that with moose feet.

Ay xa ch'ah nah'ogn k'ahdu' t'eey k'a hǫǫ' hidąy k'ahdu'.
And they out there don't do that nowadays.

T'oot'eey dąą' ch'a nąy.
Even [if you don't need it you do] thus, he
said.

Ch'idhahxįį de' nithaat dänh ch'idhahxįį de'
dahdzäl dadhah'aay.
When you kill something, when you kill
something a long way away, keep a meat
rack.

Nahugn ch'ixol' ch'ike' <<ch'idzaadn'>>
iin k'a k'at'eey natalshyeel de' hahdogn
dahdzäl maa dadhah'aay tl'aan ay k'it
dadhałeey.[6]
And when you can't bring the legs, the feet,
and the shinbones back, have a drying
rack upland and put them in there.

Hǫǫt'eey taat'eeł.
It'll still be there.

Xay hultsįį de' dahtsįį de', ay ch'a ukah ishyiit niitatdegn.
When it's winter and you're hungry, that's
when you'll go back for it.

Hǫǫ' ch'a ts'idįįgn.
That's what we would do.

Ay tl'aan hu diniign hugn diniign tsaan' ay
ay chih nįhtsay.
And also there, moose, moose droppings,
gather those as well.

Nahtsayh dą' tuu shyiit nahxot.
Gather them and boil them in water.

Ay tl'aan hahshyuugn dahkąą.
And then leave it sitting on the ground.

Tl'aan dii ch'itduul ushyii eedlay hut'aat
nitaadeh.

6   This does not need to be a proper drying rack; a platform that cannot be reached by animals will suffice.

And then the chips that are in there they
will settle on the bottom.

Ay k'it ts'änh tuutįįł eh tuu nelkon' ay
tatnįįł.
From this you will drink the hot water with
a cup.

Ay t'eey ch'a huts'änh nuht'ayy' nootaltsay.
And from that, your strength will come
back.

Ay xa ch'ale dąą' ndihnay, shta' shdįįni'.
That's why I tell you this, my father said to
me.

Nah'ogn dlegn de' t'eey, dlegn t'eey ntsuul
t'oot'eey ay t'eey taldeeł.
Out there squirrels too, squirrels may be
tiny but still you will eat them.

Utsǫǫ, utsǫǫ, shta' utsǫǫ, ts'ist'e::' nłįį.
His grandmother, his grandmother, my
dad's grandmother, she was a really old
lady.

Shyi' kah dįįtsįį de', hah'ogn dąy tah ugaał
nanetdegn ay kah ch'a dachaatl'uuł.
When she gets hungry for meat, when the
snowbirds come back in the spring, she
could set snares for those.

Dąą' maagn nahǫǫłiin.
She would fix it like this around it.

Tthek k'eh heltsįį, k'ąy' eh hohts'iik hu-
maagn hǫǫłįį.
It was like a fence, she would make it with
willow all around it.

T'eey ugaał iin ishyiit nach'ihi'iil.
And in there whatever the snowbirds eat.

Hahshyuugn daach'etl'oon.
Where she set the snare.

Ay shyiit utsǫǫ yidlǫǫ.
That's how his grandmother snared them.

Ay t'eey eldeeł, shyi' kah shyi' dįį kah dįįtsįį
    tah, ts'ist'e::::' dadihnih.
And she would eat them when she was
    hungry for meat, a really old lady, I'm
    talking about.

Ay tl'aan nah'ogn, nts'ą̈' t'eey hiiyuusi'?
And then out there, what are they called?

Kelahjǫǫ.
Grosbeak.
What they eat?

Kelahjǫǫ.
Grosbeak.

Kelahjǫǫ hiiyehnay.
They call it grosbeak.

Ay du' k'a nts'ą̈' nah'ogn k'a ts'ineh'įįgn,
    k'ahdu', nah'ogn jǫǫ nanetdegn nįh'įh?
That one, we don't see it out there right
    now, do you see the camprobbers flying
    around there?

Ay k'eh įhchah.
It is the same size as camprobber.

Ha'gaay nts'ą̈!
It is tiny!

Ay ch'ashyiit įhchah ay chih hiiyeldeeł.
And it is bigger than those, and they eat it
    too.

Ay ch'ale' hahshyuugn nihshyee dii, nih,
    dii nihshyee, ay t'eey hinehtsayh tl'aan
    hiiyeldeeł.
And also down there whatever grows, she
    said, whatever grows, they gather that
    and eat it.

Xayh.
Winter.

Xayh ts'ą̈' haathäl.
It's getting to be winter.

Noołuut, hą̈ą̈?
Fall time, huh?

Noołuut tah chih łuugn hahiłeek.
In the fall they take out fish.

Ay tl'aan nän' shyii hahihułeek, ay du' k'ąy'
    shyįį ushyii iitah nän' shyiit tah hii-
    yuułeek dänh k'ąy' k'ihiłeek tl'aan łuugn.
And then when they have it, they put it with
    willow in the ground, they put willow
    into the hole and then fish.

Ay ishyiit k'ihiłeek tl'aan tay' k'ąy' hiik'it
    hiłeek tl'aan nän' eh nahiiyitsah.
And they put it in the hole and they put
    more willow on it and then they bury it
    again in the ground.

Hǫǫ't'eey ishyiit t'eey hi'idatliidn t'axoh xay
    hǫǫłįį de' hihdįįtsįį de' ay hahiitaa'aal.
They will just leave it there (without dis-
    turbing it) and in winter, when they're
    hungry, they will take it out.

Įhjit, įhjit de' t'eey miholtsänh t'oo įį'aal de'
    k'at'eey hǫǫ' utalnay.[7]
If it's fermented, if it's fermented it'll smell
    bad, but if you eat it, it won't taste like
    that.

Hǫǫ't'eey nsǫǫ.
It is still good.
<<Jin ch'a dzinah hiiyuusii.>>
They call it dzinah (fermented fish).

_____

7   The Upper Tanana word *įhjit* is usually translated as
    "rotten," but we decided that "fermented" sounded more
    pleasing.

Ay chih jign chih hǫǫ't'eey hiiyeh'įįk.
And they also do this with berries.

Jign hihnehtsayh tl'aan k'įįtth'aak choh dąą'
įhchah hehtsiign ay shyiit hiiniłeek tl'aan
hudaadį' hitnihk'aak.
They pick berries and then they make a
large birch basket, that big [gesturing],
and put them in and then they sew the
lid on.

Ay chih nän' shyiit hiiyih'aak.
And that also they keep in the ground.

Ay chih xay de' kah.
This is also for winter.

Nts'ąą::' t'eey hidįįk.
Thus they always do it.

Hǫǫsǫǫ hug hǫǫ' all mits'etnay de' hǫǫsǫǫ
niign t'eey hidį'.
If we know all that really well, they did
things in good way.

Ay shyįį', t'axoh.
That's all, enough.

STORING FOOD

Oscar Isaac (Simeone 1987k) said an important part of taking care of meat is storing it so
that it does not go to waste. Oscar described
how to store meat in a cottonwood cache that
his father-in-law built, but Oscar said spruce is
better. This type of cache was built when there
was no time to properly dry the meat, usually
in September. Later, during the winter, the
hunter would return to pick up the meat. The
cache was about fourteen feet long and six feet
wide. The outside logs were wired together
and notched. This held the cache together
tightly enough so that bears could not break
in but not so tight that air could not circulate
through the cache, drying the meat. The meat
was hung in quarters above the ground. Drying
the meat changes its flavor, Oscar said, so that
it does not taste like fresh meat or smoked dry
meat cut into strips. Smoked dried meat seals
the juices into the meat so it tastes better. Air-
dried meat loses its flavor because the outside
does not crust fast enough to seal the juices,
and they flow out of the meat. An outside crust
one quarter of an inch forms on the dried meat.

Oscar said bones are kept separate for over
a week after the meat is prepared so the bones
dry out and the marrow can be removed. The
bones between the joints are then thrown away.
The joints are kept because there is always a little meat on them. Joints are placed in a bucket
and boiled, and if there is a lot the entire village
is invited to eat and drink the soup. The grease
on top is taken out of the bucket with a cup and
stored for use with dried meat. This grease is
different than marrow grease or fat grease
because it has been boiled.

COOKING

Dene had a variety of ways to cook food before
they began using metal pans. Meat and fish were
often boiled to produce both soup and cooked
meat. Fish and meat were often dried for later
use, but both fresh fish and meat were roasted
over an open flame or buried in hot coals. Every
part of the animal was used, from the stomach
to the hooves of caribou and moose.

In an article in the *Tundra Times*, Bessie
Walter, Maggie Isaac's mother, described how
to boil meat using hot stones. A birch bark
basket was placed in a hole in the ground, and
water and meat were placed in the basket.
Another basket full of water was placed in the
fire. Rocks were thrown in the fire and heated.
After the rocks became very hot, they were
removed from the fire and placed in the basket
with water to rinse off the ashes. The rocks were
then immediately taken out and placed in the
basket with water and meat. The stones boiled
the water and cooked the meat (Walter 1966).

Figure 1.1. Caribou meat drying at Tanacross, 1919. Photo by F. B. Drane. Photo by F. B. Drane, Drane Photo collection Alaska and Polar Regions Department, Elmer E. Rasmuson Library, University of Alaska, Fairbanks.

The Reverend David Paul (de Laguna and McClellan 1960b) provided additional information about cooking meat with hot stones.

(In) the old time, k'įį tth'áak they use [birch bark] basket for bucket. Can't put it in the fire. Cut meat and put it inside the basket. Then hot rocks—sticks. [Shows hot rocks were lifted from the fire with a pair of wooden tongs, manipulated by two hands]. Put it on the basket—make hot. Put nother rock in, nother one. Three rocks and want to get one more in. Ready to boil. Put in this last one and it boil. It kind of quit boil, put in nother rock.

When finish boil, drink soup.

Put water and meat in first [before hot rocks].

And cooking fish;

Fire in middle of the house, got hot ashes. Put them aside, make a hole in there. Put fish there. Then cover with ashes. Build a fire on top. Maybe half, maybe one hour.

Fire going down, take out fish. See if its cooked, roasted.

Take off fish skin—inside is nice and clean, white.

And cooking rabbit;

You want to cook meat, take rabbit skin, outside fur side (turn) outside.[8] Put meat inside, and cover it. Put in hot ashes. You cover it. After one hour you tear off rabbit skin. Inside meat is clean. [This technique can be used] for any kind of meat, just to keep clean.

And moose stomach;

Moose stomach—one side, the small smooth one, clean it. Me, Joe [Joseph] and I cook. (We use) that little sack. Put meat and water (and little fat—see below). Tie on top so no air come out. Hang on string, and turn around, all the time (over the fire).

---

8   When a rabbit is skinned, the skin is pulled down the animal's body, creating a tube of skin with the fur on the inside. When using the skin to cook, the fur must be on the outside.

(Pretty soon is cooked). Me and Joe we hunt that way (And cook that way).

Cut open. Cooked meat, soup. Don't want that sack too hot, or it break open, and soup is drained out. You want to be careful.

[Q] How long does it take to cook?

[A] One hour, I guess.

And we roast meat on a stick, too.

Big shot sit down like this [legs cross]. Slaves bring him food. Pretty soon big man finish to eat. He takes away plate and clean with moss. Just use (moss) once and throw away.

You can use small moose stomach for water bag. Clean, wash it. Use for out camping.

[When cooking the moose stomach] add little fat. That makes grease to mix the water, to taste good. Indian eat meat, if that meat got no fat, got to put fat with it. If you eat poor moose, no fat—that's no help [not nourishing].

We got meat is no fat on, (we) got to have little strip of caribou fat.

If cook summer the fat can spoil. Got to boil fat and put it away for keep.

Some people look for bear, because (bear) got plenty fat. Need one bear per year. Take out fat. Go hillside, get red berries. Make pot of grease—Put berries in there.

If you eat that in the morning, go out hunting, you no hungry all day. Fish oil and berries, same way, help you not to be hungry.

And berries;

Get them in fall time. Slow to get ripe. Grow low on the ground. Got white flower in the spring. Last of September is time to pick him up. [It is not cranberries]. Inside got hard seed like rock. It don't hurt you. Sometimes you chew, you take out juice, you can throw away seed. Or you can chew (and swallow seed).

[If] berry got no grease, no good for stomach they say.

"All kinds of berries"—i.e., any kind—jêg.

But don't mix the berries; (each basket has only one kind).

And sour fish;

Fish—fall time, they dig hole. Clean fish and cover it with dirt. It sour a little bit—like you say (little bit sour) fish. Some man make it too strong, but I want it just a little bit sour. Eat some, make you feel good.

Ts'A nax—that's his soup. Good for heart burn. You walk long time, you tired. You cook, make the soup. I take 2 little slice (2 inches long or wide?), cook, I eat and take the soup. Help heart burn.

In 2000, Ellen Demit described how to cook without metal pans to Don Callaway and Connie Miller-Friend (2001). Ellen repeatedly uses the phrase *Ts'edoghanih*, which means to be prepared for any situation.

If you got no bucket, you know what you doing.

You know how to cook out there.

You got out there and you got no nothing.

You take some part of the moose. You goin' wash it [the meat]. You goin' dig the ground. You heat up with rock. With clean stick you put rock in that thing and meat already thin' cook for yourself if you know what you doing.

Roots [tsaath]—dig them up out of ground, taste like potatoes, mixed with a little rice.

We gonna smoke fish, but our fresh fish goin' be, we smoke a little bit, whole fish, we smoke a little bit and we put away in the cache.

Grease, moose head soup we goin' chopped up. We goin' make grease out o' moose fat. Sometimes we put berries and fish oil. We gotta fix it. We boil fish oil. We put water in there. We boil it. It just tastes like, come out like bacon grease.

Figure 1.2. Annie Denny and Archie Denny, Tanacross 1937. Caribou meat is spread out on the ground. In the background is a sweathouse. Photo by Lucille Wright, William E. Simeone photo collection.

And we mix with dry blue berries. It's for old people.

Rose hip, you got your porcupine. You cut up porcupine fat. You get grease out of porcupine. You mix with rose hip. That's just vitamin C. And we make dry meat.

But then we take moose stomach, whole moose stomach, we take it out. We dry, and we have a lot of dry meat.

We pound the meat soft.

We put the moose stomach inside the ground. We put stick around. We put grease in there. After grease cool off, we put our dry meat.

That's real special food. We never eat big either, just a little piece. That's enough to last up. Old people real careful for their food. Never eat all time just gotta eat good. (Callaway and Miller-Friend 2001: 19)

This one I want young people to listen. He always wash food too much and flavor out. Ruin that food when you wash too much.

You got your fresh meat up there. Leave on meat cache. You smoke it a little bit and go ahead and work on. Put it away.

You don't wash your food too much. Us native people, we don't like that. Make sure you cut your meat good. Clean. Make sure

you gotta have something under your moose meat before you skin. Make sure you prepare. (Callaway and Miller-Friend 2001: 22)

Cooking liver in the fire

From there, and my grandpa used to cook caribou liver.

He just, he clean it and he put campfire.

You just push those dirt.

Me, I stand watch, not goin' eat.

And my grandpa, he throw that liver in the fire.

Nothing in there.

He covered with dirt, he don't care.

Guess what, when after we come back, we pack meat all day we come back, my grandpa break those marrow and take caribou liver and he clean it with out there on branch, clean special branch and he clean it and he slice it and eat it.

Boy, delicious, eat.

That's what I say, "you gotta learn how to cook campfire." (Callaway and Miller-Friend 2001: 47)

Ellen said that when her father butchered a moose, he skinned it perfectly. He knew which meat was hard and tough, which should be boiled, and which could be roasted. Ellen described preparing different parts of the moose, including sinew, dry meat, and moose stomach.

> We camp.
>> We camp and we dry a lot of back sinew.
>> We call tth'eex tthiin'
>> And we make dry meat special way.
>> We take sinew out and English we goin' say, "back sinew."
>> And we take it out, that one, whole you got take our sinew put for sewing and then cut that dry meat real thin.
>> Just huge dry meat.
>> We have caribou meat and moose meat dry together.
>> And moose stomach, if you take care.
>> You take it out without 'n hole [in the stomach].
>> That moose stomach, one moose stomach, just think four different kind [stomachs] in there, and I cannot talk.
>> One we call sausage, and one we call a ch'etthiinikónn' [stomach lining], ch'enad-huht' een, ch'etel.
>> With we call moose stomach and "ch'emet."
>> Connect with moose stomach.
>> You take it out real good, without 'n tore.
>> It looks like little liver.
>> You goin' cut open. You goin' stuff with moose fat.
>> With all full of moose fat and you goin' build fire and you goin' cook it with campfire till real burned, and you goin' take it down and you slice it. Moose stomach— . . . moose stomach you open the outside that look like net you goin' take it out real clean and wash that ch'enadhuut'een. (Callaway and Miller-Friend 2001: 49–50)

Ellen emphasized again that nothing was wasted, and she talked about saving for emergencies when food was in short supply. She again used the word *ts'edoghanih* to describe how her mother filled an old tin with a little bit of fat, dry meat, tea, and sugar to be used in emergencies. Years later, Ellen found the can hung in a tree along with a bunch of caribou feet.

> Caribou feet, caribou, moose, my mother climb the tree with it.
>> Tie to tree good.
>> My mother say "ts'edoghanih."
>> Ts'edoghanih mean you prepare.
>> You goin' go someplace, you got stuck, you goin' 'member that.
>> You hungry, you goin' 'member where you put that caribou feet.
>> My mother have a can, old fashioned lard can.
>> She puts a little bit o' sugar, little o' tea and little bit o' dry meat, little bit o' fat. (Callaway and Miller-Friend 2001: 54)

Oscar Isaac (Simeone 1987k) also described saving caribou feet for hard times and how to prepare them.

> Caribou feet soup is made during hard times. Caribou hooves are split down the center and hung up in trees. Long strings of hooves are wound around a big tree with large branches that keep off the rain. These never spoil. When you want to eat you soak them in water, then boil them and the soup appears like milk, white and the same consistency. There is also grease. It is the number one animal soup but you cannot drink too much. You also eat the foot, it is like pickled pigs' feet. Moose fat is also eaten, this is very rich food.

Silas Solomon said some caribou meat was eaten fresh, but most was smoked or dried. Silas said they had to keep the rain off the meat because rain makes the meat hard. They mixed caribou meat with fat, or tallow, so the meat would be soft. Fat came from animal bones. Dried caribou meat was put in underground caches. Caches remained at a constant temperature, so the food would not spoil or freeze.

In this interview Martha Isaac (Simeone 1987l) recalled how her family cooked food, particularly caribou, when she was growing up in the 1920s.

During the day just watch meat and wash clothes. No cooking like now, just fry meat, or on a stick and when my dad stay home in evening he make bannock and we save it for another lunch. Both mom and dad cooked. Cook bones, don't want to throw it away. Huge pile of bones from caribou and they split bone and cook it for marrow and grease and that grease go in little stomach and that too they cook it and put it in stomach and they flatten it out and in winter cut it into little strips like wrapping paper and they can get grease from it. Caribou, extra little stomach, make sack for grease. Fat is left open some place but grease is saved in stomach. Grease is kidney fat, kidney is big and they have to cook it fast because it will sour. Most of that work done by women and women tan skins. If they have time [at camp to] start to tan skin, clean it so it's easier to make skin when they get home. Old time they cook grease, water and leave little stomach by fire and water keeps it from burning [Martha said she never saw that kind of cooking]. Men kill the caribou, and butcher and then hang the meat until it's a little dry. After it's a little dry meat is easier to cut.

Photo-montage by Hal Gage.

2 LIFE ON THE LAND

The Seasonal Round 1910–1940

Today upper Tanana Dene no longer live exclusively from the land yet their ties to the land remain strong. While many Dene live in villages, modern life is still regulated by the seasons. In summer many families go to fish camp, and during the fall they make an effort to pick berries and hunt moose, traveling in automobiles and seldom spending the night away from home. The economics and physical labor of trapping make it unattractive to most upper Tanana Dene. Those who continue to trap use snow machines, which make it easy to return to the village instead of spending nights on the trapline. While many people continue to hold traditional beliefs about animals, some elders lament that many young people are ignorant of what is injih or forbidden.

The narratives in this chapter are recollections of a different time, before all of the modern conveniences we take for granted. Trapping was the only way to make money. Food could be abundant one year and scarce the next. Animals were not always at the same place, so people had to move and look for food in many different places. The narratives show how ingenious and resourceful Dene were at living in a harsh environment. Traveling in extreme cold required discipline and an exact rhythm. Men moved ahead, breaking trail, setting up camp, and finally bringing the family to the new campsite. Women and men had specific tasks. Women cut meat, tanned skins, picked berries, snared rabbits, and took care of children; men hunted and trapped.

Figure 2.1. Brittan Jonathan on winter trail near Mansfield, 1986. Photo by William E. Simeone.

These narratives are linked to previous history and include continuity with the past but also speak of significant changes. Until the construction of the Alaska Highway in the 1940s, the upper Tanana region remained relatively isolated. In the nineteenth century, trade goods were only available if Dene traveled outside the region, so reliance on trade

https://doi.org/10.5876/9781646423347.c002

Figure 2.2. Jessie Mark making overnight camp, 1969. Photo by Marie-Françoise Guédon, courtesy of Bee Paul. William E. Simeone Photo collection.

Figure 2.3. John Luke at George Creek. Jeany Healy Photo Collection UAF-2000-181-129.

Figure 2.4. Lucy Adams gathering berries, 1969. Photo by Marie-Françoise Guédon. Courtesy of Bee Paul. William E. Simeone photo collection.

goods developed slowly. Firearms came first, and Titus David mentions that his father used a muzzle loader while Titus used a level action rifle. Access to trade goods, such as tea, flour, sugar, and rice, made starvation less of a threat. Avis Sam recalled that food was more plentiful once the traders arrived, but people still experienced shortages and hunger.

Figure 2.5. Little Frank and family. Indians moving camp. This is near Paul's Place. We left Tanana Crossing April 11th, very warm, water under ice on river." Photo by F. B. Drane. Drane photo collection Alaska and Polar Regions Department, Elmer E. Rasmuson Library, University of Alaska Fairbanks.

In the context of increasing White encroachment and restrictive regulation, the elders' accounts are often political. Chief Andrew Isaac constantly reminded anyone who would listen that Dene used all the land: "Indian don't stay in one village year around," he would say. They moved to intercept the annual caribou migrations and spread out across the land. Then, to emphasize this point, he would mention the many different places people used in their annual round.

> Indian don't stay in one village year around, summer, spring got to move dry place, dry ground. Us we move where caribou herd going, we know certain day certain time when they going to go that's why we got so many camps from Lake Mansfield, over to Big Hill, Old Cache, Stone House, Little Denison, Long Cabin, Wolf Creek, Mosquito Fork, Indian Creek, Rock Creek,

Creek this side of Indian Creek on the hill, Flint Hill, Hay Creek and Ketchumstuk. (Isaac 1984a)

ELDERS' NARRATIVES

PAUL KIRSTEATTER: HEALY LAKE

In a 2000 interview with Connie Miller-Friend and Don Callaway, Paul Kirsteatter described how Healy Lake people spent a year. Healy Lake people practiced the "cycle," as Paul called it, until World War II. Kirsteatter was married to Margaret, whose parents were Gus Jacob from Ketchumstuk and Agnes Sam from Healy Lake. Paul was a serious student of Dene culture and wrote out long descriptions of Dene culture that he sent to Robert McKennan (appendix A).

Winter was spent up the Healy River at the village of Joseph, or Tehluug Niindeex Ndiig,

Figure 2.6. The Reverend David Paul at Camp Lake. Camp Lake, or *Niindeeyh Mĕnn'* ("Stopping Lake"), was part of David Paul's trapline. Jeany Healy Collection, UAF 2000-181-156.

"Whitefish Moves Creek." Paul said Healy River people had a caribou fence in the area and they fished for grayling and whitefish in Joseph Creek.

> The Spring they come back [to Healy Lake]. It was a cycle. They come back here for the moose, beaver, and fish. They weren't dependent too much on the fish, but although they did have fish that mostly, and there's not salmon come up this, this part of the Tanana, very few so they depended mostly on whitefish. But they had traps down there on the Healy River, traps up the Healy River for whitefish. And then in the fall they'd gather berries and all. They went up in the Alaska Range over here for sheep and marmot. And the women and all would go along too and they pick berries and the women would pack and snare the marmot and the men would hunt sheep. Then they would come back here and prepare to go back up into their caribou fences, up the Middle Fork as far down the Middle Fork as Joseph Village. That was Healy Lake people's area up there. (Callaway and Miller-Friend 2001: 125)

JULIUS PAUL: TANACROSS

Julius Paul was born in 1913. In 1987 he described to the author his experiences out on the land as

Figure 2.7. Joe and Salina Joseph on the trail, spring 1919. The children are wearing caribou skin pullovers. The little girl sitting in the sled has a hood decorated with cloth and buttons. Photo by F. B. Drane. Drane photo collection Alaska and Polar Regions Department, Elmer E. Rasmuson Library, University of Alaska Fairbanks.

a young man (Simeone 1987a). When Julius was young, Mansfield (not Tanacross) was the primary village where people stayed during holidays like Christmas and in the summer to fish. Fall and early winter were spent on the trapline working out of Camp Lake (*Niindeeyh Mĕnn'*). Summer was spent fishing at Mansfield. People went wherever they thought they could get moose. Sometimes Julius's family went to Sand Lake (*Ch'inchedl Měnn'*) to hunt moose or hunted sheep in the Alaska Range. When possible, extended families hunted together, but when food was scarce each family struck out on its own or joined up with relatives who had food. Throughout his narrative Julius connects people with places. He also refers to Sam Thomas, who was highly respected for his abilities as a hunter and provider. Paul points out that when the family ran short of food, they visited Sam Thomas.

[The family] hunted for moose at Camp Lake, tracking it and using lookout [to spot moose]. Never saw them use snares [to take moose]. There was snare fence on Little Tanana, Annie Denny's daddy made it when mission was there. Also, there were snare fences located at Indian Creek, which is close to Ketchumstuk.

Hunt, dry meat for winter: caribou, moose, and bear. Cook and get grease, save that. Go to Camp Lake via Billy Creek trail. Whole family camp there, sometimes four of five families [these included Julius's brother, David Paul, Joe Joseph who was married to Julius's sister Salina, Henry Luke who was married to Julius' aunt Jennie, sometimes Peter Thomas and Sam Thomas, who were Julius's maternal uncles]. Group splits up and go off in different directions because everybody can't go one trail, not much room.

Went to [Camp Lake] Niindeeyh Měnn' in September and they could catch both moose and caribou. Stay there for about a month to dry the meat. Make trip to Mansfield to haul meat. Also make high cache at Camp Lake until snow came then haul meat into Mansfield.

From Camp Lake went back to Mansfield. Winters spent out on trap line. Some people leave Mansfield before Christmas and come back for Christmas; others stay until after Christmas, leave the village in January, and come back about April. Some-

times one or two family stay in village but the majority left.

People go wherever they think they can get moose. One time we move down to Sam Creek [Taak'etth Ndiig] for one winter, almost to Sand Lake. Sometimes we go to the same place two years running but other times we go to different place; have to change around. Went to Long Cabin [Dechenh Ghajenįį'ah Denh] after Christmas for a while because there is lots of meat up there in caches. That year we didn't go out and we don't have much meat. Moses' [Thomas] daddy [Sam Thomas] up there and Kenneth's [Thomas] dad told my mother to go up there and stay with him. We go up there and hunt around there. Come to spring we move around down to Wolf Lake and trap for muskrats and then return to Mansfield.

One time, in the fall, we go to Sheep place [Demee Ndaag, in the Alaska Range]. Joe's [Joseph] family, Henry Luke's family, David's family, our family. It took three camps [nights] to get there, small kids slow you down. Mansfield to Tanana River one day, next day to Cathedral [Demee Ndaag], and third day to Sheep place, bottom of the hill. We saw sheep every day, shoot them with rifle. Caribou live down there, kill moose, and bear; got enough meat that time. From there we go across the river and cut across the country to Mansfield. [note: Demee Ndaag means sheep lick so there were several places with that place name].

Most of the summer spent fishing in Mansfield. Fall go out short way for moose. Long Cabin and Paul's Place [Nataatey also referred to as Paul's Cabin] are farthest away from Mansfield. Paul's Place is where my daddy live. Old Paul and Chief Isaac's trapline was in the vicinity of Paul's Place which just like their village. People live there all the time. Two or three or four families live there. Blind Henry lived there too, he was chief after my daddy.

Mouth of the Tok River, Thirty-mile Hill, Johnny Jonathan's family and Charlie James were the people who used that trail. From Wolf Lake (Shós Měen) they walk up river clear up to Porcupine Creek, make raft to come back.

Sometime went to Mosquito Fork for muskrat and wolf. Hunted wolf for the 15-dollar bounty. Never went to Ketchumstuk when I grew up, only went there when I was kid. Hunted muskrats in Tetlin when I was older. Also went clear to Northway, wife's daddy spent spring up there. He went to Tetlin because my brother was there and it was easy for him to hunt. Go up there around April and come back in June time. (Simeone 1987a)

ISABEL JOHN: TANACROSS

Isabel John was born in 1922. In this interview conducted by Bella Paul, the daughter of Julius Paul, Isabel provides a woman's perspective of life on the land after people had begun settling around St. Timothy's Mission at Tanacross. Missionaries pressured people to settle down, grow gardens, and send their children to school, but they also realized that people had to be on the land to survive. After planting a garden in May, almost everyone left the village to spend the summer and fall fishing, hunting, and gathering food for the coming winter. Isabel talks about many of the activities women did throughout the year, including snaring rabbits, gathering duck eggs and birch bark, tanning skins, picking berries, and digging roots. Her drawing of a camp illustrates some of the different women's activities, including tanning skin and tending to the meat-drying racks. Isabel also talks about many of the places her family visited, like Big Hill, Long Cabin, and Camp Lake. She notes that they also went to Tetlin and Northway and describes how people used the rivers to travel, the dangers of the Tok River in the Alaska Range, and who hunted and

trapped up the Tok River. Isabel ends the interview by talking about getting groceries from traders like Tom Denny and the trails used to reach the Copper River.

Grandparents always treat us good and teach us to hunt. Take us out hunting, set snare for rabbits. Learned mostly from my grandma, taught us how to cut meat, trapping for muskrat. Busy with us more than our mother. Cut our clothes, taught us how to sew, make moccasin. Mom told us how to clean the skin, that is mostly what my mom did.

Grandma took us out in May to look around for eggs, duck eggs, all different kind of colors. Put in the water, if it sinks that's good, if it floats a little bird is in there. Eight-pound lard can of eggs boiled.

Pick mushrooms, grandma tell us which is good, fry mushrooms in grease. That's how we learn what to do. After grandma died we remember what to do.

Birch bark, go around and pick lots of that kind. August make baskets for blue berries and cranberries.

May went down to Big Hill [Teyh Chox] and Long Cabin to make dry meat. My mom tell us to help her cut some meat and we got to make a good fire under dry meat and smoke it. Put smoke under skin and help her tan skin. They busy with us all that time. Everybody have dry meat and grease and fat. The whole village help each other to have enough dry meat and fish. Busy for their food all summer, after school. Now we come back before September.

Go to school early. First of May school is out so whole village all go out, only a few people left in the village, whole village all go out to Big Hill and Long Cabin and Camp Lake, they just go here and there where they fishing and hunting. They come back in September and dig garden out.

Tthihdzeen, a little way from Big Hill, stay there all summer and come back in

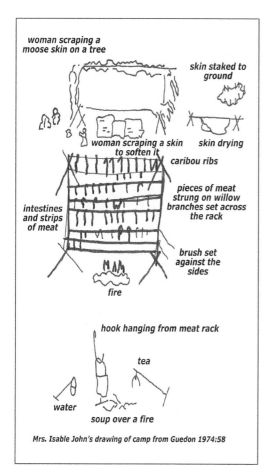

woman scraping a
moose skin on a tree

skin staked to
ground

woman scraping a skin   skin drying
to soften it

caribou ribs

pieces of meat
strung on willow
branches set across
the rack

intestines
and strips
of meat

brush set
against the
sides

fire

hook hanging from meat rack

tea

water

soup over a fire

Mrs. Isable John's drawing of camp from Guedon 1974:58

Figure 2.8. Sketch of camp by Isabel John, redrawn from Guédon (1974: 58).

Figure 2.9. Bell Abraham tanning skin, 1937–1938. Photo by Lucille Wright. William E. Simeone photo collection.

August. Then we went to Big Hill and then Long Cabin. No name for Long Cabin so they call it that. I went as far as Dick Ranch walking and hunting. Stay in Ketchumstuk all summer and go over to Dick Ranch. That is our country you know for our camp, we go through all our camp in summer for berries. From there we go short cut to Camp Lake then we come through Camp Lake trail with walk.

And during Christmas they just go around with sled and one sled filled up with dry meat and fat and grease and berries. And another sled is filled with cabbage, carrots, and potatoes. That's for cook, that's the way they used to do that in the old village over there. We put away all our garden. Just like we raise up Alaska food. Grandma take us out and dig up some roots in September and grandma put away for us in grease, fish grease. And we help my grandmother to skin, to make babiche [rawhide cut into thin strips used as webbing in snowshoes]. She teach us how to make babiche. Gee that was really good to do that but I don't know why we don't do that. That's really good to make that.

I think it's really good long time ago when teenagers help mom and dad and do everything, that's how we learn everything and right now we use it. We gotta help teach our grand kids like that.

Figure 2.10. Doris Charles working on skin, with Bessie Walter standing in the background. Note the frame for smoking the skin. Photo by C. Heller, Anchorage Museum of History and Art.

Figure 2.12. Maggie (Demit) Isaac collecting birch bark at Tanacross, 1937–1938. Photo by Lucille Wright. William E. Simeone photo collection.

Figure 2.13. Wringing out a moose skin at Tanacross, 1937–1938. Photo by Lucille Wright. William E. Simeone photo collection.

Figure 2.11. Martha Isaac tanning skin. Photo by William E. Simeone.

Figure 2.14. (*right*) Maggie (Demit) Isaac working on moose skin at Tanacross, 1937–1938. Photo by Lucille Wright. William E. Simeone photo collection.

We have log cabin and all summer we stay in tent, Big Hill and Long Cabin. Visit Tetlin, go through and stop one night. Have dog team, go to Tetlin and stop one night. Go to Northway and stay there and my daddy get ready for potlatch for uncle. So we stay there all summer, Mom cut dry fish and we came back in July with boat. Old man Northway bring us back. Just Tetlin and Northway we visited when we were young. (B. Paul 1987a)

TITUS DAVID: TETLIN

In this wide-ranging 1980 interview, Tetlin elder Titus David talks about growing up, learning to hunt, and how to behave properly. As a child, Titus said, he knew nothing about hunting, not even which way the wind blew. Later he learned how to hunt by watching his parents. He hunted on the Ladue River, the Dennison Fork of the Fortymile River, and the Tanana River at Riverside. Moose were not abundant, and people had to travel a long way to find them. Titus provides details about hunting, including catching molting ducks and using dip nets to catch muskrats.

I was born February 28, 1904.
Ever since I was a boy, began walk, follow my dad where he go. My dad want to get away from every time. I cry. I know where he went.
I try to catch him.
He chase me back home.
Got no right to go hunting.
Which way wind blow.
Later go by myself.
[Stay in] Skin tent go out hunting.
Kids get little wood, birch bark, grass. Start, make fire. Use fungus and bow drill.
Ask question, they don't tell us.
Had canoe, little bow and arrow.
Hunt ducks with bow and arrow and canoe.

Show me how to paddle.
Go up stream, down stream. July month easy to get ducks.
No feathers.
Go up to them and grab them.
Show me how to make arrow. Shoot in shallow place.
Fall time mom and dad hunt rats with babiche dip net. Chase them out of the house. Spring time cut open muskrat house and kill the rats and they climb out. Club them.
Big Game. My dad show me how to skin moose. Young people don't know how. Know how to cut moose muscle. Heart and stomach, put grease and berries in stomach.
Ladue and Dennison, Riverside [places where Titus hunted]. No moose those days. Have to go a long way to kill moose. Never moved all the meat, cached it.
No traps, use spring traps for wolverine.
[I was] Ten years old steel traps come in—1910. John Strelic brought steel traps into the country.
Hunt caribou on the Ladue River.
At Tetlin there were lots of caribou but after the road [Alaska Highway] came through never see caribou herd. Have to go to Eagle.

Titus finished the interview by saying how important it was for young people to listen to their elders and obey the rules so they could survive off the land.

Listen to old people. I listen so people will think I am a man. Even today I listen to my boy who turned out alright.
Have to help everyone, even an old dog who is left to die. Don't laugh at anyone, you get punished if you laugh at old people. Have to give something before you go by. Don't bother small little animals, might bring bad luck. Use to bother little ducks when learning how to hunt.
Show us how to survive. Dig roots out.

Show us which ones to eat.

Lots of things to eat but some young people don't know.

Never went sheep hunting. My mother used to tell about hunting sheep. (Simeone 1980a)

ANONYMOUS SOURCE: LAST TETLIN

In the late 1960s Marie-Françoise Guédon (1974: 44) interviewed a female resident of Tetlin about life in Last Tetlin. The village of Last Tetlin was a good example of how Native people situated their homes to take advantage of local food sources. The community was so well situated that people did not often have to travel very far from the village. There was a fish weir in front of the village and to the west was a caribou fence, while minutes away from the village were lakes with beaver and muskrat.

> March. April, we trap rats on lake. Late April, the rat houses go down [through the ice]. We wait until May when open lake, rats come out. We set trap and we shoot them. This spring, I stay in my dad's camp, Last Tetlin. Ducks come in May. June time, fish run, we dry fish, moose, caribou all year. Caribou are coming back spring time. We make dry meat for winter. Better in August time. In September, it's too late—too cold.
>
> Summertime, we stay Last Tetlin. Then we pick berries. Old time, we never use groceries. Roots, we get in September, October. Tsüü root, take off and leave for winter, taste sweet and good. Ducks go out in September, October.
>
> Fall time, October, we get fish at Last Tetlin. Fish grease we use for some berries. Wintertime you use fish grease; summertime you cannot; it tastes something. . . . November time, they use dip net, Last Tetlin. Sometimes they can take ten, thirteen fish together, November, you get pike on the ice. Ch'į̂o', or "hook" with line to

Figure 2.15. Building a birch bark canoe. In the Tanacross language the word for canoe is *k'įj ts'eyh*. Drane photo collection, Alaska and Polar Regions Department, Elmer E. Rasmuson Library, University of Alaska Fairbanks. UAF-1991-0046-00455.

Figure 2.16. "Rat canoe" made of canvas. Jessie David, Roy David, and Walter David. These canoes were lightweight, could be easily carried by one person, and were used to hunt muskrats and to tend fish nets. Photo by C. Heller, Anchorage Museum of History and Art.

> catch ling cod, you use on ice. Little pike, ch'uljüüdn you catch with Ch'į̂o'too.
>
> December, creek freezes. No fish, no beaver open. My mom's dad, chief Luke, he stays Xaal Männ; he used to trap there. We stay with him wintertime when were small. We use to come to Tetlin for Christmas, then go back Last Tetlin. Wintertime, we

trap, [gather] k'įį, birch bark, they leave berries in it. They don't use caches [elevated caches made of logs] like now, but they dig holes. Make clean inside with bark. They leave food in there, berries, grease, everything. Ch'ishyagn, marrow, my mom used to take all that ch'ishyagn out, put in bag. Then they take dry meat, put inside; we eat in wintertime, all good.

"Rotten fish" [fermented fish], they do that too. Good for old time people; my grandma, my mother's mother, used to do that. By this time, September, they clean fish, put in cache in ground. Take off October time, make grease with that thing; save it for winter; it stinks too. They make soup. Lugnetsiil, little bit rotten fish in cache, but not really rotten fish.

Figure 2.17. Drying meat at Nabesna, 1930. Photo by Robert McKennan, courtesy William Workman.

AVIS SAM: NORTHWAY

In 2001, Avis Sam was interviewed by Olga Lovick (Sam, Demit-Barnes, and Northway 2021: 84–97). Avis was a member of the Old Nabesna band who had fish camps on the lower Nabesna and Chisana Rivers and traplines and hunting areas in the Ladue River drainage. In this interview, which was conducted in the Upper Tanana language, Avis gives a detailed description of life on the land. She begins by describing life on the trapline on the Ladue River and how the family's only food was animals killed by her father. There was a discipline, a rhythm, that ensured survival in extreme cold. Avis's father first broke trail, then set up the tent and stove before moving the family. Everyone had to pitch in: the boys chopped wood while the girls melted snow. Avis tells us she was born when it was minus 50 degrees, and to keep her warm, they wrapped her in a squirrel's nest. Avis then talks about spending spring at Lower Nabesna and the fish camp called K'ehtthîign Niign where people dried fish and stored them in underground

Figure 2.18. Elisha Demit and family on the trail, 1930. Photo by Robert McKennan, courtesy William Workman.

caches. She also talks about gathering berries during the summer and the moment the traders arrived with flour, rice, sugar, and tea. "And that's probably when we eat well." Avis also refers to a time when there were no stores and people ate only what they could kill or gather, such as muskrat candy.

Shihǫǫłiin dą'
When I was born

Shnąą eh shta' eh Ladue Hill degn' nee-htiłeek xay tah.

My mom and dad would take us up into the Ladue Hills in the wintertime.

Daa' hǫǫt'ay eh, daa' hut'eegn eh.[1]
It used to be just like it is now.

Shta' eeł idlaak.
My father used to set traps.

Tl'aan udzih eh diniign eh įhxąą.
And he killed caribou and moose.

Nts'uu'aal xah t'eey shyi' kol.
So we could eat, there was no food.

Jah ts'änh ts'idek tah xał eh,
When we would move on from here with a dogteam [sled],

neełįįgn' neełiign' dahdiłeegn tl'aan xał t'eey nahdegn' ts'idek.
They would hitch up dogs and then we would go up with the sled.

Shta' neettheh tąy hohtsiik.
My father would break trail ahead of us.

Aayh eh tihaak na'ahdegn' <Ch'uh tl'ayh> hinih niig.
He would go with snowshoes up there in what they call "glistening place."

Tl'aan ay ay tl'aan łįį iin hudegn' tihaak tay'.
And then he would go up again with the dogs.

Ay ishyiit t'eey t'axoh taathüh eh stove eh taałeeł.
And then finally he would bring the tent and the stove.

Ay hunadegn' ndeh k'eh ni'ihhaagn dänh taathüh ni'ehnay.

He went up as far as he could and then he would set up the tent.

Ay tl'aan ch'a na'idaak neekah na'edaak t'axoh mbeh ts'idek.
And then he'd come back, he would stay for us, and finally we would go with him.

Tseenaa, t'axoh tseenaa nahdegn'.
We'd move there, finally we'd move up there.

Neexonh ts'iikeey gaay ts'įįłįį t'oot'eey tsidek!
Us, we were children, young children but we would walk!

K'at'eey xał shyiit neehidlaak.
They wouldn't take us in the sled.

Xał shyiit dzeltth'ih de' eli::h tsaałeel ch'a'.
If we'd been sitting in the sled, we would have gotten cold!

Hu'eh tsidek.
We would walk with them.

Ay tl'aan t'axoh ishyiit nits'inįįdeeł de' ishyiit dzaltth'iił tthee di'eel' natnal'įįl xah.
And then when we'd finally get there we will stay there for a while so my dad could check his traps.

Ay and ay tl'aan udzih dhehxįį de' nah'ǫǫ niitaałeeł.
And if he killed a caribou, he'd bring it back in from outside.

Ay tl'aan diniign dhehxįį de', ay chih hah'ǫǫ niitaałeeł.
And when he kills a moose too he'd bring it back in from outside.

Ay tl'aan ishyiit ts'änh t'eey eeł taadlaał.
And from there he will set traps.

1   It was also winter and snowing hard at the time of the interview [footnotes are in the original translation].

Hudegn' tsidek tah taathüh shyiit dzeltth'iik.
When we'd go around, we would stay in a
tent.

Ay tl'aan neexonh ts'iikeey choh ts'įįłįį
shǫǫnüü iin łaakaay helt'eh ay iin tsät
hittheeł.
And then us, we were big children, and I
had two older brothers, they would chop
wood.

Neexah tsät hah'ogn nts'ą̈' tah ts'änh tsät
hittheeł tl'aan niihiidelshyeek.
For us they would chop wood out there and
bring it back to us.

Ay tl'aan t'eey ay tl'aan tsät hittheel tl'aan
neexonh ts'exeh ts'įįłįį du', nah'ǫǫ shyüh
daats'elshyeek tl'aan tl'aan daats'elshyeek
tl'aan stove k'it na'ulxįį xah.
And then they would chop wood and us
girls, we would bring in snow from outside and, we would bring it back in so it
would melt on the stove.

Tuu ts'ixą̈ą̈.
We were making water.

Shyüh ts'änh tuu ts'ixą̈ą̈ ishyiit du' shną̈ą̈
yeh ch'uhmbia xah.
We were making water from snow so that
my mother could cook with it.

Tl'aan chih ay tl'aan neeshyah xah tuu
tsaaxą̈ą̈ tl'aan łįį xah chih tuu tsaaxą̈ą̈ ay
du'.
And then, when we'd made water for our
house we would make water for the dogs
too.

Shta' łįį teedlah de' na'inshyah de' hushyi'
nach'ihuu'aal xah hushyi' ts'ehmbiah.[2]

When my father would take the dogs and
would come back, their food, so they
could eat it, we'd cook their food.

Dziin tah hǫǫ' ts'edį'.
We did that during the day.

Ay tl'aan t'axoh eeł įįdla' ishyiit t'axoh
ch'ookol de' tay' t'eey ch'iduugn tąy noot-
ahtsay.
And then he finally would have set traps
and if then there'd be nothing in it, he
would make trail again to somewhere
else.

Aayh eh taahaał tąy.
He will go there with snowshoes on the
trail.

Ay tl'aan t'axoh ishyiit nts'ą̈' ts'ineey de'.
And then it would be about time we moved
there.

Neets'ädn' ishyiit ts'änh jah nits'inįįnah
dänh nts'ą̈' ch'idänh nts'ą̈' natsetneey
t'eey.
Our stuff, from where we moved there, we
would start off to a different place.

Neets'ädn' noo ch'ittheh nitaałeeł.[3]
He would move our stuff ahead.

Ay ay tl'aan t'axoh tsineey de', taathüh
naatahnek.
And then when it's time to leave, he would
take the tent down.

Ay eh hahde::::gn' tsaaneeł.
And we will go a long way up.

Ddhäł tah neexonh shyįį' hugn neexonh

2   It was the children's jobs to take care of the dogs while
Avis's dad would go into the tent to rest. He'd have a team
of eight or nine dogs and would often come back late at
night.
3   Tent and stove would be left until last, so that his family would be comfortable while he transported everything
else.

shyįį' hugn natsetdiik, shta' eeł uudla'
niign.
Among the mountains, only us, only us
would walk around there, on my father's
trapline.

Ishyiit ch'ale ch'ittheh niits'inįįnaa tl'aan
tay' ahde::gn' nats'etnaan eh.
This was the first place we'd move to then
again we would move up there.

Shtaay Joe Mark mǫǫsi'.
My paternal uncle Joe Mark,

Shtaay or shee'eh?[4]
Paternal uncle or maternal uncle?

Shee'eh, hunh.
My maternal uncle.

<Shee'eh> Joe mǫǫsi' di'aat eh dits'įįkeey eh
neek'eh hihnįįdeel.
My maternal uncle Joe, his wife and his
children they would come behind us.

Ay tl'aan shta' mǫǫnüü Bill Northway
mǫǫsi' di'aat Liza eh chih ay iin chih all
<neek'eh> nahtetdek.
And then my father's older brother Bill
Northway, his wife Liza too, they all
followed us.

Hiixah nįįdeeł k'eh ch'a doodeltsįį.
It sounded like they followed him.

Niithaat tah hǫǫ' shihinay, ch'eładn idhag-
nnüh.
A long time ago they told me this, I forget
some.

Eli::h hǫǫłįį, xay.
It was cold, winter.

Shnąą uts'iiniin uteełe'.
My mother was about to have her baby.

Ay t'axoh ts'iiniin muuteełe', ehnih, Martha
Mark sheh naholnegn tah dihnih.
And she was about to have her baby she
said, Martha Mark told me what I'm
saying now.

Ay ch'ale shnąą eh įįda' ay ts'iiniin mihǫǫłiin
du'.
And she was sitting with my mother while
she was giving birth.

Ts'exeh gaay nłįį.
It was a little girl.

Ay ch'a shiy.
And that was me.

Martha eli:::::h hǫǫłįį ehnih taathüh shyiit.[5]
Martha, they say it was really cold inside
the tent.

Ishyiit dą' laa down blanket ihitnay ha' ts'ät
ts'ät mädn gaay shyįį' t'eey hǫǫłįį ishyiit
dą' t'ay shyįį.
Back then they didn't know there's such a
thing down blanket, the only thing they
had was a small flimsy blanket.

Ay eli::h hǫǫłiin eh Martha nah'ogn dlegn
hut'oh de' kah natidaak.
And because it was so cold, Martha began
walking around out there looking for
squirrel nests.

Hǫǫ' shehnih.
She told me that.

Dlegn t'oh uudįh'aan ay nadįįdlah.
She found a squirrel's nest and took them
down.

---

4   Different words are used for "my father's brother"
(shtaay) and "my mother's brother" (shee'eh).

5   Avis was born in late February. She says the temperature was in the −50s.

Dlegn t'oh shyiit tl'oh.
Inside the squirrel's nest was grass.

Nįį!
Look!

Ushyii tl'oh su'.
In it is fine grass.
Nice!
She said it was like chuyh! Chuyh k'eh
    nt'eh.
She said it was like down feathers! It was
    like down feathers.

Ay ch'a ts'ät shyiit idįįdlah tl'aan.
And she packed that in the blanket and,

ts'ät shyiit idįįdlah tl'aan ay shyiit shįhtįį
    nagntän ch'a' le'.
she put that in the blanket and then she
    put me into it to prevent my freezing, I
    guess.

Ay Martha Mark hǫǫ' shehnay ch'ale ay
    dihnay.
And I'm saying it the way Martha Mark told
    me.

T'axoh nidhihshyąą, nidhihshyaan eh
    hǫǫ't'eey hudegn' shta' naneetiłeek.
And then I grew up, and when I was grow-
    ing up my father still would take us up
    there.

Ay ch'ale dadihnay that ninaholnek dą'
    natsetdek ndihnay.
That's the one I was telling you about when
    I was telling you the story, we went off, I
    told you.

Neexol' eh natsetdek.
We were walking on our legs.

Hahde:::gn' udzih įhxąą ay kįį' dzeltth'ih.
Up there he killed a caribou and we lived
    on it.

Ay tl'aan ahdǫǫ natsetdek tah, ahdǫǫ
    natsetdek tah k'at'eey keey niitsetdegn.
And then when we came back from up
    there, when we came back from up there,
    we would not go back to the village.

Ha'anoo datth'uugn neeshyah gaay hǫǫłįį
    dänh shyiit dzänh de' kah niitsetdek.
Up ahead a little ways toward the river we
    had a little house, there we went back to
    see if there's muskrat.

Ay tl'aan t'axoh łuugn t'axoh łuugn uteełe'
    de' łuugn natetłeek de',
And then, finally fish, when there was final-
    ly fish, when the fish come back,

Fish camp hinih dänh, shyiit dą' K'ehtthiign
    Niign mǫǫsi'.
At what they call fish camp, where they call
    it K'ehtth'iign Niign.

Ishyiit niitsetdek.
We would go back there.

Keey deltth'ii ay iin shyii all shyiit łehchin
    niihetdek łuugn de' kah.
The ones staying in the village all came to
    gather there to see if there was fish.

Łuugn heh'įį:::k tl'aan hiiyehgąy.
They take lots of fish and then they dried it.

Chinh shyiit hiiyidlaak xay xay uudih
    yuu'aal xah.
They would put them into the pole cache to
    eat them all winter long.

Łįį xah chih łuugn hit'üü, ay du' ch'its'ąą
    hiiyit'üü.[6]
They would also cut fish for the dogs but
    they cut it differently.

---

6 For people, they separate the sides and cut tails off. For
dogs, they keep the tails on and keep the fish in one piece,
just cut the ribs out.

Kelältseey hiiyehniik ay łįį shyi'.
Kelältseey they call it, the dog food.

Chinh shyiit ukol de' nän' shyii haahuhta-
ałeeł.
When there's no more [food] in the pole
cache, they take it out of the ground.

Nän' shyiit hahuhtaałeeł ishyiit dänh.
They take it out of the ground right there.

Dahshyuugn k'ąy' eh k'įį eh, k'įį hiishyiit
diłeek.
Into the hole they put willow and birch.

Ay k'it dishyi' k'ihiłeek shyi' łuugn eegąy
and shyi' eegąy chih heedlah ay de' chih
hiishyiit k'ihiiyįįleek.[7]
And on it they put their food, dry fish, and
if they have dry meat then they also put
that into the hole.

Xay tah hahiiyi'aak, hiitaa'aal xah.
They take it out in the winter so they can
eat it.

Ay du' hiik'it ch'iiłeek tl'aan ay k'it nän' eh
hiiyitsah.
And then they cover it [with spruce bark
etc.] and then earth, and they bury it.

Xa::y hǫǫłįį de' k'ahdu' November hǫǫłįį,
yeah, December, January le', hihdįįtsįį
de', hahiitaa'aał.
When it is winter—now it is November, yeah, maybe in December,
January—when they're hungry, they will
take it out.

Ay tl'aan ay ch'a hiikįį' deltth'ii.
And then that's what they live on.

Jah ch'ihuukeedn dänh shyiit ch'ookol hu.
There was no place where they could buy
anything.

Hushyi' kol de' hah'ogn nuun de' kah statah-
dek, dineh iin.
When they had no meat, they would go out
looking for little animals, the men.

Dii uhdih'aan, dii uhdih'aan hiitaa'aal
hiiyixąą.
Whatever they found, whatever they found,
they would kill [so] they could eat it.

Ay tl'aan ay kįį' hihdeltt'ih.
And then they would survive on that.

Ay ay tl'aan hǫǫ' ch'a xay uudih hihdeltth'ik
tl'aan dąy nootet-łe' de', hihdįįtsįįl t'axoh.
And in this way they lived all winter and
then when spring arrived again they
would finally be hungry.

Hushyi' kol.
They had no food.

Ay ay xah ch'ale' nihts'įįl de' kah hiiyuudeel
ay ch'a hiikįį' deltth'iik.
That's why they would go for muskrat candy and they would live on that.[8]

Ay chih hiiyi'aał.
They would eat that, too.

Shiin nahut-łįį de' ay xah ch'a ts'exeh iin
hah'ogn dii niishyeey ay t'eey hiinehtsiik,
hiinehtsiik, hiinehtsiik.[9]
When it became summer again the women
whatever grows out there they would
gather and gather and gather.

_____

7 They dig down three to four feet, so that animals
wouldn't dig it out. Then they'd put birch and willow and
then birch bark or spruce bark to keep the food clean.
Then they'd fill the hole up again.

_____

8 Muskrats store roots in the ground that are similar to
a potato and Dene would go out find the muskrat cache
and eat it. It was one way of getting vegetables in the
winter.

9 Ts'igǫǫ ("wild rhubarb") is eaten in spring but not
stored, according to Avis it's good for the stomach.

Ay du' ay du' xay nahut-łįį de' hiikįį' dultth'i xah ch'a hiiyeh'ąy.
So when it is wintertime again they can live on it, that's why they do it.

Nah'ogn jign, ntl'ät nihnayh and tsüüh and <noołuut de'>.
Out there, blueberries, lowbush cranberries, bearberries, and edible roots in fall.

T'axoh hutneltänh de' hǫǫ't'eey łuugn, hǫǫ't'eey łuugn hǫǫłįį de' hiitalshyeek tl'aan ha.
Finally it freezes, and if there's still fish, if there's still fish they will take it.

Ay du' ay chih nän' shyiit hiiyełeek.
And that too they will put into the ground.

Elih hǫǫłiin k'a hiitahgąy.
Because it's too cold they won't dry it.

Hǫǫ' ihchah nts'ą̈' nän' shyiit hiitaałeel.[10]
They leave it whole and put it into the ground.

Ay chih hugn hǫǫ't'eey hiiyehthįįk ay chih hihdįįtsįį de' ay hiitaa'aał.
They just leave it like this [frozen], and when they are hungry, they will eat it.

Tl'aan ay ch'ale dzinah hiiyehniign.
And then there's the one they call dzinah (fermented fish).

Dzinah mǫǫsi', łuugn.
Dzinah is its name, fish.

Hǫǫ' įhchah nts'ą̈' t'eey nän' shyiit hiiyiłeegn.[11]
They put it in the ground whole.

_____
10 Gutted but whole, head and tail still on. As soon as it's out of the water it freezes.
11 Again the pit is lined with willow first.

Hahiiyįį'ąą de', shnąą iin eh shta' iin eh tsǫǫ iin hiitaa'aal>.
When they take it out, my parents and grandparents would eat it.

<Midhagnnüh.>
I don't remember.

Ts'iikeey iin k'a hiiyi'aal? Yaa hii'agnnay, nän du'.
Children didn't eat it? I don't remember, you!
I ate some when I was a kid.

Ishyiit dą' laa freezer ts'įįdlah ha'.
At that time we didn't know anything like freezer.

Dii dii hįįxaan hiiyehgąy shyįį'.
Whatever they killed they only dried.

Dii hįįxaan hiiyehgąy.

Whatever they killed they dried.
Dąy hǫǫłįį, dąy hǫǫłįį de', diniign hiidhehxįį de' nelgąy.
In spring, in spring, if they kill a moose it is lean.

K'ah kol.
It has no fat.

Ay hiiyehgąy hant'eey t'eey igąy.
And they dry them, they dry fast.

Ay ch'ale hiinehtsay shiin tah.
That's what they gather in the summer.

Tl'aan noołuut t'axoh huteełe' de' ay chih hǫǫ't'eey diniign, hǫǫ't'eey diniign hįįxaan.
And then when it becomes fall, they still kill moose.

Ay chih hiiyehgąy.
And they dry them also.

Tl'aan ch'ik'ah diniign huk'ah ay hiiyidlaag naxat shyi' eegąy eh hiiyuu'aal xah.[12]
And the fat, the moose fat, they keep it so they can eat it with the dry meat.

Ay tl'aan diah dineh dahdǫǫ tth'itu' niign ts'ayh eh nįįshyay ch'a.
And then there was the man who came from downriver on the river with the boat.

Łiat, saay, sǫgay, ldil> nįįdlay.
Flour, rice, sugar, and tea he brought.

Ay ay eh tah hǫǫsu' ts'i'aał le'.
And that's probably when we eat well.

Ts'inishyeeh dą' Roy, Roy eh ts'inishyeeh dą' dzįįtsįį.
When we grew up, Roy, Roy, when we grew up, we were hungry.

Shta' iin shnąą iin hushyi' ookol eh neexon t'eey all nts'ą' dzįįtsįį neeshyi' kol eh.
Our parents had no food, and all of us were hungry because we had no food.

Nts'ą' shyi' ehdänh nts'ą' niithaad, niithaad tat'eey shyi' ehdänh dzeltth'iik.
Without food, for a long time, a long time we stayed without food.

K'a nants'e'iil nts'ą'.
We didn't eat.

Shnąą iin łuugn eegąy ntsiin eedlah de' ay łahiitnahch'ił tl'aan neetl'ayitahchik ay xah t'eey ay xah t'eey ts'idüh.
My mother, when we had even a little bit of dry fish, she would tear it apart and she would give it to us and that's what would sustain us all day.

---

12 They save the fat from the fall moose to eat with the very lean meat of moose killed in spring.

3 UDZIH AND DINIIGN/DENDÎIG

Caribou and Moose

Of all the animals, caribou and moose are the most important to upper Tanana Dene. In the nineteenth century, caribou were more important, providing food, skins for clothing and tents, and bones and antlers for tools. Moose were much scarcer and did not become abundant until the 1930s. Both animals are woven into the fabric of people's lives, providing not only meat but also an important cultural link to the ancestors. In this chapter Dene elders talk about traditional methods for hunting caribou and moose.

Caribou (*udzih* [UT, T]) are migratory animals that cross the upper Tanana region in large herds. To kill large numbers of caribou efficiently, upper Tanana Dene employed an elaborate system of fences to divert the migrating animals into corrals where they could be easily killed. Clan leaders directed the construction and maintenance of the fences and corrals in a way that allowed for the interception and slaughter of migrating caribou at specific times of the year. The best-documented caribou fences were operated by Dene from Ketchumstuk and Mansfield and were used to take animals from the Fortymile caribou herd.

Moose are solitary animals, so they could not be taken in such large numbers as caribou. Nevertheless, moose were harvested using snares placed in a fence or barricade. Snares were more efficient than bows and arrows, especially in extremely cold weather. If the hunter missed his first shot, the sound of the bowstring was so loud it often frightened the animal. Firearms were more efficient, and McKennan (1959: 48) reported that Dene understood the habits of moose so well and hunted them so effectively with modern rifles that moose were scarce around the more frequently used campsites.

UDZIH (CARIBOU)

Upper Tanana Dene hunted several caribou herds that crossed through the region: the Fortymile herd, the Chisana herd, the Mentasta herd, and more recently the Nelchina herd. Dene whose traditional territory included the uplands between the Yukon and Tanana Rivers and Fortymile River drainage hunted the Fortymile herd. Dene living to the south of Tanana River hunted the Chisana and Mentasta herds. The Nelchina caribou herd now migrates through the region from their calving grounds on the upper Susitna River, but according to Northway elder Louie Frank, no Nelchina caribou came around Northway until the 1950s (USFWS 2011: 4).

During the summer, food is abundant and adult bull caribou store great quantities of fat, mostly along the back and the rump (Skoog 1956: 117). In September, adult bulls join existing bands of cows and young animals for the rut and remain with them through most of October. Most caribou mating takes place during the first two weeks of October. Calves are born after a thirty-three-week gestation,

https://doi.org/10.5876/9781646423347.c003

We use caribou for our clothing. Sometime we kill a little caribou in July. If we want a little longer hair, we kill caribou in September. Little more long hair we wait till October. October hairs start to break loose. Still they make parky. Women make all the clothes for kids, grown people and old people. They sew and they tan skin. All the stuff we use we don't feel cold, our legs, not even our feet.

from the second week of May until the third week of June, with the majority being born during the latter half of May (Skoog 1956: 137).

In the early 1900s, the Fortymile caribou herd was the largest in Alaska (Valkenburg et al. 1994: 11). Written reports provided by prospectors, missionaries, and others describe the movements of the herd at different points in time. Archdeacon Hudson Stuck ([1914] 1988) reported that in October 1909, 100,000 animals crossed Mosquito Fork and Ketchumstuk Flats. In 1921 the naturalist Olaus Murie (1921a) interviewed local people about the condition of animal populations in the area. At the time, the Fortymile caribou herd was vast, and Murie estimated there were 586,000 animals. At Chicken he interviewed Jack Fitzpatrick, who said that in September 1920 thousands of caribou crossed the Fortymile River. The migration lasted four or five days and stretched over twenty miles.

In the 1930s, the Fortymile herd started to decline. Various reasons were given: predation by wolves killing calves, humans killing adult caribou, and overgrazing by the caribou. In the early 1950s, the herd increased but then declined, probably due to hunting pressure. In the 1950s, roads in Alaska and Canada provided hunters increased access to the herd. By the 1960s, the herd numbered approximately 20,000 animals (Valkenburg et al. 1994: 12).

HUNTING CARIBOU

Silas Solomon recalled that when he was a boy there were "so many caribou. Caribou by the million thru twice, three times in the summer." Silas said the caribou came through as they moved from Alaska to Canada past Taylor Mountain and Ketchumstuk. People hunted caribou in April and May, when they were calving, then again in August when the herd moved toward Canada. The only time caribou were not hunted was during the fall, in October, when the animals were in rut and smelled so badly that people "can't even eat" (Solomon 1984a).

Gaither Paul said people relied on the knowledge and skill of leaders such as Sam Thomas, who knew from experience when the caribou would arrive. Runners were sent out to determine the location of the herds. People were told not to kill the leaders of the herd because the herd follows the leaders. An elder explained:

> The first lead. They follow that one. [Caribou] have one boss. One lead in the front. All medicine men say, "Don't kill the lead—he leads the rest." If they kill that one then they have to make sing [song]—"I making trail. Why is gun in my stomach?" Medicine man sleep and dream. "Go after and find that lead and bring." Then he [medicine man] gives caribou another lead. Gives that caribou which leads. (Andrews 1975: 48)

CARIBOU FENCES ON THE UPPER FORTYMILE RIVER

Up until the beginning of the twentieth century, upper Tanana Dene built long fences to divert the caribou into corrals, where they could be easily killed. The caribou fences in the upper Fortymile River drainage were famous and attracted Dene from as far away as Mentasta, Northway, Eagle, and Healy Lake. Beginning in the 1880s, the caribou fences in the upper Fortymile River drainage became a part of a complex economy that included hunting and trading. In the early 1880s, American fur traders established stores on the upper Yukon River, and upper Tanana Dene began making frequent trips there. The location of the caribou fences thus served a dual purpose, as they provided a reasonably secure source of food and were near the Yukon River trading stations. The village of Joseph, for example, was important because of its proximity to the annual caribou migration route and because it was relatively close to trading posts on the upper Yukon River. Once Dene obtained repeating rifles, the complex system of fences and corrals was abandoned, although Dene continued to use shorter snare fences for caribou and moose into the 1920s.

Caribou fences were built in two basic forms: straight-line drift fences and surrounds (Bales 1904). Straight-line fences were long structures with openings at various intervals, with a snare inside each opening. Surrounds were circular enclosures that could be a mile or two in diameter. There was an opening at one end and two drift or wing fences extending away from it. When the caribou herd encountered the drift fence, they were directed into the corral. Dene put snares in the corrals, and the snared animals could then be killed with a spear, knife, or bow and arrow (Solomon 1984a).

Chief Andrew Isaac explained the use of the snare fence and corral, and then talked about how to prepare different parts of the caribou.

One way we catch enough caribou for dry meat is with fence. When people think caribou will start to run they make tripod and hang snare. That snare is twelve or twenty-four strings [sinew] twisted together. They stretch them together so it gets as strong as cable. It's ten or twelve feet long. They make loop in it while it is wet.

When I was a boy we get up early, no breakfast. We run to the caribou fence. If they get a caribou, we take the snare off and drag it off by the horns. We take it away so animals coming in won't smell stomach, fresh meat, or anything. Two of us can drag a caribou far as we want. Almost everybody gives a hand to it. Even old people go there. That's the people help cut.

We bring all the caribou heads into camp to one pile. We skin them and cut all the small pieces off. We break the jaw and take the tongue. [We eat] everything in the head. Just the bone we throw away. We cut brain and put one place too. They use that to tan

Figure 3.1. Caribou lookout station, Ketchumstuk. National Archives.

skins. The liver we throw in the fire and cook it on real hot wood. Top is all burned, but the inside is fresh. We take a wood meat-hammer and pound that liver and brain together. Then we leave it on the cache to dry out. It turns a little sour and we put it away. Never take it out of the sack. Just put it away. (Yarber and Madison 1988: 24–25)

Silas Solomon (1984b) said the fences were constructed out of willows and small trees burned to harden the wood. The fence was braced to withstand the push of the caribou and built high enough so the animals could not jump over. Silas said you had to be careful the caribou did not break down the fence.

Lots of time they break the fence. You got to repair that quick. They make a trail and all the other ones gonna follow. They even do it at night. There were fences all along the creek drainages. No nails were used in the construction, no wire, use the willows, see like this to tie in the crotch you know. Tie with willow. The fence rails were supported by tripods that could not be tipped over.

Murie (1935: 2) described two types of lookouts: trees trimmed of their upper branches and platforms made from poles. There were lookouts on the Mosquito Fork of the Fortymile River, the head of the west branch of the Dennison Fork, and an elaborate pole structure on a hill near the Ketchumstuk corral.

CARIBOU FENCE AT KETCHUMSTUK

The longest and most elaborate fence in the upper Fortymile drainage began at the winter villages of Saagés cheeg (Ketchumstuk) and Mbehts'eh Těyy' (Flint Hill) and ended near Birch Lake. Figures 3.2 and 3.3 show the location of caribou fences in the upper Fortymile drainage in the vicinity of the village of Ketchumstuk. Figure 3.3 was made by the BIA and includes the names of villages and geographic features in both English and the Tanacross language. To the left is Saagés cheeg (Ketchumstuk). The caribou fence is represented by the dashed line. In the middle is the village of Mbehts'eh Těyy' (Flint Hill) and the double corral used to catch caribou. From Mbehts'eh Těyy', the fence continues on to Indian Creek past an "old village," which is labeled Crow Nest Village.

The map in figure 3.2 by Silas Solomon shows the caribou fence and several villages. As shown on the map, the fence between Ketchumstuk and Birch Lake was several miles long. Shorter fences, some only hundreds of feet long, were located at various places in the upper Fortymile River drainage. One was at Long Cabin, or Tthek Ła'chii (literally "end of caribou fence"), another at the head of the Little Dennison River. During the summer of 1921 Murie (1935: 2) located the fence on the Little Dennison, describing it as about a mile long and following the old Eagle trail. The fence was in good condition, built in sections, and four to five feet high. Murie also learned of a caribou fence that ran from a point about one mile up the North Fork of the Fortymile River to within one and half miles of the mouth of O'Brian Creek. Snares made of telegraph wire were placed at intervals where there were gaps in the fence. At one place, a short piece of fencing was placed at a right angle, with a gap for a snare; the right angle forced the animal into the snare (Murie 1935). There was also a fence near Mount Fairplay (Tets'enkeen) and another located between the mouth of Fish Creek and

Tanacross called Stsey Undaagh' Kol Tthěg (literally "my blind grandfather's caribou fence") used by Sam Thomas.

In the summer of 1890, the newspaper reporter E. Hazard Wells (1974: 211) traveled through the upper Fortymile River drainage and visited Ketchumstuk, where he saw the caribou fence. Wells wrote:

> On July 27th the expedition followed up the basin of the Forty-mile keeping well to the ridges but passing through scrubby timber. A brush and pole fence was soon encountered which we knew to be one of the wings of a caribou corral . . . It was doubtless the property of the Kittschunstalks [Ketchumstock Indians]. Caribou fences in central Alaska are extensive affairs, running for many miles across the country and converging into U-shaped corrals. The deer [caribou] cross the country in the fall in immense droves and running against these fences follow them down to the corral, where the natives make a surround. . . . There was a well beaten trail along the fence, and we followed it toward the south. At noon the deserted Kittschunstalks [Ketchumstock] village was reached . . . The march was resumed that afternoon, and we traveled some six miles, keeping near the caribou fence, and about sun-down reached a wide and picturesque depression through which the Forty-mile threaded its way in two forks, one crossing to the west, while the other wound away to the south.

Sometime between 1901 and 1903, Lieutenant William Mitchell (1982: 50) visited the Ketchumstuk area and described the caribou fences:

> For miles along the low range of hills bordering the Mosquito Flats they had constructed a series of fences about eight or nine feet high. These led into pens something like a fish trap. When the caribou began to come into the vicinity of these stockades, Indians

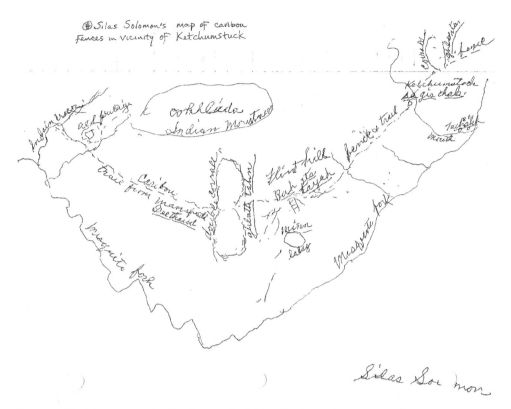

Figure 3.2. Silas Solomon's map of caribou fences in the vicinity of Ketchumstuk. Source BIA 14(h)1 project.

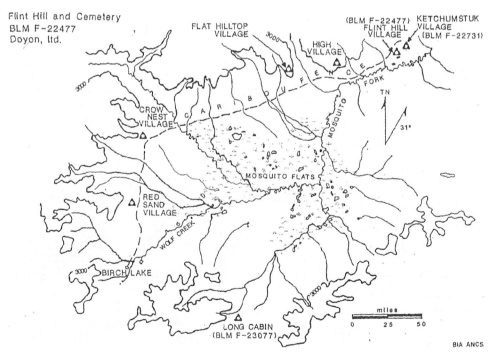

Figure 3.3. Cartographers rendition of Silas Solomon's map of villages and caribou fence, upper Fortymile River. Source BIA ANCSA 14(h)1 project.

posted on eminences would signal to others waiting on each flank where the caribou herd was located. They signaled by means of smoke from a fire built in a hole . . . The Indians would then run out on their snowshoes and surround the caribou, driving them along the fences and into the pens. Once they were secured the squaws and children attacked them with bows and arrows and spears and butchered them.

Murie (1935: 2–3) also described the caribou fence at Ketchumstuk, which was a more elaborate structure composed of a line fence extended westward about six miles. At the east end of the fence Native people had constructed a corral. The entire structure was well built, with the different parts fastened with willow. Murie reports the corral had an inner pocket six feet high, reinforced by vertical poles placed close together. The entrance was guarded by a number of people. One person on each side would shoot caribou with a bow and arrow or stab the animal with a knife lashed to a pole.

The Reverend David Paul (1957b: 15–16) of Tanacross described two fences within the Fortymile River drainage, the first a short fence located at Long Cabin, and the second the more elaborate setup at Ketchumstuk.

My grandfather and uncle have caribou camp on tundra [above tree line] at Long Cabin. This fence maybe 4.5 feet high so animals not jump over, and it won't upset because this fence braced against run of these caribou. Each brace maybe six inch at bottom. This top maybe two, three inch. This only small fence at Long Cabin. At Ketchumstuk, old Chief Isaac had caribou fence with just trap part mile deep. People go out all around and spread out and start driving caribou to trap. Only two or three stay there [at the entrance to the trap]. They shoot big, fat caribou and let thin ones go.

According to Silas Solomon, the corral at Ketchumstuk was located on a big flat on the other side of the creek from the village. The pocket was very solidly built, approximately six feet high and tied together with willow (Simeone 1987d). David Paul said two bowmen were stationed at the opening of the corral. People drove the caribou toward the opening, and the "best arrow men stay at the mouth of the trap. Only two or three stay there, they shoot big, fat caribou and let the thin ones go by" (Paul 1957b: 16).

Silas Solomon said different clans cooperated in the construction and maintenance of the caribou fences at Ketchumstuk and Flint Hill. However, there was a "boss" who mobilized the young men to build and repair the fence. The fence at Flint Hill, which had a double corral so caribou could be intercepted coming from two directions, belonged to the Dik'aagyu clan, while the Ketchumstuk fence belonged to the Naltsiin clan. The Dik'aagyu headman was named Stsêey Netłé'. He directed the operation and maintenance of the fence and is said to have invited his relatives from Northway and Tetlin to use the fence (Simeone 1987d).

By the 1920s Dene stopped using caribou fences, in part because they had repeating rifles and a relatively stable source of ammunition. It was also against the law. In a 1986 interview, Gaither Paul described hunting caribou when he was a boy and young man in the 1920s and 1930s. The interview ranged across several subjects, including how Sam Thomas directed the caribou hunts, the impact of the Taylor Highway on the Fortymile caribou herd, and beliefs surrounding the hunt.

Herd of caribou cross Sixty Mile Butte, they call it. Indians call Tthihdzen. And that man [Sam Thomas] knows just about exactly when that's going to go across up there. When its nice and sunny day I remember him go out of his house and he start speaking, he speaking loud, he speaking to all of the village people. When man said that, everybody go out and sit outside and listen. And he give a lot of advice and then finally he said, now its time for the caribou herd to cross the hill up there. Some young guys run up there and take a look, he would say. Us young people would say, I'll go, I'll go, we love to run up there.

We run up there, sure enough its starting, there is fresh tracks, I don't know how that guy know, but he knew just about the time the caribou crossing up there.

He tell people to check, its time to check up there. All those kind of advice he give people.

And people, Fortymile herd they call it later, that's what crosses the Sixty Mile Butte. Native people didn't have a name for the herd, but that's the herd Tanacross people live on for years and years, probably for centuries.

When we go up there, when first herd of caribou crossing, old people tell us not to shoot, not to shoot, first ones, let the first one go. If you're hungry, shoot one and just lay low and let it go by. When you know the leaders went by then you can start shooting any way you want to, [otherwise] you disturb the leaders. I don't know why it's, from when they cross its wide [the herd] as from Big Hill to Long Cabin. That's how wide it is, probably farther down, that's how wide, I don't know how you would disturb the leader but that's the rule.

Even when people have caribou fence, long caribou fence, when the first herd of caribou come the runners go through the snare and hang it up and let it [the leaders] go by. Because if you turn the herd, disturb it, you force them back, force them to go someplace they not supposed to go, they can't survive.

There is so many animals, Indians say they need to go where they are going to, to survive. They know where to survive. That's why you cannot disturb the leaders. But we had it ever since, even when I was a boy in early teenagers.

When Taylor Highway is built, that's right in the path of the caribou migration, when caribou hit the road the news flash all over. And people they don't know, you know, they just block it in, just first day. There some went by but not all of them go by, it's completely block off. They probably moved some place and didn't survive, that's what I think, that's my own personal thinking. Because that's what going to happen, old people say. And they are really careful for that, you got to let the leaders go. That once was a top rule, that you don't disturb the first one.

When people move up [to hunt caribou] [they] make camp anywhere near water or wood, and when caribou migration come, they either come to your camp and you can shoot right around your camp, or go a little ways.

There is stone or little hill here and there where people have tea and campfire and they wait for it and it will come. And then they shoot them. Skin it and then haul it. The hunters did the skinning, and the women haul it. When caribou migration come people work long hours for meat. Old people, young girls cut meat, dry it and us boys, they fill up dog pack, and we relay dry meat to Mansfield, stuck them in cache and go back, make more. That's mostly our work, old people and young women cut. They work long hours because it just only last about week or ten days.

SIMEONE: How many caribou do people shoot?

As much as they can take care, but people never over kill, it's superstition to waste meat in Indian way, it's they call injih, you waste your meat you don't get that kind of luck again.

So you have got to take care of everything you got, you got to take care.

Even if you left bones where you killed moose, you cannot take the bones, most of the time the bones are taken and split the ends and cooked, cooked grease out of it, nothing wasted. But you have to throw away bones, you can't leave them scattered all the way around. Get them together and put them under a tree or something. If there is creek near by throw in creek or lake. If bear come around and scatter your bones, its not you, you took care of your bones when you left. Old people use to tell us that too, don't left your bones scattered all around.

SIMEONE: Why do people have to take care of bones?

I think its some sort of superstition. That's the way I was told. I was told don't just let your bones scattered all around where you killed moose or caribou.

If you going to throw away the bones gathering them up and put them under a tree. If there is river then just throw it in the river so its not kicked all around.

After you leave there if bear or wolf come around and scatter all your bones, its not your fault you took care of your bones, they told me.

Its just some kind of superstition, if you just throw your bones all around its not good.

If you don't take care of your stuff like that you'll be bad luck, you wouldn't see caribou or moose again, that's why you gotta take care what you get.

Nature provides and you lucky you got that meat, you should take good a care of it, that's what I was told. And, a lot of people say Indian over killed stuff. The way I was taught, there is no waste. The way I was taught, there is no waste, I was told not to waste any meat, if you don't need it, you just don't shoot anything for nothing, its bad luck. You waste the whole good food. So that's why I never see Indian, when I was a boy, when even they get lot of meat,

when caribou migration come, people have a lot of meat, but nothing is waste. Even the guts have a lot of fat, There is a way to get the fat out. Even the bones, the end of the bones with soft they cook up all of the grease out of it and take it out on top of the boiling bucket. And nothing waste, everything is cut off. Little streak of meat on it old lady cook those. (Simeone 1986a)

DINIIGN (UT)/DENDÎIG (T) (MOOSE)

Moose have been present in Alaska for thousands of years (LeResche and Bishop 1974). In most of Alaska, moose numbers have risen and fallen over the last 150 years. According to some Dene elders, at the end of the nineteenth century moose were not as abundant in the upper Tanana region as they are now (Simeone 1987d). Since the 1950s, numbers of moose have increased throughout the state, largely in response to the regular occurrence of wildfires, which create moose browse (LeResche and Bishop 1974).

> Dene elders have stated a preference for moose meat, its quality being that it "fills you up" unlike sheep and caribou from which "you get hungry right away." The person who killed the moose was expected to make a "potlatch" or party with the ribs, brisket, and head of the moose while the rest was divided up among the other hunters: "That man he got no meat." (Andrews 1975: 54)

In the 1920s, Olaus Murie saw numerous moose tracks throughout the upper Fortymile River area. Little Frank, a man from Tanacross, told Murie that when Indians encountered a moose, they constructed a snare fence and then chased the moose toward it. Snares were made of babiche, strips of moose rawhide (most often from a summer hide) that was twisted and stretched between two green trees bent together until the snare was dry. The snare was embellished with paint. Caribou hide was not strong enough. Little Frank said that in the fall moose fight, and their hide must be thick to withstand their exertions and possible puncture with horns. So, the summer/fall hide is the strongest, and the winter hide too thin because of the thick hair grown for winter protection (Murie 1921a).

Oscar Isaac of Tanacross said hunters could kill animals because they had knowledge of the environment, the lay of the land, habits of animals, and the weather. When hunters look at the land, they see where things are: spruce, willows, hills. Hunters must also know the habits of animals: what they will be doing at certain times of the day. Oscar said that moose, for example, sleep at 9 a.m. Before they lie down, they backtrack on themselves so that they are protected by brush. When the wind comes up their trail, the smell of any predator following them will come first on the wind. Hunters go to high places to watch for moose, and they can then go after the moose with the wind in their face. This requires detailed knowledge of the country and careful appraisal of the whole situation. Sneaking up on a moose requires considerable skill, and there are incantations taught to young boys so they can grow into the skill. The reason some people get meat and others don't is because some people don't know how to hunt moose. Oscar said hunting moose is a learned skill, and if people don't pay attention, they won't know how to do it. Some people are too lazy and follow downwind, so the moose gets their scent and is gone (Simeone 1987e).

The Reverend David Paul provided an explanation of how to hunt moose.

> Native people know about animals. They know moose eat early morning and lie down during day and eat again before night. He know moose hear good and when wind make noise in tree and grass he can get closer to this moose. He knows if wind blow this man-smell to moose he will run away so he stay down-wind from this moose and know that this moose cannot run fast in deep snow nor swim fast in water and, in winter, when this snow is deep and crusted and cuts his legs and belly this moose will hunt a place to live where snow is just little. This man knows that before he sleep he will turn back on trail little to one side so he smell those that follow before they find him.
>
> Native people know all these things and they keep cutting this moose trail until they don't find track—then he sleeps and they follow his back trail until they find him just sleeping.
>
> My uncle go early in morning find moose and this moose run and my uncle run and always my uncle go around other side to chase him close by the camp. He always think just ahead of moose. But my grandfather say, "Don't chase moose too hard—kill it and makes it taste like moose." This meat look like water when it run too hard and get too hot.
>
> My great grandfather make little fence for moose between two hills and little creek run between these hills. This was just little fence maybe one mile long, not too strong, with snares every little way. Over this snare, men put just little willow. Moose push it with head to break it—just small willow maybe one quarter inch. When men and dogs chase this moose to fence, he get head in snare, can't get out. (Paul 1957b: 13–14)

A lone hunter might follow fresh moose tracks for hours or days and kill the animal after it bedded down, or, as the Reverend David Paul explained, several men sometimes hunted moose together, placing snares at intervals along a brush fence at the base of a hill. Some of the hunters positioned themselves at the opposite side of the hill before daylight, and then shouted at the approaching moose or set fires to drive the startled animal over the hill and into the awaiting snares. A moose killed a long way from camp was skinned, gutted, cut into six pieces, and cached in spruce boughs until it could be transported back to the camp (Paul 1957b: 13–14).

At the end of August we would build a we

Afterward, in 'the month of leaves turning yellow' [early September], we would dry split whitefish.

When it turned to 'bull moose month' [late September], we would freeze the whitefis on the ice.

We would dry the surface of the split fish for half-dry fish and freeze it and then we would store it for winter.

Next we also would make fermented fish.

Sometimes they would make forty fish into fermented fish.

We would live all winter on that.

Photo-montage by Hal Gage.

4 FISHING

Fish are an important source of food for upper Tanana Dene because they can be taken in large numbers, have predictable habits, and can be dried and stored for relatively long periods. Historically, fish were important because in times of scarcity, especially in late winter and early spring, they could always be found in lakes and did not require a lot of energy to catch. As described in chapter 1, the oral history of Dihthâad (Mansfield) is an example of the importance of fish as survival food. Dene discovered Lake Mansfield when they were living at Fish Lake and starving. They were saved from death when a young man caught a pike. In the spring the grandfather climbed a hill and saw Lake Mansfield off in the distance. He went there and discovered Mansfield Creek and "lots of fish." When he returned home, he told the people they should move "down on real good fishing place." They settled in Dihthâad (Andrews 1980).

A fair number of fish species live in the upper Tanana drainage, including burbot or ling cod (*ts'aan* [T, UT]), Arctic grayling (*seejel* [T], *seejil* [UT]), broad whitefish (*tehshyüü* [UT]), humpback whitefish (*łuug* [T],[1] *tehshyüü* [UT]), round whitefish (*xełtįį'* [T, UT]), least cisco (*xaal* [UT]), suckers (*tats'aht'ôl* [T], *taasts'ät* [UT]), and northern pike (*uljaaddh* [T], *jüüt* [UT]). Of these, the various species of whitefish are the most significant to the local economy. Salmon (*łuugu delt'äl*) are rare in the upper Tanana drainage and therefore a minor source of food.

---

1 The word *łuug* is also the general term for fish.

LUUG (T)/LUUGN (UT) (WHITEFISH)

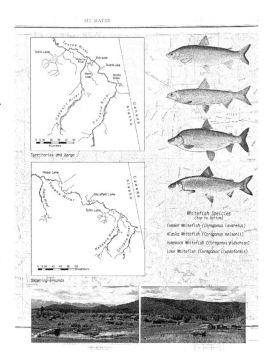

upper Tanana Dene harvest whitefish in July and August, when the fish are migrating between the lakes and main rivers in small clearwater streams. At this time of year fish were especially fat, and spawning females, plump with eggs, were especially favored. Mary Tyone (1996: 13) provided a synopsis of fishing for whitefish in the Scottie Creek area. The interview was recorded in the Upper Tanana language by Jim Kari.

https://doi.org/10.5876/9781646423347.c004

Figure 4.1. Fish weir at Tetlin, 1968. Photo by Frederica de Laguna, courtesy Alaska State Library.

Figure 4.2. Fish weir at Moose Creek, Frank Sam with net, 1930. Photograph by Robert McKennan, courtesy of William Workman.

End of August k'adn nats' ihohtsiik
At the end of August we would build a weir.

Ay tl'aan Ch'it'aan' Tsiik Saa łuugn ts'ehk'
    aay ts'ehgąyh
Afterward, in "the month of leaves turn
    yellow" [early September], we would dry
    split whitefish.

Niichoo Saa ii 'aagn eh łuugn tänh tänh k'it
    łuugn ts'ehtän.
When it turned to "bull moose month" [late
    September], we would freeze the white-
    fish on the ice.

Mba' ts'ehk'aay wuka'itgąy eh ts'entänh tl'aan
We would dry the surface of the split fish
    for half-dry fish and freeze it, and then

Xay kah nits' iłeek.
We would store it for winter.

Tl'aan dzännax chih ts' ehtsiik.
Next we also would make fermented fish.

Łuugn sometimes dän deetaan dzännax
    hehtsiik.
Sometimes they would make forty fish into
    fermented fish.

Xay uudih wukįįy' dzeltth'iik.
We would live all winter on that.

To catch large numbers of whitefish, Upper Tanana Dene built a weir or fence with one or two openings into which they placed a trap or a dip net. Dene had fish weirs on the Healy River, in Fish Creek at Mansfield, at Tetlin and Last Tetlin, and at K'ehtthîign (old Northway). Silas Solomon (1984a) described fish trap used Ketchumstuk.

Figure 4.3. Logan and John Paul Luke, George Lake. Jeany Healy Collection UAF-2000-181-50.

> We had one right in the village, but this [trap] caught bigger fish. That's why they had the trap down at the mouth [of Ketchumstuk Creek]. They dammed Mosquito Fork [and Ketchumstuk Creek] both. Get whitefish lots on there. They're big. Graylings. Get tired of eating graylings. There's more food value to the whitefish than graylings. They don't have much, its good for frying. That's, there's a dam put straight across not the other way, slant. River goes like that, banks along here. That's poles we drive, poles down same as a fence [poles driven into the bottom of the creek].

The fish were stored in two underground caches set side by side along the bank of the creek.

Frederica de Laguna described the weir at Tetlin, which she observed during her visit to Tetlin in 1968 (de Laguna and Guédon 1968b).

Figure 4.4. Fishing in Tetlin. From left to right, Eva Joe, Jenny Joe with net, Clara Joe and Annie Joe, Tetlin photo collection UAF-1987-114-09.

> The fish weir is built across the larger channel of the Tetlin River, here a small stream that divides around a little grassy island. The whitefish entering the channel with the weir are blocked by it and by the large circular dip net that just fits the single opening. The others can ascend via the other channel.
>
> The weir is built for everyone in the village. There is a small platform and a rickety walk leading to it from the bank. If several people want to fish they apparently wait their turn; the one at the weir is said to yield his or her place quickly.

> The person using the net puts it vertically into the water to close the opening in the weir. The handle is lashed to an upright post at the side by a winding of string. The fish entering the net pushes against it, and the person lifts up the net. Dumps the fish onto the platform and kills it with a small club. Usually have a little brush (willow branches) handy to keep off the sun and flies from the fish. Will wash them in the stream after they have been strung on a cord or branch as one is coming ashore.

The net is made of a hoop of wood, almost a yard wide, fastened to a pole about six feet long. The pole crosses the circle of wood at one side (not through diameter of circle). The net is of twine made very deep. When not in use the net is laid across the platform.

The dip net mentioned above was made out of a wooden hoop, measuring three to four feet in circumference, with a four- to five-foot-long handle. The net itself was made from the inside bark of willow and little roots from small spruce trees.

According to the Reverend David Paul (1957b: 19), "These small tree [spruce trees] have little fine root sometime four feet long. Men peel this root. Hold teeth and with little sharp knife split this small root and make dip net."

Fishing was done mainly at night, when the fish were moving. In the dark the fish or dip net could not be seen, so the fisher placed a long, thin willow wand in the net; when the fish entered the net, the willow wand moved. Reverend Paul (1957b: 19) explained: "Man can't see fish, can't see dip net, but he take end long, dry pole in hand and other end this pole down in net, not too tight he hold this. When fish go in net, touch this stick with his tail, this hand feel little move in stick. Quick he lift out dip net and he get fish."

Whitefish were also caught during the winter under river ice. An elder from Northway described fishing with nets in Moose Creek and the Nabesna River: "What we did, we cut a hole, cut hole about every five foot and then we push our net to the next hole with stick and pull it out and then we set the whole net to catch fish in November" (Godduhn and Kostick 2016: 34).

OTHER FISH

Jessie David of Tetlin spoke to de Laguna and Guédon about fishing for grayling, pike, whitefish, and ling cod or burbot and the various

Figure 4.5. Frank Sam's fish weir. Photo by Robert McKennan, Robert McKennan Collection UAF-1985-98-760.

methods used to catch them. She then talked about a bird that heralds the arrival of fish and is a portent for bad weather.

> August month, we like to go to big lake [Tetlin Lake], fish net use. Some place they got creek, lot of fish around there, near little creek, whitefish. Some grayling too, but we don't put with nets. Some use hooks. In clear water, if too many we see, we can hook whitefish too.
>
> Pike, we use hook on the lake, we open ice; some [fish] don't smart; some [fish] smart, [you can't take out,] some big sometimes.
>
> Ling cod or burbot; the meat is fed to the dogs, people eat only the liver.

INTERVIEWER: Any kind of birds that bring [or show] good luck?

> [Jessie] Ya, . . . Tzi Tzi [imitating the sound] he call it means fish coming lots of fish. I don't know the name, just hear it. Some kind of ducks . . . with green feather. They fly around, they go, they come, I saw some yesterday, they come around, village, big lake; qo qo qo qo qo they said. That means rain, bad weather. (de Laguna and Guédon 1968c: n.p.)

Figure 4.6. Alfred and Mildred Jonathan with northern pike at Mansfield, 1987. Photo by William E. Simeone.

Fish traps were also used to catch Arctic grayling and whitefish. The Reverend David Paul described a fish trap with a funnel-shaped opening larger at one end and smaller at the other so the fish could not escape the trap.

> this trap has little basket inside big basket. Fish can go in but too little come out. Sometime people put two, three trap cross river and tie then with spruce root to trees in water. This tree guide fish to trap. Man lift out trap; pour fish on bank. (Paul 1957b: 18)

Oscar Isaac described a trap used at Ketchumstuk to catch Arctic grayling. A box made of logs was placed in the middle of a stream. A platform was built behind the box with a slight incline. On each side of the platform, fences or weirs were placed that forced the fish to swim up the platform and fall into the box (Simeone 1980b).

Some fish could only be caught using a spear of baited hook and line. Northern pike were harvested with a spear or with a baited line or jig, the same method used to catch burbot. Laura Sanford of Tanacross recalled using a piece of rabbit or squirrel as bait to catch pike. David Paul said,

> People make spear from birch with three sharp points like pitchfork, maybe ten, twelve feet long the handle. He wait and watch when water clear. Pretty soon he see pike. Quick he spear him, hold him there little while, then hard and quick he throw him on bank. (Paul 1957b: 18)

Fishing for small pike was an important activity in the fall. The anthropologist Robert McKennan saw Tetlin people fishing for pike

Figure 4.7. Tetlin fish weir. Tetlin photograph collection, UAF-1987-114-10.

on a small lake near Tetlin in early March 1930, where warm springs kept the water open.

> The place was literally alive with small pickerel [northern pike] about four to seven inches long. The Indians were flipping them out by the hundreds by means of a small wire hook attached to a small stick. Not much sport and the fish are too small to eat so the Indians boil them up for dog feed and dog feed is an omnipresent factor in northern life. (Mishler and Simeone 2006: 99)

The harvested fish were frozen, placed in birch bark baskets, and stored in outdoor caches for later consumption and to feed dogs.

In the 1980s, Tetlin people were still using the same time-tested technique for catching small pike as previously described by McKennan in the 1930s.

Figure 4.8. Spearing whitefish near Healy Lake. Jeany Healy Collection UAF-2000-181-03.

Figure 4.9. Annie Moses in front of a fish rack at Mansfield. Annie was mother to Emma Northway. Jeany Healy Photo Collection UAF-2000-181-183.

Just prior to freeze-up, usually near the end of October, yearling pike (5"–10") referred to as "pickle," are harvested in small sloughs, rivers, and along lake shores. They are taken with a sal—a handcrafted hook attached to a long wooden pole that resembles a gaff. . . . Since they are taken in the fall, they are also easily frozen and stored in outdoor caches. . . . "Pickle" taken earlier in the fall are often used as bait [on a handheld line and hook for catching burbot]. (Halpin 1987: 51)

FISH PREPARATION METHODS

Men and women caught fish, but women did most of the processing. As with the processing of any animal, there were rules around fish handling to ensure that the fish would return year after year. Fish were eaten fresh, dried, smoked, boiled to make soup, and put into the ground to ferment. Tetlin elder Shirley David

Figure 4.10. Fish camp at Nabesna. Photo by Robert McKennan, Robert McKennan Collection UAF-1985-98-757.

Jimerson said there were two ways to cut up whitefish:

Ba' is for eating and ts'ilakee is dog food. Mom prepared ba', but she let us children cut up fish for ts'ilakee.

We took the fish up to our family's campsite to clean and smoke. Each fish cutter had his own fish cutting board made from a split log. Mom and we children sat next to our cutting boards and worked until all the fish had been cut.

After a fish was properly cleaned and prepared, it was hung up to dry on a pole in the smokehouse. My mother and grandmother kept a smokey fire going all the time. Besides smoking the fish, they had to keep the flies out. A good, big rotten log will burn all night with no tending.

Sometimes we dried the eggs along with the fish, and sometimes we just fried the eggs and guts and ate them right away. Dried fish eggs are better! (Jimerson 1975: 40–41)

Fish heads were boiled, and the grease skimmed off and put into a bag. The meat from the heads was eaten and the remainder given to the dogs. The grease was fermented and used in potlatches or to entertain important guests (Anderson 1956: 11).

To make fermented fish, the fish were placed in pits in the ground. The bottom of the pit was lined with poles and birch bark. Laura David Anderson said:

Then everyone would bring this fish and the Chief would mark this fish and this fish and with one and this one and they were to be his. Then all the fish, but not the livers, they put in the hole and covered with more birch bark and then dirt.

Around Christmastime the chief would make a speech and point at this one and that one to go and dig up this hole. The fish was soft and smelled strong but they would pull it out and start cutting off chunks and eating it mama said. (Anderson 1956: 11–12)

Laura Sanford remembered the taste and smell of fermented fish. "My dad would cut the fish and put it in the birch basket and put it underground and let it kinda rotten a little. You can smell the rotten fish" (Paul 1987b).

MAJOR FISHING SITES

Most fishing took place on clear-water tributaries of the Tanana River. Every summer Dene gathered at prime fishing spots where there was a weir, drying racks, and storage pits to keep fermented and dried fish. Some of the most well-known fishing sites were *K'ąąy Kę̧ę̧'* on the Healy River, Dihthâad and Mansfield on Mansfield Creek, Old Northway or K'ehtthiign, and Tetlin or Tee łay and Last Tetlin or Nahk'ädn.

Healy Lake people fished in the Healy River at a place called *K'ąąy Kę̧ę̧'*, or "marmot den," where Chief Healy had a house and trapline. Paul Kirsteatter talked about this place. He said there was a village there with evidence of fish cache pits.

That was more for caribou and fish than the upper Tanana [river]. They had upper Healy River fish. Upper Healy River they had by the old chief's cabin there, they had, well there was a number of cabins there. And they had camps and there's also pits up there where they had, they had covered you know, with skins and bark, and all along the river there's still cache pits in evidence, where they had their fish there, their whitefish, they put in those pits, you know and they put, lined them with bark, put a layer or grass there, fish, layer of grass, then later they would cover them with log 'n soil 'n moss, n later dig them up. Then they dried 'em, quit a bit of fish. (Callaway and Miller-Friend 2001: 127)

Ellen Demit added this information about fishing in the Healy River.

Now, I got talk about Healy Lake, Healy River.
   Ts'aadleey Nediig ["least cisco whitefish creek"]
   That's stand for the fish
   Big fish come out in the creek.

Figure 4.11. Bridge and fish weir at Mansfield, 1971. Photo by William E. Simeone.

They call big fish Ts'aadleey
That's why he call Ts'aadleey Nediig
It connect with K'aay kee'
And, but it's hard to explain English,
But that's our chief's home.
Our chief trapline, our chief's house.
(Callaway and Miller-Friend 2001: 45)

People from Ketchumstuk fished at the mouth of Ketchumstuk Creek, or Taacheeg, where it joined the Mosquito Fork of the Fortymile River. Silas Solomon said, "You go down to the mouth of the creek, there's good fishing. People moved up there in September. They fished for grayling mostly. Round whitefish" (Andrews 1980, n.p.). Oscar Isaac described the different kinds of fish people caught at Ketchumstuk.

Down Ketchumstuk we had trap for grayling. That other fish, almost like whitefish, that kind of fish they can cut it like whitefish and dry, but grayling you cannot

dry. And pike, when you dry just like wood. And sucker, all those they just take out of trap and boil for dogs. Some people split pike and grayling and sucker and hang up for the dog food. Old people like sucker because it's fat and greasy but a lot of fine bones, too dangerous. (Simeone 1987f)

In 1946 anthropologist Walter Goldschmidt visited the residents of Tetlin, Tanacross, and Northway to document their use of the land, including where they fished. Charlie David Sr. told Goldschmidt, "I fish at Tetlin and Last Tetlin. I also fish in the fall up Bear Creek. Everybody goes to these places." Titus Paul said he fished in Tetlin Creek in June and July. Paul Joe told Goldschmidt, "Up Bear Creek there is a good place to get fish in the fall just before freeze sets in. I catch whitefish and freeze." People said they fished at Last Tetlin for whitefish "cod" and lake pike and fishing lasted from June until September. "Everybody fishes right below the village and at Old Store Creek" (Goldschmidt 1948: 26).

Tanacross people told Goldschmidt they had a fish camp at Mansfield. Peter Charles said, "In summer all the people go there together. There are thirteen houses at Mansfield, mostly small cabins." David Paul said he went to Mansfield to fish. John Jonathan said, "On Mansfield Creek there is a fish trap for the whole village which is used all summer. Pickerel, whitefish, grayling, suckers and ling cod are caught." Jimmie Walters said there was a fish camp at Billy Creek (Goldschmidt 1948: 36).

Goldschmidt wrote that at Northway there were two fish camps and a number of other locations where people fished. Steven Northway told Goldschmidt:

> At fish camp we fish for whitefish, pike and sockeyes [sic]. The whole village goes there. We generally go to the fish camp about June 7 after the rat season is over and stay there until the end of July. We generally divided the fish between the people of the village. There are two fish camps about a quarter of a mile apart. There are eight tents and three houses. The houses belong to Abraham Isaac, Bill Northway, and Andrew Jim. These fish camps are about ten miles from where the Northway road comes into the Alcan Highway. The camps are about three miles south of the highway. (Goldschmidt 1948: 50)

Today, most people harvest fish close to home and in places that have been used for generations. Tanacross people fish mainly in Lake Mansfield and Fish Creek and in the Tanana River. Tetlin residents fish in the Tetlin River, while Northway residents fish in the Nabesna River and various lakes and streams. Healy Lake residents fish in the Healy River and Healy Lake.

My mother and father almost the same [clan], not quite, but I belong to my mother's people. All children belong to mother's [clan]. Young people must know these things to know who are his friends; who fight with him in war; who he must give meat when hunger come; and who he can marry ...

Photo-montage by Hal Gage.

5 DESCENT, MARRIAGE, AND TRAINING OF YOUNG PEOPLE

In traditional Dene culture, clan identity is vital. Knowledge of clan histories and genealogies is given great significance, and men and women who possess such knowledge are held in high esteem. Knowing who their relatives are enables a person to act appropriately and avoid injih or dangerous situations. Upper Tanana Dene have strict rules governing interpersonal relationships, which include interactions between different clans, between one's maternal and paternal relatives, and between different members of one's family. To break or disregard these rules is injih.

CLANS AND MOIETIES

Upper Tanana Dene trace their descent through their mother's line. A person belongs to the same descent group as their mother. Some Dene refer to these descent groups as tribes. Anthropologists call them clans. A clan is a group of people who descend from a common ancestor. In Upper Tanana culture, clans are arranged into opposite sides or moieties called raven or crow and seagull. Each side is composed of four or five clans (figure 5.1). This arrangement separates clans and individuals into "opposites" who marry, help one another during life crises, and entertain each other at potlatches. Tanacross elder David Paul explained it this way:

My mother and father almost the same tribe [clan], not quite, but I belong to my mother's people. All children belong to mother's tribe [clan]. Young people must know these things to know who are his friends; who fight with him in war; who he must give meat when hunger come; and who he can marry. (Paul 1957b: 1)

Clans are not localized or limited to one village but spread over a large area, although clan names vary from group to group. For example, clans found in Tanacross and Tetlin also exist among the Ahtna of the Copper River and in villages farther down the Tanana River. When traveling, individuals can expect hospitality from their clan mates in a distant community even when they have no other ties.

CLAN ORIGINS

Details about each clan's origins vary, but there is general agreement that Ałts' ą' Dineey (UT) or Ałts' į' Dendeey (T) originated in Midway Lake in the upper Tanana Valley. Naltsiin are said to have come from up above, while the Ts'ikaayuh (UT) or Dik'aagyu (T) floated down from the sky, and the Ch' ichelyuh (UT) or Ch'echĕelyu (T) came from the Yukon River. Tetlin elder Cora David (2017: 181–185) briefly names the clans and their origins. The text was translated and transcribed by Olga Lovick with the help of Roy and Avis Sam.

https://doi.org/10.5876/9781646423347.c005

Tanacross Language	Upper Tanana Language	Englilsh Name/Symbol	Literal Translation	Notes
Ch'echeelyu	Ch'ichelyu	fish tail	"fish tail people"	chĕel' or cheel' fish tail
Ch'âadz /Ch'aaddh		seagull	"others"	ch'áa or ch'ishyuuy different
Ałts'į'Dendeey	Ałts'ą' Dineey	marten	"one way or right way people"	ałts'į' or ałts'ä' right way or correct
Dik'aagiyu	Ts'ik'aayu	silver fox	"cottony people"	dik'aag or dik'aayu fluffy seed of cottonwood or fireweed
Niisaas	Nisüü		"open country"	nén' land "from Canada"
Tsesyu	Tsisyu	ochre/wolf	"ochre people'	tseyh ochre
Naltsiin	Naltsiin	sky people	"the ones made from above"	tsįį made
Wudzisyu	Udzihyu	caribou	"caribou clan"	wudzih caribou "mostly Ahtna"
Taandîidz altsiil	Ch'itoonia		middle clan	taania in the middle

Figure 5.1. I have not ordered the clans according to moiety because people have different ways of doing so. Nor is this a definitive list of clan names; it represents the clans I was told about. Where I have listed nine clans, Guédon, for instance, listed seventeen. Source: Holton 2002, Alaska Native Language Center Archives, and Kari n.d.

Doo iin nah'og hihdeltth 'ii iin łahtthagn hoo shnąą
I name all the people living out there the way my mother told me

Naltsiin iin
The Naltsiin

dogn nts'ą' nahaltsįį huhenih.
came from up above, they say,

Tasina danh ch'a huxa hijįį' aan.
Tansina is named for them.[1]

Ts'ikaayuh iin du'
The Ts'ikaayuh

ahugn nts'ą'
there

dahtiitth 'aag'
they floated down like feathers

they say.[2]
hiiyehnay.

<K'ahdu'du> ay iin
Today,

ts'anh ha'altįį,
that's where they come from,

Ts'ikaayhu.
Ts' ikaayuh.

The Ałts' ą' dineey iin du'
The Ałts' ą' Dineey

naat Toochinh danh nts'ą' hahaltsįį.
come from down there 'sticks-in-water'
    (Midway Lake)

Ch'ąą iin du'
The Ch' ą' ą' iin

Naltssiin iin
to the Natlsiin

neech 'ąą didhaltth'ih
they were staying close to them,

henay xa t'eey
'they say that's how

hoo hu'oosi'.
they got their name.

---

1 The Naltsiin are the first clan.
2 Roy Sam adds that when they hit the rock, they turned into people. This rock is called Naateeł and is a gathering place for Ts'ikaayuh.

Seagull tribe, Ch'ąą.
Seagull tribe, Ch' ą̈' ą̈'.

Ch' ichelyuh, iin
The Ch' ichelyuh,

nts'aa hahaltsąh nts'ą' t'eey
where they come from

hits 'ishniign ay iin.
I've forgotten.

Ch' ichelyuh, iin.
The Ch' ichelyuh.[3]

Nisüü iin du' nahugn
The Nisüü

gah dhüh
rabbit skin

<eek> k' eltsiin nahdelshyay ay xa t'eey
they were wearing vests that's why

Nisüü hu ' ich 'ihnįį' ąą.
they named them Nisuu.

Ka'at'eey
Not

k'at'eey ay hiiłay t'oot'eey
It wasn't like that but

hu 'ich'inhdehłe' niig ch'ale hu'oosi'
they way they named them was their name,

neenaattheh dą'.
long before us.

Ay tl'aan
And then

Dzihyuh
the Dzihyuh.

Dzihyuh iin du'
The Dzihyuh

Uszih ts'anh
from the caribou

hadįį [deeł]
they come.

Ay shyiit ts' anh hu'oosi' hehtsįį, Dzihyuh
That's where name comes from, Dzihyuh.

Udzih k'e hu'oosi'.
They are named after the caribou.

Ay iin <chih> Tah hugn
And there

ndee nts'ą'tahįįdeeł tah
where they come from,

da'an ch'ale
down there

ntl'aan t'eey Dzihyuh iin
there's lots of Dzihyuh

Ahtna dą'
in the Ahtna area.

<Ay> jah du' hu'ełaan iin
And their partners

neetah nįįdeel eł.
And their partners

Roy uta'
Roy's father,

Titus David jah Dzihyuh.
Titus David, was Dzihyuh.

---

3   According to Roy Sam, the Ch'ichelyuh "fish tail people" come from the Yukon River area. When people from
the Upper Tanana went there, they were given fish tails to
eat; that's the origin of that name.

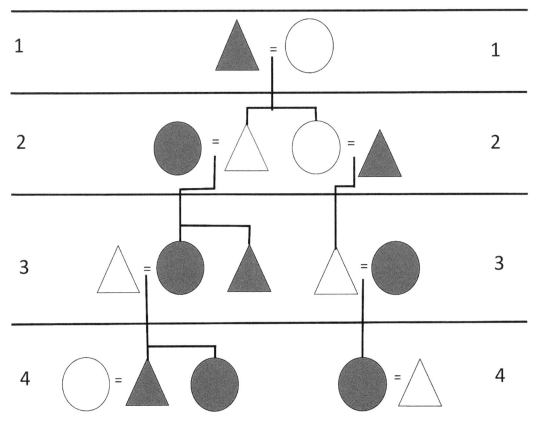

Figure 5.2. Linking clans through marriage. Triangles represent males, circles represent females, and equal signs indicate marriage between two people. Gray and white clans are represented in four succeeding generations, 1, 2, 3, and 4.

MARRIAGE

Traditionally, moieties and clans are exogamous, which means a person is supposed to marry someone from a different clan in the opposite moiety. For example, a person from clan A in the seagull moiety marries a person from clan B in the crow or raven moiety. It is also preferable for a person to marry a member of their father's clan (figure 5.2). A Tanacross man explained that by marrying a woman who belonged to his father's clan, he raised children for his father's clan. He pointed out that he was also following the tradition of the Ałts'į' Dendeey and Dik'aagyu marrying each other across the generations.

> My wife is same tribe [clan] as my dad. . . .
> I married my dad's people [clan]; just for

that, my dad is satisfied. I raised my children for my dad's tribe [clan].

From way back, two tribes [clans] started doing it [intermarrying]. My grandpa, my mother's dad, married Ałts'į Dendeey, same tribe [clan] my daddy's father. From way back, they still marry to each other, Dik'aagyu and Ałts'į Dendeey. We like it that way, which is old time way. (Guédon 1974: 87)

Because opposite clans are supposed to marry back and forth—for example, Ałts'į Dendeey and Dik'aagyu marrying each other—a man's grandchildren are said to be worth more than his own children. This is because a man's own children belong to their mother's clan, but the grandchildren will be members of his father's clan. There is a saying "we work for nothing," meaning fathers work for their natural children who don't belong to them—that is, are not in their clan. It is also said, "We lose our work but all of that comes back through grandchildren" (Simeone 1987b: n.p.).

Walter Isaac of Tanacross said that if a man married a woman from one clan and she died, the man was obligated to marry another woman from the same clan. He also said that after the marriage, the man moved to his wife's village.

> If Dik'aagyu marry Tsisyu first and she
> died, he must marry Tsisyu again. . . . Man
> always goes to woman's village or usually
> trouble. Walter married Ketchumstuk girl.
> When his father died people claim Walter
> for chief and sent word. He came down [to
> Mansfield] from Ketchumstuk with wife.
> She didn't like it. Went back etc. Finally she
> come to think of this Mansfield as home.
> Stayed there. (Pitts 1972: 75)

RELATIONS AND FRIENDS

Dene elders stress the importance of knowing who your relatives are. Strict rules guide a person's behavior toward those considered friends and those considered relatives. To disregard these rules is injih. Upper Tanana Dene distinguish between a person's maternal relations, who are classified as relatives (wude'egken [T], -ah'üü [UT]), and a person's paternal relatives, who are classified as friends (shtlęę [T], shtlųų [UT]). As friends, they are ideal marriage partners and referred to as "sweethearts" and "partners" (Guédon 1974: 112). They are also people one can joke with, whereas one is supposed to be more careful when interacting with one's relatives.

An example of a special relationship between cross cousins or friends is the partnership between persons of the same sex. In the Upper Tanana language, the word is shtlųų; in Tanacross, it is shtlęę. In the case of males, partners are often brothers-in-laws, and so they are from opposite clans. Partners

are supposed to treat each other very well. They hunt together, share food, and assist one another in times of stress (McKennan 1959: 50). If a man killed game, he was supposed to give his partner the best parts of the animal. Andrew Isaac said a partner is to be trusted, and it is important to extend them every courtesy. Gene Henry is the friend Andrew is talking about. He recalls how Gene's parents needed help after one of their children died, so the Tanacross elders sent Andrew to Batzulnetas to render assistance. Gene was born at Batzulnetas on the upper Copper River. Andrew talks about how a person is supposed to treat his shtlęę or friend:

> We have to be proud about, like Gene. He is
> our friend, Indian way shtlęę.
> We are not supposed to talk against shtlęę. We
> really trust the shtlęę.
> Really proud about the friend in Indian way,
> trust them, treat them right. Happen if they
> comin in our village, our trap line we give
> room to stay, if he got dog with them, got to
> feed that dog too. This is one way [i.e., right
> way], Indian way, Indian, Athabascan Indian
> really proud about trust their partner. Don't
> talk bad against it, don't treat bad, take care
> of them. Longs they're our partner because
> his mother is grandma to us. His father is
> special to be our uncle, we got right to go for
> one of his family's death.
> His brother Jimmy [Henry from Northway].
> Now he growing up, just as soon as they
> see me they hug me up. [Andrew then talks
> about when he went to Batzulnetas on the
> upper Copper River to attend a funeral.]
> By foot, [I went] across the country, along way,
> you comin in our village, help us to our
> family to bury my sister.
> Right now today, how great that you doing
> walk across the country, through the water.
> Old Gene he come over [to Tanacross] mother
> need help, daddy need help. All old chief,
> Tanacross community hall, in front of
> them, big pile of log.

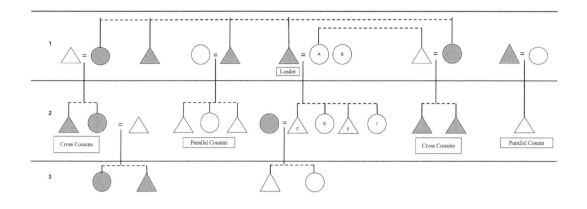

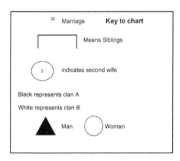

Figure 5.3. Matrilineal descent. This diagram shows a hypothetical group consisting of three succeeding generations (1, 2, 3). Triangles represent males, circles females. Triangles and circles connected by dashed lines are brothers and sisters. Equal signs signify marriage; the leader has two wives, A and B. Two clans are represented in the diagram: gray and white. A person born into a gray clan marries a person born into a white clan. The children of the marriage belong to the mother's clan. Parallel cousins are members of the same clan; cross cousins are members of the opposite clan.

"You grandpa want to see you down there [at the community hall]. I go down there."

"Your grandma need help, Batzulnetas, it's a long way, long walk, we know you the only one can go do that work."

He send his boy over, Gene and other boy Elgin, Fred John's eldest brother. Packed up my dog, walked. Gee! I thought through the mountain just dry. That's worse in this kind of country, wet water, gee! too much water. Sometimes we swim across. We lose Elgin down the Tok River, high water. He got pack on, he put stick all six, seven of us. He slip off, fall off and he got pack on and went down river. Elgin he holler he thought he drown, he hit the bank, he grab the grass and he going up the bank. Even we go through that time. (Simeone 1987h)

In a society based on matrilineal descent, a child's maternal uncle has authority over his maternal nieces and nephews, who treat him with great respect. The maternal uncle is responsible for training and disciplining his nephew, and in some cases boys live with their uncle. Because the nephew and maternal uncle belong to the same clan, the uncle teaches the boy clan stories and is involved in all affairs concerning his nephew's relations with the clan, even after the nephew is married and his own children (Guédon 1974: 124). A boy's relationship with his father and paternal uncle is much less restrained, and the boy's paternal uncle is often treated as a father. Both the father and the paternal uncle teach the boy to hunt, and when it is time for the boy to marry, the paternal uncle often directs him to choose a wife who belongs to his father's clan (Guédon 1974: 125).

Oscar Isaac (Simeone 1987m) described how his father, Walter Isaac, and Chief Sam of Northway were members of the same clan, so Chief Sam was like Oscar's paternal uncle. For this reason, Oscar said that Chief Sam was just like his father. Chief Sam always treated him well. In fact, Chief Sam's son, Frank Sam, made speeches about Oscar, saying how Chief Sam had taught Oscar to be a good man, an "old time man."

GROWING UP: TRAINING OF YOUNG PEOPLE

Young women and men were both brought into society by stages and trained to be physically and mentally tough. At puberty, they were sequestered away from the community and put through rigorous training that included the strict observation of rules to ensure good health and a long life free of afflictions visited upon old age.

According to Mary Tyone (1996: 17–22), who was brought up at Scottie Creek and Northway, both girls and boys were secluded away from the community. In the Upper Tanana language, a girl in puberty was called *ts'axt'iin*, "the one with a hat or hood." Both girls and boys had to wear puberty hoods adorned with raven feathers so that their hair would not turn gray in old age. The anthropologist Guédon (1974: 183) was told that women wore a hood or a hat with fringes hanging down about six inches in front of the eyes "so [they] could not see anything." The hood was also designed to "hide your face from the sun, too, if sun hit your face, your skin going to be brown." According to Helen David Charlie (Anderson 1956: 16), the hood worn by young girls was made of "moose skin maybe two moose skins long and so heavy it had to be tied to poles to keep from falling." The hood was designed to fix the young woman's attention so

she could concentrate on the specific tasks she needed to learn for her family to survive.

A complex set of restrictions was imposed on both sexes. Girls, for instance, could not drink cold water through their mouth; they had to drink water through a swan's windpipe so water would not touch their teeth. They had to keep their legs tucked underneath them, otherwise they would get leg cramps. Both boys and girls had to wash their faces with their hands moving upwards so their faces would not sag in old age and chew spruce boughs to make their teeth strong. According to Cora David (2017: 165–166):

Tagoh thuul' shyiit ay ishyiit
ch'a tuu ihetniign.
Ts'exeey in <chih>
ay hugn
nah'ogn ts'oo niidee'aay ay <<thuuchin>>
ay
ditthi' hii' eł etsade hetsiik nts'ą'hii eł ditthi
ets'iit.
Dila'eł k'a diithi' hets'iign, įįjh, huheniik.

Through a swan's windpipe
They drink water.
The women too
there
Look for spruce standing out there and hooked branch
And
They make comb out of it and scratch their heads with it.
They may not scratch their heads with their hands, that's įįjih, they tell them.

While secluded, girls practiced their sewing. Girls who sewed with tiny stitches were called "mouse women" and those who used large stitches were called "rabbit women." Mary Tyone said that women who sewed with tiny stitches were better and would make a lot of money. Also, men would not marry women who sewed large stitches (Tyone 1996: 17–22). Cora David (2017: 164–165) said that:

Ishyiit ts'anh noo	From then on,
tihniishyah de'	when they have their first period,
k'at'eyy ha'ogn t'eey tihtaahaal	they may not go outside;
dinįį'	their faces
dinįį' nach'ihudeh-niik	they cover their faces
nts'ą'nahugn t'eey k'a hohnanh' iil.	and they don't look around.
Naach'ihnaak' ąą'	They have to sew
natl'ade eł.	with beads.
Nahugn ttheeh tah,	Sinew,
diniign tthee'tah	moose sinew
mbeł ch'ikee julkąą xa hii'eł	in order to sew slippers with it
hiinetdat nts'ą'	They twist it
hugn tah hehxąą.	They make them like that.

Elder Ellen Demit (Callaway and Miller-Friend 2001) said that training began at a very young age. All this training was to make a person strong and able to withstand privation and extreme cold. Young people had to get up and go outside to get fresh water and wood for the fire. Water that stood overnight was considered stale and undrinkable.

If old people talk to young people, just don't ignore. You better stop and listen that. Old grandpa, old grandma say something, you drop everything for them. Respect. Listen. You goin' learn something out of them.
    The baby, even newborn baby, if snow out there. We have to grab a baby.
    Run.
    Run one mile.
    Huge branch out there, just wet, freeze, we just put out babies when run.
    We don't walk slow either.
    Train.

That way when cold weather, our baby already train.
    You don't have to worry about your baby goin' be cold.
    That's what it mean, "You gotta train your baby."
    Make sure it's clean.
    But you have to train.

Ellen then said that a mother took a piece of the baby's diaper and placed it on the trail of the caribou.

Caribou walk around.
    Caribou light.
    Caribou's not heavy.
    Our little baby when he grown up he started doin' her own life.
    That baby we train already, she not goin' be tired.
    Maybe how many mile, mile that whoever we taught goin' work, get moose and the food. That's why we do that.
    And beaver, beaver we don't train our family for cause they live on dirt. If we use beaver too much our little baby goin' be poor.
    He no goin' to make money.
    He goin' to be lazy.
    So we take a little part out the beaver bone, shoulder bone and the baby goin' be real, real strong.
    No one goin' to beat that baby if you train with beaver bone to your baby.

Women rendered the cod oil and use it to oil the child's body. By doing so the child—when he eventually hunted moose as an adult—would know which moose is fat and which is skinny. Because moose are so heavy, babies are not trained with moose—that is, young people are never supposed to eat baby moose; that is left for the elders. If children eat baby moose meat, they will become too heavy and will not be able to run fast like caribou.

He [caribou] goes mile, mile, but no baby moose.
    So old people it's all eat.

Also young women are not supposed to eat moose heart.

Ellen then described rules regarding young women:

Under blanket you use that special branch to sleep on.
He put a special tent.
When we begin woman we never stay inside.
We go out.
He let us move out, out of the house.
Our mother and daddy he get us tent.
The tent is placed away from the house.
Girls make lots of sinew and sew and sew. They are not supposed to use thread, just sinew. If the man is hunting you don't watch him shoot, that's injih. (Callaway and Miller-Friend 2001: 21, 36–38, 39)

In 1960 Frederica de Laguna and Catharine McClellan interviewed Maggie Isaac about how children were trained. Like Ellen Demit, Maggie talks about being trained to withstand cold and to be a productive member of society.

MAGGIE: Woodpecker eat worm under the wood. My dad cut wood, find that. My dad rub on our hands—both. Then we can do any kind of work—not lazy. Nothing hard for us.
Early in the morning we sleep. And first snow come, and throw us out of doors in snow. I don't mind snow. And we run right in the brush and pull trees, pull snow down on us. With no moccasins. And we could sit on our dress and get a little warm. And we run and change clothes and start to eat. Every fall, boys, they throw in ice water.

INTERVIEWER: To make you tough?
MAGGIE: Yes, I never have trouble with cramps. Never know much cramp. Now my niece always have cramp. We not supposed to eat much meat, no tendons.
We just exercise real hard, when we turn to first woman. When turn to woman we

sure really get trained up good that time. Sew, any kind of work, moccasin, everything: anything people want to sew—what we live on, this world. Nowadays, girl turn to woman, we don't know. Just act like whites.

INTERVIEWER: Did women wear a hood?
MAGGIE: You ask my sister Doris [Charles]. I never see.

To avoid endangering a man's luck, young women could not share their food with anyone. Maggie says bears did not like menstrual blood, so women had to stay out of the bush and men had to stay away from young women.

MAGGIE: We eat alone, and never eat with nobody else. And don't bother nobody's food, too.
Old time, bear is against woman, when sick [menstruating]. They sure don't like us. I don't know some reason. We don't go in the bush. That's why when we get sick, men don't come out [to our] place, and we got to stay alone. Me, I stay with my mother. I'm the only one. They love me so much. My mother keep me in the house.
They sure train us good. My mother train us good for hard work so me . . . our lifetime. My girl, I just break her in, my girl. Make her cut fish and meat. I cut meat—break her. [Now it is] no different between white and Indian. Lazy people don't have better place to sleep. Only good rustler got good place.

INTERVIEWER: Were men trained to be tough men in war?
MAGGIE: Train early—either no war; (even) no war. Early in the morning, they run out and pull brush; get excited. Cut wood—anything! Pack water. Whatever his parents work for.

INTERVIEWER: Special training for husband when the couple has their first baby?
MAGGIE: Yes, both of them have to train up again. When she first turn woman, and

if she don't work, when she got first baby, that last chance. If she don't (train then) then, bad luck. Just only two times. (de Laguna and McClellan 1960c)

As a young man, Walter Northway began his training as soon as his voice changed. His father told him to leave the house and stay secluded from the community. According to Walter, all this training was to stay "strong and young."

> When I was around fourteen or fifteen my voice changed. My dad instructed me to pack up and move out. I had to move about five miles away from home. I had to build a tree house to live in.
>
> Then I was given materials—a thin moose skin to count days and two small, dry sticks, one short and one long. The short stick was to use like a toothbrush in order to have straight teeth. The long stick was to chew for strong gums and strong teeth. Then I had to weave sinew through my fingers. In the morning when I awoke, I warmed up water, put a small amount of moose grease in the water, and wet a dry, flat twig in my mouth. I had to drink the water for three days without eating. Just drink that water.
>
> I used that twig for my teeth. I also had to bite and bite on the long stick. That is why I don't have a problem with my teeth to this day. They fall out now by themselves. No toothache. While sleeping I had to keep my legs bent. I was not supposed to straighten them out. I had to eat early too, before the women got up. I couldn't drink straight out of a cup. I had to use a swan leg bone as a straw. My dad also tied a swan windpipe around my neck so I could have strong, loud voice. (Yarber and Madison 1987: 38–40)

When a child made their first kill, their parents or maternal aunt and uncle distributed gifts to the child's father's relatives. In the case of a small animal, such as a rabbit, the meat along with a gift of two or three blankets or money was given to an elder. If the child killed a large animal such as a moose or if the family was wealthy, a potlatch was held. With his first kill, a young man became a full-fledged member of society, able to provide and share. He came into being socially as a provider who was now a vital part of other people's lives. His hunting success demonstrated not only his practical skill but his coming into awareness and ability to connect with the world of animals. This was vital to his personal survival as well as the survival of others. Likewise, a young woman's ability to sew, concentrate on vital tasks like butchering fish or caring for meat, and keep herself clean meant survival not only for herself but her family.

YOU SHOULD TEACH THEM

In this interview with Olga Lovick (Sam, Demit-Barnes, and Northway 2021: 217–234), Darlene Northway comments on some of the problems brought about by 100 years of colonialism. The primary result is that no one has taught young people their language, traditions, or how to live from the land. She says, "They live instead like White people." Darlene says it is important to know who your maternal and paternal relations are, and that only your maternal relations are your relatives. She laments that young people now mix indiscriminately with their maternal relatives. She then talks about how the land can provide food and money, but the children today don't know how how to find them—they don't know how to dig roots or what kinds of plants there are. They don't know the names of the fish or the names of the internal organs of a moose. "The children are lost out there," she says. Darlene comments that young people are not disciplined today. Instead of staying home, they go in and out when there is a potlatch. Only older people have any business being in the community hall during a potlatch. Darlene is also disturbed that young women are not told what is įįjih so they endanger their own and their children's well-being. Young women were once sequestered and not allowed to mingle with young men; otherwise the young men would lose their luck—"they won't have money in their pocket." This was the last recording Olga made with Darlene, who died not long afterward.

Hudziit hahheeyh
You should teach them

Dziin k'ahdu' hǫǫłįį nee'eh, jah nts'ą́ą́'
    nats'iholnegn xah.
Today, we are here to tell stories.

Olga shaa ninįįshyah tl'aan sheh eedah.
Olga came here and sat with me.

Shaa nts'ą́ą́' niłts'udzelkan xah.
About how we are related for me.

Ay nts'ą́ą́' niłts'udelkanh xah ts'iikeey iin
    niłts'ihetniign niłhii'udelkanh nts'ą́' t'eey
    nił'eh nahdeltth'ih.
And the children don't know how we are
    related to each other; they are related yet
    still live together.

Neeshyah, neets'iikeey iin neeshyah nee'eh
    hihdeltth'ii iin ay ishyiit ts'änh ch'a
    neets'iikeey iin hihtatnayh.
Our houses, our children living with us in
    our houses should know this.

Neexon ch'a, hunąą ts'įįłiin hutsǫǫ ts'įįłiin
    nts'ą́' neexon ch'a hudziit hutsaaheel
    tl'aan, "Hǫǫ' ch'a nuh'uudelkan iin ay iin
    ay iin ch'a," hudzaanił.
Us, being their mothers and grandmothers,
    it was us who should have advised them,
    "These and these and these are your rela-
    tives," we should have told them.

Ay iin ch'a ts'iikeey iin nił'its'ihetniign
    nił'ehłaadn nłįį nts'ą́' t'eey nił'eh nah-
    deltth'ih.

And the children do not know who they are
    paternally related to and they live with
    each other.

Hiits'ihetniign eh ch'ah hetdąy.
They don't know so they do that.

Hunąą iin, huta' iin, hutsǫǫ iin, hutsay
    iin ay iin hudziit hihǫǫheey de' k'a hǫǫ'
    hihtaadįįl.
If their mothers, fathers, grandmothers,
    grandfathers and others, taught them
    they wouldn't be doing that.

Neexon' ch'a neek'eexaagn ch'a <ts'iikeey>
    iin.
It is our fault kids are doing that.

K'at'eey hǫǫsǫǫ hidąy ha'ogn ts'iikeey iin hu'.
They're not doing well, the kids out there.

Neexon ch'a hunąą ts'įįłįį nts'ą́' hįįtsuul nts'ą́'
    t'eey neek'eh huts'ą́' ts'utaaheel chih,
    k'at'eey chih neek'eh huts'ą́' ts'ihǫǫheey
    nts'ą́' neek'eh k'at'eey hiihetnay.
We, though, we are their mothers and
    when they were little, we should have
    spoken to them in our language; we did
    not speak to them in our language and
    now they don't speak our language.

Neek'eh shyįį' huts'ą́' ts'ihǫǫheey de' hiit-
    suul dą' ts'änh, neets'iikeey iin huts'ą́'
    ts'ihǫǫheey de' ch'a neehihtdaatth'egn
    <k'ahdu'> dziin.
If we had spoken only our language to
    them from the time they were little, if we
    had spoken to our children they would
    understand us today.

Hah'ogn nts'ą́', ts'iikeey iin ts'ą́' hiihunay
    ha'ogn nän' k'it, huxah chih hushyi',
    hu'elsüü' įį'eh tah ha'ogn nän' k'it hǫǫłįį
    t'oot'eey hiits'ihetniign nts'ą́'.
Out there, the children can work out there,

out there on the land also their food,
their money and so on, it is on the land,
but they do not know it.

Doo t'eey k'at'eey jah ch'a huts'änh nelsüü'
ut'ah nt'ah utaałeel ch'a ts'iikeey iin
idzaaniił.

Anyone around here could use anything
around to put money in their pockets, we
should have told the children.

Nah'ogn k'įįy įį'eh tah ch'a mbelsüü hǫǫłįį
ts'oo įį'eh tah ch'a ay iin hugn t'eey nts'ą̈'
hihtnahtsayh.

Out there is lots of birch, that is money, and
spruce too, and they should gather them.

Hii'eh naach'ihniką̈ą̈ xayh.
They sew with it, spruce roots.

Ts'oo ts'änh ch'a mihǫǫłįį, xayh.
It comes from spruce, those roots.

Hugn iin t'eey its'ihetniign nts'ą̈ xayh t'eey
k'at'eey hihndehtsay.

They don't know about roots, and they don't
gather roots.

<Ts'iikeey> iin hu'ihuushyaak ha'ogn.
The children are lost out there.

Neexon' ch'ah neek'įįl neets'iikeey iin
k'at'eey hiihetnay.

It is our fault, that our kids don't know.

Tay' ahugn hudziit ch'eedlay iin noodlee::
noodlee k'eh shyįį'.

The people with headphones, white people,
only the white people's way.

Nuhts'iikeey xah <dii t'eey> huxah ahkeet.
You buy anything for your kids.

Ndehdą̈' nuhtsǫǫ nuhtl'a'yįįdlay ch'a
dahdą̈y'?

When did your grandmother give you these
things, why are you doing this?

Na'ogn tsüüh kah t'eey shyiit k'at'eey
ts'iikeey iin staats'iłeegn.

Out there, we don't even take the kids out to
look for edible roots.

Jign įį'eh tah, jign įį'eh tah nts'ą̈ą̈' u'et-sih
nts'ą̈ t'eey hits'ihetniign.

There are berries, there are berries and they
don't know what they are called.

Neek'įįl ch'a hǫǫ' nt'ay.
This is our fault.

K'ahmänh tah tsi'ahdek nts'ą̈ t'eey
nuhts'iikeey iin nahugn hihdeltth'iign
iin t'eey hutah dahdaltth'iign tl'aan
nuhts'iikeey iin: "Jin ch'a udidhįlkan, jin
du' k'at'eey udįlkan, k'at'eey neełeegn
įįłay <jin ch'a>," ts'iikeey iin itdzaaniil.

In the morning, when you wake up, your
children right then are sitting around
them you all are sitting around and your
children: you are maternally related to
these children, you are not maternally
related to this one, this one is not your
close relative, we should tell that to our
children.

Nah'ogn łuugn huxah taanuu hanohshy-
ugn xaniign ay iin łuugn įį'eh tah hǫǫłįį
t'oot'eey, ndehde' ishyiit ts'iik'eey iin
nitahłeeł, tl'aan, "Dą̈ą̈' ch'a łuugn k'it
ts'etnay::," ch'a tdahniil.

Out there there's fish for them, there is an
island down in the creek where there's
white fish, but when you going to bring
the kids down there and "This is how we
work on fish," you should teach.

Łuugn chih mǫǫsi' hǫǫłįį, nts'ą̈ hįhdlą̈ą̈
nts'ą̈ <łahtthegn'> mǫǫsi' hǫǫłįį.

Whitefish too has names, as many as there
are, they all have names.

Łuugn k'it nahugn hudzeey, huthät, humbät <łahtthegn' nts'"ą̈> hugn t'eey ch'a
   <ts'iikeey> iin xah utahsih.
The fish out there, their heart, their liver,
   their stomach, you should name them all
   for the children.

Łuugn tthi' t'eey ch'a k'at'eey tth'ats'ihłeey.
We don't throw away even fish heads.

Hugn t'eey ch'a k'ąy' eh ts'i'iah tl'aan hadogn dahdzäl k'it dahiiyihdlaak eegąy xah
   hugn tah.
There we string them with willow and they
   put them up on the drying rack so they
   dry.

Xay nihuuthek tah t'axoh dziįtsįį de' ch'itthi'
   hadogn shiin dą' įį'ąą dadhįįdlaay ay ch'a
   huts'ą̈, "Mbaa niitįįdaał ay tl'aan ay ch'a
   tuuthäl mbeh tįhtsayh."
In the winter time, when we are hungry
   those fish heads which we put up there
   while it was summer, "You go back for it
   and make soup with it."

Ay ts'änh t'eey ch'a nt'ayy' nootat-łeel.
And you will get strength back from this.

Dii t'eey k'at'eey tth'ats'ihłeey.
We don't throw away anything.

K'ahdu' ts'iikeey iin hǫǫ't'eey hits'ihetniign.
Right now, the children still don't understand.

Neek'eexaagn ch'a ts'iikeey iin, ts'iikeey iin
   k'at'eey hǫǫsǫǫ dąy.
It is our fault that our children don't do well.

Neek'eh nah'ogn hiihutįįł dänh chih
   ch'ah hihutįįł tah doo ehteek dą' chih
   ch'a ishyiit dänh chih ch'a ts'iikeey iin
   yahnįįshyeek, yahnįįshyeek hanoo' ndee
   naach'ihi'aał dänh.

Where they give potlatches too, they potlatch when someone dies from something, the children come in and go out
   where people are eating.

Ay chih k'at'eey hǫǫsǫǫ hiidąy.
They don't do things right.

K'ahdu' ch'itįįł dą' t'axoh nahditįįk tah
   ts'iikeey iin, "Shyiign didhaltth'ih
   nuhshyah," ch'a huheniik.
Right now at a potlatch when they carry the
   coffin they should tell the children "Stay
   in your houses."

K'ahdu' du' k'at'eey hǫǫ' hudziit hudetnąy nts'ą̈' k'at'eey hǫǫ' hudetnąy nts'ą̈'
   yahnishyeek yahnishyeek.
Nowadays they don't teach them this and
   they don't tell them this and they go in
   and out, in and out.

Nts'ą̈' ts'iikeey iin än hihdel'aak.[4]
They used to keep the children away.

Ch'itay iin, ch'itsǫǫ iin ay iin shyįį' ch'a
   nach'ihi'įįł dänh< łahtthegn'> ishyiit
   niihitdegn.
Old men and grandmothers, they alone
   may go where they will eat.

Hugn tah ch'ihdee'aag iin ts'iikeey iin du'
   k'at'eey dą' huhiłeegn.
And when they sing, they don't bring the
   children in.
Hushyi' huxah shyi' nihełeegn tl'aan huts'ą̈
   tah hiitelshyeek ch'inąą iin.
They put their food down for them and
   their mothers bring it to them.

Dziin du' k'at'eey hǫǫ' hidąy.
Today they don't do that.

_____

4   Roy Sam commented that when he was a child, they
were not allowed to attend funeral potlatches, but that it
changed soon after.

K'ahdu' uts'iiniin hǫǫłiin iin t'eey ts'iiniin k'ahdu' mihǫǫłiin t'eey nahtehmbik
   ha'ogn ch'ehteek tat'eey.
Right now, the ones who have newborn
   babies flaunt them even though someone
   is dead.

K'at'eey hudziit ch'ihuha' iin ch'a dąy hugn
   iin hǫǫ' hitdąy.
They weren't taught that is why they do
   that.

K'at'eey ts'iikeey iin xah!
It is not for young children!

Hunąą iin hutsǫǫ iin ay iin ch'a hǫǫ' huht-
   daaniił nts¨ą' "Ena', sǫ' hugn natǫǫdaagn
   k'ahdu' nts'iiniin hǫǫłįį du' dineh dineey
   iin tah sǫ' natǫǫdaagn," nts'ą' dits'iikeey,
   dits'iikeey iin ihtdaaniił.
The mothers, and the grandmothers, they
   are the ones that should tell them: "No,
   don't go anywhere, you just had a baby,
   don't go among people," they should tell
   that to their children.

Nshyaats'e' uts'iiniin hǫǫłįį de' ay ch'a hǫǫ'
   utdįįnįįl.
If your daughter has a baby you have to tell
   her this.

Tthiinįįshyah de' chih ay chih ena'.
When you become a woman also, that's also
   no.

Ts'exeey gaay iin tthihiihaak tah ishyiit dą'
   ch'a "Ina'," hinąy, "ishyiit ch'a įįjih."
When young girls are going through puberty, they have to tell them "No, this is įįjih."

"Įįjih sǫ' hugn, nduugn dineey iin natetdek
   dänh ishyiit hugn sǫ' natǫǫdaagn."
"It's taboo, wherever the people go, don't
   walk around in there."

"Dineey iin sǫ' ǫǫdloo eh nųh'iign įį'eh tah,"
   neehehniik.
"Don't smile and look at men," they used to
   tell us.

"Įįdloh de' jah duugn nxu' ts'ehkah taa'aal ay
   ina'," neehenih.
"If you smile around here it will show your
   teeth plainly, that's a no," they say to us.

Ts'exeey gaay iin tthihiihaak tah, k'at'eey
   dineey iin nah'ogn.
When young girls go through puberty [they
   may not encounter] men outside.

Diniign kah nahtetdek tah ay iin dineey iin
   ay iin ch'a įįjih nts'ą'.
They are going to go for moose, and it is
   taboo for the men.

Ts'exeey iin tthihiihaagn iin ay iin ch'a an'
   ihdel'ay, nah'ogn neetsay nah'ogn ts'äl
   shyiit nłiin ay ts'exeey iin tthinįįshyay
   itsidel'ay nt'eh.
They keep girls going through puberty out
   there away because there are bears in
   the brush and they don't like girls going
   through puberty.

Ay xah ch'a dineey nts'ą', "Än hihdalshyah,"
   huhinay.
That's why they told the men "Stay away."

Ay chih hut'ah t'eey k'at'eey nelsüü taa'aal.
And also they won't have money in their
   pocket.

Huch'a' italch'ee ts'exeh tthinįįshyay
   itahch'ee.
[Money, success, luck] will stay away from
   them; the one who becomes a girl
keeps it away from him.

Nah'ogn stsay, shoh.

Out there is my grandfather, bear.

Ay ts'exeey iin hǫǫ' hįįt'ay eh t'eey nts'iiniin yeh natidaak de' nshüü ay naadlih
itaambah.

And the women who are that way [i.e., have
their period] if your child go to them, he
might fight your son by mistake.

Ts'exeh hiits'änh tahtsänh.

They are going to smell it from the woman.

Ay xah ay dineh itaambah.

That's why he will fight the man.

Ay xah ch'a dineey iin "Ina', duugn ts'exeey
iin dishyįį' nahdeltth'iik tah huch'a' än
idalshyah," huhenąy.

That's why they tell the men, "No, the wom-
en who stay by themselves, she should
stay well away from them."

Ay chih k'at'eey dziin k'at'eey ts'iikeey iin
ts'exeey gaay iin k'at'eey hǫǫ' huhinay
nts'ą́.

Today, they don't tell the children, the little
girls about this.

Hunąą in hutsǫǫ iin k'iheltth'ek ts'iikeey iin
hu'ihuushyay hah'ogn.[5]

Their mother and their grandmother have
fallen into the wrong teachings the kids
are all lost out there.

Noodlee k'eh naadlįh hihunayh.

They live instead as white people

Nił'udzelkan ay nts'ąą nee'uu'et-sii iin ay
iin shyiit ch'a neets'iikeey iin <łahtthegn>
hu'eh nats'uutalnek nts'ą́ hits'etnąy.

We're maternally related to each other and
the way we call our clans we all need to
teach them how they related [the clans,
etc.].

_____
5   "Fallen into the wrong teachings" is an attempt to
translate _k'iheltth'ek_, which literally means something like
"fallen by the wayside."

Nts'ąą ntsay iin ntsǫǫ iin naak'ay iin nts'ąą'
nahiholnegn, doo iin udelkan, ay iin
udelkan ay iin dįįtth'egn ay hǫǫ' nts'ąą'
ndatnį' ay ch'a nts'iikeey iin nchaay iin eh
nootįlnegn.

What, [this is] your grandfathers, grandmothers, aunties, what they told you,
who you are related to, listen to what you
are told and then keep telling it to your
children and your grandchildren.

Jah hits'itniign nts'ą́ nats'iholnegn chih k'a
huusuuy.

We don't know and when we tell stories it's
not good.

Hii'innay łą́ą' hii'innay.

When you know, you really know.

Ay ch'a ts'iikeey iin eh nats'utalnegn.

That's why we have to tell the children.

Hutsay iin nts'ąą' ch'ihdhehxeek tah,
chih ch'ihdhehxeek tah, nts'ąą' diniign
nathuuhehte' ay doo hii'etnąy, hutsay
hu'ee'eh iin hiihetnąy iin ch'a.

When their grandfathers killed something
[moose], who knows how they cut up the
moose, in the way that the grandfathers
and their uncles knew.

Dichaay iin dąą' ch'a diniign nathuuts'ehte'
ch'a dichaay iin ihtdaanil.

Their grandchildren, this is the way we cut
our moose, they would tell their grandchildren.

Hashyuugn nts'ąą u'et-sii humbät eh <łaht-
thegn nts'ą́> udzeey nts'ąą u'et-sii ay iin
ts'iikeey iin hiits'ihetniign nts'ą́.

Down there, what they call the stomach and
what they call the heart, the children do
not know that.

Neexon, neexon shyįį' jah dugn niits'in-

įįdeeł nts'ą̈' neexon ch'a neets'ą̈' udee'ah ch'a neets'iikeey iin eh nats'utalnegn.
We are the only ones going around that know that and we have luck and it is up to us to tell our children.

Hugn dits'än nanatdäl.
The ducks are coming back.

Danoo ts'änh dits'änh iin <łahtthegn> nahnatdäl t'eey chih ay chih ay nts'ą̈ u'et-sii hahdogn nts'ą̈' nanatdäl ay.
From there the ducks are coming back and what they called, the ones flying back up there.

Nts'ą̈ hu'u'et-sii nts'ą̈' dįįtth'ek nts'ą̈ <ay ch'a> ch'atnay itdahnil <ts'iikeey> iin hǫǫ' itdahnił.
What they are called, listen to the sounds they make and then tell that to the children.

Taagoh nanaat'ah de' ishyiit ch'a chih hǫǫsǫǫ tdįįtth'ek nts'ą̈' nts'iikeey iin ay nanatt'ah hutdįįnįįł.
When the swans fly back, listen well and tell your children that they [swan] fly back.

Nahugn ts'aht'udn nanatdäl <chih> <ay> chih <ay chih> ha'ugn ogn nts'ą̈' ch'ih-deh'ą̈ą ay ch'atnay dą̈ą' ch'a ch'uusi' dą̈ą' ch'a ts'iikeey iin itdahnįįł ay nih.
Out there the birds are coming back too, that one and that one, and they're singing somewhere out there, and by the noise they make, you should tell the children their name.

Hah'ogn k'ąy', k'įįy, <łahtthegn> nts'ą̈ą' hu'et-sih niign ay t'eey ch'a ts'iikeey iin hǫǫ' itdahnįįl nts'ą̈' hu'et-sih nts'ą̈'.
Out there willows, birch, the way they call are called, you guys need to teach the children what they're called.

T'axoh neets'iikeey iin ihuushyaak, noodlee k'eh shyįį' hiihetnayh.
Finally our children are all lost, they only know the white man's way.

Hah'ogn nän' jign t'eey chih its'ihetniign le' k'ahdu'.
Now, they don't know the bog cranberries out there, I guess.

Ndäl iin ishyiit de' nanatdäl nanetdeeł heniik.
The black scoters when they're flying back, they say they're flying back.
Näl nanetdeeł.
The black scoters are coming back.

Dits'ayy' gaay hah'ogn mänh shyiit hiłeek tl'aan hiikah tikeek.
They would put their little canoes in the lake and paddle for them.

Na'elk'ah dänh ch'a hiikah tidegn.
When they get fat, they would go for them.

K'ahdu' elk'aa::::le'.
Right now they're really fat, I guess.

Diniign chih already k'ahdu' hugn t'eey just stsay iin hahne' jah dugn hihnįįną̈ą.
The moose too already now, the grandfathers moved in the area upriver.

Stsay iin stsǫǫ iin shǫǫndüü hu'eh eedah.
My grandfathers, my grandmothers and my brothers were staying with them.

Shǫǫndüü hihnehshyą̈ą.
They raised my older brother.

Ay hu'eh eeday jah dugn hihnįįną̈ą tl'aan hanogn łuugn keey.
And while he was staying with them they moved up here for fish camp.

Ishyiit tah dahdzäł choh da'eh'ąą stsay.
At that time he had a big fish rack, my
   grandpa.

Ts'ayh shyiit įįshyah tl'aan hanugn mänh
   choh k'it ts'ą' teeshyah k'ahmänh hǫǫłiin
   eh.
He went by canoe and he went onto a big
   lake in the morning.

Hǫǫt'eey ts'ehtiat nts'ą' t'eey stsay hahnogn
   tah t'axoh natehxeel eh stsay hadǫǫ
   na'atkeeł.
We were still sleeping, and then upland,
   and just before it got dark, my grandfather would paddle back from up there.

K'ąy' k'ąy' gaay unuht'aagn ts'änh hadee'ah.
A little willow was sticking out from his
   back.

Stsǫǫ: "Hahnǫǫ ntsay na'atkeeł," nee'ehnih.
My grandmother said to us: "From up there
   your grandfather is paddling back."

Hanoo k'üdn k'it daagąą'ts'elshyah stsay
   ts'ineh'įh.
We ran over to the platform and saw my
   grandpa.

Uts'ay' titeełaat k'eh eltsįį.
His canoe looked like it was about to sink.

"Stsǫǫ!"
"Grandma!"

"Stsay, stsay du' ts'ayy' ishyiit ts'änh k'ąy'
   hadįį'ah," udihnih.
"My grandfather, from my grandfather's
   canoe, willow is sticking out," I told her.

"Ch'idhehxįį!" shehnih.[6]

_____

6   Her grandfather had put willow into the bottom of his
canoe so there would be airflow underneath the moose
he killed, and so the blood wouldn't get all over the canoe.
The willow sticking out and the way his canoe was sitting

"He killed something!" she told me.

Stsay neexah nii'inshyay eh hashyuugn chih
   ch'ik'a' na'inkįį.
My grandfather came back to us and he
   brought back its fat.

Na'įhxeel eh stsǫǫ hanoo ch'ibät <eh>
   ch'ichąągn ch'ishyuutth'än įį'eh tah
   tthinįįttheeł eh chih tl'aan tl'aan
   tthiitl'aydįįkąą.
It was getting dark, and my grandmother
   upland its stomach, its ribs and its bris-
   ket too she chopped them and put them
   in a container on the fire.

Geez łąą' t'eey łąą' t'eey ch'a suu' ts'inelthänh
   nts'ą' nants'įį'aał.
We were really happy to be eating this
   meat.

Hǫǫsǫǫ:: t'eey nants'įį'aał!
We ate so good!

Shǫǫnüü du' hǫǫ' hiinehshyąą nts'ą' hi'etnayh.
My brother, they raised him and he knew.

Neexon du' jah dugn tah neenąą nee'eh
   eedah shta' du' ehtįį.
Us, our mother lived with us [because] my
   father passed away

Jah dugn tah nee'eh eedah tl'aan stsay stsǫǫ
   du' hahnugn tah ishyiit hugn ch'a my
   shǫǫnüü hihnehshyąą.
There she stayed with us and my grandfather and grandmother up there raised
   my older brother.

Dii du' hii'etnayh neexon du' hiits'etniign.
He knew all about it, but us, we didn't
   know.

_____

low in the water are signs that her grandfather had had a
successful hunt.

Họọ' neeshyąąn eh hii'etnayh.
He knew because he grew up that way.

Stsay na'atkeel hii'etnay k'at'eey họọ'
  nee'ehnay.
He knew that my grandfather was coming
  back but he didn't tell us.

Shiy xah "Ahugn k'ąy' hadee'aa," stsọọ
  idihnạy just stsọọ họọ' shehnạy.
Me, "Me's got willow sticking out," I told my
  grandmother, and my grandmother told
  me:

"Ntsay ch'idhehxįį," shehnih.
"Your grandfather killed something," she
  told me.

Stsọọ iin stsọọ k'at'eey jah dugn hihnįįnaan
  de' k'at'eey hiitishnay họọ'.
If my grandfather and grandmother hadn't
  moved here, I wouldn't know anything.

Họọ' hihuunay niign hunak'ąy eh ch'a
  dihnạy.
I say this from the way I saw them live.

Hugn ch'iłįįgn, ch'iłįįk!
And songs, songs!

Hehteek tah ch'ehłiik hehtsay ay chih ch'a
  muteeshyaagn ay chih ch'a nts'ąą' łaan
  dats'uuniih?
When they die they would make songs and
  those too will be lost soon, how are we
  going to figure them out?

Hah'ogn k'at'eey ch'ehłiig k'at'eey hehtsay.
Out there, they don't make songs.

Shk'ąy' shch'a ehtįį dą' niit Ch'atxąą Männ'
  hahne' Ch'atxąąh Männ' k'it ishyiit ch'a
  diniign kah dineey iin dineey iin ishyiit
  ch'a niihetdek dą'.
When my husband died from me, down

there by "something is killed lake," up
  there by "something is killed lake," the
  men used to go there for moose.

Diniign hįhxąą dänh ch'a họọłįį ishyiit dänh.
This is the place where they kill moose.

Ishyiit dänh huke' k'eh họọłįį huke' k'e.
There were foot tracks.

Hashyign hugn họọłįį.
There were lots there.

<Łahtthegn> k'ahdu' hu'ookol iin.
Now the people are all gone.

<Łahtthegn> hu'ookol.
They're all gone.

Huke' k'eh shyįį' họọłįį aniit.
Only their tracks are down there.

Ishyiit dänh ch'a Ch'atxąą Männ' dänh ch'a
  shk'ąy' shch'a ehtiin eh ishyiit Ch'atxąą
  Männ' k'it ch'a ch'ehłiign mbaa hadih'ąą.
There, at "something was killed lake," when
  my husband died and there at "something
  was killed lake" I made a song for him.

Neets'iiniin' Teddy Jr. mọọsi', kon' dįįk'ąą
  ishyiit
Our child, Teddy Jr. is his name, a fire was
  burning there.

Tayh kon' cho::::::::h nahtän kon' dihk'ąą.
Hill, there was a big fire, thunder and light-
  ning started the fire.

Hahnugn hahnugn tah ishnah, shiy du'.
  Up there I was working, me.

Olga wrote that "At this point, a visitor
arrived, and I turned the recorder off. Darlene
was so exhausted that I left a few minutes later
so she could get some rest." Olga said, "I believe

this is what Darlene was going to tell me: after her husband's death, she made a song for him. In that song, she grieves for his tracks, which were taken away by the fire."

CONCLUSION

Historically upper Tanana Dene lived in small, autonomous groups, with two or more groups composed of closely related kinsmen. Individuals were born into their mother's clan and remained members of that clan throughout their lives. Clans were organized into two sides, or moieties. In times of food shortage, the clan-based kinship system provided people with multiple linkages to other groups, allowing them latitude to seek assistance from a variety of kinsmen. Marrying outside the group and cross-cousin marriages (so that people married outside of their clan) reinforced connections to other groups.

In the twenty-first century all upper Tanana Dene live a settled life in permanent communities whose residents are usually the descendants of one or more regional groups. The extended family and the village are the centers of social life, although clan affiliation continues to serve a function, especially during potlatches. Among upper Tanana Dene, kinship affiliations are extensive, reaching beyond the village and providing people with a network of kinsmen from which to seek assistance in times of need.

Contemporary Dene have a strong sense of identity with their community and the surrounding landscape. These are not simply backdrops or stages for some activity, or a place of residence, but a home in the sense of a place of belonging, so that when a person says, "I am from Northway," she or he is asserting an identity associated with a specific place and group of people.

Photo-montage by Hal Gage.

6 XÁXKEH/XASKEE'

Rich Men

In the Tanacross and Upper Tanana languages, the word for "headman" or "boss" is *xáxkeh* (T) or *xaskee'* (UT). Another word is *dineh*, which is also the word for "rich man" and for man or person. The word "chief," introduced by non-Natives at the end of the nineteenth century, is sometimes used when describing rich men, but elders make a distinction between the modern elected chief and the old-time rich men. Modern leaders are not the same as the old-time rich men.

Helen David Charlie, in her book *According to Mama*, provided a concise definition of a xáxkeh: he was rich with lots of possessions, had many wives, and was a good hunter.[1] Helen said:

> If a man was rich he had more wampum [dentalium shells] and more wives and this way people knew it. And if this man was lucky at hunting and had many goods besides, soon people started calling him Chief. (Anderson 1956: 2–3)

According to Bessie Barnabas of Salchaket, xáxkeh were strong and fearsome characters who were rich, were often mean, and had considerable supernatural powers. She said:

> The people had to provide him with food and obey his commands. He decided where they would hunt and how long. He told the men when it was time to make a war party and they were afraid to go against his wishes. This was because he had powerful magic. Chiefs were also medicine men who could kill any man with magic if he didn't obey. (Baggen n.d.a)

In an interview recorded by Guédon, an unidentified person from Tetlin emphasized the importance of luck in being a chief. Luck, combined with being "smart," enabled a chief to kill game easily, without apparent effort.

> Who is lucky, that man is just like chief, everything they hunt, all kinds of game. Moose, anything, they get just like nothing. You know, Chief, he is smart man; he is lucky too. That's why they say. "he is lucky man." (Guédon 1974: 142)

OLD-TIME RICH MEN

In traditional Dene society, leadership rested with charismatic, enterprising individuals who combined an interest in others with a degree of personal cunning and economic calculation. These men were often bigger than life, with huge personalities, and their actions raised them above other members of the group. *Xaskee'* were hunters of considerable skill and knowledge; had considerable wealth measured in food, heavily decorated clothing, and large winter houses; and were trained in clan histories and the special language used in potlatches and trade. A rich man's prestige

---

1 Tutchone from the Yukon Territory gave similar explanation for a chief. A man from Burwash Landing said "to be a high person" the man had to "kill" the most fur, have the most meat, and be "a good rustler . . . just like now, who got lots of money—they are high people" (McClellan 1975: 490).

Figure 6.1. Chief Isaac, 1908. Chief Isaac was a noted xáxkeh, or rich man. Silas Solomon said Chief Isaac came originally from the Goodpaster River. According to John Hajdukovich, Chief Isaac lived at Chief Creek near Dot Lake, where he raised his three sons: Titus, Follet, and Walter. After that he moved to Joseph Village and then to Ketchumstuk. Silas said Chief Isaac moved into the upper Fortymile River to be closer to the traders on the Yukon River. Photo taken from a scan of a photo in the *Alaskan Churchman* 4 (4), August 1910. William E. Simeone photo collection.

SILAS: Direct the people. Tell them. Like these guys around here lay around doing nothing. There's jobs here they won't work. If there's chief here he'd say "get out of here go hunt." Everyone, anything you can use to benefit you. You will go out, don't lay around go hunt that's the thing tell them how to do it. Keep your house clean, get wood, all that.

INTERVIEWER: Would he tell the people where to go, where to hunt?

SILAS: Yeah he'd do that cause he knows better the way to go.

INTERVIEWER: Why does he know better?

SILAS: I don't know, cause he's been there, been told him by years. He goes out and kills a bear upon the mountain. He goes out there, climb a steep mountain. Rocky cliffs. And people fall off the mountain too, if the chiefs don't tell them how, not to go there. If they fall off—dead, killed.

INTERVIEWER: So he is responsible for the welfare of the people?

SILAS: That's right. He gotta be telling them right from wrong.

INTERVIEWER: People answered to the chief?

SILAS: Yeah. They got to do what he say.

In *The Upper Tanana Indians*, Robert McKennan (1959: 132–133) outlined the history of Chief Sam of Nabesna, illustrating the characteristics of a leader. As a young man Chief Sam was industrious and shrewd. McKennan wrote that before Chief Sam was married, he had made three potlatches, thereby establishing himself as important and generous. He also made annual trips to trading stations on the Yukon, bringing back beads, guns, and ammunition with which he made more potlatches. For years he was a man of importance, but as he got older Chief Sam lost his edge. When McKennan met Chief Sam in 1930, he was poor and had lost his influence.

While authority was concentrated in the hands of rich men, there were other important

was based on his ability to distribute food and goods, especially in times of need. He had the authority to settle disputes and to give out punishment, including killing someone if necessary. Xáxkeh usually had many wives and an entourage of maternal nieces, nephews, and poor relations who did all the manual labor in exchange for food and shelter.

Silas Solomon (1984b) outlined the chief's duties and responsibilities:

Figure 6.2. Chief Sam and family, Lower Nabesna, 1919. Robert McKennan (1959: 132–133) wrote that Chief Sam was a good example of a xaskee', or rich man. Photo by F. B. Drane. Drane Photo collection, Alaska and Polar Regions Department, Elmer E. Rasmuson Library, University of Alaska Fairbanks.

men in each community recognized for their special skills. According to Jerry Isaac of Tanacross (Simeone 1987n), each clan had a historian who knew clan histories and the genealogies of important people. There were also orators who knew the esoteric language used in potlatch speeches, and "potlatch men" who attended to the people's social needs and wants during a potlatch. Jerry said this man was diligent, saved to make a potlatch, economized, and able to spread wealth. Jerry believed there was a "class" system based on material wealth. In the case of an extended family where there was an imbalance of wealth, the rich took care of the poor or less fortunate. Two other important figures were the doctors or oracles (*deshen* [T] or *dishin* [UT]), who had special powers to foretell the future and cure an ailment, and war leaders, or *mbaah tthi'* (UT).

Xáxkeh were economic lynchpins. They did little labor themselves but organized the work of their kinsmen and followers. For example, Andrew Isaac (1984b) said his grandfather (Chief Isaac the elder) organized construction and maintenance of the caribou fence at Ketchumstuk. Silas Solomon (Solomon and Isaac 1987) said chiefs from Mansfield "owned" different sections of the caribou fence and made sure they were maintained.

INTERVIEWER: So there were different men who owned these fences?

SILAS: The sections. They were chiefs. They're from Mansfield.

INTERVIEWER: The men that owned the fences, did they build them?

SILAS: The workers do that. Just like, for instance, if I was a chief. I had a few relations, you know young boys, if they got ambition. The chief, I'd keep it after them. If they go someplace after they got finished built [it] up, I'd be watching you know.

Repair it. Before the herds came through.
People watch every day. Caribou. Then
when once caribou herd's going to come
through they wait.

INTERVIEWER: That one at Flint Hill is the
biggest one?

SILAS: Yah. That's the biggest one.

Xáxkeh also organized trading expeditions
by employing young men to carry furs to the
trading posts and goods back to the homeland.
According to Maggie Isaac, chiefs paid their
relatives to pack trade goods and took care of
the people who worked for them.

> Great Grandpa go to Tanana, first of June my
> grandpa go down, they go by canoe, bring
> all his nephew and all his uncle, all go down
> to Tanana. All people go together, bought all
> that shell [ammunition], tea, chew, whatever
> they use, come back when berries ready to
> ripe, August or September. Hard trip but old
> people pay so much a day for the packing.
> His own relative pack stuff for them, the
> leader old people take care. If chief hire you
> and do it for them they give you stuff if you
> get hard up, they share with shell, tea, and all
> that stuff. The chief keeps up all his people,
> just like one family. (Simeone 19870)

In the late 1960s, François-Marie Guédon
(1974: 65) was told that Upper Tanana Dene villages were identified with a particular xaskee'
who controlled that village. They were identified specifically in the genealogical record
and recognized by certain emblems, including
eagle feathers and dentalium shells. One Tetlin
elder told Guédon:

> Eagle tail, white one, who is chief, put one
> feather on his head. And where he goes
> in, in his house, they put feathers on top
> of that door. Tudi [bald Eagle], long time
> ago that eagle was a chief. That's why every
> chief's house they put feather, and he puts
> feather on his head, on the right side.
> (Guédon 1974: 141–142)

Rich people were distinguished by the deco-
rations on their clothes, and accouterments
such as their gun cases and arrow quivers
as well as their clean and neat appearance.
One elder said . . . "if everything clean, you
look like rich people, they visit you . . . lot of
money." (Guédon 1974: 181)

Helen David Charlie said that chiefs had
large amounts of "wampum," or dentalium
shells, they used to decorate themselves.

> Just rich people and Chiefs and their
> wives could wear wampum [dentalium
> shells] in wide collars around their necks
> and long earrings hanging clear down to
> their shoulders and even longer some-
> times. Some wore headbands of wampum
> too, and sometimes where there was a
> potlatch, Mama said the Chief put on a
> neck piece with beads just solid and big,
> big breast plate all over beads and he
> was beautiful. He had, too, a knife-case
> covered with wampum and both of these,
> the breastplate and the knife-case, had
> little eagle feathers all around the edge.
> (Anderson 1956: 2–3)

Even today, dentalium shells, ch'ink'ón (T)
or ch'iik'unn' (UT), have special significance in
Dene culture as a sign of wealth as well as prestige and respect because they are rare, coming from outside the region. Several stories
have been recorded about how upper Tanana
Dene got dentalium shells. In both stories a
stranger from outside the area, described as
having a big nose, big bones, and big joints, has
the shells. In one story an upper Tanana man
kills the stranger and takes the dentalium. In
another story the Upper Tanana man saves the
stranger from a bear. The stranger tells the man
to clean a nearby birch of all its limbs so that it
can be easily seen. The stranger then tells the
man to return to the tree in the spring and take
whatever he finds hanging on the tree. When
the man returns, he finds dentalium shells
hanging from the tree (Paul 1980).

Figure 6.3. Andrew Isaac, Walter Northway, and Lilly Northway wearing traditional regalia including dentalium shell necklaces and "chief's coats." Photo by Terry Haynes.

Dentalium shells have an emotional resonance. According to Larry Jonathan of Tanacross (Simeone 1986b), when a child is especially loved or cared for, the parents will give them a dentalium shell necklace. Larry said dentalium is worn not for wealth but for love. In the past certain men wore belts or bandoliers of dentalium around their bodies.

Guédon recorded a Tanacross elder talking about the ideal leader, Chief Healy from Healy Lake. The elder emphasized that Chief Healy worked hard, was generous, and was reserved in his behavior, except on special occasions when he displayed his personal wealth in the form of highly decorated clothing and personal adornment. The elder also alluded to taboos in the form of dietary restrictions that Chief Healy followed to help ensure his good luck. As Guédon notes, no man was expected to succeed in so much work unless he was helped and protected by a good deal of luck.

Old Chief Healy, I hear story. He was living yet in the country when I was growing up. When his family eats, he does not eat. He eats all by himself. . . . His wife cooks for him special way. Poor looking clothes, hard working. He goes out hunting, moose, everything. All hard works. He hunts fish, ducks, all kinds; he kills rabbits, cuts spruce tree, puts them in cache. When poor people, he just gives away to them. Lazy people got poor living. Only certain day, one day, he (Chief Healy) dresses good; maybe once a year. Puts on all rich clothes, walks around. Sometimes, he would look for the whole village. That's the only time he would dress. Also when potlatch, 3 days . . . walks around, does nothing, visits friends. (Guédon 1974: 143)

While leadership was achieved through hard work and luck, it was also an ascribed status.

Figure 6.4. Chief Healy. Jeany Healy collection
UAF-2000-181-23.

Figure 6.5. Chief Peter and family, 1919. Photo by F. B. Drane.
William E. Simeone collection.

Figure 6.6. Chief Luke and his wife Helen. They were the
maternal grandparents of Cora David. Chief Luke was from
Mentasta but lived in the Tetlin for a good part of his life.
Photo by E.A. McIntosh, William E. Simeone collection.

People were recognized because of their training and background. Andrew Isaac (Simeone
1987h) talks about how he was trained to know
who his relatives were and how to speak. The
importance of knowing who your relatives were
is a constant theme of the elders. Information
about relations in other villages was critical so
that when a person traveled, they knew where
they could get support and who they could rely
on in times of need. According to Andrew Isaac:

> Indian people, ever since generation, they
> tell us, young people, tell us story. Old
> people even tell us. Our relatives go through
> the village all the way up to Northway and
> Scottie Creek. In our home, our parents
> tell us which relative we belong to, which
> cousin we belong, so that's the way we know
> our relatives to other village. As a young
> boy once in while I walk with the other
> going down to Tetlin [he names prominent
> men in Tetlin]. I got my uncle Chief Peter,
> Paul Joe, Jimmy Joe, Andrew David, Charlie
> David's daddy, and Old Joseph, Chief Luke.
> Chief Luke he is my uncle. Which uncle we
> got in other village. Through our parents

Figure 6.7. Chief Luke in the 1950s. Photo by C. Heller, Anchorage Museum of History and Art.

they tell us, they got the Indian name, like white man name now, everywhere. All even, Gene's [Henry] daddy, little Bill is my uncle down Copper River. Cross the country they married, they take cousin, cross the country to other village. A lot of white guy ask me, how come you got [relatives] long way [from] village and how did that girl get there? That's how us Indian know our relative. I raise in Ketchumstuk. Chief Isaac [Andrew's grandfather] is chief over down Healy River, [he] move up to Boat Bottom, go down to Joseph village, stay there, go down to Ketchumstuk. Them people they move in that area. My grandfather is chief in that area.

Us Indian people we living under the chief. We can't pass, we can't boss alongside the chief, to put our self [ahead] unless the old man let us to say some word, that's the only time. Grandpa Big Albert, his daddy old man Charlie, Charlie James's daddy old Jim, and Peter Onion, all them people been

learned while they young people raised, and learned to speak [using a certain type of oratory] just important person. Only that people, Old Saul, Chief Healy down Healy River, whoever chief in other village they tell us the name, they tell us the relative, they telling us how many children they got, how many cousins they got in the village, and all that our old people in our village tell us. Even if we never been that village we know our relative there. Someday somehow, we got chance to get in the village we know who are relative, right off. We coming in village we want to stay with special person, with that person, where they stay, we go in our relative place, they took us, show us where us where to stay.

Indian people watching the young generation. Not the land, like I tell a little while ago, not the land to rush [make quick decisions], not raised rush, watch old people, [they] say no, we stop right away. Mothers, daddies, uncles, aunt, grandma,

Figure 6.8. Sam Thomas was born in 1859 and was a highly esteemed spokesperson and leader, but according to some people, he was not considered a xáxkeh. Andrew Isaac said that when Sam Thomas spoke, people had to be very quiet out of respect "so they could put their minds to good things and know about so as to pass them on to our children and the world." From left to right, unidentified woman and baby, Albert Thomas (Little Albert), Bessie Thomas, Sam Thomas, and Tommy John, who was from Salcha. Photo by E. A. McIntosh, William E. Simeone photo collection.

all our old people, grandpa, uncle, all our long relatives they are boss. I go through that stuff [training], boss, that's how I learn I understand, how we are to talk, along old people teaching you, [to] look forward, go through the village, watch the other people, watching other village people how they treat themselves for living, watch. (Simeone 1987h)

Gaither Paul of Tanacross (Simeone 1986a) describes the importance of "background" or ancestry using the example of Sam Thomas, who was a well-known figure in the upper Tanana region in the early twentieth century. Sam Thomas was born between the villages of Ketchumstuk and Mansfield in about 1860. He was a member of the Dik'aagyu clan and was recognized locally as the most senior member of that clan.

When Gaither was growing up in the 1920s, Sam Thomas was a partially blind elder and still considered a spokesman and advisor with considerable prestige because of his own

achievements and because he was descended from a long line of "chiefs." This meant Sam Thomas was a descendant of people who were known to possess knowledge and abilities that made them "great" or "rich." It was widely accepted that all the prestige acquired by these ancestors had come to rest in Sam Thomas. Because Gaither was related to Sam Thomas, he too had some of that prestige. What Gaither remembered most about Sam Thomas was his skill as an orator. This skill was based on Thomas's extensive knowledge of local genealogies and his ability to mobilize that knowledge in speeches made at potlatches. Gaither Paul said:

I remember people look to him [Sam Thomas] as advisor, spokesmen, because that man knows everything. [His name was] Gah Xąą' Ta' "Father of an Arctic hare's front leg" or "Rabbit Arm." Everybody look to him for advice on old ways, he know it all. This man, in Indian way, his forefathers are chief, in Indian way nobody can beat him in debate, because he can use the greatness of his father and use that with his talk. And everybody know they can't beat him in debate. Those are all forgotten now, but that's the way it was then. He is the spokesman, he is the one that knows everything about old people.

He is oldest brother of my daddy's mother. So this, in Indian way, make him my grandfather too. So in Indian way, those Dihthâad people [people from Mansfield village] are known for their greatness, or richness, or whatever, he come from those people. In any kind of debate, he can use those words as his weapon, and nobody can beat him. In that debate, I remember that M-shaped mountain that sign of Mansfield, that is mentioned and pointed to and stuff like that [here Gaither is talking about Nax-ęy Xú', the mountain in the Alaska Range].

Because I come from those people. Because I come from those people like Sam Thomas, his daddy and all those people at Mansfield. Because they are my grandfa-ther, if today Indian feel like those days, even if they know I am poor man, people respect me, just on account of those people before me. Even if I got nothing, I am still come from those people and people just respect me for that.

One old man told me, this is Mark's [Henry] daddy, one time he told me. If old time people, you and your brothers, if you know a lots of old time people, and if peo-ple think about old time, think like old time if you know everything like that man Sam Thomas, stuff like that, nobody can beat you with debate, any kind of argument. Even you have nothing, you can have those people behind you. I guess that's the way Indian feel. But its all gone now, nobody feel that way anymore. (Simeone 1986a)

Rich men were spokesman of power and authority, and their ability to persuade an audience was extremely important. Oscar Isaac of Tanacross (Simeone 1987p) explained how senior clan leaders were supposed to keep young people out of trouble.

When all the old people die, in the case of all the old, important Ałts'įį Dendeey peo-ple, when they die off, the one left, and the one who is the eldest, takes care of the kids with his talk. If the children respect him he will become a big shot. That is why some old timers, who aren't worth a shit, have no money, are well respected, because they keep the people out of trouble with their talk. (Simeone 1987p)

Oscar added that in the past this was partic-ularly important because it was necessary that people keep out of trouble. He said:

Headmen should be good people, not bad, to avoid war, to avoid trouble. Bad men can use their talk to get people into trouble. In a family with lots of men the eldest might be bad so the family takes as headman another person, second or third son.

Rich men were identified in the genealogi-cal record, and well-educated Dene could often recount the succession of chiefs at a particu-lar place. In an interview recorded by Mertie Baggen, Bessie Barnabas named the chiefs at Salchaket to Healy Lake.

"Wai-nul-at" was Bessie's father and chief at Salchaket. Before that Hu-u-chat was chief. Old John was chief at Goodpaster and he inherited leadership from his father Ska-xil-taq. All of these except Hu-u-chat were Ałts'įį Dendeey. There were two chiefs at Healy, Nat-selta and Xi-tza-saga (skinny old man). Another group lived on the Little Delta River whose chief was Datchet', father of Chief Thomas at Nenana. Gotsul-ch' ti' was chief at Chena (Chief Hanley?). (Baggen n.d.a)

Two of the most famous rich men in the Tanacross area were Ketl'aad Tá' and Stsêey Netlé'. In 1885 Lt. Allen (1887) met Ketl'aad Tá', and there is a photograph of the chief, his son, and a medicine man named De̲shen Gaay in Allen's report on his expedition. The photograph, which was taken on the Yukon River in 1883, is the earliest known photograph of Upper Tanana Dene. Stsêey Netłé' is also mentioned in the written record as the "Indian Chief" "Adam" whom the reporter E. H. Wells (1974) met on his trip into the Fortymile country in 1890. According to Kenny Thomas Sr. (Thomas and Mishler 2005: 218), the name Stsêey Netłé' translates as "really my grandfather or truly my grandfather"; Thomas said that he was also known as Ch'aadh Che'et'aandiidz—"the main person for the Ch'âadh or Ch'âadz clan."

Chief Andrew Isaac (1984a) said Stsêey Netłé' was known as Adam: "Now they call white man name Adam—Indian name Stsêey Netłé', biggest chief at Lake Mansfield." Stsêey Netłé' is remembered as mean, and David Paul (1957b: 28–29) recounts a story about him murdering two boys in a fit of rage:

> My great grandfather big chief but he have hard time. No commissioner, no jail! He kill two boys and people don't feel too good for my great grandfather.
>
> The grandfather hides out with his wife, brother, and nephew. But he decides hiding out is not a good idea and returns to Mansfield, accepting the fact that he might be killed in revenge. Stsêey Netłé' has a good friend who lives in Mentasta and intercedes for Stsêey Netłé', not out of love or true friendship but for business. Stsêey Netłé' and the man from Mentasta are trading partners. The Reverend Paul says the man from Mentasta is a big chief. When Stsêey Netłé' goes to Mentasta the man put both arms round my great grandfather so he won't be hurt too much and some other men beat him up but not kill him.
>
> Then his friend help him up and talk and talk to his people to get grandfather out of trouble, just like a lawyer! My grandfather tell these people. "I don't want no more trouble! I don't want no strings on me, no more people follow me! Whoever hard feelings with me, I pay. Tell me how much!"
>
> No one know how much he pay to get rid of this trouble but he give many gifts. Big trouble! Big gifts! Then he tell people in Mansfield, "My trail no good! Don't follow my trail! I'm big, big man but don't do what I do," and he put stick across his trail and say, "Don't cross my trail. Is no good."

This story includes several details about "old-time" leadership and relationships. Stsêey Netłé' is held accountable for the murder, but he has an important friend who can intercede for him. It may be that the Mentasta chief is Stsêey Netłé's "partner," shtlęę (T) or shtlµµ (UT), a close friend who is a member of an opposite clan. The Mentasta chief does not protect Stsêey Netłé' out of affection but for reasons of commerce or trade. Stsêey Netłé' avoids being killed because the Mentasta chief talks for him, "just like a lawyer," and Stsêey Netłé' has enough property to compensate those he has wronged.

Another characteristic of traditional leadership is revealed in stories about Ch'inchedl, who lived at Sand Lake, probably in the early 1800s. In the stories, Ch'inchedl is portrayed as war leader, but it is unclear whether he was considered a xáxkeh. In a letter to Robert McKennan in 1964, Paul Kirsteatter wrote about Ch'inchedl, a great warrior and mercenary captain who carried out raids into the Copper River and as far as the coast. To carry out his raids, Ch'inchedl called out every available man in the Sand Creek/Healy Lake area to fight and would hire men from Northway and Tetlin to raid people south of the Alaska Range. After Ch'inchedl died, his people spread out to Mansfield, Ketchumstuk, and Healy Lake. Kirsteatter said Chief Walter Isaac told him Ch'inchedl was buried on a hill at Sam (Sand) Lake (Kirstteater 1964; see appendix A).

In another story, Mansfield people gave Ch'inchedl a young woman in marriage as part of the payment for defending them.

Figure 6.9. Ketl'aad Tá'is standing in the middle, to right is his son, and to his left is Deshen Gaay, or "little medicine man." Taken in the summer of 1884 or 1885 near Eagle on the Yukon, this is the oldest known photo of Mansfield/Tanacross people. Ketl'aad Tá' was a xáxkeh, or rich man, who lived at Dihthâad. Annie Denny said there were five brothers: Ketl'aad Tá' and Stsêey Netlé', a man named "No Gun," and two others (Annie Denny, December 16, 1986, interview by Bill Simeone). Alaska State Library Wickersham State Historic Sites Photo Collection, P277-0170.020.

The Reverend David Paul (1957b: 29–30) said that by marrying the young girl, the big chief becomes a "friend." "Once old days Mansfield people needed help and they talk with one big chief and ask, 'how much you want me pay you help me fight?'" The big chief says nothing, and the Mansfield people start to pile furs and goods in front of him. He says nothing. The Mansfield people put out more goods, but the chief remains silent. No one knows what the big chief wants. Reverend Paul then says, "This old man got cousin, a young girl. This one man he think, 'We pay him our cousin and make him marry and make him good friend.'" For a moment the big chief says nothing and then says, "Early in morning, I go. You tell crew."

According to Gaither Paul (Simeone 1986a), Ch'inchedl was a famous mercenary who lived on the Tanana River at Ch'inchedl Teyy' or "nose hill." Gaither said Ch'inchedl had many well-trained young men at his disposal. Their favorite weapon was a caribou horn club

studded with obsidian and soaked in grease to increase its weight. When not in use, the club was carried in a bag. According to Gaither, effective use of the club required considerable training and a very strong wrist.

Lee Saylor (Ferguson 2012: 72–73) recounted the story of three brothers who were so agile and fast that they were named Na'thee dek, "chips exploding in water." The younger brother was a troublemaker who got into fights and killed people. No one complained because his uncle Ch'inchedl, "Big nose chief," protected him. Ch'inchedl had his headquarters between George and Sam or Sand Lake at Big Nose Village. During times of war, Ch'inchedl hired out as a mercenary. One day this favored nephew got into a fight with one of his brothers and was killed. Upon hearing of the death of his nephew, Ch'inchedl wiped out the village where the brothers were staying. The two older brothers escaped and eventually made their way to Tetlin, but people were too frightened to help them, so they kept going south and finally settled in the Eklutna area.

CHANGING LEADERSHIP

Colonialism produced a shift in hierarchy. In traditional Dene culture, the man with lots of stuff was leader. The stuff represented his practical expertise and his ability to touch the world of animals so that animals came to him and gave themselves to him. When the Americans arrived, they had unlimited supplies of stuff and claimed the country. Dene began to look toward the American government to supply the necessities of life, food, ammunition, tents, and traps.

Beginning in the early 1900s, Dene leadership changed as new institutions introduced by the Americans took over many of the duties of the xáxkeh. For example, US marshals took over administration of the law. Chief Andrew Isaac tells a story about an incident at Ketchumstuk in which a non-Native ignored the wishes of xáxkeh, so they had to ask the marshal to intervene.

Sometime around 1910 Jack Long started a saloon at Ketchumstuk and the Native people got drunk so the old Chief Isaac (Chief Andrew's grandfather) told the saloon keeper to pack it up and move. Long said he didn't have to move—"I got license and insurance." Walter Isaac, old Chief Isaac's son, who was one of the first Dene to understand English, tried to get Long to move. But Long refused. Walter Isaac asked the mailman to tell the marshal to come up from Jack Wade with dog team. The marshal went into the saloon and told Long to pack up now, "chief wants you to move so move." That afternoon Jack Long left (Isaac 1987).

The change in the xáxkeh's authority also reflected changes occurring in Dene society. Where the traditional culture emphasized communal living, with the xáxkeh at the center of economic and social life, American frontier culture emphasized individual initiative and freedom from constraints. Young Dene

Figure 6.10. Chief Walter Isaac, 1913. Walter Isaac was the son of Chief Isaac. Walter was the first elected chief of the Tanacross village and instrumental in negotiants with the US military during World War II. Chief Walter began the tradition of elected leaders. His son Oscar and grandson Jerry followed in Walter's footsteps. Photo by C. Betticher, courtesy Episcopal Church Archives, Austin, Texas.

people especially were influenced by the freedom offered by mining camps and frontier towns like Dawson and Fairbanks. This was a constant concern of the missionaries. In 1938 E. A. McIntosh wrote that young people had lost faith in the elders:

> The young people are becoming enlightened and having lost faith in the leadership of their elders are becoming confused. They are coming more and more in contact with white people of various stages from being mildly interested in Christianity to those opposed to it which is also confusing. One

Figure 6.11. Chief Oscar Isaac, 1981. Oscar was born in 1914 to Walter Isaac and Maggie Demit. For several decades he was the elected chief of Tanacross. Highly esteemed throughout the upper Tanana region and beyond, Oscar worked tirelessly for the good of his people and, like his cousin Andrew, was instrumental in the land claims movement.

Figure 6.12. Chief Walter Northway was born in 1876 at K'ehthiign, near the present-day village of Northway. During the Chisana gold rush a Captain Northway gave the name Northway to Walter's father, Taaiya Ta'. Walter eventually became chief of Northway Village and was renowned as a woodworker, hunter, and orator. He was one of the last who could use a particularly stylized form of oratory known as 'chief's talk'. Walter was married to Lilly John who was from Scottie Creek. Walter died in the 1990s (Yarber and Madison 1987). Walter is wearing a dentalium shell necklace, a sign of his status, and is holding two pieces of his woodwork. Photo by Terry Haynes.

of their greatest weaknesses is their desire to be a good sport and agreeable to those around them. Thus, they are easy prey to those who have no scruples about making bad examples or spreading undesirable teachings. (McIntosh n.d.: 14)

At the same time missionaries were busy undermining traditional leadership by emphasizing election of leaders, who were often not as esteemed or respected as the old xáxkeh. These new leaders were younger men, often adherents of Christianity, who knew and understood the English language, which made them more convenient for missionaries and government agents. Goldschmidt writes:

The effect which the chief [Walter Northway] deplored was the weakening of the bonds of the community and the powers of the older men in controlling the behavior of the youth. Native society rested upon the respect for elders, their superior practical knowledge and experienced leadership. The undermining of these values tends to destroy solidarity of village life in an area where the unity of the village is essential for survival. (Goldschmidt 1948: 48)

Photo-montage by Hal Gage.

7 TĮĮŁ/XTÍITL

Potlatch

In the Dene languages of the upper Tanana region, *tįįł* (UT) and *xtíitl* (T) are translated as potlatch. A potlatch is a distribution of gifts in which the hosts, who are members of one clan, give gifts to the guests, who are members of an opposite clan. There are different reasons for hosting a potlatch. Gifts are distributed to celebrate a significant event in a person's life, such an adoption or a child's first hunting success, or to heal an injury or insult, including an offense as grievous as murder. The most compelling reason for holding a potlatch is a person's death. The most elaborate and important is a memorial potlatch held several years after a person dies. Chief Peter John of Minto explained:

> The memorial potlatch is one of the biggest events the Athabaskan culture hold. We honor the person who passed away and lay down our grief. That's why when they gather together for that occasion, they give everything they got. This kind of potlatch calls for the best—no second hand. . . . The Athabaskan culture calls for that. (John 1996: 61)

Using Christian metaphors, Chief John also explained that just as Jesus gave his flesh and blood, his everything, so do those who give a potlatch.

> That's the one [memorial potlatch] we call last supper. The last supper is when people give the best they got. The Bible talks about the last supper when Jesus brought his disciples together. He offered the wine and food as his flesh and blood. . . . That's what we have in the memorial potlatch. We give lots of blankets and guns and everything. They just give it away with love. The memorial potlatch is a way for us to put away the grief we feel over the loss of a person who dies. (John 1996: 59)

At the beginning of the twentieth century, Episcopal missionaries attempted to stop or curtail the potlatch, but their efforts failed because Dene refused and told the missionaries not to interfere. Today the potlatch thrives, providing a strong sense of continuity with the past and representing a spirit of community through unparalleled generosity, shared grieving, and celebration of life. At the same time, like any dynamic ritual, the potlatch has changed. When talking about the potlatch, all the elders expressed concern about the changes that have occurred in the ceremony. Some felt the younger generation did not take the ceremony seriously enough. To the elders, the potlatch is full of injih, and some of the problems faced by contemporary Dene are believed to be the result of not paying attention and being too lax in following the necessary restrictions, for example, allowing young women and children to attend the ceremony.

POTLATCH ELEMENTS

A potlatch is composed of several elements that, when combined, offer the entire community

https://doi.org/10.5876/9781646423347.c007

a way to express their grief, the joy of being together, and the achievement of putting on an important ceremony. In the past a potlatch lasted as long as there was enough food, but today potlatches are often held over a weekend and usually last two or three days. Every potlatch follows the same pattern: The guests arrive, and there is an exchange of speeches. Every evening the guests are served a feast, which is followed by singing and dancing. On the final night there are speeches and a feast, and after the singing and dancing is over, the hosts distribute gifts.

Cora David (2017: 191–193) describes the sequence of events at a potlatch for the dead. First the hosts collect the gifts, including blankets, and dentalium shell necklaces. In the community hall they hang up scarves that people use when dancing. On the third day the hosts present their guests with a feast of all the best foods. There is singing and dancing, and the hosts lay out the gifts in the middle of the floor. The gifts are laid out on the tarp and it is įįjih, or bad luck, for the children to walk close to the gifts or step on the tarp. Once the gifts are distributed, the people sing and dance with their presents.

Ts'ihootįįł xa ch'a unihheeyh
I am talking about potlatch

Ts'ihootįįł tah
When we make potlatch

Adogn
up there

ts'at eł dats' ehłeek tl'aan ch'ik'on' uk'üü
we collect blankets and dentalium necklaces and

dats'ehłeek tl'aan hushyign dats'etiik.
we bring it in.

Ay tl'aan eł
And then

ay tl'aan eł
and then

dogn nats'oonehtl'u'
we tie rope across up there [across the community hall].

K'oniit'ay dog tah ts'ehłeek tl'aan hii' eł

dzi'ulshyee xa.
We put up scarves for dancing during sad songs.

Ay eł dzihelshyiih.
And then they do the mourning dance.

Taagn udeetaan k'e
After three days

Hugn ch'il tahehłeek.
they give out gifts.

Taagn hoołįį de'
On the third day

shyi'eł hugn dii eł
meat and whatever [the best stuff]

hehmbiadn eł.
they cook.

Noo ts'ihaałeel dineey nataa'aał
We put in the middle for the people to eat.

Ay tl'aan eł
And then

ch'ihtahxał nts' ą' ch'ihtaldzüh
They play drums and dance.

Dzihtalshyee
They will do a mourning dance.

Ay tl'aan eł
And then

ts'at dahtaał, k'a',
they will bring blankets, guns,

lsüü, hugn k'onitt'ay tah unaanetk' ąą,
money, whatever, scarves, and what they
    have sewn,

ushyii dzel'iadn
footwear,

ushyi' dzelniign įį'eł,
mittens and so on,

hugn,ne' dahtaał tl' aan noo nitsaałeeł.
whatever, they will bring it all in and put it
    in the middle.

Ts'iikeey iin k'a hii'aaxah łootahaal, įįjih,
    henih.
Children may not walk close to it, that is
    forbidden, they say.

Ts'iikeey iin k'a hiik'it dą' taahaal.
Children may not walk on it.

Ay ahnoo hitsehniik.
And we put [the tarp] in the middle.

Ay tl'aan eł
And then

k'a'eł
guns,

jiyh e
mittens,

lsüü eł
money,

k'oniit ay łe
scarves,

ts'uutaanak tl'aan.
we will get.

Naltsiin ihłįį nts'ą'
I am Naltsiin and

Ts'ikaayu iin
Ts'ikaayu

tl'atihłeeł.
I will give them things.

Ay tl'aan eł
And

hoo'üü
as many

hoo'üü įįdlah nts'ą hoo tsaałił
as many as there are, we will give all of
    them [a gift].

Ay tl'aan
And then

hii eł chaldzüh.

they dance with [their potlatch gift].

Ch'ełiik
A song,

noodlee k'e t'eey
English

hiishyiit tnay.
they speak in it.

I got gun ay eł ch'ehtaldzüh.
I got gun and they will dance.

Tsiin' įį eł ch'ehtaldzüh.
Thank you, and they will dance.

Hoo shyįį' dhniił.
I have said all.

Figure 7.1. Ahtna lined up for the potlatch of Chief John of Mentasta, 1918. Photo by F. B. Drane, Drane Photo collection Alaska and Polar Regions Department, Elmer E. Rasmuson Library, University of Alaska Fairbanks.

WELCOMING GUESTS

The tenor of contemporary potlatches is different from those of the past. Descriptions of historical potlatches indicate a tension created by the presence of a relatively large number of people, accentuated by the anxiety and grief caused by death. Ellen Demit described how the hosts once greeted their guests with rifle fire and made speeches to ensure "everything okay":

> From village our chief goin' shoot two time.
> Other chief goin' shoot two. That's four
> shots. And then he goin' meet. This is really
> bad part I talk about. He goin' meet each
> other, chief. He goin' [to make] speech out
> there where he meet each other. Other one
> from other village and other one from this
> side. They goin' speech. They goin' talk over.
> If everything okay, then they goin' come to
> village. (Callaway and Miller-Friend 2001: 29)

In the past the guests entered the host's community dressed in their finest beaded clothing. Rifles were fired and songs sung as the hosts welcomed their guests. Important

Figure 7.2. "The Receiving Line." Tanacross people lined up to receive their guests at the potlatch for Chief John of Mentasta held in Tanacross in 1918. Photo by F. B. Drane, Drane Photo collection Alaska and Polar Regions Department, Elmer E. Rasmuson Library, University of Alaska Fairbanks.

men gave speeches accompanied by aggressive gestures that were supposed to intimidate. Today the competitiveness that characterized past potlatches is almost gone. Hosts do fire rifles when a body is brought into the village, and both hosts and guests make speeches welcoming and praising each other.

ORATORY

Oratory was and still is critical in a potlatch, especially a potlatch for the dead. As Ellen Demit indicates, oratory sets the tone so there are no misunderstandings or bad feelings (Callaway and Miller-Friend 2001: 29). In the past spokesmen made competitive speeches challenging one another in an archaic language, sometimes referred to as "chief's talk," often using obscure references to clan histories, ancient wars, and former potlatches. Today no one has the knowledge to participate in such exchanges, but visiting clan leaders and important guests still give speeches of condolence praising the deceased. The hosts reciprocate by thanking the guests for coming and helping them in their time of need.

A major part of a potlatch for the dead is the public expression of grief. In the past expressions of grief were much more intense than today. Helen David Charlie, who was born in about 1867 on the Goodpaster River, described what happened when a man died.

> People . . . cut off all their hair and threw it on the fire. And all the sharp things they hid from these relatives so they couldn't drive them through their ears or arms and make cuts on their bodies until they were covered with blood and would roll in the snow or moss. (Anderson 1956: 22)

During the potlatch, the relatives of the deceased sat around the fire while

> other people watched and these relatives cried and wailed for this dead man. Then this dead man's people cut off their hair and threw it on the fire and they would bend forward and singe the rest of the hair from their heads. This was a great sacrifice . . . for it took many years and much work to make these thick braids. (Anderson 1956: 24)

Chief Andrew Isaac explained that it took strong words from a well-respected man to restrain the grieving relatives from hurting themselves. Death is final and people should mourn, but not too much.

> At potlatch they've got to have speech. Got to have a good word, strong word, and old-time story. Put it up all the time. Today there is nothing. They pass out blankets and forget about it.
>
> Potlatch means the death. Indian death the last time we die. Turn back to ground, earth, dust. That's done. Right now we go to funeral, all the women cry. Eyes red and walk around. Don't pay attention; don't feel worry, not even sorry. Used to be different. You don't believe it, go talk to Walter Northway.
>
> Walter Northway and his wife rub their face right on the ground. Burn their hair and tear their shoes off. That's the way live people treat themselves over death. That bad. When we do that, only one old important man can talk and tell them to stop. (Yarber and Madison 1988: 47)

FEASTING

Feasts are a required part of the potlatch. When preparing for a potlatch, the hosts send young men to hunt moose. Because moose meat is essential to a potlatch, the State of Alaska protects the right of Dene to kill moose for this purpose. Much of the meat, including the head, is cut up and made into soup, which is cooked out of doors by the men. Other wild foods include salmon (from the Yukon or Copper Rivers), duck, porcupine, caribou, and beaver, which are also prepared by men on wood fires outdoors. Women do their cooking indoors, preparing foods such as fry bread and spaghetti. Only men are allowed to serve the food. Elders are given the choicest food, including moose meat, porcupine, and beaver. All the food left over at the end of the potlatch is distributed to the guests.

Photo-montage by Hal Gage.

Left to right

Figure 7.3. Cooking moose meat for potlatch in Tetlin, 1979. Photo by William E. Simeone.

Figure 7.4. Potlatch feast at Tanacross, 1986. Photo by William E. Simeone.

Figure 7.5. Cooking at Tanacross potlatch, 2012. Arthur John to the left, Brady Henry in the center, and Brittan Jonathan with back to the camera. Photo by William E. Simeone.

Figure 7.6. Arthur John preparing moose meat for Tanacross potlatch, 2012. Photo by William E. Simeone.

Figure 7.7. Brady Henry scorching ducks for Tanacross potlatch, 2012. Photo by William E. Simeone.

SINGING AND DANCING

Left to right

Figure 7.8. Potlatch drummers (left to right): Huston Sanford, Andrew Isaac, Kenneth Thomas Sr., Charlie James, and Abraham Luke. In the background are Roger Retano and Tom Denny Jr. Photo by Terry Haynes.

Figure 7.9. Singing a sorry song at Tetlin (left to right): Helen David, Bella Demit, unknown, Laura Sanford, Lilly Northway, Annie Denny, and Isabel John. Photo by Carol Buge, courtesy of Terry Haynes.

Figure 7.10. Drummers at Tanacross (left to right): Buster Gene, Titus David, Oscar Isaac, Paul Joe, Charlie James, and Charlie David Sr. Photo by William E. Simeone e.

Figure 7.11. Charlie David Sr., Tetlin potlatch, 1979. Photo by William E. Simeone.

Left to right

Figure 7.12. Northway potlatch (left to right): Ellen Demit, A. Sanford, Northway Man, Walter Northway, Lilly Northway, Annie Sam, behind her is Silas Solomon. Photo by Terry Haynes.

Figure 7.13. Tetlin potlatch (left to right): Oscar Isaac, Stephen Northway, Dorothy Titus, Ada Gallon, Helen David, and Ena Albert. Courtesy of Ellen Thomas, William E. Simeone photo collection.

Figure 7.14. Tetlin Potlatch, 1969. Steven Northway drumming, Maggie Isaac, Kitty David, and Annie Joe dancing. Photo Francois Marie Guédon, courtesy of Bee Paul, William E. Simeone photo collection.

Figure 7.15. People dancing with *gunhos*, dance sticks introduced by the Han at the funeral of Chief Isaac, Tanacross potlatch. Note the rifles hanging on the wall next to a potlatch sign painted by David Paul. Photo by William E. Simeone.

Figure 7.16. Tanacross potlatch, 1960s. Photo courtesy Martha Isaac. William E. photo collection.

3

Figure 7.17. Dancing at Tanacross, 2018. Photo by William E. Simeone.

Figure 7.18. Potlatch song (left to right): Ada Gallon, Laura Sanford, Walter Northway, Kenneth Thomas Sr., Huston Sanford, Andrew Isaac, and Oscar Isaac, Tanacross, 1978. Photo by William E. Simeone.

Singing and dancing are fundamental to the potlatch as an expression of grief and joy. Guests are expected to dance hard, because movement in the dance is supposed to "break out the good time" (Simeone 1987e). That is why people say that to dance at someone's potlatch is do a favor for the hosts. Dancing hard is especially important at funerals, where the hosts are expected to lift the mourners' spirits.

Songs performed during a potlatch fall into three types: sorry or mourning songs, dance songs, and the potlatch song. Song leaders are expert at using music to lead the mourners into their grief and then bring them back into joy. At a funeral potlatch the mourning process begins with a sorry song made expressly for the deceased and sung only by the host and their

relatives. The guests then join in, singing a succession of sorry songs from previous potlatches, ending with the song especially composed for the recently deceased. By singing different sorry songs, the guests are reminded of their loss and are able empathize with their hosts' grief.

The mourner's mood is expected to change when they dance joyfully with long strips of calico. Dance songs are joyful, loud, and playful. Bodily movements, especially for the men, are flamboyant and emphatic. Their feet planted wide apart, the men jab the air with a scarf to the beat of the drum. The women dancers form a circle around them, moving their arms and upper bodies to the beat. Songs are about familiar topics such as fighting forest fires, the beautiful women of Northway, or driving a car to Fairbanks.

The potlatch or wealth song is sung before the distribution of gifts. Each potlatch song is composed for a special occasion and is sung once at the potlatch. It then becomes the property of the host's clan and may not be sung by another clan unless they pay for it. It is injih to sing a potlatch song outside the potlatch because it is just for the host's clan's luck.

Andrew Isaac (Simeone 1987h) said the potlatch song must be sung precisely. If a person made mistakes when singing it, they could be physically harmed. Andrew gave the example of Frank Sam's father's potlatch song, which is in two parts: the first was an expression of grief and loss expressed in the words "daddy don't go away from me." The second part had to do with the potlatch gifts and with keeping your luck. When singing the song, people used to burn a plant that filled the air with scent. Together, the song and scent were supposed to ensure a person's luck or good fortune.

The only instrument used in the potlatch is a drum—*ch'elxĕ* (T), *elxal* (UT)—made of caribou skin or moose skin stretched over a round wooden frame. Andrew Isaac (1987: 15) talked about the drum:

> Ch'elxĕ we use today, use part of it for potlatch. Drum is like person, makes noise, makes good news. I like drum. People use drum but don't know the story. Drum important for xtíitl potlatch—important Indian law. Don't rush with drum—treat it right or injih. Lead Potlatch—makes lot of noise. Person hears drum thinks something is wrong. Remind the old people, Indian feel the drum, feel something like great person.

The Upper Tanana Dene music repertoire is extensive, containing some very old songs. Maggie Isaac of Dot Lake talked about the history of song and dance in the region (Simeone 1987q). According to oral history, the Han, who live along the upper Yukon River in the communities of Eagle and Dawson City, were noted dancers and singers. During the gold rush of 1898, Chief Isaac, the Han leader whose territory included Dawson City, was concerned his people's songs and dances would be lost, so he gave them to the people of Mansfield during a potlatch for their leader, whose name was also Chief Isaac. Maggie described how young men returning from a war were greeted with the news that four young boys were just born and in celebration they danced. According to Maggie, that is how the dancing started. She then goes on to tell how the tradition was carried forward

Figure 7.19. Laura Sanford arranging gifts to give away over her grandson who had caught his first fish. Tanacross, 1987. Photo by William E. Simeone.

Figure 7.20. Steven Northway holding a drum he made. Photo by Terry Haynes.

by Chief Isaac of Dawson and his brother Esau, who practiced dancing in front of a large mirror, and how, when they came to Mansfield for the funeral of Chief Isaac, they danced like spruce hens.

> Dawson people make this song and potlatch people come through. Then [they] have relative [living in] Lake Mansfield, and Ketchumstuk, those Dawson people. Early days ago, lots of war going on, you know, and war people going up, and Dawson people come back, four young men born, new baby born. Somebody meet them and he say he got four more boys come, then those two him, they come home and they dance with it, he say. That's first to start with it, come out like that, that's what my parents told me. And that Moosehide [Chief Isaac] and his youngest brother, youngest brother named Esau, mama told me. He is headquarters in dance, all that territory. So when they start to dance all the people behind them. They used to have big mirror, that headman, Moosehide, his youngest brother come behind what he dance, they way he watch his brother with mirror, he said.
>
> You know those spruce hens, they dancing on hillside? They do same no different, mama say. They all paint their face and they use [head] band, they us blankets, they use dance clothes, some they really dress up. Depend on what tribe they belong to they dress up. So Lake Mansfield there is big potlatch for grandpa [Chief] Isaac, that's the time way far a way village people come, Eagle and Dawson. My brother told me for two months straight they stay in Mansfield. All that many days people dance every night and have big cook. (Simeone 1987q)

In addition to bringing their songs, the Han brought the *gunho* or dance stick, which they gave to the people of Mansfield to use. Gaither Paul described when the Han brought the gunho to Mansfield in 1912 for the potlatch of Chief Isaac.

> I heard Mansfield had a big potlatch, I guess it was over Chief Isaac. And people from Dawson is invited and they came all the way from Dawson. And there too my grandmother told me story about it.
>
> They bunch up across the lake [Mansfield Lake], and they start shooting across the lake, [to announce their arrival] and they knew they were coming, and dog team after dog team just line up across the lake.
>
> They stop at the edge of the lake someplace and tie up their dogs and there too they had a fire going but nobody went over to the lake to greet them. Man come from Dawson, but nobody greet them!
>
> They dress and they came into Mansfield like, like what I said Copper River [people] did. And this one I heard, you know that Charlie's [James's] house over that trail? They coming up there, and when they coming over that hill I remember people say they come over just like spruce hen. You know they dance like that, they coming over just like that, just like spruce hen coming over. Their leader is the only one standing up and behind him is just like a bunch of spruce hen.
>
> That was part of the dance. They use to dance that way, they don't dance like that any more, like spruce hen.
>
> That is probably 1912, they said.
>
> That is the year that gunho come to Mansfield.
>
> That Moosehide chief brought it up and he left it, he brought it up, and he come ahead with it. Gunho come from Dawson people, started that. I don't know the meaning, too. I hear speech that Moosehide chief left that at Mansfield as a gift when he came. And he left there without it, to be used in dance. That is the start of gunho in dance. Moosehide chief brought it in.
>
> I don't know the original one [gunho], what happened to it, but I saw it. It was painted really beautiful, beads or yarn hanging down and when you shake it, it kind of rattle, that is what he carried

ahead. He left that with Mansfield people. That is the start of use of gunho in Tanacross area. That is what I heard, my father told me this. Just like the chief at Dawson left that as a gift at Mansfield when he came that year. From there they copy it and always use it in dance. (Simeone 1986a)

DISTRIBUTION OF GIFTS

Potlatch gifts, *jąą'* (T) or *jaann'* (UT), were once tanned skins, furs, clothing, and food. Ellen Demit (Calloway and Miller-Friend 2000:

30–32) described how in the past the chief sewed together tanned caribou skins to place the potlatch gifts on.

> He put it on the floor. Each one that place he got to put skin in there and put blanket and gun and arrow and moose skin, beaver skin, lynx, all kind animal skin out there on the land.

Today people give away rifles, blankets, beadwork, household appliances, and money. Potlatches are supposed to be lavish displays of wealth and generosity. In the past, the hosts were expected to give everything away

Figure 7.21. Potlatch gifts arrayed on the floor of Tanacross community hall, 1987. Photo by William E. Simeone.

Figure 7.22. Potlatch blankets on display at Tanacross, circa 1930s. Photo by E. A. McIntosh, William E. Simeone photo collection.

Figure 7.23. Blankets displayed at Tanacross. Jeany Healy Collection UAF-2000-181-22, Alaska and Polar Regions Department, Elmer E. Rasmuson Library, University of Alaska Fairbanks.

Figure 7.24. Gifts on the floor waiting to be distributed at Tanacross potlatch, 2012. Photo by William E. Simeone.

to cleanse their grief. Nowadays, hosts are still expected to provide guests with an abundance of food and gifts, but they no longer give away all their possessions. Gifts are distributed in a particular sequence. Young men of the opposite clan who dug the grave, made the coffin, and built the grave fence receive the first gifts. Next are elders of opposite clans, followed by special guests and other members of the opposite clans. In the case of unexpected tragedy, such as the death of an only son, the host's family can give gifts to the family in mourning to show support of their loss.

Introduced in the late nineteenth century, blankets and rifles are now staple gifts. Both were once displayed outside on a fence especially constructed for the potlatch. Culturally, the most significant gifts are the white-striped "point blankets" once obtained from the Hudson's Bay Company but now purchased from Pendleton Woolen Mills, and .30-30 Winchester rifles. The color and warmth provided by blankets represents love and respect. Rifles provide the means to make a living and feed one's family.

Andrew Isaac (Simeone 1986c) talked about the importance of the potlatch and the gifts as expressions of love and respect. He used the word *diichâagh*, loosely translated as "respect." The root word is "big" or "large" (*chox* [T], *chaax* [UT]). Oscar Isaac (Simeone 1987r) explained this word means all of the people in a particular clan are great. He said it is like "glory"—"glory come down as in the bible, not directly like glory but something like it." He then said that Indians don't explain things directly. A person is supposed to understand what they are being told by the context in which a word is used. For example, at a potlatch in Chistochina, Walter Northway made a speech to the host using the word *diichâagh* ("respected person"). Walter talked about the host's ancestors, pointing to Mount Sanford, the mountain that stands for those ancestors. By extolling the host's ancestors, Oscar said, Walter had "hung diichâagh around their neck, just like he had hung a dentalium shell necklace around their necks." Later on, Oscar said potlatch speeches are supposed to contain references to diichâagh for the other clan: "say how great they are, then the speaker can talk about how great his own people are and then everyone has to be satisfied. There can be no recriminations, no unhappiness because everyone has been satisfied."

Using the word "diichâagh," Andrew explained the gifts are the very essence of respect. In the past, potlatch gifts were made by hand, and the labor, as well as the objects, represented the host's love and respect for their guests. White men introduced blankets and guns, both of which became symbols of love and respect or diichâagh, with the striped Hudson's Bay blanket taking on special significance. Andrew also said it was important to show love for your partner or friend (a person in the opposite clan) who buried your deceased relative and helped you to grieve.

Diichâagh—something really important or really important man. Indian blanket—little blanket in the old days people gave what they had—fur, moccasins, glove, parka, what ever Indian use gave at potlatch. Old ladies work hard to keep man going. Whiteman brought blankets—what is their idea of shiny blanket—bed sheet. White blankets make a real potlatch.

Friend work for me (partner) I have to—why didn't show my love? Show my love—thank you, you give hand to me. Thank you, you make my feeling different. What feeling I got for my person whom I lose. I trust you to help me bury my loved one. See, Grandpas make potlatch with double barreled shot gun. Show how much love they have in their heart for their relatives breakin heart. Straighten them out. Really glad they make potlatch over their loved ones.

Means great love, pretty close to good book, tells us to love one another, Indian people love children, aunts, uncles. Skin coat, cut up skins, all tanned stuff. 1914 old John H. Flannagin. Herman Kessler bring blankets—Canadian blankets. (Yarber and Madison 1988: 20)

While gifts are an important part of the ceremony, a potlatch is not simply about giving things away but about using objects in a specific way, to assuage or wipe away grief as well as to cement, preserve, or maintain sometimes tenuous relationships and to enhance one's own reputation and that of one's clan. At the same time, gifts are not "freely" given but given in expectation that at some future date the guests will reciprocate, and the wealth will "come back." In one sense, the gifts never leave the realm of the potlatch. Once a potlatch is over, there is a lively trade in guns and blankets, as the guests who received these items sell them to other guests, who then store them away in caches for future potlatches.

POTLATCH RESTRICTIONS

After a potlatch, the host was once subject to a number of restrictions. For 100 days he could not sleep with his wife; he could not eat meat from the heads of animals but had to subsist on soup made of animal fat. He had to suck drinking water through a swan-bone tube and not cut meat lest he get blood on his hands. To scratch his face he had to use a stick and not his hands, and scrape his face with a piece of plate to keep it smooth. For shorter periods, the host was not to extend his legs when lying down; when sitting, he had to keep his arms folded over his hands (McKennan 1959: 137–138). Not observing these rules was injih and could produce terrible consequences in that animals would avoid the hunter, causing his family to starve. These restrictions are generally ignored today.

The death of an individual makes the community vulnerable to powerful and unpredictable supernatural forces. Excessive distribution of food and gifts "may draw the attention of the nonhuman powers to the participants, especially the donors who, by giving away so much wealth, seem to claim they are rich" (Guédon 1981: 581). Ostentatious displays of greed and pride can attract the attention of powerful supernatural forces and bring calamity.

To stay in harmony with these forces, participants have to be very careful how they conduct the ceremony and act when everything is finished. Ellen Demit said:

> You have potlatch you never talk about again.
>   Superstitious, you don't talk about.
>   You don't brag about how big potlatch you got either. (Callaway and Miller-Friend 2001: 43)

In the past, women were only allowed to attend a potlatch when no longer capable of bearing children. Young women could not attend the ceremony and were not allowed to serve or handle food. Young women were kept away from the gifts lest they contaminate them with their menstrual blood. For this reason, the gifts were brought into the hall through a window and not a doorway used by anyone since it was contaminated. Likewise, gifts were never set directly on the floor.

By the 1970s, some of these restrictions were relaxed, but even today gifts are brought into the community hall through a window and never set directly on the floor. A person from Tetlin observed,

> That door, young girls come. Some women they are not careful. Young girls [during their puberty]—that's why we got to use the windows. That way, good luck. Potlatch things [gifts] must be careful. You cannot take through where women are walking. (Guédon 1974: 224)

Photo-montage by Hal Gage.

I attended my first potlatch in the winter of 1971 after several people died suddenly and tragically. Dene from all over the upper Tanana and Copper River attended, as did Dene from Fairbanks, Nenana, and Minto. The potlatch lasted several days, but it was the first night that left a lasting impression. There was a feast, and once the remains had been cleared away, some of the visiting elder men walked to the middle of the floor and spoke. In a mixture of English and Dene, they expressed condolences to the bereaved parents and siblings of the deceased and gratitude for being invited to the potlatch. Then Walter Northway walked onto the floor. Displaying a shock of white hair, he wore suspenders and knee-length moose skin boots trimmed with beaver fur. As he spoke, his voice grew ferocious. He stabbed the air aggressively, pointing first at the deceased's relatives and then toward the mountains. He told the mourners they had to withstand their grief and be strong like the mountain peak that stood above them as a symbol of their ancestors. Abruptly, he stopped speaking and sat down. A man who had been sitting in the audience went over to the Walter, shook his hand, and gave him fifty dollars. The speechmaking was over.

After an interval, a few women formed a circle in the center of the hall; several men, two of them holding drums, stood outside the circle. One of the drummers struck up a "sorry song" made especially for the deceased. The women commenced dancing in a counterclockwise direction, moving their hands up and away, pulling the grief from their breast. The deceased's mother and sisters pulled their hair over their faces so that it hung down like a black veil. Waves of grief rose from the mourners as song after song was sung, in memory not only of the deceased but of people who had died ten, twenty, and thirty years before. When a mourner swooned, the circle of dancing women tightened in a display of physical support. Everyone in the hall was pulled into the vortex of grief. Finally, the lead singer stopped. People shifted uneasily, and some of the mourners left the floor.

MARGARET KIRSTEATTER: HEALY LAKE

Figure 7.25. Dancing at Healy Lake potlatch. William E. Simeone photo collection.

In 1980 Margaret Kirsteatter talked about a potlatch that took place at Healy Lake in 1927. This was considered to have been the largest potlatch ever held in the region. Robert McKennan (1959: 137) said the traders, who supplied the goods, told him it cost between $15,000 and $20,000. Automobiles were ordered from Fairbanks to go to Copper Center to pick up the Ahtna guests, and two river boats were hired not only to bring those guests to Healy Lake but to go over 150 miles up the Tanana and bring down guests from Northway, Tetlin, and Tanacross. Healy Lake people built a large cabin as a potlatch house, importing "matched boards" from Fairbanks for the floor, doors, and windows. Stoves, dishes, pots, kettles, and pans were purchased, as were cans of fruit, bags of rice, raisins, flour, coffee, tea, sugar, and moose meat. Hundreds of blankets were also bought, as were rifles, ammunition, tobacco, coats, and socks.

As a young girl of nine or ten, Margaret remembered the guests destroying the dishes after each feast. According to Margaret, this was a test of the hosts, to see how they would respond: "Just play, see how they doing. See if somebody feel bad or another." The hosts, on their part, simply brought out a new set of dishes. Margaret continued:

> And about the potlatch going on, and it's in the middle of the summer. They got meat and everything, fish, and gas boats full of groceries and guns and blankets, calico, tobacco, you name it. And they gathered up people and then they have potlatch going on. Okay, they have so much you know the groceries just put away summertime, of course everything is wasted. They just dump and then cook some more fresh one. Cook some more fresh one. Potlatch time begin. They dance and they throw that . . . they throw [dishes] up [in the air] there like they play ball, you know and they do that in that game and begin to eat. And the first one they eat. Second time they eat, they throw dishes and pots and pans throw it out. And they come back next day eating time and they put another set out. They do that for I don't know how many days. And begin all that happen now they just play. See how they doing. See if somebody feel bad or another. They [the hosts] just put it back, new set back again.

After the potlatch, the guests from Mansfield walked home. Margaret described the trip:

> From Healy Lake all the way. All the potlatch people, all walk back. On the way, just close to Mansfield, other side of Billy Creek, hillside, some where I guess they all the people gang up and they got one moose. They're hungry, they travel. They kill moose. Nothing left. Not even meat to save. So many people. Long days middle of the summer. Children, half my age, you know like, young girl, young boy and all that. That's what happened, 1927. (Andrews and Huntington 1980)

OSCAR ISAAC: TANACROSS

During a 1987 interview, Oscar Isaac described potlatches he had attended in Tetlin as a boy in the late 1920s. When they arrived in the village, the Tanacross people lined up across from the Tetlin people. Peter Thomas, who was from Tanacross, and Old Joseph, from Tetlin, made speeches using a special kind of language accompanied by gestures that appeared aggressive and angry. The speakers tested each other with riddles, each trying to outsmart the other. Oscar's father explained this to him, stressing that it was all in fun.

OSCAR: I remember potlatch in Tetlin, 1928 and 1929, both time I been up there. Old Joseph made potlatch over his wife.

Them days was really old time, today is a lot of different, almost just like White people, just like you go in lodge and eat. White people put it up for some reason, some good time, they put it up all kinds of food, I seen it quite a few times what they doing, and that's just like modern potlatch.

Oscar then commented on how he thought things had changed. In his view, people today do not really understand the significance of the potlatch as it relates to the relationship between clans.

OSCAR: 1929, just looks to me like Indian tribe [clan] is still up, today you lost that tribe, we never know, we not really know, but that's the way it look to me.

Oscar then described what he saw at Tetlin.

OSCAR: In 1929 when we comin in, the Tetlin people line up to the Tanacross people, and when the Tanacross people comin close to them they also lined up. They shootin gun to each other and the man get out in the middle of the people and he make a speech, play speech, out smart in other word [tries to trick the other speaker with a riddle].

That old Joseph make a speech to Peter Thomas and it looks like that man is mean, mean talk, sounds like that to us, we young kids, we thought they fight talk. Then after, through speech, he say Na', here "he said," and he laugh and went back across from where he came out and he stand and that Peter Thomas he just come right after him and point him like this all the way across, and all old people laugh.

And, he really give him hell, Na' he said, then he go back, and gee three time they done that, go back like this. And, then they, all old Tanacross and Tetlin people laugh, they look like they have a lot of fun.

And, that night when we stop in a tent, Frank Sam loan us tent, and he have big tent set and we were right close to him in his tent.

And, when we go to sleep I ask my daddy why they have fight talk, my daddy laugh and he say no they don't fight, just like out smart, play with, out smart. He didn't say that way, but he said, they just make a speech to each other, whoever, which guy the smarter than each other, they make speech all right, but they just test to each other, they relative [member of the same clan] to one another and no way someone can get pissed off.

And that way, relative to relative, and they let everyone hear that, all different tribe [clan] people heard them and they know which man is more smart, or know better. For that part they just play talk, lots of time they do that and that one nobody going to get mad, Tanacross and Tetlin old people just laugh to die and that make them more mad and they really give him hell to each other. People like that, he told me.

And by that they know that Joseph and my uncle, Peter Onion [Thomas], by that tribe know somethin lot, something good sense, and that's going on with the story all the time to somewhere in the country. Those people in the country who don't know either Joseph or Thomas, they heard about those people, smart people and give them more careful when they comin to potlatch.

INTERVIEWER: What did they give away?

OSCAR: Just like right now today, except a few pairs of moccasins, gloves and mittens. Those just go to certain people. Like whoever important man, those guys.

Sometimes they have one whole tanned moose skin.

If there are too many people they cut the skin in pieces and give to man. Blanket and gun, but those go to special people, not odd guys, like young people.

Last three days.

A lot of dry meat, save it, even year old, can save it and when they cook it just like a month ago. Caribou is not as good when it's old. Fat, when one year old is strong.

And more than year old is pretty strong, you get heart burn.

INTERVIEWER: Who cooked?

OSCAR: Like the people doing right now today, women and man both, but just man served.

INTERVIEWER: Who were big chiefs?

OSCAR: Chief Joseph make potlatch, Chief Luke, Big John. Them, its like part of their business. They are cousin somehow. Each one of them take part of it with speech and they make a speech, like that time I heard Big John going to make speech for Joseph, his shtâay [father's brother or paternal uncle] and Big John is shee'eh [mother's brother]. My daddy, big John is his uncle.

Toward the end of the interview, Oscar stressed how the potlatch is powerful, full of injih, and if people do not watch themselves, act responsibly, and follow the protocols before, during, and after the ceremony, they will suffer.

OSCAR: That's the way the potlatch go, potlatch is awfully great, really important to the Native life. Really be careful for all the young girls got to watch I, like young girls have month sick, not supposed to be coming in there, otherwise, if they do, don't watch themselves they going to die quick, some way they going to get into trouble and die for that part there's lots of injih in potlatch.

Potlatch have more injih than anything, any kind of injih in the world. They got take care, certain way for long life. If we don't take care right the people going to die out of that place.

Some new boys, young people, they don't understand injih, hardly anybody understand, and if we don't understand we don't know whether its true or not. Potlatch time injih, that's really important to the people.

Now today so many people don't believe, think that potlatch deal can done do no wrong to them, but it does make something wrong to the people when they don't handle it right. That's why from way back, we don't know how many generation doing those potlatch and the potlatch business what injih they bringing along with that potlatch, and the people don't care right now, hardly anyone believe.

Maybe that's why the people are beginning to die, drown, shoot each other, stab each other or maybe house catch fire with them, drown, a lot of them. You see all those [kind of accidents] happen before White people come to Alaska, [but] we don't have that many, accident, shot a few, that's about all we have, that's before White people come up. I think what they ruin, drug, I don't know what that mean, drug,

and marijuana, I never even see either one, those and liquor, liquor life, that's make them do a lot of things they shouldn't do it.

And also they don't know about injih, they don't believe injih, I think its better for them if the Indians want to have right life they have to believe in injih and care [about] those, then we might come out better life. If we don't care what we hear from our old people, we won't understand or care and yet we misunderstand injih. (Simeone 1987f)

Oscar also told a story his father, Walter Isaac, told him (Simeone 1987f). He told the story twice, the second time offering more details, which were supplemented with an explanation from his wife, Martha. At one time, the people of Joseph Village came to Ketchumstuk for a potlatch. The people danced, sang, and shook hands as usual when entering the village. Walter Isaac played an accordion for the visitors so they could dance and sing, but according to Oscar the real purpose for the accordion was that Walter was "fishing for a speech" from Chief Joe, who was chief of Joseph Village. To prod Chief Joe, Walter came up to him, dropped the accordion in front of, and smashed it with his foot, crushing it to pieces. This action was reciprocated at a later potlatch the Ketchumstuk people attended at Joseph Village. When they arrived, Chief Joe was playing a fiddle. When Walter saw this, he understood immediately what the fiddle was for and "he knows he has got it coming." The Ketchumstuk people danced and sang their way into the village to the accompaniment of the fiddle. After the greetings, Chief Joe made a speech and then stomped the fiddle, smashing it into pieces. Oscar said this was just for fun, and therefore was not seen as aggressive or hostile. He said, "For fun these two men act like chiefs." Chief Joe bought the fiddle just so he could destroy it and reciprocate Walter Isaac's breaking of the accordion. Oscar added that his father and Chief Joe were not relatives;

"they just play with each other" and were not trying to offend one another.

The second time Oscar told the story he added an additional detail. Walter Isaac not only broke the accordion but broke it in front of Chief Joe's mother. At this point Oscar's wife, Martha, interjected and said Walter destroyed the instrument because they all thought that Chief Joe's mother was a great woman. Oscar added that when Chief Joe broke the fiddle in front of Walter, he did it because Walter had honored Chief Joe's mother. Oscar explained that Chief Joe's grandmother had delivered "our daddy, and for that reason she is worth more than any other woman—so we have to love her very much." Oscar added this was not foolishness, this was very important.

I include this story because Oscar thought it important enough to tell it to me twice and because it reflects both the intricacies and importance of relationships as they are played out in a potlatch. It emphasizes the insignificance of material goods compared to relationships and illustrates the importance of knowing and acknowledging relationships made possible by one's own life and the relationships that made one's life possible (i.e., the relationships into which one is born). By acknowledging Chief Joe's mother, who delivered "our daddy," Walter Isaac acknowledged his father's relation—in other words, those people who had made his life possible.

MARTHA ISAAC: TANACROSS

As a young girl Martha was not allowed to attend potlatches but she could see the welcoming ceremonies held outdoors. She talked about what her mom told her about a potlatch at Mansfield. This was the potlatch for Chief Isaac that Martha thought it was held in 1916 or 1917.

> I don't know what they do, I don't understand. When they make potlatch we didn't stay there, not like kids now, we stay home.

Figure 7.26. Martha Isaac and Charlene Jonathan at Tetlin potlatch, 1969. Photo by François-Marie Guédon, courtesy of Bee Paul, William E. Simeone photo collection.

At Mansfield there was potlatch but we didn't see who got potlatch.

People start coming to village and they start dance, we going to dance and they dress up, they not dress like now days. Only mans who going to make potlatch wears the fancy coat. Paint their face a little bit, paint it red. If they paint face black means they are going to do something, paint one side of face red the other black and people are afraid. That was before us, mom tell story.

Mansfield people dance outside, and they came out from Julius's [Paul's] house and they were down there by Laura's [Sanford's] house. Stand in front of big community hall that Follet Isaac built and dance and shoot. People wear suit of clothes, man whoever going to make potlatch wear fancy coat. Visitors don't wear nothing but suit of clothes, old time they use to use clothes [suits] even they work.

Never see men with long hair, use to have long hair before minister came but minister told them to cut their hair. Speeches were made after they dance, Kenneth's daddy [Peter Thomas] really good for speech, he really smart, more than anybody.

The gifts were left outside on fences, blankets and roll of calico, all what they going to give away is put outside to show, rifle is hung inside they put on the nail, what they going to give away they put up there. Now days you put it out and somebody going to steal it.

In the old days use to leave gifts outside two or three days and when it rains they have to bring it back, bring in the house and put it back in cache. Really sunshine they put it out. Potlatch last three or four days. Chief Isaac potlatch lasted forty-five days, no one short of food or short of dog food. They feed them both together, men and their dogs.

Potlatch is a little bit different now days. Not as strong, but look like it, one year they can make lots of potlatch, like this summer [1987]. Two time there have been potlatch here, no three times. Long time ago not like this, not as often and cheaper too. And when people die I don't think they make potlatch too, they just have tea. Potlatch after they die.

They said they cannot let it go, a person die they cannot let go right away so they cannot make potlatch right away. Grandpa Sam, his son is dead in 1918 and 1920 he make potlatch, by then he plan to let it go his son by now, that's what they use to do. But now they make change that way so now there too much accident right now and they don't want to wait, they want to let go right away.

Who ever want to make potlatch they all join in together, all have to get together let it go one shot that's only time people have potlatch. (Simeone 1986d)

GAITHER PAUL: TANACROSS

When he was a boy, Gaither Paul witnessed several potlatches. Gaither talked about the opening speeches and they impression they made on him. In 1928, Chief John of Mentasta died, and his potlatch was held in Tanacross. Gaither described the arrival of Ahtna from the Copper River. He also mentions taking a small piece of blanket that would be given away in a potlatch and keeping it to ensure that what the host gave away would eventually return.

I remember potlatch 1928 they got rack [fence for displaying gifts] clear down, in front of Tanacross village, almost to the church. And then one up in the middle of the church [yard]. Full of blanket, is hanging over it. And every section there is two guns tied together, tied together and hanging on both sides of the rack. I think the year was 1928, I was little boy but I still remember the potlatch.

I really remember the speeches, I remember most clearly the Copper River people came. They said somebody brought the news that the Copper River people are across the river, but nobody went over to greet them. People just all walk down to the front, to front street. So many people, Healy Lake people were there, and so was Tetlin, I think. People all the way across, and they just waiting for Copper River people to come. And they stop across the river and they build big bon fire, we can see smoke over there. And they dress and put on their dancing coats and dress. When they start to come they start shooting, just like thunder going across there. And they stop and Tanacross people start shooting their rifle and after that you can hear drum across there and they start singing and they coming across, row after row. I think they had really good songs those days. And they marching across, and Tanacross people waiting for them up front. And up the bank they dance and they stop at the bank and they dance there for awhile. And then their leader, I can't remember who he was, he came forward and he make a speech. He make kind of friendly talk like that. And pretty soon he is getting louder and louder and louder and pretty soon he look serious and pretty soon he looks really mad and he start pounding his fist into his hand and pointing at Tanacross people.

And after that he went back, then Sam Thomas of Tanacross, he is spokesmen or leader, advisor, everybody look to him for advice on old ways, he know it all. This man, in Indian way, his forefathers are chief, in Indian way nobody can beat him in debate, because he can use the greatness of his father and use that with his talk. And everybody know they can't beat him in debate. Those are all forgotten now, but that's the way it was then. He is the spokesmen, he is the one that knows everything about old people. And when the Copper River leader went back to his men Sam Thomas came out and he start speaking slow and friendly greetings and like that and pretty soon he too is getting louder and louder and louder, and pretty soon he really looks mad and he pointing at Copper River people and pound his fist in his hand. I don't know all what's said but when he come back, right behind him is Copper River chief and he too is pointing his finger at Sam Thomas and Tanacross people and he looks really mad. And several times this exchange happen. And then they go away laughing and everybody greeting each other.

At first I though they were going to fight, you know, I was a kid, the way they look they look really mad at each other, but there is no mad involved in it. I guess it goes with the potlatch those days, you have to do that. I don't know why they did it. Probably which people knew more, probably [who was more knowledgeable]. I don't know why they did that. But those debate with another village was one part of potlatch, you got to have it with a potlatch. So that's why Sam Thomas is Tanacross spokesmen, he always win the debate.

And I was told too, one time, I don't know if they did it with guns, but I was told

if you make potlatch take a little piece of your blanket, not to damage blanket, put little piece of it and keep that in safe place it will keep coming back. What you give out will keep coming back. I don't think people do that anymore. But they supposed to take a little piece of it.

When I was a boy there was lot of calico given away in potlatch too. Calico, women make dress out of it. I remember them use to measure by hand like this, several hand and then tear it off. But today no calico in potlatch.

They gave it away to make their clothes. Just like giving clothes.

Gaither also said:

I remember it was a really big one. Blankets folded, not open. There were several (potlatch) after that, but that's the only really big thing I remember. People dance across the river. In early days that's the way visitor come to potlatch, if bunch of villages invited you cannot just come in. You gotta come in like they did. (Simeone 1986a)

JESSIE DAVID: TETLIN

Jessie David told Frederica de Laguna and Marie-Françoise Guédon about a potlatch in Tetlin that took place in 1968 and about changes that have occurred in the ceremony.

INTERVIEWER: Did they hang gifts on the line?
JESSIE: No, not this time. Before us born, old time, they make show, make line with it.
INTERVIEWER: How did the guest come?
JESSIE: Sometimes by plane, sometimes by boat, sometimes by snowgo. This time by plane and boat.
INTERVIEWER: Did they shoot guns?
JESSIE: No. Long time [ago] used to do that. Not this time. First they come in, go to community hall. Have to eat before go around the village.

Figure 7.27. Potlatch at Tetlin (left to right): Bertha Demit, Agnes Abraham, Lilly Northway, Doris Charles, and others. Photo by Terry Haynes.

Figure 7.28. Tetlin funeral, 1980. A Hudson's Bay blanket is draped over the coffin as sign of love and respect. Photo by Terry Haynes.

INTERVIEWER: Did the Tetlin Naltsiin eat with them?

JESSIE: Some people, some not. They used to be that way, long time [ago]. No used to eat with their cousin. Now this time can eat with it. They sing sorry song. [When] they through, they can dance Indian dance. First sorry song. Dik'aagyu and Naltsiin—all that.

INTERVIEWER: Who danced first?

JESSIE: Got to be Dik'aagyu—father's side. Mother's side we call "cousin" [they are considered relatives as opposed to the father's side who are non-relatives or friends]. All Dik'aagyu dance first: Tetlin, Tanacross, Northway. Lots of dances. All some together they help—Tanacross and Northway. Lots of dances. Sometimes one or two guys they get smart that way [start to compete in dancing]. They try to beat [each other] with dance.

INTERVIEWER: Did they used to dance against each other long time ago?

JESSIE: Yes we hear story about it. Those who's cousin, kids die, who don't like [what] somebody say, they get mad, give some kind of grease, strong tea. If you talk to me and I don't like the way you talk—that's how people get mad.

INTERVIEWER: Do they get sick from the grease and tea?

JESSIE: They throw up. And those make [tobacco] chew in water [then make people drink it]. Then give special present. Lots of pair of blankets. Lotsy—2, 3, 4 pair of blankets and money—is 20, 30 dollars sometimes.

INTERVIEWER: Any good luck medicine for potlatch?

JESSIE: Not since old people die off. We don't feel that way. That's way of time. Now no one can use. . . . Way ahead of me when I born. When somebody make potlatch, use something like perfume. Take from ground. Some chew it up. That's bring good luck for everything.

INTERVIEWER: Did everybody do it?

JESSIE: They can make smell. Start fire. Use little pan. Start fire. They burn slowly. That means good luck. Quick burn fast—don't smell so much—that's bad luck. Different on chew and burn. Like grass take out from wet ground. Can burn [it]. Can dry up—so when start to potlatch. Same one to chew. My daddy used to carry from mountain. He takes roots of that. That one too smell.

INTERVIEWER: Did the potlatch giver stay away from his wife?

JESSIE: Yes, I think one month.

INTERVIEWER: Did they stay quiet?

JESSIE: He got to take care of himself, take

care of body. Women take care of self too, when make potlatch. Take care of her body.

INTERVIEWER: Can he work?

JESSIE: Not to work. They can cut wood, bring water, but not go round village. They don't like to step on dog . . . one that dirty thing. That bring bad luck too. [They are not supposed to laugh]. Not do that. If they laugh, if who take care of his or her body, that bring bad luck too. [They have to do this for every potlatch they give].

INTERVIEWER: What kind of bad luck?

JESSIE: Money. (de Laguna and Guédon 1968c)

JERRY ISAAC: TANACROSS

Jerry Isaac (1974) wrote this description of the upper Tanana potlatch for the student journal *Theata* in 1974 while an undergraduate at the University of Alaska in Fairbanks. This is a slightly edited version of the original article.

A potlatch in our particular way is an occasion to present visiting people with a big feast and gifts. Friends and relatives gather in a large building, usually a community hall, and the joyful people carry on for the next four days. On the fourth day of the potlatch, the sponsor gives away gifts, like guns, blankets, mittens, moccasins, knives, scarves, and axes. A potlatch is a respected event, and therefore taboos are practiced. For instance, while the gifts are being given out, the teenage girls are not supposed to walk around in the building.

In the old days, before there were many white people in our area, only the chiefs or those who were fairly wealthy sponsored

Figure 7.29. Left to right: Jerry Isaac, Kirby Thomas, Kenneth Thomas Sr., and Roy Denny. 2012. Photo by William E. Simeone.

Figure 7.30. Mildred and Alfred Jonathan, 2012. Photo by William E. Simeone.

potlatches. The modern potlatch is sponsored by anyone who feels like presenting one in memory and honor of a loved one who has died, a loved one who has had a near death from an accident, or just a person the sponsor wants to honor. It is also an expression of great love for that person. The only time the people of a village and the neighboring villages are heartbroken and sorrowful at a potlatch is when the potlatch is for a sudden death which has occurred within a family. Then grief fills the hearts of many, and condolences are always expressed to that family.

Often a group of three or four people will get together to present a potlatch. When a person decides to sponsor a potlatch, he sends invitations out by sending a messenger to several villages. Sometimes the person sponsoring the potlatch asks for a particular person to be present at the potlatch because he is or was a close friend of the person whom the party is being given for, or because he belongs to a certain clan. The person invited will be a guest of honor. This does not mean that this person is the only one invited. After this specially invited person is informed of the coming event, he in turn tells his village people. Anyone is welcome to attend a potlatch providing he finds his own transportation; although at times, the sponsor may even hire people who own cars to go to the other villages and offer rides to those who need them. Anyone is welcome to feast with the rest of the crowd and join with the dancers afterwards at his own will. The visitors can stand around, sit and watch, or if they want to, participate in the dancing.

By 6 p.m. the supper starts and food like wild berries, moose meat, ducks, soup, wild roots, fish (white fish or salmon), salad, jello, homemade doughnuts, bread, wild rhubarb, canned fruits, and tea are served. The eating lasts for an hour or two. Then the plates, cups, dishpans, and silverware are picked up, and the dishwashers are again hard at work. The floor is swept by two or three girls so it will be ready for the dancing.

The visitors and the villagers at first just sit and joke with each other, although some of them help clean up to get the hall ready for the dancing. Then after a while, the older men, all sitting on one side of the hall, maybe the far end of the hall, which is in the back, start singing, first sitting. After fifteen or twenty minutes of warm-up singing they all get up and begin dancing. The songs are well-known among them; therefore everyone joins in. The songs have a unique effect on people, like the modern hard rock music has on young people. It inspires the people to participate in the dancing which makes everyone feel happy and carefree. The women participate in the dancing right along with the men. Usually the women encircle the men because women stand in one place to dance, moving only occasionally, while men dance making all kinds of motions. The men are always inside the circle of women.

The drum which keeps the beat is painted with designs. It is made by stretching a wet moosehide over a nicely smoothed birch hoop about five inches wide and twenty inches in diameter. The dancing is now underway, and the hall is filled with spectators and dancers. Dancing may look easy, but for the men it takes good wind and leg muscles to keep up with the other dancers.

After an hour or two of dancing passes, the dancers have a special song calling for water, juices or soft drinks. They sing this song so someone will bring in three or four cases of pop. This is why at every potlatch there are always ten or fifteen cases of different soda pop. After the exhaustion and sweating, cold pop refreshes the dancers. After the dancers rest up, they all start singing again, inspiring the resting ones to come and rejoin in the dance. Then a roll of calico is brought out which the dancers grab hold of in a tug-of-war, usually between the dancers and the spectators at the doorway. After one side wins, the calico is put away and dancing starts again. The dancing goes on until midnight or later, until people feel like quitting.

The next morning, gradually the village comes alive again. The visitors go out to visit, and some of them go to the community hall for their breakfast. This is the fourth day of the potlatch, so the day of work is hastened a bit. By noon lunch is served. More people flow into the village around three o'clock, creating a bigger multitude.

In the meantime, singing rings out of the hall attracting the attention of many, thus increasing the number of people in the hall. Different songs are sung, each signifying a different dance, but no matter what song is sung, usually the style of dancing is the same. This is the last day of dancing because the gift-giving time is near. The people sing and dance until about four or five; then they eat the last big feast. The feast on the last day is bigger since there are more people and more leftovers from the previous days. About 6 p.m. the sponsor and some of his helpers spread a big sheet or blanket in the middle of the floor; this indicates that the giving away of gifts is now commencing. The gifts are brought in by way of a window because of the belief that bad luck will come in with the gifts if they are brought in by way of the door. After everything has been brought in, the blankets, guns, and so forth are neatly stacked, and then a person makes a speech concerning the potlatch. This is usually done by an old man from the home village.

After the speech, the sponsors form a small circle. A song or two will be sung

Figure 7.31. Tanacross men with gunho, Tetlin potlatch, 1919. Photo by the Reverend Frederick Drane, Drane photo collection Alaska and Polar Regions Department, Elmer E. Rasmuson Library, University of Alaska Fairbanks.

Figure 7.32. Burial of chief David at Tetlin, 1919. Photo by F. B. Drane. Drane Photo collection Alaska and Polar Regions Department, Elmer E. Rasmuson Library, University of Alaska Fairbanks.

over the materials or gifts. This type of song has a distinctive sound, making it recognizable to all. These songs are sung because of the belief that the sponsors will hold on to the good luck they have had and that the money which is spent will someday gradually come back to them. The music has a slow beat and the words are also slow. After these songs are sung, the giving away begins. The gifts are given to people according to the clan in which they belong or because they were or are friends of the person whom the potlatch is presented for.

The person who is given gifts is not supposed to be related or belong to the same clan as the person whom the potlatch is for. This process of passing gifts around takes as long as five or six hours, so the giving away begins around six in the evening. It proceeds by Indian time, which is defined as proceeding until the event ends, with no limits. By ten o'clock, some of the lively children are asleep or their eyes are heavy with sleep. This seemingly monotonous event drags on, but the adults patiently sit around and joke quietly while the giving away continues. As the blankets and the various gifts are still being passed around, maybe someone will make a few pots of tea, and tea drinking pries itself into the activity. Finally the giveaway finishes and the people who received guns get up and sing a song that includes the English words, "I got gun," mixed with our own Native chants. This song is known very well and is commonly sung at the end of a potlatch. Singing and dancing take place once more for a short while, and then everyone bids each other good-bye, says, "I'll see you sometime," and departs remembering the joyful last four days. After the potlatch, the community hall is cleaned up, and all is quiet again until a few months or a year later when the next potlatch begins, and the joyful crowd returns to the village.

Archdeacon Frederic Drane attended a funeral potlatch held at Tetlin in May 1919 for Chief David. As he neared the village, Drane was greeted by twelve rifle shots (Drane thought the number had some particular meaning). The people were drawn up in a large semicircle "chanting their mournful lament over the death of Chief David. Over and over again they sang their song of sorrow that pierced even my heart, though I knew not a word that they sang. Tears streamed down the cheeks of the men as well as the women" (Drane n.d.b: 76).

> As the women sang, they leaned over from the waist, and with an up and down motion of the arms, and a twisting of the shoulders they worked over a silk handkerchief. This was the regular dance of sorrow, to be seen at the "potlatches," or feasts in memory of the dead, so common on the Tanana. But the song they sang this time was a more penetrating dirge, than I had ever heard before. The men had rattles made by putting pebbles in a baking powder can, and these they shook violently throughout the lamination. (76).

Following the dances came the speeches; one was made by Joseph, a "medicine man" married to Chief David's daughter. Meanwhile, the men were busy making the coffin by sawing a large spruce tree it into boards. The corpse was covered with a "handsome blue mantel" decorated with a double row of "pearl buttons" lined with some red scarlet cloth. Each night the chief's youngest son and his wife slept beside the body of the dead man. Drane wrote, "I have heard that after death the soul or spirit of a man lingers for a certain length of time . . ." (79).

After the coffin was finished, it was brought into the cabin through the window and carried out through the window; then the window was nailed up so that the spirit could not find its way back into the house. The mantle was draped over the coffin. Drane told the people that it was appropriate to take the coffin out the door of the cabin, so they did that instead. One man tossed two silver dollars into the coffin and the money was rubbed over the bottom of the coffin and to the four corners then returned to the owner.

The graveside service was Christian. After the funeral a feast was held at the house of Chief David's eldest son that included sweetened tea, sweetened biscuits, and quantities of boiled dried moose, caribou meat, and dried whitefish. The feast was gay and happy in contrast to the previous day's events. The remaining food was divided up for the people to carry home.

The family of the chief brought out presents for those who had helped with the funeral. Big Frank, a distinguished guest, was given several expensive blankets, a Winchester rifle, $40 in gold coins, and several pairs of beaded moccasins and mittens. Singleton [the teacher], who made the coffin, was given a dish full of biscuits, a Hudson's Bay blanket, a pair of trousers, and a shirt. Drane was given $5 "to be applied to expenses," a pair of beaded moccasins, and a pair of beaded mittens. The chief's eldest daughter gave him a Hudson's Bay blanket. The daughter who gave Drane the blanket made a speech that was translated. She said: "Now that my father is gone I am asking you to be my father and live and cherish me as he did. Unless you do this my heart will be heavy and sad. And now, my father, I am giving you this warm blanket to protect you on your long journeys. Take care of yourself as you travel, and come see us often" (Drane n.d.b: 81).

Photo-montage by Hal Gage.

8 THE FUR TRADE

Upper Tanana Dene participation in the fur trade dates back hundreds of years, long before the arrival of Europeans in Alaska. In the seventeenth and eighteenth centuries, almost all European manufactured goods that reached Upper Tanana Dene came through Native intermediaries. Russian trade goods came from Ahtna and Dena'ina, English goods from Han and Tutchone, and American goods from the Chilkat Tlingit. After Russia ceded Alaska to the United States in 1867, Upper Tanana Dene began trading directly with American traders on the upper Yukon River. It was not until the beginning of the twentieth century that American traders penetrated the Upper Tanana homeland and established stores at Healy River, Tanacross, Tetlin, and the lower Nabesna River.

EARLY FUR TRADE 1780–1900

Up until 1900, when American traders established stores on the upper Tanana River, Upper Tanana Dene could only obtain trade goods through Native middlemen such as the Han, Tutchone, Ahtna, Dena'ina, and Chilkat Tlingit or by traveling long distances to trading posts on Cook Inlet, Prince William Sound, or the Yukon River. Information about the fur trade in eastern Alaska before 1867 comes from Ferdinand von Wrangell, governor of the Russian America Company from 1830 to 1835. Wrangell was intrigued by the wide distribution of Russian trade goods in Alaska and published a map showing trade trails connecting

the upper Copper River, upper Susitna River, and Tanana River (Wrangell [1839] 1980: end sheet). He thought English trade goods obtained by the Dena'ina, for example, came from Hudson's Bay Company posts on the upper Yukon River while American goods came via the Chilkat Tlingit who traded with American ship captains trading along the Northwest Coast (Ketz 1983: 31). Lt. Allen (1887: 138–139) observed the extent of this trade when he was at Tetlin in the summer of 1885. There, Allen saw an axe made in Montreal, Canada, a pair of sailor's trousers, and a Tlingit blanket that came from the Chilkat Tlingit, who likely got the trousers from an American war ship stationed at Sitka.

Annually, Tlingit traders met Tutchone and upper Tanana Dene who traded furs and tanned skins for English and American goods. Tetlin elder Titus David (Simeone 1980c) said his father traded directly with the Chilkat Tlingit at a place on the Yukon River above present-day Dawson City. In exchange for their furs, people received buttons, beads, blankets with pearl buttons, and leaf tobacco.

One place where Upper Tanana Dene and Tutchone met to trade was North Fork Island (Tl'ooo Gayh K'it, "on the white grass") on the White River near the present-day US–Canada border. In *The Upper Tanana Indians*, Robert McKennan (1959: 129) writes that trade occurred annually, lasted one month, and was accompanied by singing and dancing. He also writes that Upper Tanana Dene would sometimes go to the Copper River to continue trading.

https://doi.org/10.5876/9781646423347.c008

In his field notes, McKennan says the women did not accompany the men on these trips and that trade took place in winter, around Christmastime. Trade items included dentalium shells; big red, blue, and white beads; and Hudson's Bay Company beads that came from the village of Champagne in the Yukon Territory. McKennan cites Chisana Joe as saying Dene traded furs and skins for Hudson's Bay blankets from the Tutchone who lived on Kluane Lake for one or two skins per blanket. Other prices mentioned by Joe were cross fox that went for $2 or a blanket; red fox for 50 cents; and beaver, marten, and lynx all for $1. Chilkat ceremonial robes with a button design cost as much as $50. Moose and caribou hides were traded. Some copper was traded, which was made into bullets for shotguns (otherwise people used pebbles in their firearms) (McKennan 1962).

There are various accounts of how firearms reached Upper Tanana Dene. Chisana Joe told McKennan that rifles came from the Yukon River, the town of Fortymile Mile, Salt Creek, and Stewart River. Joe said when he was small, Dene obtained flintlock rifles; later, these were followed by rifles of various calibers: .45/70s, .44s, .38 Winchesters, .30/30 Winchester, and .30/40s Winchester (McKennan 1962).

Bessie John, from Scottie Creek, said Herman Kessler had a trading post at Northway where the people first got repeating rifles. Before, people used muzzle loaders that came from the Tutchone and Chilkat Tlingit. Bessie said people from the crow clan were the first to obtain guns, which gave them the right to claim or "own" them, making the crow clan the top people (Simeone 1985b). Gaither Paul of Tanacross said the first person to obtain a gun was a man named Cha Dan Esha. He ended up with two guns he got from a white man who taught him to use them. Because he had two guns, Gaither said, it somehow "upgrade his tribe" (clan). Gaither said a Mansfield clan was supposed to be the top clan, but now they

Figure 8.1. Old Paul wearing a button blanket he may have obtained in trade, 1936–1937. Photo by Lucille Wright, William E. Simeone photo collection.

were surpassed, so the Mansfield people purchased the guns for a lot of money. When there is a potlatch, the old people mention these two guns in their speeches (Simeone 1987t).

NOOCHULOGHOYET

In 1847, the British-owned Hudson's Bay Company built Fort Yukon. There is no evidence that upper Tanana Dene visited Fort Yukon, but they did travel to the mouth of the Tanana River to trade at Noochuloghoyet with Russian, English, and Dene. After the Russians sold Alaska to the United States in 1867, Americans replaced both Russian and British traders and in 1868 built a store near the mouth of the Tanana River.

In 1867, the American explorer Frederick Whymper met Tanana River Dene at Noochuloghoyet and left a vivid account. Whymper did not indicate exactly where on the Tanana River these Dene came from, but he believed them

to be the most unsophisticated Indians to be met with at the present day. They were gay with painted faces, feathers in their long hair, patches of red clay at the back of their heads covered with small fluffy feathers, double tailed coats and pantaloons of buckskin much adorned with fringes and beads and elaborately worked fire bags and belts. (Whymper [1868] 1966: 210)

Whymper also described the greeting ceremonies as each group arrived:

On some occasions their gatherings have numbered 600 persons. . . . On landing at this village a ceremony had to be gone through, possibly to test whether we had "strong hearts" or not. The Indians already there, advanced whooping and yelling, and brandishing their guns till they reached us, and discharged them in the air. We, with the Indians just arrived returned the compliment. (210)

Several Dene elders told of their grandparents going to the mouth of the Tanana River to trade. Maggie Isaac remembered her great-grandfather went to Tanana. She said:

Great Grandpa go to Tanana, first of June my grandpa go down, they go by canoe, bring all his nephew and all his uncle, all go down to Tanana. All people go together, bought all that shell [ammunition], tea, chew, what ever they use, come back when berries ready to ripe, August or September. (Simeone 1987o)

Gaither Paul told a story about when Mansfield and Goodpaster people went down to Tanana to trade that portrays the tenor and a sense of the competition accompanying the trade when Dene from different parts of Alaska

met. At Tanana. the Mansfield and Goodpaster people met a Koyukon wrestler who defeated everyone he wrestled. Gaither said the Koyukon man stood with his feet planted wide apart and challenged each opponent to grab him and try to throw him. Each failed and was thrown. On seeing this, the Mansfield chief decided to have his man challenge the Koyukon. Before the match, the Mansfield chief made a speech saying they had come a long way and it would be good if the Koyukon did not hurt their man. Then the Mansfield man wrestled, and was immediately picked up by the Koyukon and gently lain down. This taunt angered the Mansfield chief, who had his runners go get a Goodpaster man. He came down at the beckoning of his own chief and wrestled the Koyukon, throwing him (Simeone 1987u).

Andrew Isaac said that his grandfather Chief Isaac had a large cache on Chief Creek (Tthee Xaaddh'), just north of the Robertson River. It seems the purpose of this cache was to store goods obtained at Tanana. Apparently, these goods, which included cans of gunpowder and lead shot, were to be given away at potlatches.

My father's people—Follet Isaac, Walter Isaac, my daddy, and all four boys they up Chief Creek, right here Chief Creek. My grandfather make big place like village above right there, they build big cache. And people going down with the boat down to Tanana they go down with it. They tell me story, ten young men like you, that can pack 40, 50, 60, 70 pounds, that people go down with them, and they get the boat and buy outfit and all pack out and they cross Sand Creek coming up and build big cache up there, they got all outfit. . . . Chief Isaac had cache.

John Frank, me, Peter Charles we working for John Hajdukovich, and he ask us what kind of people use that area, use land? We tell him story and that's why they name Chief Creek, after Chief Isaac. My grandfather got fence from that place go over across the country way down to Robertson bank, moose fence. That's how he build big camp, set up, up there. (Simeone 1987h)

Bessie Barnabas said her father, John, traveled to Fort Gibbon in the 1880s to trade furs, and her aunt once walked to Valdez before there was a post at Tanana. Fort Gibbon was at the confluence of the Tanana and Yukon Rivers. Bessie's mother saw her first white man when her family walked there. Bessie said it was a trading post then; the military had not yet arrived. They didn't use dog teams then but traveled with sleds. The men pulled them, two men to a sled, and there were usually six to eight men in the party. Bessie walked to Fort Gibbon when she was a child and remembers it was a very hard trip. Some of the women became so tired they staggered and cried, but the men wouldn't stop or slow down for them (Baggen n.d.a).

UPPER YUKON TRADE 1874–1898

In the years following the purchase of Alaska in 1867, American trading companies opened stores along the upper Yukon River. These companies employed steamboats to bring goods upriver, increasing both the amount and type of trade goods available. Steamers towed four or five barges, with each barge holding ten tons of supplies. This allowed traders to stock not only traditional items like glass beads but bulk foods such as flour, repeating rifles, canvas for tents, and exotic items like china teacups (Clark 1995).

In 1874, the Alaska Commercial (AC) Company built Fort Reliance on the Yukon River, just below the present town of Dawson City. According to Francois Mercier (1986), the post was opened at the insistence of the Han chief Catsah, who was leader of the Tr'ondëk Hwëch'in (or Klondike) band of Han. Mercier

also said he established Fort Reliance to bring the trade closer to upper Tanana Dene. Fort Reliance was important for two reasons: upper Tanana Dene now had easier access to trade goods, and the presence of Fort Reliance helped facilitate mineral exploration in the upper Yukon River basin. The discovery of Yukon gold would ultimately have a profound effect on Upper Tanana Dene.

Upper Tanana Dene visited Fort Reliance on a regular basis. In 1883, Lieutenant Frederic Schwatka met a group of Dene led by a man he called "Chil-Tah," whose name sounds very much like the name Ketl'aad Ta', a leader at Dihthâad. Schwatka wrote that during the time of his visit there were "evidently" many people from the Tanana country visiting Fort Reliance (Schwatka 1900: 340). At Last Tetlin, Lieutenant Henry Allen encountered Dene who had been to Fort Reliance and noticed "their clothing indicated more easy communication with a trading stations than did that of the Atnatánas" or Ahtna (Allen 1887: 75).

In 1880, the Western Fur and Trading Company opened a store at Belle Isle near a Han community called David's Village, close to the town of Eagle. This store lasted only two years and was replaced by another near the same spot operated by the AC Company. In 1884, gold was discovered on the upper Yukon River, and in 1887 American traders built a store at the mouth of the Fortymile River, largely to supply miners prospecting on the Fortymile River.

With direct access to goods from Fort Reliance, Belle Isle and eventually the town of Fortymile, Han living on the upper Yukon became middlemen in trade between upper Tanana Dene and Upper Ahtna and established a trading partnership with Tanacross-speaking people from Ketchumstuk. A rare glimpse of this trade appears in the unpublished journal of the Anglican missionary Robert J. Bowen (n.d.), who arrived on the upper Yukon River by steamboat in 1895. That winter Bowen accompanied the Han on a trip to Fort Reliance and a trading expedition toward the Tanana River.

According to Bowen, the Han relied on hunting and fishing to feed and clothe themselves but measured their wealth in terms of Hudson's Bay blankets, which they obtained from the traders. He wrote the "wealth of a native consisted of and was designated by the number of four point Hudson's Bay blankets he possessed." This wealth, along with the ability to provide for his wife's parents, was taken into consideration when a man wanted to marry.

The trade in furs was critical, and the Han jealously guarded their position as intermediaries with the Dene living south of the Yukon River. On a second trip, Bowen accompanied a Han trading party traveling from the town of Fortymile into the hill country south of the Yukon River. Bowen writes:

> A tribe of Indians, known as the Ketchem Stock [sic] Indians also joined the Takudth [Han] Indians toward the head waters of the Fortymile Creek. These Indians were in touch with a tribe from beyond the Copper River area and made annual trips to their country for trading purposes. . . . He goes on . . . the time arrived when the Takudth Indians decided it was time to for them to make their trip over the Alaska Border, to do their trading with natives less experienced than themselves.

For this trip the Han had arranged to rendezvous with the Ketchumstuk people and then venture farther south to meet with an unnamed group of Natives, but at the final moment Bowen was prevented from meeting these "less enlightened" Natives, whom he refers to as "Indians of the Interior." Bowen speculates that if the "Indians of the Interior" met whites, the Han monopoly would be broken.

> The Indians of the Interior had seen me at the head of our dogs and sleighs and they went into the timber and would not come

out again to trade. The Ketchem Stock and Forty-Mile Indians [Han] had to go into the bush to a place decided upon before the Interior Indians would either trade or expose their furs. Only those who were deputed [sic] to trade went into the bush, the others, with myself and dogs remained in camp. I really believe I was refused this meeting through intervention of the Ketchum stock and Forty-mile Indians. It evidently was a preserve they did not wish to have interfered with either by missionary or white trader for fear the Interior Indians would be influenced to cease trading. The monopoly was worth something and must be held at all costs.

Later in the day, the party arrived at a Han hunting and trapping camp. Bowen's description provides a snapshot of late-nineteenth-century Dene. Bowen writes that the camp was in a "well selected spot with plenty of standing dry timber and a good creek from which to get water and ice. The skin tepees [sic] were erected so that the shoulders of the hills would protect them from heavy winter winds." Bowen estimated seventy people lived in the camp. The men were busy trapping marten, lynx, ermine, and fox and hunting moose and caribou while the women tanned hides, which they used for moccasins and clothing. They had flour, baking powder, syrup, and raisins, along with plenty of dried caribou meat, roasted caribou heads, and tongues.

UPPER TANANA TRADE 1900–1940

Once gold was discovered on the Upper Yukon in the 1880s, trading opportunities for Dene increased. By 1900 Upper Tanana Dene were trading at Dawson and Eagle and on the Fortymile River at Steele Creek and Chicken Creek. Oscar Isaac said Big John of Tetlin told

Figure 8.2. Healy Lake Trading Post. William E. Simeone photo collection.

Figure 8.3. Strelic's store at Tanana Crossing, 1919. Tishu V. Ulen Collection UAF-1989-88-29. Alaska and Polar Regions Department, Elmer E. Rasmuson Library, University of Alaska, Fairbanks.

him Tetlin people traveled to Dawson via the Dennison and Walker forks of the Fortymile River. Along this route they had some "moose lakes" where they hunted moose during the trip. They went to Dawson to buy ammunition and tea and returned to Tetlin before freeze-up. They used canoes to cross Midway Lake (Simeone 1987r).

Steele Creek, a minor tributary of the Fortymile River, had both a roadhouse and store established in 1898. Tanacross elder Julius Paul

recalled the first store was at Eagle, then came Steele Creek on the Fortymile River and then Chicken. Old Paul, Julius's father, made trips to Steele Creek when Julius was a boy. Julius never went to Chicken, because by the time he was grown there was a store in Tanacross that they went to all the time. Before that the Steele Creek store was the only one.

W. H. Newton was one of the earliest traders on the upper Tanana River. When he opened his store at the junction of the Healy and Tanana

Rivers in 1907, the Healy River people began to settle semipermanently at Healy Lake. On August 26, 1931, Newton (1931) wrote a two-page letter to Robert McKennan relating the early history of the fur trade on the upper Tanana River. Newton makes clear how difficult it was to start a trading business there.

Newton wrote that his memory "only goes back to 1906 when I started poling up the river." Before 1908, when Newton "poled up with a ton of goods," there was John Martin who had the mail route but left the area in 1907, the same year Newton opened his store on the Healy River. In 1912 Newton opened a store at Tanana Crossing and cached goods at Tetlin and at Nabesna with Chief Sam. Two years later he sold out to John Strelic, who stayed for four years. Tom Denny bought out Strelic but went broke. In 1909 Captain Northway made it as far as Tetlin but then lost everything the following year.

Newton said the discovery of gold at Chisana in 1913 brought a rush of traders, including Sam Shucklin, who lost everything when the price of furs dropped. Other traders included a man named Merritt who tried to make it to Chisana but lost his boat and cargo below little Delta. Newton recalled traders Herman Kessler, Ole Frederickson, and Jim Slaterwhite at "Sampson Landing," who lost his boat in the spring ice and stayed for three years before quitting. Flannigan started a store at Gasoline City on the Chisana River in 1913 but lost his boat and entire cargo the following year and went broke. In 1916 fur prices rose, attracting John and Milo Hajdukovich, who eventually bought out Flannigan in 1929. Newton sold out to Emil Hammer in 1925.

John Hajdukovich began trading on the Tanana River in 1918 and the upper villages in 1919. When Hajdukovich started his business, he dropped off goods at spots along the river and Dene would pick them up. He also cached goods at Tanana Crossing and Tetlin. Later he traded more often in villages when trappers returned to the community to trade; some came once a month to get supplies, others more often.

Figure 8.4. David Joe with beavers. Jeany Healy Photo Collection UAF-2000-181-26. Alaska and Polar Regions Department, Elmer E. Rasmuson Library, University of Alaska, Fairbanks.

Figure 8.5. Brittan Jonathan and Ricky James beaver trapping, 1971. Photo by William E. Simeone.

Herman Kessler opened a store on the Nabesna River in 1920, trading primarily with Dene from Nabesna Village. Kessler also had a store at Gardiner Creek, where he traded with Scottie Creek people. Kessler reported the

Figure 8.6. Silas Henry hauling freight. Photo by Lucille Wright. William E. Simeone photo collection.

Indians trapped fox, mink, beaver, marten, and lynx, but muskrat furs were the primary trade item. Beaver was not plentiful until the 1940s and was closed to trapping until 1948. Marten season closed periodically. Fox were important in the early years but declined in value so Native people made little effort (Brown 1979: 12).

Transporting goods into the upper Tanana region was expensive and time-consuming. Goods came by steamboat to Fairbanks, then along the Richardson Highway to McCarty, near present-day Delta Junction. During the summer, goods were transferred to shallow draft riverboats for the trip upriver; in the winter, they were hauled by dogsled. Because transportation was limited, it was more profitable for the traders to handle expensive luxuries like portable phonographs and lady's rayon bloomers instead of the cheaper, bulkier items considered necessities. Traders charged high prices for everything, and Dene were frequently indebted to the traders (Brown 1984: 91–92). One trader estimated he gave an annual credit between two and three thousand dollars (Brown 1984: 144).

Figure 8.7. John Healy on traders' boat at Delta Junction. Jeany Healy collection UAF-2000-181-138. Alaska and Polar Regions Department, Elmer E. Rasmuson Library, University of Alaska, Fairbanks.

Ted Lowell worked for Hajdukovich and had his own business on the upper Tanana River. In an interview Lowell (1979) said much of the trade was conducted during the winter, when the traders used dog teams to reach the villages and sometimes went to remote trapping camps. During the summer, the traders were busy hauling freight by boat. The best time to travel by boat was June and July, when the water was high. Lowell said during the summer he and Hajdukovich made six to twelve trips

Figure 8.8. Catching a ride on the traders' boat after ratting season. Note the dogs on the roof of the boat. William E. Simeone photo collection.

Figure 8.9. Launching the traders' boat into the Tanana River, 1936–1937. Photo by Lucille Wright, William E. Simeone photo collection.

hauling freight to the upper Tanana villages. During the spring, when Native people were muskrat hunting, the traders traveled from camp to camp using outboard motors. Lowell said Herman Kessler operated a thirty-foot-long boat with a twelve-horsepower kicker motor. John Hajdukovich owned several boats, one with the capacity to haul six tons of freight. Lowell estimated that some 500 to 600 gallons of gasoline were needed to power the boats during the summer season.

Tea was highly desired, and one trader said that he had sold 3,000 pounds of tea, mostly to upper Tanana Indians. Other items included finished clothing and raw materials such as bulk calico and cotton; food supplies, especially staples such as flour, sugar, and tea; and tents, traps, rifles, ammunition, and related supplies. Lowell said ammunition was cheap: a box of .22-caliber shells cost seventy-five cents and box of .30-30 shells cost two dollars. Nonperishable goods were not traded because of the storage problems. Appendix C has a selection of documents related to the fur trade on the upper Tanana River in the 1920s and 1930s. The documents provide a glimpse into the trade, showing the amount and types of furs trapped and traded, the types of goods traded, including the large number of Pendleton blankets, and the debt incurred by individual Dene.

Figure 8.10. Potlatch blankets at Big Delta. William E. Simeone photo collection.

JOHN HAJDUKOVICH

John Krist Hajdukovich was the best-known and most influential trader on the Tanana River and was well remembered by all Dene elders. Hajdukovich had an outsize role because he was not just a trader but a prospector, roadhouse proprietor, hunting guide, and advocate for local development (see chapter 10). Until his death in 1965, he was widely recognized as the authority on the economic and social conditions of the upper Tanana region. While Hajdukovich achieved many things, his crowning achievement was the establishment of the Tetlin Indian Reservation in 1930.

Hajdukovich described how he began trading on the upper Tanana River:

> After I sold the roadhouse to Rika Wallen, I made a trip upriver in 1919 to 1920. I started in a small way, just got started. I got the trading post in both places: Tanana Crossing and Tetlin. I hauled lots of freight. Quite a few tons over the Goodpaster Trail. Finally I had three trading posts Tanana Crossing (they call it Tanacross), Tetlin; Nabesna, that's Northway now. We took supplies up the Tanana. Pretty rough going: Tanana River. I had two gas boats and could haul four or five tons of freight each. Took five, six, seven sometimes eight days from Big Delta to Tanacross. (quoted in Ferguson 2009: 29)

In 1937 a *Fairbanks Daily News-Miner* article described the trade on the upper Tanana River, mentioning Milo Hajdukovich, John's cousin:

> Wolves are about evenly divided between the blacks and grays. The latter bring a high price. Rabbit and fox are plentiful but fox prices are low. Because of the higher rabbit cycle, lynx are coming back. Outside, there is a good demand for lynx; they pay as high as $40 for a No. 1 prime pelt. Hajdukovich reported that back in 1928, he bought more than 1,000 lynx pelts. . . . Milo estimated that there are 25 native trappers at Tanacross, 12 at Tetlin, and 15 at Nabesna. (quoted in Ferguson 2009: 36)

MUSKRATS

Perhaps the most important animal trapped by Dene was the muskrat. In 1938, for example, Kessler reported that he and Hajdukovich handled 28,000 muskrat skins (Brown 1979: 140). In 1938, Dene killed so many muskrats that Hajdukovich needed permission to exceed the limits of his mail contracts with the US Post Office. In February 1939, the teacher

Figure 8.11. Oscar Isaac at muskrat camp, 1977. Photo by William Simeone.

Figure 8.12. Eddie Joe's spring camp, 1970. Photo by Francois Marie Guédon, courtesy of Bee Paul, William E. Simeone photo collection.

at Tetlin, John A. Singleton, informed the Post Office the traders would be taking their June mail to Fairbanks in their own boats because the amount of muskrat skins they were going to ship far exceeded the 500-pound limit. The Post Office approved the request, letting Hajdukovich transport one way not more than 5,000 pounds of mail at eight cents a pound from Tetlin to Big Delta. The emergency contract was renewed in 1940 and 1941 (Brown 1979: 141).

According to Ted Lowell, muskrats or "rats" were sold to the traders almost as fast as they were dried. Steven Northway once took 110 rat skins overnight. In 1931, the traders purchased three skins for one dollar; at other times the prices were considerably higher, and traders gave two dollars a skin and up to four or six dollars a skin. Lowell said muskrat trapping took place during the late winter and early spring when the lakes started to open. He described how Nabesna people hunted musk-rats. In the spring, they moved out of the hills where they had been trapping and down to the flats where the lakes and muskrats were. Dene would set up tents along the lakeshore during the season. They used small boats or canoes as well as thirty-foot-long poling boats. At a good lake, they would pitch their tent and make it headquarters for their muskratting, then walk from lake to lake. Since lakes thaw from the edges, there would be a patch of ice out in the middle of the lake so Dene could take a canoe and go around the edge and hunt muskrats (Lowell 1979).

The significance of muskrats to the local economy is reflected in a letter written by John Hajdukovich to the Alaska Game Commission. In 1926, the commission changed the reg-ulations on taking muskrats. In the letter Hajdukovich (1927) explains why the new reg-ulations would not work in the upper Tanana region and that a change in the regulations would benefit both Dene and traders.

DENE ELDERS' RECOLLECTION OF THE FUR TRADE

GAITHER PAUL: TETLIN

Tanacross elder Gaither Paul narrated the chronology of traders who entered Upper Tanana territory beginning around 1900.

> John Strelic was the first, he had stores at Healy Lake and Tanacross, his store was Tom Denny's old house.

Newton, who was second, also used that house. He had stores at Healy Lake and Tanacross. He was called Newty.

John Hajdukovich was third, his cousin Milo traded as well, they had stores at Tanacross and Tetlin. Hajdukovich lived mainly at Big Delta. He would travel around during the winter to trapping camps and buy fur. Hajdukovich gave peo-ple credit and they paid up when they had some money. Hajdukovich would drop off supplies at the mouth of Billy Creek where Jimmy Walter had a camp. He told Jimmy to take supplies: sugar, tea, and flour to David Paul at the head of Billy Creek.

Flannigan was at Tetlin then Herman Kessler who had stores at Tanacross, Tetlin, and Northway. Kessler lived at all these places. [Gaither worked for Kessler driving a boat upriver from Tanacross; they didn't go downriver because of rapids.] Kessler was at Northway after World War II.

Hajdukovich hired the Clark Brothers—who wintered around Mount Fairplay trapping and prospecting. There is a story that Felix Pedro struck it rich on one of these creeks. [Gaither thought it was the Ladue River so Hajdukovich hired these guys to find the strike, but they never did.] (Simeone 1987v)

TITUS DAVID: TETLIN

In an interview with Frederica de Laguna and François-Marie Guédon, Tetlin elder Titus David talked about the fur trade. He described making trips to the mouth of the Tanana River and then to Dawson City, Yukon Territory. He also talked about John Hajdukovich and Herman Kessler.

> They [Upper Tanana Dene] go down from here to Tanana to buy leaf tobacco and shotgun and shell [ammunition]. Come back half way by canoe. Maybe as far as Fairbanks and walk the rest of the way.

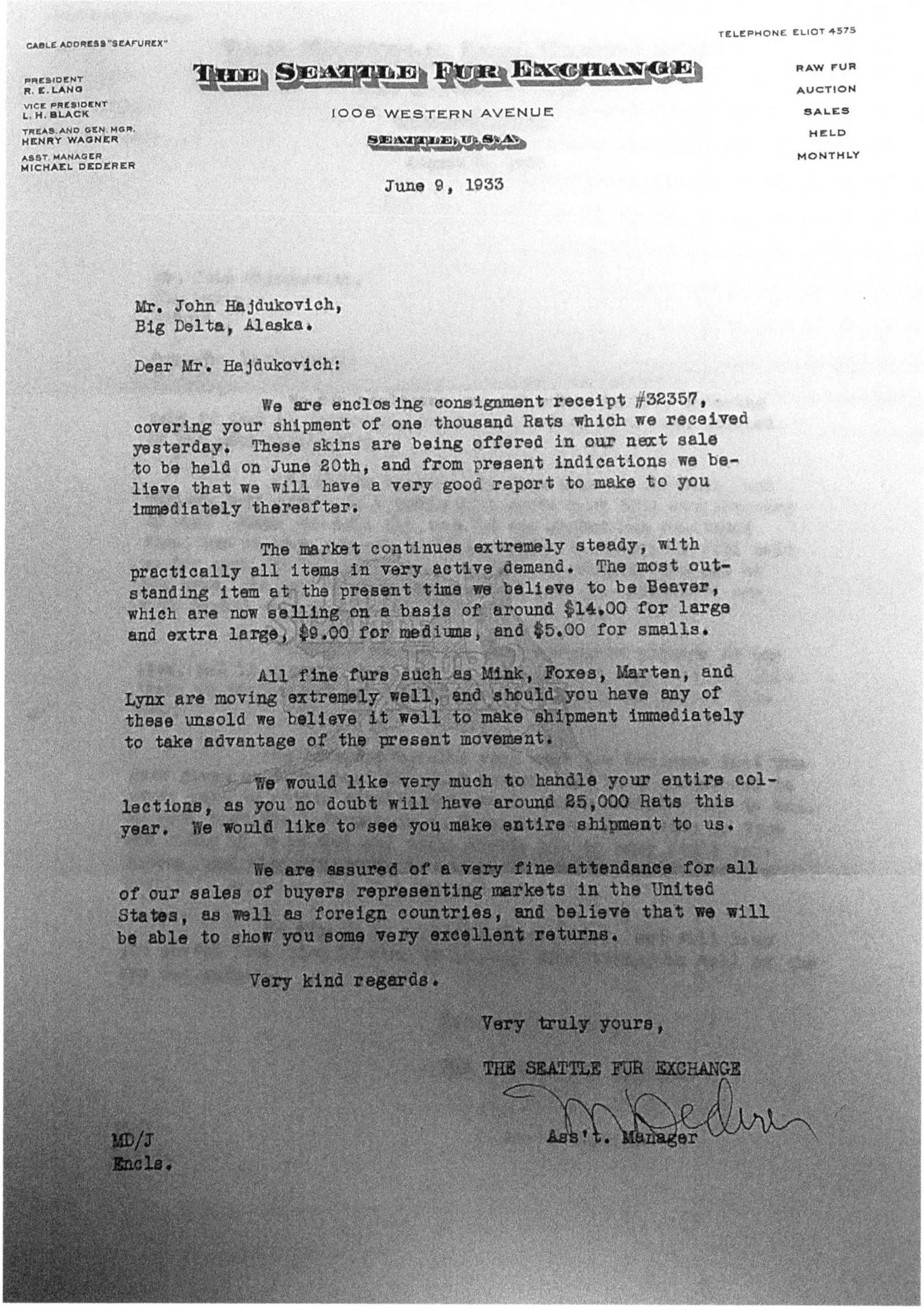

TELEPHONE ELIOT 4575

PRESIDENT
R. E. LANG

VICE PRESIDENT
L. H. BLACK

TREAS. AND GEN. MGR.
HENRY WAGNER

ASST. MANAGER
MICHAEL DEDERER

THE SEATTLE FUR EXCHANGE

1008 WESTERN AVENUE

SEATTLE, U. S. A.

RAW FUR

AUCTION

SALES

HELD

MONTHLY

June 9, 1933

Mr. John Hajdukovich,
Big Delta, Alaska.

Dear Mr. Hajdukovich:

We are enclosing consignment receipt #32357, covering your shipment of one thousand Rats which we received yesterday. These skins are being offered in our next sale to be held on June 20th, and from present indications we believe that we will have a very good report to make to you immediately thereafter.

The market continues extremely steady, with practically all items in very active demand. The most outstanding item at the present time we believe to be Beaver, which are now selling on a basis of around $14.00 for large and extra large, $9.00 for mediums, and $5.00 for smalls.

All fine furs such as Mink, Foxes, Marten, and Lynx are moving extremely well, and should you have any of these unsold we believe it well to make shipment immediately to take advantage of the present movement.

We would like very much to handle your entire collections, as you no doubt will have around 25,000 Rats this year. We would like to see you make entire shipment to us.

We are assured of a very fine attendance for all of our sales of buyers representing markets in the United States, as well as foreign countries, and believe that we will be able to show you some very excellent returns.

Very kind regards.

Very truly yours,

THE SEATTLE FUR EXCHANGE

Ass't. Manager

MD/J
Encls.

Figure 8.13. Letter from Seattle Fur Exchange to John Hajdukovich describing the price of fur and acknowledging the receipt of 1,000 rat skins. Source: Hajdukovich collection. Journals and Ledgers, 1922–1948 Accounts Hajdukovich ledgers Box 3 Tanana Crossing 1931–32, 1937, 1929–31, 1932 and 1939. Box 5 Accounts 1927–1930. Alaska and Polar Regions Department, Elmer E. Rasmuson Library, University of Alaska Fairbanks Archives.

Figure 8.14. Franklin Paul, Gaither Paul, and Baily Paul at Billy Creek or Dendeyn Ndiig ("bearberry creek"). Jeany Healy Photo Collection UAF-2000-181-219. Alaska and Polar Regions Department, Elmer E. Rasmuson Library, University of Alaska, Fairbanks.

And Dawson Stampede [time] they had store there, and they walk over to Dawson, buy tobacco. My dad used to talk about Jack McQuesten, made store at Dawson. I grow big, and my brother–step brother Andrew David used to go.

First trader was in 1921. Came from Big Delta, all the way. Was John Hajdukovich. From Yugoslavia. Same fall Herman Kessler come up. I used to work for him. Smart guy. 1924 steam boat come. John H. used to be U.S. Commissioner and later on he was man for Game Commission. He hauled mail Big Delta. Mail once a month. Sometimes two months. He got big bunch of horses—18 horses. Each got sled. They came as far as Tanacross—hauled mail from Eagle to Tanacross by horse. Now every 4 days we get mail.

We work on steamboat. We get two and a half [dollars] a day. Steamboat is [up the Tanana River] till Big Delta. $4 a cord for steamboat. I cut 7 cords, I quit [Titus cut cord wood for the steamboat engine]. (de Laguna and Guédon 1968d)

Captain Northway, who sank his boat and never started a store, was the first trader Titus met. Titus said that before 1914, there were not many white men on the upper Tanana River, but the Chisana gold rush drew them into the region.

There was no store in Tetlin. Few cabins at Tetlin, mostly people lived in tents. These were hand made tents, buy cloth from the traders, Flannigan. In 1924 Flannigan built a store. Use steam boat. Herman Kessler and Hajdukovich came after. Tanana steam boat go to Chisana in 1915.

Titus used to run the boat for Kessler and Hajdukovich.

Cut cord wood at 2.50 a day for Flannigan. In 1928 Flannigan sold out to Hajdukovich. Tried to cut out Flannigan by cutting prices.

The trail to Dawson City start at Midway Lake then over to the Ladue, then over to the Denison, down to the Sixtymile River all the way to Dawson in wintertime.

Riverside [location on the Tanana River] to Ladue, walk halfway down then [take] skin boat to White River down to Yukon and to Dawson, summer trail.

Dawson was a major source of store food before Flannigan. Another trail: Fortymile Road house [at the junction of the Taylor and Alaska Highways] to Denison and then past Mt. Fairplay to Chicken on down to Fortymile. Scotty Creek down to Northway—1202 on the Alaska Highway—go into White River and to Dawson. (de Laguna and Guédon 1968d)

In an interview with the author (Simeone 1980a), Titus talked about trade items, including buttons, beads, and blankets with pearl buttons, his father received from Tutchone and Tlingit. He said the trade took place on the Yukon River above Dawson City, which is where Titus's father met the Chilkat Tlingit and learned about leaf tobacco. Titus said they did not trade much copper because they could get copper from creeks around Tetlin and did not have to trade with Ahtna. Later, he said, "[Dene] made their own shot from lead bars. Pack the bars over from Dawson." At the end of the interview, Titus added, "Go to Tanana [Noochuloghoyet] with canoes" (Simeone 1980a).

OSCAR ISAAC: TANACROSS

Oscar Isaac said the law limited the trapping season to November 1 through March 15, which he did not feel was an inconvenience because March was a good time to trap. In March Oscar traded his fur for flour, rolled oats, baking powder, lard, tea, coffee, macaroni, sugar, dried prunes, dried apples, and raisins. Between March and November, he had no money—only the supplies he got from trading in his furs. When these supplies ran out, the people got along without. (Simeone 1980b).

After his family moved to Tanacross in the late 1920s, Oscar and his father, Walter Isaac, went back to Ketchumstuk, spending several weeks at a time trapping. Oscar would go to Chicken trade his furs. The trader shipped his furs outside, and when the trader was paid, Oscar collected the balance owed him after purchasing all the supplies he needed. Much of what Oscar learned about white culture was learned from the stories he heard while hanging around the stores. Without these stories, Oscar said he wouldn't know anything about white people. One time, while visiting Chicken, he stayed with an Irishman who talked to him about Christianity. The man wanted Oscar to stay and work, but Oscar said the work was too hard and he had only come to Chicken for groceries (Simeone 1987w).

Oscar had to go to Chicken to buy food because it was hard to get an assortment of groceries at the store in Tanacross. His interview reveals two things: by the 1920s, Dene relied on groceries supplied by the traders, and Dene had become familiar with a wide assortment of foods.

> Down here [Tanacross] hard to get anything, not much grocery in store. Most of the time they have rice, flour, sugar, tea and hardly for the dry fruit, not much can fruit when I was kid, very few. Mostly fifty pound, eighty-pound dry fruit in box and they weight it by pound. How much they charge, how much they want to buy weight it by scale. Dry apple, peaches, apricot, pear, raisin, and later on raisin come out with package. I think they had package, but they [Dene] want to buy cheap, and you know those business people want to make money. Now, today I think that way. At Chicken, we can buy canned fruit, #2 1/2 can. Down [Tanacross] here you cannot buy that kind when I was a kid, later on they have it. But store is closed for month, because store keeper has to take care of three villages. Canned foods: Any kind, canned soup, Eagle brand milk, canned fruit, peaches, pears, apricot, always #2 1/2 can. (Simeone 1987f)

BESSIE JOHN: SCOTTY CREEK

Bessie John (Simeone 1987b) said people from Sourdough, Pepper Lake, and other places went to Scottie Creek to wait for the fur buyers, who came in boats from Big Delta and Nenana. The fur traders would not give credit but sold food for cash. Items included canned peaches, crackers, canned corned beef, long bricks of chewing tobacco, beads, .30-30 rifles for $27, and .22 rifles for $7. Traders also came from Dawson to Pepper Lake using horses.

WALTER NORTHWAY: NORTHWAY

Walter recalled:

> Before the Alaska Highway was built store owner, Herman Kessler, hauled his store supplies to Northway by river from Fairbanks. He had his store here from about 1921 until he died in the 1950s. He's buried at Northway cemetery. During the

same time, I worked for other store owners here in Northway: John Hajdukovich & Teddy Lowe [sic]. They also hauled their supplies by river boat from Fairbanks to Northway. And I hauled supplies for them by river boat from Northway Village up the Chisana River to people living along the river all the way up to Scottie Creek. (Northway 1979)

SHERRY DEMIT-BARNES: NORTHWAY

In this narrative recorded by Olga Lovick (Sam, Demit-Barnes, and Northway 2021: 146–150), Northway elder Sherry Demit-Barnes describes how her father, Joe Mark, combined hunting, fishing, and trapping with wage labor to feed his family. In the summer her father worked for Herman Kessler hauling freight from Big Delta to Nabesna. When it started to get cold, they went trapping, hauled wood, and caught whitefish. Sherry said here parents always worked and never sat still.

Ts'ayh eh noodlee shyi' kah heltąy
They brought groceries with a boat

Hanaan' nohtsąy tah neekeey hǫǫłe', dih-nih.
Our village used to be on the other side [of the Nabesna River], I said.

Ishyiit ts'änh <noodlee iin k'eh udzeldįį dänh> įį'eh tah.
The school is there too.

Ndzeldįį dänh, ndzeldįį dänh įį'eh hahugn tah hihnįįdeeł.
The place where we are learning, they went here.

Ay tl'aan shta', Joe Mark, ch'ehłaadn iin doo iin tat'eey hidhagnnüh, Fred Demit, ts'ayh choh ishyiit hada' shyi' and hahugn <<dii hiyeldeel>> telshyeegn.

And then my father, Joe Mark, some of his friends I forget, Fred Demit, they went downriver with a barge for meat and other groceries.

Hermann Kessler ts'ayh choh hǫǫłįį ehtąą.
Hermann Kessler had a barge.

Hada' Delta, Delta nahįltąyh.
They made trips downstream to Delta.

Ishyiit ts'änh tah hadugn Herman Kessler dii ay telshyeegn <<noodlee iin hii-yeldeel>> ishyiit ts'änh tah hiyuukeet nts'ą́ ishyiit tah ts'ayh choh shyiit hadǫǫ įį'eh natetkeek.
From there they bought groceries, white man's food from Hermann Kessler and then they returned from downstream with the barge.
<<Chief John Healy's Cabin.>>

Tanacross niihetdek ishyiit ishyiit chih hach'ihiłeek ay tl'aan hanegn' Tetlin nts'ą́.
They would make a stop in Tanacross there and would take [the groceries] out and then [go] upland to Tetlin.
Tanana River was their route.

<Tth'itu' Niign> ishyiit ts'änh hanegn' <Teedląy niign> hiiyehniik.
From the Tanana River, up what they always call Tetlin Creek.

Tetlin ne', Tetlin Teedląy nįįłąy huhnegn' tah tthiihikeek tl'aan ishyiit chih.
Tetlin upstream, where Tetlin "Current flows" is flowing, they would go out upland there by boat.

Ahuugn dii hiiyuukeedn Delta Junction ts'änh nahiiyalshyeel ishyiit chih hahiiy-iłeek.
Whatever they bought from Delta Junction they would bring back there and they would take it out there.

Ay tl'aan <Teedląy> ts'änh jah duhdǫǫ
    Northway nahetdek.
And then from there from downstream
    they would return to Northway.

Hįhdląą ts'ą̈' t'eey hahiiyiłeek.
Many of them take [the cargo] off the boat.

Doo iin, doo iin yaa etnah nts'ą̈' t'eey
    hits'ishniign hidhagnnüh <<ihtsuul
    eh>>.
I don't know who worked for him, I forget,
    <I was too small>.

Shta' hǫǫ' dį::', shta' hǫǫ' dį::', shiin nahot-
    łeek ts'ą̈' t'eey hǫǫ' dįįk.
My father would do that and do that, all
    summer he would keep doing that.

<<Hu'eh natehk'üüdn eh>> tänh įį'eh tah,
    tuu niign, mänh įį'eh tah ishyiit tah ch'a
    t'axoh hihdeltth'iik nts'ą̈'.
When it got cold for them and there was
    ice on the rivers and in lakes from there,
    then finally they would stay at home.

Eeł hidlaagn xah staahetdek.
They would go out to set traps.

Tsät įį'eh tah t'eey nihdiłeek.
They would also go for wood.

Ay tl'aan hane' Scottie Creek.
And then upriver to Scottie Creek.

Łįį eh <xał eh> shyiit hune' łuugn kah heltąy
    <<hihteedeeł>>.
With dogs they went in sleds upriver for
    whitefish.

Tuu nįįłąy shyiit ts'änh łuugn hahiłeegn.
From where the water is flowing they
    would take out whitefish.

Hǫǫ' neltänh nts'ą̈' t'eey nahiiyelshyeek,
    Scottie Creek ts'änh.

It froze and they would bring it back from
    Scottie Creek.

Hǫǫ' shyįį:: <<ch'a>> hidį'.
They would always do that.

K'at'eey shyah hihdeltth'iign.
They wouldn't stay at home.

Dahniit <<hetnah>> eeł įį'eh tah, tsät įį'eh
    tah, łuugn kah heltąy įį'eh tah, naxach'ih-
    delshyeek įį'eh tah, huugn įį'eh tat'eey
    niihelshyeek <<Scottie Creek ts'änh>>.
They would always work, trapping, wood,
    they'd go for fish, they'd go hunting, and
    they would bring all of that back from
    Scottie Creek.

Diniign <eh> udzih įį'eh tah, gah įį'eh tah
    t'eey ch'a nahtalshyeegn.
Moose and caribou as well as rabbit, they
    would bring back.

<<Shta' ch'ah hǫǫ' dįįgn>>.
My father would always do that.

Nihiinįįdlah xay hutaltsay ttheh: jign,
    tsüüh, hashyuugn nihts'įįł t'eey ch'a
    hahiłeegn, xay tah.
They would put it there before it turned to
    winter: berries, edible roots, down below
    they would take out "muskrat candy," for
    winter.

Christmas time tah nihts'įįł nats'i'iił, hi'ag-
    nnayh.
At Christmas time we would always eat
    muskrat candy, I remember that.

Ndehde' jah dakich'ihtdalshyaał?
When are they going to relax?

Dahniit hitnah t'oot'eey k'at'eey huugn
    dakich'eł'aagn ha'ogn ahda'.
Always working but he never relaxed, out
    there, downstream.

Bertha or stsǫǫ Anna, hutsädn' kol de' tsät kah huxa <niidalshyeek>.
Bertha or my grandma Anna, if their wood was gone they would bring in wood for them.

Ay iin chih naxät doo iin t'eey hutsädn' kol ay xa t'eey tsät <<niidalshyeek>>
Others too, when someone did not have wood he would bring back wood.

Nts'aa' k'at'eey tsaadiil niign t'eey ch'a hįįdįį'.
There is no way we can do what they did.

K'ahdu' du' dakidzelshyah.
Today we kick back.

CONCLUSION

The fur trade was one part of the colonial process by which Dene culture and society was transformed. The process began slowly. Few goods were available, and it was necessary to travel great distances to reach a store. But as the trade expanded, it became entrenched in Dene culture. People spent more time on traplines and became accustomed to a wide variety of goods, including groceries that were used to supplement the larder when wild food was scarce, as Northway elder Sherry Demit-Barnes describes at the end of this chapter. While Dene altered their lives to participate in the trade, people did not simply abandon their old values and institutions. As the anthropologist Steve Strong (1973: 239) points out, trade goods were used to enhance Dene culture and particularly the potlatch. In the process, the rifles, blankets, and beads distributed as gifts became "indigenized," or took on meaning and value that was completely Dene (Simeone 1995).

Dene elders born in the first three decades of the twentieth century spent a good portion of their lives on traplines or working for traders as river pilots, freight handlers, or wood cutters. Everything from firearms to food, clothing, hardware, beads, and even record players could be obtained from traders. By the 1950s, however, trapping declined. Fur prices dropped, and trapping was no longer as lucrative. Dene began to rely seasonal employment, particularly construction work and fighting forest fires, to obtain cash to purchase food at local stores. Today, trapping is one way to supplement a household's income, but it is no longer embedded in Dene culture like it once was.

Photo-montage by Hal Gage.

9 UPPER TANANA DENE AND THE EPISCOPAL CHURCH

Colonization is "often less a directly a coercive conquest than a persuasive attempt to colonize consciousness, to remake people by redefining the taken-for-granted surfaces of their everyday worlds" (Comaroff and Comaroff 1991: 313). Christian missionaries and their families are major actors in colonizing the consciousness of Indigenous peoples (Manville and Maller 2009: 4). When Russia ceded Alaska to the United States in 1867, US government policy toward Native Americans was shifting toward assimilation. As the 1869 annual report of the US Board of Indian Commissioners stated, "The religion of our blessed Savior is believed to be the most effective agent for the civilization of any people" (Purcha 1975: 133–134). During a relatively short period of fifteen years, beginning in 1880, Alaska was divided into spheres of influence for nine religious denominations, including the Episcopal Church, which assumed jurisdiction over the Tanana River.

Upper Tanana Dene may have first encountered Christian missionaries when visiting American trading posts on the Upper Yukon River in the 1880s. Lieutenant Allen reported young men from Last Tetlin had learned the letters of the alphabet from the Canadian Anglican missionary V. C. Sims at Fort Reliance in 1883 or 1884 (Allen 1887: 75). The first Episcopal missionary to travel up the Tanana River was the Reverend Jules Prevost. On December 15, 1892, Prevost left St. James Mission Nulukayet (i.e., Tanana) and traveled 370 miles up the Tanana River with a dog team. He came across eight winter camps and over

Figure 9.1. The Reverend Vincent Sims preaching at Fort Reliance, August 18, 1883. Sims was one of the first missionaries the upper Tanana Dene encountered. P277-017-021. Alaska State Library Wickersham State Historic Sites Photo Collection.

360 Dene. He reported baptizing 346 people: 96 men, 95 women, and 155 children under the age of eighteen. From the Tanana River, Prevost crossed the mountains to the town of Fortymile, arriving there on January 17, 1893. There he met the Anglican Bishop William Bompas, who had been near the headwaters of the Tanana and baptized twenty-six Dene[1] (Prevost 1893).

Two years after Prevost visited Fortymile, Peter Trimble Rowe was elected Bishop of Alaska. Bishop Rowe set about establishing missions along the Tanana River, first at

---

1   It is likely Bompas baptized the old Chief Isaac, David Paul, and other upper Tanana Dene.

Figure 9.2. Martha, Polly, Follet, and Sarah, at Nabesna, circa 1930. William E. Simeone photo collection. Follet Isaac was from Ketchumstuk. He lost his first wife to tuberculosis and later married Polly and moved to Nabesna. Follet was a well-known doctor or shaman who combined traditional healing with Christian beliefs. He was interviewed by Robert McKennan (1959: 151).

Figure 9.3. The Reverend David Paul, in front, walking to Tanacross with the Reverend Frederick Drane, 1918. Jeany Haly Collection UAF 2000-181-227

values and save them from unscrupulous white people who had invaded Alaska during the 1888 gold rush. Bishop Rowe believed the only way to do this was to isolate Native people, urge them to abandon their hunting way of life, settle down, live in log cabins, and grow vegetables. On the other hand, the Archdeacon of the Episcopal Church in Alaska, Hudson Stuck, believed that removing Native people from the land would destroy them and make them paupers (Stuck [1914] 1988: 288–289).

Nenana in 1907, then Chena in 1908, Salchaket in 1909, and Tanana Crossing in 1912. Episcopal missionaries had limited influence throughout the region; their greatest effect was on the people of Mansfield and Ketchumstuk, since St. Timothy's Mission at Tanana Crossing was in their territory. As a result, the church has special meaning for the people of Tanacross. They say it was their elders who requested the Church establish the mission, and one of the elders, the Reverend David Paul, became the first Dene deacon in Alaska. Upper Tanana Dene have integrated Christianity into their culture and history, and today most would call themselves Christian.

In addition to converting Dene to Christianity, the Church believed its role was to instill Native people with strong white middle-class

ST. TIMOTHY'S MISSION TANANA CROSSING

Tats'áltey ("trail crosses water"), or Tanana Crossing, was located where the trail from Mentasta Lake crossed the Tanana River. In his report, Lieutenant Allen (1887: 79) says the headman Ketl'aad Tá' had a series of caches at the crossing. On August 24, 1902, the two ends of the Washington–Alaska Military Cable and Telegraph System (WAMCATS), connecting the tidewater port of Valdez with Eagle on the Yukon River, were joined at the Tanana Crossing.

The first buildings were a telegraph station and trading post. In 1910, the US government abandoned the telegraph line and station, selling the buildings to Bishop Rowe, who

Figure 9.4. Original caption: "A View of the Mail Carriers cabin and warehouse, where he sold and traded meager supplies to the Indians for Meat & Fish, which in summer were many. The Tanana is slightly shown. Hoepple was at this station early in 1905, when the first Special Steamer ever to go this far on the Tanana River—" [Written on reverse] "Store-Roadhouse, Tanana river (ice covered) at Crossing Tel. Line Tanana Crossing Alaska." Hoepple Collection UAF-1986-0188-0002. Alaska and Polar Regions Department, Elmer E. Rasmuson Library, University of Alaska, Fairbanks.

Figure 9.5. Original caption: "I was Operator in Charge at this Place, 'Tanana Crossing' on the upper Tanana River, year early 1905, after that was Opr In charge at Eagle Alaska, 1906 I am standing center, with A rifle. Two on left are Siwash Indians from Lake — Mansfield, 6 miles distant from the Tanana River I built part of this cabin." Hoepple Collection UAF-1986-0188-0005. Alaska and Polar Regions Department, Elmer E. Rasmuson Library, University of Alaska, Fairbanks.

purchased them using money donated by St. Timothy's Episcopal Church in Catonsville, Maryland. The first missionaries arrived in 1912, and the mission stayed open until 1927. It closed temporarily for lack of funds, but missionaries returned in 1931 and opened a post office. Several years later, the Bureau of Indian Affairs opened a school, and a district nurse was stationed at the mission.

St. Timothy's Mission at Tanana Crossing was the last Episcopal mission established on the Tanana River, and for many years it was the only mission on the upper Tanana River. The "Crossing," as it was often called, was considered strategically located due to its proximity to all the upper Tanana villages. One missionary later described the location as "the hub of a wheel and the Indian villages of Mansfield, Tetlin, Last Tetlin, Nabesna, Ketchumstock [sic], and Mentasta form the spokes" (McConnell 1920: 73). One of Bishop Rowe's objectives was to assemble all upper Tanana Dene into a single settlement so they could be easily controlled, preached to, educated, and protected from

corrupt white people. Because of their relative isolation, Bishop Rowe thought upper Tanana Dene were better off physically than most Native people because "they have not been hurt by the evil white element," and game and fur were plentiful. A mission at Tanana Crossing, he wrote, would put the Church "in possession and control of the whole Tanana River" (Rowe 1910–1911: 67–69).

Both written and oral histories emphasize Chief Isaac's role in the decision to establish the mission. According to the missionary E. A. McIntosh, Chief Isaac had been to Eagle and seen the Episcopal Church and mission and had heard about the Episcopal missions at Fort Yukon and Salchaket. In the fall of 1909, Chief Isaac went to Fairbanks to petition the church to send a missionary to his people. In 1910, Archdeacon Stuck was sent to the upper Tanana to assess the situation. In his book *Ten Thousand Miles with a Dog Sled*, Archdeacon Stuck wrote that Chief Isaac requested a mission be built at Mansfield or Tanana Crossing since "farther down river was not so good for their hunting and fishing" (Stuck [1914] 1988: 262). Stuck's account is consistent with oral history. Tanacross elder Silas Solomon (1984a) said:

> 1912 was when [Arch]Deacon Hudson Stuck and Bishop Rowe came through. They talk to Chief Isaac, ask him "can we lead a mission here?" Chief Isaac, innocent man, no fighting, no cussing, just friendly, he feed a lot of people. He feed a lot of the people, that's why he became chief. In the early days. He said yeah, they'd like to have mission here.

Gaither Paul also knew about Chief Isaac's involvement in establishing a mission. Gaither emphasized that Chief Isaac and Archdeacon Stuck were considered equals. In the winter of 1910, the archdeacon caught up with Chief Isaac at Paul's Cabin, the camp of Old Paul, a prominent elder and leader who was Gaither Paul's grandfather. According to Gaither, Chief Isaac consulted Old Paul, saying, "Some important man wants to meet with me, but I don't think I am important enough." Old Paul told Chief Isaac not to think that way: "You are a leader, and you can talk to Hudson Stuck man to man" (Simeone 1987c).

Margaret Graves and Celia Wright were the first missionaries. Graves had been stationed at Anvik while Wright, the sister of Arthur Wright, had spent most of her life at Nenana. Because of Wright's outdoor skills and ability to speak the Dene language, she was considered essential to the mission's success. In the late summer of 1912, the two started their trip up the Tanana River on the steamboat *Tana*, but within 100 miles of their destination were forced to return to Fairbanks because of low water. Eventually they made their way to McCarty, near present-day Delta Junction, where another missionary, the Reverend Charles Betticher, and four Dene men joined them. The four men—John Paul, Sam Charlie, John Sam, and Joe Joseph—pushed and pulled the missionaries and their boats the remaining 100 miles to the crossing. The party left McCarty

Figure 9.6. Missionaries in boat on Chena River, headed to St. Timothy's Mission, Tanana Crossing, summer of 1912. Photo by C. Betticher, courtesy Episcopal Church Archives, Austin, Texas.

Figure 9.7. Lining the boat up the Tanana, summer of 1912. Photo by C. Betticher, courtesy Episcopal Church Archives, Austin, Texas.

on September 8 and arrived at Tanana Crossing on September 26 (Betticher 1913: 75–77).

Graves wrote that tuberculosis was rampant; in the first several months after she arrived, there had been nine births and five deaths. Like most missionaries, Graves advocated making planting gardens and introducing vegetables instead of a diet of straight meat and fish, which the missionaries thought primitive. She also thought the "Indians extravagant" and with tastes far beyond their ability to satisfy with money earned from trapping. "Most of

Figure 9.8. Reloading the boat after it capsized going up the Tanana River to establish St. Timothy's Mission at Tanana Crossing, summer 1912. Photo courtesy Episcopal Church Archives, Austin, Texas.

Figure 9.9. The mission house at St. Timothy's Mission, Tanana Crossing, 1912. Celia Wright and Margaret Graves standing in front of the mission house. Photo courtesy Episcopal Church Archives, Austin, Texas.

the Indians," Graves wrote, "are industrious; were they less wasteful and could be made to abolish the potlatch system among themselves, I believe there could be very little real need" (Graves 1913: 73–74). Abolishing the potlatch became the missionaries' primary goal.

That first year, Graves held church services and started teaching school. In the spring, several families from Mansfield built cabins and planted a community garden. Graves also initiated an election for chief. Old Chief Isaac had died at Mansfield the year before the missionaries arrived, so Graves convinced the people to hold an election. Walter Isaac, Chief Isaac's son, was elected chief (McIntosh 1941: 3–12).

Silas Solomon remembered Graves as the "woman preacher, [a] single woman who wasn't married" and recalls her providing some rudimentary schooling.

> No church house. Old station. Tanana Crossing station. Signal Corps station. Had a big building over there. That was the biggest building anyway. For potlatch house—just a tent. The building has one story up, one story high. Downstairs, in wintertime, they had church in there, first floor, ground [floor]. People stay in Mansfield.

Figure 9.10. Because of her country skills and knowledge of the Dene language, Celia Wright was considered essential to the mission's success. John Paul, Sam Charlie, John Sam, and Joe Joseph stand in between Wright and the Reverend Charles Betticher 1912. Photo courtesy Episcopal Church Archives, Austin, Texas.

> They [Native people] got no place over there [in Tanacross] so they walk [from] Mansfield to church every Sunday. Walk. Go to church. Walk back same night. [That was] telegraph station. That must be built 1903. About 40 feet long. Kitchen [in] back there, for the soldiers, I guess, where they stay, bunk, you know. Just right back of the church [at Old Tanacross] that's where we had school, mission school. No government school. Preacher started teaching. Was a school teacher, too. Go there every summer. A month or two. Those other guys

Figure 9.11. "Drilling for Turnips, we take turns being the horse." The missionaries insisted Dene plant gardens because they considered an all-meat diet to be unhealthy and primitive. Photo by F. B. Drane, courtesy Episcopal Church Archives, Austin, Texas.

Figure 9.12. David Paul and Joe Joseph taking a wood raft down the Tanana River, 1937–1938. This wood was used by the village and the mission. Photo by Lucille Wright. William E. Simeone photo collection.

Figure 9.13. Confirmation class, St. Timothy's Mission, 1915. Back row (left to right): David Paul, Jessie Joe, Adina Jonathan, Annie Denny, Silas Thomas, Peter Charles, John Jonathan, Titus Paul, and Maggie Isaac. Photo by F. B. Drane, courtesy Episcopal Church Archives, Austin, Texas.

Figure 9.14. Mansfield people gathered at the mission 1915. Left to right: Jessie Joe, Frank Jonathan, Jennie Jonathan, Laura and David Paul and daughter Nancy, Charlotte Chorettees, Silas Henry, and Annie Moses. Photo by F. B. Drane, courtesy Episcopal Church Archives, Austin, Texas.

there they go to school all summer. Learn Ten Commandments, apostles, gospel. Not much school book. Book One, Two, that's all. That's the highest book we got. I went through that fast. (Andrews 1980)

At the time, Mansfield was the nearest village to St. Timothy's, and people had to walk seven miles one way to attend church. The

Reverend David Paul recalled making that walk and the planting of the community garden.

We always walk seven miles to church until we all build home here at Tanacross. The missionaries stay with us all winter and next spring it was time to plant things. The missionaries want to show us how to plant vegetables. We want to break up the ground

Figure 9.15. The Jonathan family, 1915. From left to right: John Jonathan in decorated coat; Jennie holding baby, unnamed girl; Little Frank Jonathan; and Timothy Jonathan. In the background are Mary Paul, Annie Denny, and Peter Charles, 1915. Photo by F. B. Drane, courtesy Episcopal Church Archives, Austin, Texas.

Figure 9.16. Ellen Follet, 1919. Photo by F. B. Drane, courtesy Episcopal Church Archives, Austin, Texas.

and we had some plow and we got no horses to pull plow. So we hitch up eleven men like double harness and they pull plow and we plant turnips, potatoes, and carrots in community garden. Since then we always make gardens here at Tanacross. (Paul 1957a: 8)

In 1980, Elizabeth Andrews (1980) interviewed Annie and Tom Denney and Julius Paul about the early history of Tanacross. Annie Denny told Andrews:

They [Mansfield people] come down all the time. Most of the time, they live down here and move back. Like that [back and forth]. Even at Mansfield, church morning, they come down. Before church. They all come down here. And they stay church. In the evening they stay church and they go back Mansfield. Sometimes they don't stay too long. Sometimes Christmas and New Year's all that stuff, they stay here. So that's the only time they really down here.

They got no cabin. Some they got tent, before. Before, they got tent up. When I was a little girl, they put tent up. Not hard for them. They just come down, put tent up.

ELIZABETH: The first houses were built?

ANNIE: I know Harry Luke got house. I don't know which one they built first. Maybe Big Albert's house, I guess. Or Harry Luke. And that Big Frank. And the other one behind Albert's house and my house.

ELIZABETH: When did your parents move from Mansfield to Old Tanacross? To stay year-round? Do you know about how old you were?

ANNIE: I was good enough girl. Maybe around 18 years. They moved back down here. But they don't stay all the time. They moved back all the time [back and forth between Tanacross and Mansfield]. Summertime, they cut fish.

ELIZABETH: Do you know who worked on building that church?

TOM: The whole village. All pitched in and helped.

ANNIE: Yah. But that old house, they using before that. Old store. They used that one.

ELIZABETH: Who's store was that?

TOM: Stots. Was one of the names.

ANNIE: Mission used. They used for store, too, out here. They used that one for store, and

Figure 9.17. Mansfield/Ketchumstuk people, 1913. Group photo taken at the departure of Margaret Graves, the first mission-ary assigned to St. Timothy's Mission, and the arrival of Mable Pick (far right in black with a cross and standing to the left of Graves). Photo by C. Betticher, courtesy Episcopal Church Archives, Austin, Texas.

mission used it for church. And Sunday school and knit, teaching, all that. They [missionaries] lived upstairs. I remember when I was a kid. And little bit, long time. Then they built one old one down that way. Where that school building [is now], they built one there. But everybody, I guess. Macintosh [E. A. McIntosh served as mis-sionary], I think he was up there that time. Just about everybody working there. Lots of people work there. After Macintosh go away and Arthur Wright [another mission-ary] come up and lived there. And up that way he built some kind of church. They have church there. And then long time, house getting old. And new one over there, that's the last one they built. But one beside burned down too. Burned down and then built another one. That's the one everybody in the village built a raft down [to get logs]. That church getting old, so they start build-ing that one [the one that's still there]

JULIUS: The way I heard it, 1912, when the mission starting here, coming up. That's when they start. How they start village over there. Used to got store, some white people store, other side, each store, like this. I don't know how big, but good size and got one story high. And mission bought this one, this one old time trad-ing post [that] used to be in village, and mission bought this one. This white man and this white guy he left the country. He just sold the place off and just took off and went outside, I guess. That's how mission got started over there. Then from then on they stay here quite awhile then they start making mission house. When I was a kid I see that house. When I was around 15 or something, 16. I see that house; I used to play around there all the time. Somebody living there that time, in that house. Big house. He got another back there two bedroom, or kitchen I guess. After this log house. One story, this big one. Used to be store, trading post. Then Army, what you call that telegraph station people, used to have station over there right in that village.

Figure 9.18. Salina Paul and Laura Paul, 1913. Photo by C. Betticher, courtesy Episcopal Church Archives, Austin, Texas.

Figure 9.19. Bridge over the Little Tanana, built to facilitate access to the mission at Tanana Crossing. Philips Collection UAF-185-72-125. Alaska and Polar Regions Department, Elmer E. Rasmuson Library, University of Alaska, Fairbanks.

Figure 9.20. Celia Wright at Tanana Crossing, circa 1919. Philips Collection UAF-1985.72.132. Alaska and Polar Regions Department, Elmer E. Rasmuson Library, University of Alaska, Fairbanks.

ELIZABETH: Before the mission?

JULIUS: Before mission. Got house behind there. So I don't know when telegraph come through with telegraph line here. When them guys left I don't see any Army there. I'm too small I guess when they left. And so I see all the empty house over in there when I was a kid. Because somebody use it. Mailman used to be from here to Eagle, mailman come through here stay there all the time. That's how we know when everything still there when I was a kid. I don't see them, Army, that telegraph station people. I don't see them, I see the place. I'm too young I guess, that time, when they come through here.

ELIZABETH: When did your family move to Old Tanacross?

JULIUS: Well really, 1920 or 1925, something like that. When you had school over there 1930, 1932 something like that.

Figure 9.21. Caption on back of photo: "Constructing the new church at Tanacross located between the old church and village." Photo by Lucille Wright, William E. Simeone photo collection.

Figure 9.22. Mr. and Mrs. Arthur Wright. From 1922 to 1927 the couple was posted to the mission at Tanana Crossing, serving as missionary. The Reverend Wright was instrumental in forming a village council, with an elected chief, and he tried to curtail Dene participation in the potlatch. UAF-1991-0046-00802. Alaska and Polar Regions Department, Elmer E. Rasmuson Library, University of Alaska, Fairbanks.

In 1914, Graves went on furlough and was replaced by Deaconess Mabel Pick. Almost the entire communities of Mansfield and Ketchumstuk walked down to the mission to see Graves off. The Reverend Charles Betticher, who had accompanied Pick, took a group picture as well as individual portraits. Pick's tenure

was marked by construction of a bridge over the Little Tanana so that people could travel more easily between Mansfield and the mission.

In December 1915, Pick went on furlough, and E. A. McIntosh and his wife, Veta, took her place. At the same time, Celia Wright left St. Timothy's. McIntosh employed local people to build a twenty-six-foot-by-fifty-six-foot mission house, and his wife started a day school attended by young people, including David Paul. The McIntoshes left in 1918 and were replaced by the Reverend David McConnell, who stayed only a short time; Arthur and Myrtle Wright replaced him.

Arthur Wright (1890–1948), the son of miner Henry Wright and his Dene wife Annie (née Glass), was born at Old Station, Alaska, on the Yukon River. Arthur was raised bilingual in Dene and English. In his late teens and early twenties, he traveled through Interior Alaska with Archdeacon Hudson Stuck as his attendant and interpreter, then studied agriculture and carpentry at schools outside Alaska. On his return to Alaska in 1914, he was put in charge of agriculture at St. Mark's Mission in Nenana, and in 1922 he was ordained a deacon in the Episcopal Church. That same year he married Myrtle Rose, a missionary nurse, and the couple was posted to the mission at Tanana Crossing from 1922 to 1927 (Wright 1977: 53–56). Arthur Wright was involved in forming a village council, with an elected chief.

One of the Church's goals was to undermine the authority and power of the shamans, who were considered part of the "old order" and not only evil but also competitors for the people's hearts and minds. In 1970s anthropologist Mertie Baggen (n.d.b) interviewed Myrtle Wright about her experiences as a missionary at St. Timothy's, including how she came to realize the shamans were not evil.

Myrtle recalled driving down the Richardson Highway to Big Delta, and John Hajdukovich took them to the mission in his gas boat. In some places, the Tanana River has a strong current, so it was necessary to line the boats using a rope from shore to pull the boats upstream. It was customary to camp at night and travel during the day. Progress was slow; it took half a day to gain a mile when the current was swift. Myrtle thought it took about ten days to make the trip between Big Delta and Tanana Crossing. Most of the families who lived at the mission in 1922 had come from Mansfield. People from Nabesna and Tetlin came occasionally but did not settle.

One of Myrtle favorite stories had to do with Little Charley, who translated for Claude Denny, Tom Denny's brother, during church services. Claude would speak a few sentences and then Little Charlie would translate into the Native language:

Denny went on with a few more lines and Little Charley told the people in Athabascan "He is saying the same thing over again." After more of the service in English Little Charlie advised the people "Well he's just telling us the same thing he said in the first place."

Myrtle said she often wondered what the interpreter was really saying.

Myrtle concluded that:

the medicine making wasn't near as sinister or ominous a procedure as the missionaries presumed it was. They got together simply to find out whether the hunting was going to be good the next day and to enjoy the social gathering with singing. There were few of the dark deed so feared by the missionaries.

One of the medicine men, a man named Old John, told Arthur Wright that Myrtle, his wife, was a medicine woman whom he met when his spirit traveled around the world at night. In 1927, a flu epidemic ravaged the village. Myrtle said several of the old people died and so did a couple of the medicine men. The Wrights and the traders cared for the sick, going house to house with food and making sure that the stoves kept going. This, he said, proved Mrs. Wright's medicine was strong and that she was a better medicine woman than the Indian medicine men.

The longer Myrtle lived at Tanana Crossing, the more aware she became of an extra-sensory perception that was the stock in trade of the medicine men. Through dreams, Myrtle said she was able to predict the arrival of strangers. According to Baggen (n.d.b):

Dreams were vital part of the medicine man's function and in spite of her missionary training, Mrs. Wright realized eventually that the medicine man's sensitivity, extra-sensory perception, or whatever one chooses to call it, was not a frightening evil magic, but an attempt to correlate important events with signs, concrete or otherwise.

Missionaries were so intent on battling the devil that they failed to understand the basis of an animistic religion. They are totally unaware of the concept, in fact, and feel that their work is to impress Christianity upon the Indians, any other kind of religion being wrong and the work of the devil.

While the missionaries had some success with "stamping out" the traditional doctors and seers at Tanana Crossing, their influence did not extend into other parts of the upper Tanana River. In the winter of 1929, the anthropologist Robert McKennan attended several traditional curing ceremonies on the upper Nabesna River at the village of Cross Creek, which he described in detail (McKennan 1959: 152).

The Wrights left in 1927, and the mission closed due to lack of funds until Mr. McIntosh returned in 1931. While the mission was closed, Tanacross people continued to hold services under David Paul's direction. When the mission reopened, Mr. McIntosh established a post office and petitioned the postal service to have the village name changed to Tanacross to avoid confusion with Tanana. Mrs. McIntosh taught school for several years, and then a Bureau of Indian Affairs teacher and a nurse settled in the village. While St. Timothy's was the primary focus of the Church, Mr. McIntosh traveled throughout the region, holding services in other communities, including Northway.

McIntosh thought church attendance was satisfactory but set his hopes on the young, who had broken away from the old ways (McIntosh 1941: 11). McIntosh reflected on the role of the mission:

> Indians could not be left alone (as some had suggested). He stood squarely in the path of the white man's irresistible onward march. It was his lot to be overwhelmed by a new economic and social order. It was the business of the Church to come to his help with a new spiritual order that would give meaning to the tremendous changes that were taking place. (McIntosh 1941: 12)

Earl J. Beck, superintendent of education for the central district of Alaska, offered a different view of the situation (Beck 1930: 21–24). In the winter of 1929, Beck traveled with John Hajdukovich throughout the upper Tanana region and visited Tanana Crossing. The mission

Figure 9.23. Northway church service, circa 1931. Photo by E. A. McIntosh, William E. Simeone photo collection.

was closed, and Beck reported there were Dene who wanted it to reopen and those who did not. According to Beck, Dene who opposed reopening complained the education offered by the mission was poor and they "wanted their children to learn to read and write in preference to learning so much religion as religion was not such an important thing with them as they had a good one of their own before the white men came to the country." Beck recommended a government school be established either at Tanana Crossing or Mansfield but only if the Church withdrew from the community. Beck compared Dene living in Tanacross with those from Tetlin. He believed Tetlin people were better off because they had a government school and no missionary. Beck also believed the Tetlin people were better off because of John Hajdukovich's efforts.

In the 1950s, the Reverend Robert Greene became priest-in-charge at St. Timothy's. Reverend Greene reflected on the changes that had occurred since the first years of the mission. The "old ways," known mostly to the elders, were giving way to an entirely different way of life in which teenagers drove automobiles and appeared on TV shows. By providing a "consistent ministry," Greene wrote, the Church "has

Figure 9.24. Serving the church: David Paul (center), Jacob Isaac (left), and Frank Luke, 1960s. Jeany Healy Collection UAF-2000-181-252. Alaska and Polar Regions Department, Elmer E. Rasmuson Library, University of Alaska, Fairbanks.

Figure 9.25. Frank Luke and David Paul. Jeany Healy collection UAF-2000-181-151. Alaska and Polar Regions Department, Elmer E. Rasmuson Library, University of Alaska, Fairbanks.

been in a position to accompany the people in this period of transition." One mark of progress, according to Reverend Greene, was that in 1957, David Paul was ordained as the first Dene deacon in Alaska. St. Timothy's had four lay readers (Logan Luke, John Paul Luke, Eldred Paul, and Frank Luke), a girls' choir, and seven acolytes (Greene 1957: 2–4).

Reverend Greene and the Church pinned their hopes on David Paul, who had consistently worked for the missionaries from the beginning. In an article for the *Alaskan Churchman*, Reverend Paul wrote about his conversion to Christianity. As a young man he spent time with Archdeacon Drane, whom he admired because the Archdeacon carried his own .30-30 rifle; packed his own lunch, sleeping bag, and hand ax; and carried his Bible "right in his hand when he coming to the village." He also ate the same food as Indians. When Myrtle and Arthur Wright left Tanacross in 1927 and left Reverend Paul in charge, he began to hold service by himself. David writes he only knew the Lord's Prayer, Apostle's Creed, and General Confession, so he studied the prayer book. Reverend Paul goes on to explain his final commitment to the Church:

Then I got some kind of sick and I not well man for a few years. So trader in the village and I go to his store. Man told me "you look sick and you know what get you well?" I say I didn't. He tell me to get bottle of whiskey and you get well. And right there I think I see two men, one man right along sides the trader. And I begin to think one say I should take whiskey and other one say no good. Right there I make my mind work right. Right there I fight myself and I don't know what to do. When I think about whiskey something go in my heart and tell me go home and don't listen to this stuff. And when I went home nobody home and I kneel right down at the table and talk with the Lord just like some man I could see. And I tell the Lord what shall I do to get well. Should I buy whiskey to get well? Just tell me. By that time I feel something go into my head to say I shouldn't take the whiskey but I should take the Lord. And I get better like before and I trap like before and my wife and I get enough fur to buy groceries for the winter. (Paul 1957a: 9)

MISSIONARIES AND THE POTLATCH

From the beginning, the Dene religion and the potlatch were points of friction between the Church and the people. Many Dene maintain their ancestors knew about God long before the missionaries arrived but accepted the missionaries' Christianity because the Church was the only non-Native institution offering a way forward in the new social and economic order imposed after the gold rush of 1898. At the same time, Dene resisted many changes sought by the Church either openly, as in continuing to hold potlatches, or secretly, by taking their religious practices underground.

From the missionaries' point of view, Dene religious beliefs were at best superstition and at worst devil worship. In the Dene religion, if a person was conscientious and followed the rules, they would be able to kill many animals and feed their families. From this perspective, Dene could assume that if people prayed to God, then God should provide when the people were starving. Missionaries, on the other hand, thought it unseemly that Dene should pray for personal gain, even if they were starving. Likewise, most missionaries thought the potlatch went against the values of thrift and personal wealth and stood in the way of Dene becoming "respectable" and "self-supporting." Yet while condemning the ceremony, some missionaries admired the sacrifice people made to hold a potlatch. McIntosh wrote that if "Christian people in general would sacrifice for the cause of Christ as these people do in a Potlatch to their dead there would be no lack of funds for His work" (McIntosh 1918: 49).

Almost as soon as non-Natives arrived in the Tanana Valley, they attempted to eradicate the potlatch. As early as the 1890s, Reverend Prevost hoped Native people would give up the ceremony because they did not believe in it anymore. The Reverend Arthur Wright strongly disapproved of the potlatch, viewing it as a waste of time and resources and because it interfered with the trapping season. He thought the potlatch was "demoralizing to the whole community" because the host gives away everything he owns, "becomes a burden to the community," and is forced to rely on his neighbors and kin to support him after the ceremony is over. But he saw how deeply embedded the potlatch was in Dene culture, writing, "There is no civil or federal authority that can be enforced to regulate this system, and it is so strongly embedded in the nature of these natives that it is hard to handle without government interferences and regulations of some sort." As far as Wright was concerned, "as long as this system is continued what is the chance for any advancement in the way of good homes and a progressive providential community?" (Wright 1926: 18–22).

Wright did attempt to curtail the number of ceremonies by convincing the people of Tanacross to not accept or extend invitations between June 1 and October 1. He was marginally successful, but his success did not hold. In fact, McIntosh (1917) had to agree not to interfere with the potlatch because the Native people had specifically asked him not to. Instead of doing away with the potlatch, the people enhanced it, using their wealth from the fur trade to have more and larger ceremonies.

While the Church wanted to abolish the potlatch, the missionaries seemed fascinated by it and wrote several articles in the *Alaskan Churchman* trying to explain it. In one article, McIntosh (1918) wrote that potlatches varied from a small one for an infant, where the parents made a "little cook" and distributed a blanket cut up for mitten liners, to large ceremonies held for a chief in which all his relatives and friends combine their efforts. Interested in the details of the ceremony, McIntosh described a potlatch held in Tanacross in April 1917 for Chief John of Mentasta, who had died two years earlier. Leading men such as Big Frank, Big

John, and Old Paul gathered the gifts, which McIntosh estimated to have cost $4,000.[2] Runners were sent to invite guests from as far away as Dawson City and Moosehide, Canada. Feasting lasted for ten days or a week (as long as the food lasted). "Every night feasts were followed by singing and dancing—'sorry songs and dance songs.' All of the gifts are distributed. The further the guests came and the more distinguished they were the more they received as much as $175 being given to one man and his wife" (McIntosh 1918: 47–49).

INDIAN WAY, CHRISTIAN WAY, AND WHITE MAN'S WAY

Missionaries brought not only their religion but their middle-class values stressing individual achievement and self-reliance over the communal relations emphasized in Dene culture. To convey these values, missionaries preached to improve people's lives through the gospel and instructed them in "Christian living" and "cleanliness" since "from the concept of the clean healthy body we go to the clean healthy soul" (Drane 1915).

For Dene in the early twentieth century, Christianity was a way to mediate the drastic changes brought first by the gold rush and later by the Alaska Highway. Christianity offered a path away from the destructive habits of drinking and gambling and provided an alternative to the "white man way," viewed as self-centered and stingy. By following the Bible, Dene could get back on the "Indian way." Oscar Isaac said there were three ways: white man way, Indian way, and Christian way.

> White man way had to do with making a good living. In the White man way, you take care of your money, get into business and get rich. In the White man way, you take care of yourself, rely only on yourself and your money to get through life. But White man has no potlatch and Indian has lots of money and didn't use it for potlatch then some Indians might make fun of him. White man don't handle potlatch. With White man way if you behave, don't go to jail you might get back on the Indian way and then you can turn to be Christian. To be a Christian you have to give yourself to God. It depends on which way we want to be. If we are a good person and get help from relatives then we can get into Indian way. Indians are people who don't just rely on themselves for help. They can give and get help from all their relatives, something Whites don't do. Whites rely solely on themselves. (Simeone 1987r)

In the 1960s and 1970s, Dene elders gave speeches at potlatches urging their young people to keep the "Indian way" and to use the teachings of the Bible to avoid the pitfalls of alcohol. Anthropologist François-Marie Guédon recorded this speech at a potlatch in Tetlin:

> You have to learn Indian ways. You speak English; have to speak Indian too. Me I don't go to school much, but I know Indian language. Know your ways. White man got his way. But you got to learn Indian ways. Don't forget.
>
> There are two ways. Indian way, white man ways. Four ways altogether: Hell and heaven, white and Indian. We don't want to be stuck in the middle.
>
> Nobody wants to go to hell! All you remember your Bible, what Bible says. Some houses I feel sorry for them. People drink too much. Don't do it. No good that way. Don't forget your own ways. (Guédon 1974: 230)

---

2   About $87,000 in 2021 dollars.

{ Name of town, mining district, or creek. } Indian Village, Ketchumstuk

DATE OF LOCATING IN ALASKA.

POST-OFFICE ADDRESS AT HOME.

RELATION.

Relationship of each person to the head of the family.

Month. Year.

13th (1910) US Census, Mansfield
"Information secured at Tanana Crossing"
Enumerated February 11

Name	Relation	Date of birth	Age
Isaac, Chief	Head	1849	60
No Name Given	Wife	1879	30
Sam, Chief	Head	1859	50
No Name Given	Wife	1874	30
Albert	Son	1890	19
None Given	Son	1899	10
None Given	Son	1901	8
None Given	Daughter	1905	4
None Given	Son	1909	4m
Old Paul	Head	1871	38
None Given	Wife	1879	30
David	Son	1895	14
Salene	Daughter	1898	11
None Given	Daughter	1907	2
Chicatah	Head	1859	50
Bessie	Wife	1879	30
Jimmie	Son	1897	16
None Given	Daughter	1908	1
Big Albert	Head	1869	40
Minnie	Wife	1874	35
Mack	Son	1894	15
Walter	Son	1896	13
Unclear	Son	1906	3
Isaac, Follet	Head	1889	20
Ellen	Wife	1890	19
Tom	Head	1884	26
Maggie	Wife	1893	16
Harry, Little	Head	1889	20
No Name	Mother	1869	40
No Name	Sister	1895	15
No Name	Sister	1899	10
Charlie	Head	1858	50
Jennie	Wife	1884	25
No Name	M/in Law	1859	50
Uncertain	Son	1904	5
Mark, Big	Head	1871	38
Agnes	Wife	1879	30
Eva	Daughter	1901	8
No Name	son	1906	3
Titus	Head	1881	28
Annie	Wife	1887	22
No Name	Son	1903	6
No Name	Son	1906	3
Pedro	Head	1879	30
Sarah	Wife	1882	27
No Name	Son	1905	23
Cannot Make out	Sis/in law	1889	20
Cannot Make out	Br/in law	1885	24
Alferd	Head	1887	22
No Name	Mother	1861	42
Sarah	Sister	1892	17
Emma	Sister	1896	13
Total 56 people			

13th (1910) US Census Lake Mansfield
Enumerated February 22, 25, 26

Name	Relation	Date of birth	Ag
Charley	Head	1849	6
Jennie (Married 6 years)	Wife	1884	2
Dewey	Son	1904	5
Indian Name (unclear)	M/in Law	1854	5
Peter	Head	1877	3
Shuny (?)	Wife	1886	2
Walter	Son	1906	3
Annie	Daughter	1904	5
Joseph	Son	1905	4
Albert	Son	1894	1
Jennie	Sister	1894	1
Albert Moses	Head	1884	2
Mack	Head	1879	30
	Wife	1882	2
Eva	Daughter	1899	10
Joseph	Son	1905	4
Betsey	Daughter	1909	6
Titus	Head	1880	2
Anna	Wife	1885	2
William	Son	1903?	7
Benny	Son	1904	5
Titus Laura	Daughter	1909	6
Caluch (?)	Head	1867	48
Alferd	Son	1892	1
Sarah	Daughter	1890	1
Emma	Daughter	1895	1
Isaac Chief	Head	1849	60
Edna	Wife	1881	2
Albert Big	Head	1879	3
Minnie	Wife	1888	2
Mike	Son	1895	1
Jumbo	Son	1904	5
Walter	Son	1893	1
Cliigatah (?)	Head	1849	5
Bessie (Married 20 years?)	Wife	1876	3
Jimmie	Son	1891	1
Ella	Daughter	1909	6
Paul	Head	1864	4
Alice (Married 18 years)	Wife	1874	3
Paul		1882	1
Saline	Daughter	1884	1
Follet	Head	1886	2
Ellen (Married 1 year)	Wife	1888	2
Thomas	Head	1879	3
Maggie (Married 8 months)	Wife	1892	1
Gus	Head	1881	28
Agnes (Married 1 year)	Wife	1889	20
John	Son	1909	3m
Hamitt (?)	Head	1854	55
Harry	Son	1889	20
Julia	Daughter	1897	12
Grace	Daughter	1901	8
John Martin	Head	1859	50
Julius Struck	Head	1869	40
Thomas Hogan	Head	1873	36
Frank Britton	Head	1870	39

Photo-montage by Hal Gage.

10 NONDLÊED/NOODLEE

"Those Who Come and Go" (the Americans)

In the thirty-one years between the United States purchase of Alaska in 1867 and the gold rush of 1898, government was absent in interior Alaska, and Dene were beholden to no one. The discovery of gold changed everything. Immediate and sometimes catastrophic changes occurred as thousands of prospectors swarmed across the land, burning forests, killing game, and competing for vital food resources. Long-term changes followed, and Alaska Natives found themselves peripheral to the new money economy and without any legal rights to the land that had sustained them for generations.

Under Article III of the Treaty of Cession, in which Russia transferred ownership of Alaska to the United States, those living in the territory were categorized either as "inhabitants" or "uncivilized tribes." Alaska Native people who had never been under Russian control, which included most Dene living in interior Alaska, were classified as uncivilized. Members of uncivilized tribes were not citizens of the United States and were considered dependent subjects without any legal rights except those granted by the US government. This included the right to own land.

Citizenship, and the right to own land, was tied to White people's conception of a civilized life, which included not moving about but living in one place and disassociating from traditional culture and other Dene (Schneider 2018: 6). The idea that civilization meant living in one place appeared in laws passed by Congress, such as the first Organic Act of 1884, which said, "Indians or other persons in said district [Alaska] shall not be disturbed in the possession of any lands actually in their use or occupation or now claimed by them"—but how or if Native people gained title to that land was left to future legislation by Congress. Following passage of the Act, there was an "unspoken implication . . . that Alaska Natives, unlike other Native Americans, did not have claims of aboriginal title to vast tracts of tribal property [and] . . . Alaska did not constitute Indian country for purposes of the Indian trade laws" (Case 1984: 6).

In 1987, ninety years after the Klondike Stampede, Maggie Isaac talked about the long-term effects of US government intervention. She expressed her strong attachment to the land and said the government was helpful, especially since she had lost so many relatives. But, she said, the government treated Native people like children by sending strangers to tell them what to do. In many ways this was an affront. In traditional society, individuals had authority based on who their relatives were. Only a person of known antecedents, with proper training and knowledge, could presume to tell someone what to do. Maggie said:

> We on this land, forever, since I was born. This my really good home. We have no title. We feel free to pick berries, hunt, trapping, no one bother us, we raised like that. Cannot stand people tell us what to do; we never knew his parents, his family, his father, and mother, still people tell us what to do. We think we old enough to handle

https://doi.org/10.5876/9781646423347.c010

it all ourselves. We use it so we can stand. When we became citizens, it was promised us we would have easier time. We don't want to be bothered, to be told where to go, we belong to state, we belong to government, government feed us, that's greatest help because we lose our relatives so the government share with us, treat us right. (Simeone 1987o)

THE FORTYMILE AND KLONDIKE GOLD RUSH OF 1898

In 1882, two parties of prospectors crossed the Chilkoot Pass and entered the upper Yukon River drainage. Over the next fourteen years, they struck gold on several tributaries. Each discovery lured hundreds, then thousands, of non-Natives to Alaska, making the Dene outsiders in their own land as control over the land shifted into American hands.

Gold in paying quantities was discovered on the Fortymile River in 1886. The following year, Jack McQuesten, Alfred Mayo, and Arthur Harper moved their store from Fort Reliance to the mouth of the Fortymile River, establishing the town of Fortymile. In 1888, there was strike on the Seventymile River, and in 1894 miners founded the town of Circle City after discovering gold on Birch Creek. More gold was discovered on Mission Creek in 1895, near the present town of Eagle. Then on August 17, 1896, George and Kate Carmacks, Kate's brother Skookum Jim, and their nephew Dawson Charlie discovered gold on a tributary of the Klondike River. Their discovery started a stampede, and between 1897 and 1898 an estimated 40,000 prospectors and speculators swarmed into the upper Yukon River drainage. The gold seekers originally came to the Klondike through Canadian territory, but Americans wanted an "all American route" to the gold fields. One of these routes started in Valdez, led up the

Valdez glacier, down the Klutina River, up the Copper River, and over the mountains into the upper Tanana drainage. The trail led past Lake Mansfield and down a tributary of the Fortymile River, eventually reaching the upper Yukon and Klondike goldfields.

In the 1880s, Upper Tanana Dene had become accustomed to encountering the occasional white person, but these casual encounters were nothing compared to the thousands of people that flooded the country on their way to the Klondike. As the anthropologist Cornelius Osgood observed:

The various early gold strikes with a sizable population of miners rushing from one creek to another, building towns and then evacuating them, shooting, and fishing where convenience demanded, must have been something like having alien warring groups moving back and forth over one's territory. (1971: 136)

To survive, the miners lived off the land. For prospectors working on the Fortymile River, the Fortymile caribou herd was a convenient source of food. The first party of sixteen miners to reach the area in 1886 reportedly killed forty caribou to feed themselves. By 1894 miners had killed more than 5,000 animals (Ducker 1983: 870). Mrs. Ada Schwatka commented on the decline of moose and caribou around the mining camps:

Formerly during the winter season, a living could be made by experienced hunters in bringing moose and caribou back to camp. I heard one miner say, who had spent four winters on the Yukon, that he had seen moose and caribou so numerous on the bald hills above the timber limit, in the present gold field district, that they gave the snow a mottled gray appearance. Of course, these have now disappeared with the advance of civilization and fresh meat of any kind is now at a premium. (Urquhart and Farnell 1986: 3)

In 1900, five years after the Klondike stampede, Oscar Fish, a mail carrier, met Dene in Mentasta, Tetlin, Mansfield, and Ketchumstuk who were destitute and starving. Fish attributed their plight to the near extinction of fur-bearing animals and the killing of large numbers of moose and caribou (Brown 1984: 62). Fish wrote to the US secretary of the interior for assistance but received no reply. Through the army, the government provided large quantities of food to the Ahtna on the Copper River but nothing for upper Tanana Dene.

Little thought was given to the effects of the gold rush until 1903, when Congress created a subcommittee to investigate conditions in Alaska. The chairman of the subcommittee was Senator William Dillingham from Vermont, who clearly expressed the predicament of Alaska Natives when he said Alaska had become "White man's country" (Dillingham 1904: 29).

Most of the hearing focused on conditions in the gold fields and opportunities for developing the territory, with little attention to Native people. But the testimony of David Jarvis, the customs agent in Eagle, who had been in Alaska since before the Klondike stampede, clearly stated the negative impact on Native people:

Until the time of the Klondike excitement, outside of southeastern Alaska the Indians were the principal people in the country, but since that time the country all over has changed into what can now be called a white man's country. While the native Indian figures little in the business of the country, he is entitled to some consideration and some attention. (Jarvis 1904: 83)

Speaking about the effects of the game law passed in 1902, Jarvis thought it too "extreme" for Alaska, and he noted the law was passed in part to restrict sport hunters on the Kenai Peninsula. A law was necessary, Jarvis thought, but the current law was not "altogether applicable to a new and vast country like this where

the people must of necessity live upon the game they find in the country" (Jarvis 1904: 86).

At the same hearing E. J. Knapp, an Episcopal missionary, described the situation in more detail. Testifying to a wide range of issues, including the damaging effects of alcohol, health problems such tuberculosis, and overhunting by white people, Knapp told the subcommittee "unlicensed" non-Native trappers were a "menace to the interests of the Indians." He went on:

The Indians report the presence of increasing numbers of white men—trappers, prospectors, and miners—in the remote regions among the hills of the headwaters of the tributaries of the Yukon where they are accustomed to hunt. They say the large tracts of land are being burned over through fires being started by white men and being ruined for hunting purposes. (Knapp 1904: 130–132)

The subcommittee's presence in Alaska also raised demands by non-Natives for improved roads and a telegraph line that would connect the interior to the coast. C. B. McDowell (1904), a prospector at Chicken, circulated a petition asking the citizens to build a good winter road between Valdez and Tanana Crossing, as they could not wait for the government; the road was needed to encourage settlement, agriculture, and mineral development. McDowell thought Tanana Crossing would become a major hub because "Tanana Crossing is the best place in the interior to trade with the Indians, being surrounded by the Ketchumstuk, Mansfield, Mentasta and Tetlin tribes and their fur trade is worth having." An apparent inducement to developers was the cheap price of fur; McDowell said traders could buy black, silver, and cross fox skins for $75 to $100 and sell the furs outside for twice or three times that amount.

By 1910, the focus of mineral development had moved from the Upper Yukon and Fortymile to Nome and then Fairbanks. Mail service along the Eagle Trail was discontinued in 1908, and in 1911 the telegraph line was abandoned and the telegraph station at Tanana Crossing sold to the Episcopal Church. With no mail service, the closest post office was in Chicken, and with no roads the upper Tanana region became a backwater. Then, in 1913, gold was discovered on the upper Chisana River.

CHISANA GOLD RUSH, 1913

Chisana was the last of the Alaska gold rushes. In the fall of 1913, twenty-one steamboats left Fairbanks for Chisana, but only four succeeding in reaching the confluence of the Nabesna and Chisana Rivers (Brown 1984: 45). As Chief Walter Northway recalled:

> Captain Northway came by steamboat up to Nabesna. He was going to the Chisana gold rush. He met my father, T'aaiy Ta'. He gave him the name Northway.
>
> The steamboat used to stop at the mouth of Moose Creek. I can remember seeing lots of boats with a lot of men going up the Chisana gold rush. We used to sell them moccasins and meat. Then we would buy tea, rice, tobacco, flour, and other things from them. (Yarber and Madison 1987: 36)

In a May 5, 1975, letter to the Alaska Department of Natural Resources, Chief Northway recalled the arrival of prospectors on their way to Chisana in 1913.

> A large steam boat came up Chisana River to Nabesna river hauling freight to gold mine camp in Nabesna. The name of the steam boat was called Tana. This time the boat came up the river, it unloaded passengers at the mouth of the Nabesna River to lighten the boat so it could travel easier on up the river. The passengers (about 100–150) built log boats and poled up the river to the gold mine at Nabesna. (Cole 1979)

The gold strike on the upper Chisana River was so remote the miners relied on local resources, either killing game on their own or buying meat from Dene. The geologist Stephen R. Capps visited Chisana at the height of the stampede and estimated "2,000 sheep were killed within a distance of 20 miles of the placer camps during the winter of 1913–1914, and in that area have been almost completely exterminated." The number of caribou had also been reduced because of constant hunting (Capps 1916: 21). The wholesale killing of game forced some Native people to move out of the area, but others were attracted by the possibilities of selling meat and hauling freight and mail. The Chisana gold rush was short-lived, and in three years most of the miners had left.

DENE CHIEFS WRITE THE TERRITORIAL GOVERNOR, 1915

In the estimation of Archdeacon Frederic Drane, the upper Tanana was "Indian country." He wrote:

> The Indian of this section [upper Tanana] today is almost universally friendly with the White man. He has found it to his advantage to be so for the White man brings him ammunition, the tea, the tobacco, and other things he has learned to depend on. . . . While most of the Indians of this section are friendly to the Whites, most of them feel a great superiority to them. This is strictly Indian country. (Drane n.d.b: 62).

While the upper Tanana appeared to be Indian country, Dene were feeling the impact of white incursions. In September 1915, several Dene "chiefs" hired Daniel Bouville, a prospector at Chicken, to write a letter to the territorial governor (figure 10.1). The letter, signed by Walter Isaac, chief of Mansfield, and several "assistant chiefs" from Ketchumstuk,

Tetlin, Mansfield, and Mentasta, began by asking Governor J. F. A. Strong to plead their case to Uncle Sam and to give them a little help because they had grown "awful poor." Since they did not catch much fur over the winter, and the prices they received from the traders was low, all they had to eat was caribou meat. Later in the letter they wrote that a silver fox skin sold outside brought $3,000 but they only got $150 to $250—"not enough money." Furthermore, white people did not buy meat, because they killed caribou themselves, nor did they buy mittens and moccasins, so there was no money to purchase ammunition.

Another issue was that the miners "burn all our woods, burn lots of little furs bearers too by big forest fire," and the miners killed lots of caribou and let the meat spoil while the game wardens did nothing. So the chiefs asked Governor Strong to write to the federal government so they could get "cartridges, little tea, little star tobacco." They also wanted tents, stoves, steel traps, and some medicine. In addition, they wanted Uncle Sam to help them start a cooperative store. Bouville would purchase shares and help them out. They also heard some whites planned to domesticate caribou, which worried them (Isaac 1915). Governor Strong wrote back expressing doubt that the situation was as bad as Dene had made out, but he directed an investigation undertaken concerning conditions in the district.

Game wardens were concerned about depletion of fur-bearing animals. In 1917–1918, fur prices were high, and non-Native trappers were scattered across the upper Fortymile River basin. Special Fur Warden Christian L. Larson outlined the situation to his boss, H. F. Moore, acting commissioner of fisheries, in a June 1918 letter. Along with the letter Larson sent a detailed map of the Fortymile River basin showing dozens of trapping cabins used by non-Native trappers (figure 10.4). On the far right of Larson's map is the trail to Tanana Crossing with the caption "Tanana Indians set

Chicken Alaska Sept [illegible] 1915

27

Mr. J. F. A. Strong, Governor of Alaska.
Juneau Alaska
Dear Governor
Please we want you to [illegible] and read this Paper talk all [illegible]. we should like to see you to talk to you but too far. so it is why we are sending you this letter.
By this letter we beg want you to plead our Case to Uncle Sam Government. so that we get help. we want Uncle Sam to help us a little this year. Because we have grown awful poor. we did loose considerably of time last Winter at the Mission up Tanana Crossing. that all right for we like Mission. we like Mission peoples all good peoples. that what we want. and also we want our Children to learn at school. but we did not catch much furs. and the little we did catch did bring us little prices.

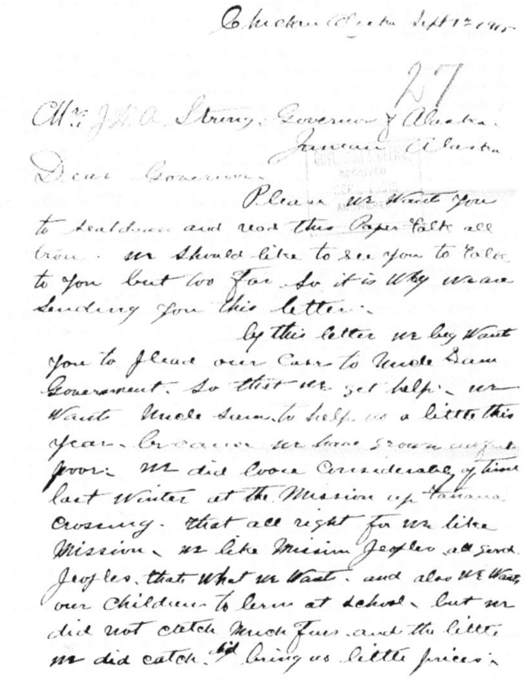

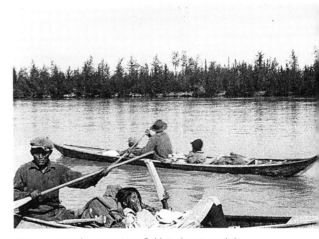

Figure 10.1. Copy of the letter to Governor J. F. A. Strong by Walter Vyeek (Isaac) and Dene Chiefs, dated September 1915. Source: Alaska State Library Governors' Papers Roll 29. Frames 212–219.

Figure 10.2. On the way to Mansfield: Andrew Isaac (left), with Minna, Big Albert's wife. In the other canoe are Big Albert and his son McConnell. Minna was sick with tuberculosis and was being taken up to Mansfield. Photo by E. A. McIntosh, courtesy of Gaither Paul, William E. Simeone photo collection.

traps along the trail." Toward the middle of the map is Ketchumstuk at the confluence of the Mosquito Fork and Ketchumstuk Creek. Noted are the telegraph station and several cabins belonging to non-Natives. A notation says, "Indians Trapping Ground." Larson has drawn in all of the creeks and non-Native traplines and cabins around Chicken. On the right of the map is the trail from Chicken to Eagle, roadhouses, and the international boundary. Larson (1918) wrote about the map:

> There were trappers located at one time or another in the winter of 1917 and 18 at all places so marked. All houses or cabins marked in many instances vacant especially at this time on O'Brien, Mosquito fork, above Ketchumstuk and Denison fork, above Camp creek. The cabins marked in those places was built years ago by Trappers or Prospectors except Mitchell where he stops part of the summer cutting hay.

Figure 10.3. Walter and Maggie Isaac and Big Albert. Photo by E. A. McIntosh. William E. Simeone photo collection.

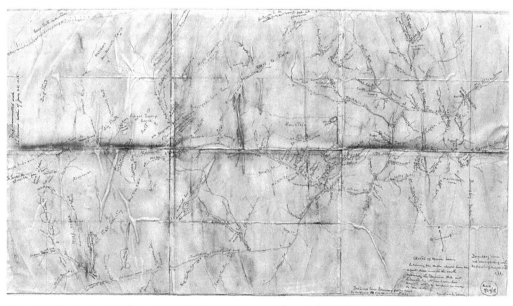

Figure 10.4. Sketch map, dated June 25, 1918, by Christian L. Larson. The map shows the upper Fortymile River drainage, traplines, and cabins. Source: Record Group 22: Records of the US Fish and Wildlife Service, 1868–2008. Records Concerning Fox Farming and Protection of Fur-Bearing animals, 1911–1928. National Archives.

He concluded:

The area is ideal country for all fur bearing animals but the few that is left will not long survive as the prices is higher than ever before. Marten is on the increase in the outlying parts where there has been no trappers in the last 2–3 years, but as the martens gets more numerous more of them will be caught in traps same for mink, weasel, foxes and lynx and wolverine, will not be able to save them, at least not in the part along the boundary [Canadian border].

GAME LAWS

In 1902, 1908, and 1925, Congress passed laws regulating the taking of wild game in Alaska. Introduced by Boone and Crockett Club member Representative John Lacey, a Republican from Iowa, the 1902 legislation was meant to curtail market hunting by creating seasons and bag limits and prohibiting the sale of meat, hides, and heads. A clause allowing "Indians, Eskimos, miners and explorers actually in need of food" to kill game for "their immediate use" (US Government 1902) was included, but the law was unpopular and unworkable since enforcement personnel were reluctant to enforce it (Woldstad 2011: 29). Dissatisfaction with the 1902 law led to the passage of the 1908 law with only marginal changes. Enforcement continued to be lax, and conservation groups continued to believe excess killing of game by Alaska Natives threatened wildlife populations (Woldstad 2011: 33).

In April 1921, the naturalist O. J. Murie visited the upper Tanana region and in May wrote to his boss, Dr. E. W. Nelson Chief, of the Bureau of Biological Survey, outlining the regional situation as he saw it (Murie 1921b). Murie had mixed feelings about Dene killing caribou and moose for food. He saw no "wanton waste" and described how Dene used every part of the caribou, including the feet.

He understood Dene needed the food, and that store-bought food, like bacon, was too expensive for them to live on. He also realized that agriculture was not a likely solution. But he was concerned that Dene were killing too many caribou to feed their dogs. He estimated that Tanacross people killed twenty-five caribou each month, and some killed between fifteen and thirty animals in two days, mostly to feed their dogs. At the same time, he realized that alternative sources of food, like rice, were too expensive to feed to dogs, and unlike on the Yukon River, there was no dried salmon. He thought one way to stop the "slaughter" of game was to limit the number of dogs.

He concluded his letter by saying that since the law had not been "rigidly enforced," and missionaries had little influence over Dene when it came to hunting, it was important to adopt a definite plan; otherwise game wardens would meet resistance. At the time, there were probably too few people living in the region to have an effect on the caribou herds, but Murie was concerned about the impact of hunting on moose populations, especially if more non-Natives moved into the region. He reported that during the winter of 1921, Dene lived primarily on moose meat. Murie heard that the Healy Lake people had killed fifty-four moose in two and half months, and that twenty-two moose were killed for a potlatch at Tetlin in May 1920.

In 1925, Congress enacted a new game law that gave the secretary of agriculture the authority to regulate Native subsistence hunting. This act, "to revise the Alaska game law" (public law 106), superseded all other game laws and authorized the establishment of a five-member Alaska Game Commission, none of which were Alaska Native. One of the biggest problems was how the Game Commission treated Alaska Natives.

Regulation 8 of the act allowed Alaskans to kill game and birds "when in absolute need of food and other food was not available." It restricted this right to explorers, prospectors, travelers, and "uncivilized natives" who had not severed their tribal relations by "adopting a civilized mode of living" or "exercising the right of franchise." Residents, nonresidents, and civilized Natives had to purchase hunting and trapping licenses, but no license was required of "uncivilized Natives." The definition of "civilized" was attached to people who had the right to vote or "adopt[ed] a mode of civilized living," which included disassociation from other tribal members (Woldstad 2011: 42).

FUR FARMS, RESERVATIONS, AND COOPERATIVE STORES: DENE ATTEMPT TO ASSERT CONTROL

Because of its isolation, the upper Tanana region was considered fertile ground for both traders and missionaries. The goal of traders like John Hajdukovich was to develop businesses that would help Dene assimilate and abandoned their traditional way of life. Hajdukovich considered fur farming to be ideal for several reasons. First, fur farms would produce a regular supply of fur. Second, Dene were becoming increasingly dependent on trade goods, but wild furs were scarce so people's incomes fluctuated; fur farms would provide a stable source of income that would enable Dene to buy more trade goods, thereby increasing the traders' profits. Third, fur farms were considered to be compatible with the Native people's way of life, creating a more hands-on education than a formal trade school (Brown 1984: 98–99). While the federal government endorsed the concept of a fur farm, neither the Bureau of Indians Affairs nor the Bureau of Education would assume responsibility for funding. This, along with declining fur prices, doomed the project from the start.

Encroachment of non-Natives on Native traplines and hunting grounds was another issue. In December 1934, Silas Solomon (1934) of Tanacross outlined the issue in a letter to the Governor of Alaska. Silas wrote he was thirty years old, had never been to school, and was used to "packing mules for wages, and prospecting with some of my white man friends."

> I am going to let you know about my peoples. They are unfortuned [sic] and unemployed. Now here we are citizens of U.S.A. why we don't get attention of all these hard life as we have been live last 20 years. There is not much game to live on, no furs to make money and most of the white peoples has been trapping and killed more game than we did. Lot of these native families are, some of them 5 to 8 children, no clothes, no food for them. They got some meat and vegetables but its small for winter. I would like you to try and get some grub for these Indians at this village more we need is ammunitions and tea matches and salt.

Silas went on the say food sold by the traders was very expensive and the people could not afford to buy it. Silas himself was "hard up," but he shared meat with poor people and the elderly. He asked the governor for a team of horses to plow and fertilize the ground. People were digging gardens by hand. He concluded the letter by telling the governor, "Don't write to those whitemans in our section about because they crooks and robbers if they got chance. Just write me a letter right soon as you decide let me know."

Four years later, in the winter of 1938, a representative of the American Association of Indian Affairs, Moses Burge, visited the upper Tanana to survey the social and economic condition. Burge thought the region could not support additional trappers, "especially white trappers who with terrible efficiency attempted to obtain the greatest number of pelts in the shortest period of time." "Trapping," Burge wrote, "was the basis for the economic life of the Upper Tanana Indians. Destruction meant almost certainly a catastrophic effect upon the Indians' society. Muskrats were the most plentiful fur-bearers in the district and the largest part of the Indian's income." Burge estimated a family's annual income at $2,000 (quoted in Brown 1984: 146). The answer, in the view of many non-Natives, was a reservation. Hajdukovich wrote about the advantages of a reservation.

> If the section in which these Indians live and trap could be established as a Reservation, many advantages would accrue. . . . A Reservation would make it possible to keep out certain white men who call themselves trappers, but who really are professional gamblers. These men gamble with the Indians for their furs. . . . The Reservation would also safeguard certain trapping grounds for the use of Indians alone so that they could build up the fur and get a dependable crop for the following season. As it is now, all sections are open to the professional white trapper who goes in and cleans up all the fur and takes it out with him and never returns. (Hajdukovich 1932: 2)

A reservation would not only prevent encroachment by non-Natives but would provide some control over Native people and especially the potlatch. Hajdukovich complained that Dene spent $125,000 a year on potlatches, "squandering" the money with "no thought of the future" (Brown 1984: 139).

Few non-Natives in Alaska supported a full-blown reservation, such as those found in the lower 48 states, but many people, such as H. Wendell Endicott, believed some sort of boundary or line that would "designate the trapping rights for these Indians and deter the influence of bad whiskey, bootleggers, outside trappers, and such interests as prey upon the Indians" was considered appropriate (quoted in Brown 1984: 101). Dan Sutherland, Alaska's delegate to Congress, and Carl Whitham, the owner of the Nabesna mine, both opposed a reservation. Whitham favored helping Native people but thought a reservation would curtail development (Brown 1984: 109). Editorials in Alaska newspapers applauded efforts to assist Native people but were apprehensive that this would set a precedent for other reservations in Alaska. Despite all objections, the Tetlin Reservation was established on June 10, 1930, with the stated purpose of promoting "the interests of the Natives by appropriate vocational training, to encourage and assist them in restocking the country and protecting fur bearing animals, and to otherwise aid in the care and support of the said Natives" (Executive Order No. 5365, 1930).

The Indian Reorganization Act of 1934, also known as the Wheeler-Howard Act, was enacted by the US Congress to decrease federal control of Native American affairs and increase self-government and responsibility. The act authorized the creation of additional reservations on land occupied by Alaska Native people and empowered Native people to create Indian Reorganization Councils and cooperative or Native-run stores. Native-run stores created competition for the traders, who then threatened to start importing alcohol. In response, some local non-Natives and Dene leaders, such as Walter Northway, advocated expanding the boundaries of the Tetlin Reservation to include all the Dene communities in the region, from Scottie Creek to Healy Lake.

In 1940, Fred A. Dimler, a teacher at Tetlin, convinced the residents to organize a village council, establish a cooperative store, and extend the boundaries of the reservation to include Nabesna Village to protect Dene from the intrusion of white trappers. Upper Tanana Dene from several communities petitioned the federal government to enlarge the reservation to include the entire upper Tanana district (Brown 1984: 149–150).

The fight to extend the Tetlin Reservation and establish Native cooperative stores pitted some Dene, missionaries, and government agencies against traders and development interests. Fearing the traders would start importing alcohol, both Chief Joe of Tetlin and Chief Walter Northway of Nabesna asked the traders be removed from the area. Chief Northway requested the removal of both Hajdukovich and Herman Kessler because Kessler was going to build a store in Nabesna against the wishes of the Dene and Hajdukovich was accused of importing liquor. According to Chief Northway, Hajdukovitch was "bitterly opposed to the co-operative movement and we don't want him in our village" (Brown 1984: 156).

From the trader's perspective, the situation had deteriorated. To counter Dene efforts, Kessler advocated traders demand cash for trade goods and let the Natives send their furs outside. Writing to Hajdukovich, Kessler (1940) complained:

> Things don't look so good at present. I believe that quite a bit of fur went away from us, and they all want to send the rats themselves. Dimler sure raised hell in Nabesna and the Indians will be hard to handle this spring. The only way I can see, give absolutely no credit from now on. Same thing I do at Tana Crossing [sic]. I told Mathew to sell only for cash and let them ship the furs themselves. Don't give Silas any more at Tana Cross or promise him a job this summer.

In the end, Hajdukovich turned against the reservation altogether and persuaded the territorial legislature to support its revocation because it stymied development. He also persuaded Chief Walter Isaac and Silas Solomon from Tanacross to write a letter opposing the reservation because it took away their trapping and timber rights. Chief Isaac and Silas told representatives of the Indian Service that the Tetlin Reservation was cutting into their trapping since the reserve was the "most lucrative section

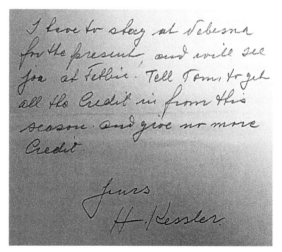

Figure 10.5. Letter to John Hajdukovich from Herman Kessler, March 21, 1940. Source: Hajdukovich collection. Journals and Ledgers, 1922–1948 Accounts Hajdukovich ledgers Box 3 Tanana Crossing 1931–32, 1937, 1929–31, 1932 and 1939. Box 5 Accounts 1927–1930. Alaska and Polar Regions Department, Elmer E. Rasmuson Library, University of Alaska Fairbanks Archives.

for muskrats." Before the reservation, Tetlin and Tanacross people had shared areas within the reservation, but the Tetlin Council was now dictating the terms by which people could trap (Brown 1984: 164–165). The issue of whether to expand the Tetlin Reservation or establish additional reservations in the upper Tanana region was not resolved until after World War II.

WORLD WAR II, 1939–1945

World War II and the construction of the Alaska Highway brought an end to the upper Tanana region's isolation as barriers to travel were removed. A military airfield was built at Northway, the airstrip at Tanacross was improved, and large military installations were built at both locations. Tok Junction began as a construction camp for the Alaska Highway and then became the regional hub.

Until the 1930s, the upper Tanana was one of the most isolated areas of Alaska. Above Big Delta, the Tanana River was difficult to navigate, and it usually took eight to ten days to reach Tanacross. The nearest post office was in Chicken. In 1928, the Alaska Road Commission built a dirt runway across the Tanana River from old Tanacross, and in 1935 Pan American Airways built a radio station to accommodate the expansion of air service in the region. Gaither Paul (Simeone 1987a) talked about construction of the airfield at Tanacross:

> McIntosh rounded up all of the men and bigger boys and we went across the river and built the airfield, all by hand. David Paul and lots of Tanacross people worked so a plane with wheels could land, before that only pontoon planes landed, few planes in winter used a grass field. The original airfield was built with all donated work, no pay. Handmade airfield, holes filled with gravel.
>
> First planes landed in back of Tanacross, not on field, regular air service used the

field, until then it was irregular. 1937 Alaska Road Commission with gas cat and hand operated grader built a regular gravel airport. The equipment all came by boat from Big Delta. Mail plane flew from Fairbanks to Tanacross. Noel Wien landed on little flat.

> There were [Native] camps on the airport side of the river. Sam Thomas had a camp over there off and on. Three or four families might live there for a time. People with tents who had no house moved around. The airport was a part of the area used by Tanacross people at different times of the year. Several trails went through the airport area, to Moon Lake and to Tanacross Flats. People picked berries around there.

The US military began using the airfield as an emergency landing field in 1941. The Tanacross Indian Reorganization Council, which had been formed in 1937, gave the army permission to improve the airfield. Gaither Paul recalled:

> The IRA council was formed in about 1937. The Council gave OK for the army to improve the airfield. David Paul [Gaither's father] said the army came to the council and asked to build an airport, the Council approved in exchange for limiting use during the war only. Afterwards the army will pull out and the village will have the airport for their own use. According to David Paul the agreement between the Council and the army had a provision that the army would provide jobs for Native people. (Simeone 1987a)

In the spring of 1942, surveyors were dropped off along the river to begin surveying the airport. This was before the Alaska Highway was built. Metcalf, Hamilton, and Kansas City Bridge Company (MHK), for whom Gaither Paul worked, did most of the work. Bechtel, Price, and Collingham worked at Northway and Tanacross. By 1943, the army had constructed a camp and operations center housing fifty people. The airfield included two-mile-long paved runways, a large hanger, aircraft refueling facilities, and support buildings.

Construction of an airport at Northway began in the spring of 1941. Supplies were flown into Tetlin, the nearest airport, and then taken upriver by boat to Northway. A crew of twenty Dene built a 100-foot-by-800-foot runway in six days (Wilson 1995: 72–73). In the spring of 1942, the army began to expand the facilities at Northway, adding a theater, church, aircraft hangar, barracks, and other buildings. The army gave contracts to local traders like John Hajdukovich to produce lumber for the buildings. When Pearl Harbor was attacked, the military realized the strategic importance of the area—and the limitations of the Northway airport, which could not be reached by road and where poor soil conditions made it impossible to expand the runway. So, weeks after the attack at Pearl Harbor, the military made plans to build another airport that could be reached by land. Tanacross already had a small airport, close to the Valdez-Eagle Trail, and the land was suitable for expanding the field. The first tractors arrived in February 1942 to begin improving the Valdez-Eagle Trail and hauling freight from Valdez.

When construction began in the summer of 1942 (Wilson 1995: 74–75), many local people got jobs, such as cutting brush for over a dollar an hour. Tok was one of the largest construction and maintenance camps along the highway. Gaither Paul said:

Some Native people took off for hunting because hunting was considered the regular life, construction was not. Hunting was still very important. Almost every man in the village worked either on the highway or on the airfield. No one refused to work, but they really wanted to hunt so had to maintain a balance. After Metcalf, Hamilton, and Kansas City Bridge Company left the army took over. People got clothes from

MHK and four-star sleeping bags—people either returned the clothes or the cost was deducted from pay. People who worked on the road stayed in camps while those working at the airfield went home. (Simeone 1987a)

According to David Paul and Joe Joseph, local Dene were generally treated well but at the beginning of the war were not allowed to eat in the mess hall, although this rule was soon overturned. Both Paul and Joseph recalled that in August 1942 there was an epidemic of measles in Tanacross and many of the elderly became ill and died. An army doctor came to the village but there was little he could do. Paul also recalled that hunting trails running through army camps and the airport could not be used, and he said he lost his trapline, as did the Jonathan boys and Charlie James (Simeone 1987t).

By the middle of the 1940s, Gaither Paul believed, many people were working wage jobs, but these were seasonal because people always quit to trap and continue to live from the land. Most jobs lasted only for the duration of the war; once the Alaska Highway was completed, there were few alternatives for employment. Some jobs opened in the mining industry. Gaither, for example, worked on a dredge at Chicken Creek in the Fortymile country. Other men, such as John Jonathan, worked building the Taylor Highway, which winds through the hills of the Fortymile River country. Like the Alaska Highway, construction of the Taylor Highway did not provide long-term employment but did make the upper Fortymile country accessible to non-Native hunters who came from urban areas to hunt moose and the Fortymile caribou herd.

After World War II, the population of Alaska grew, and between 1946 and 1956 hunting licenses more than tripled from 9,000 to 31,500. More hunters meant more regulation, which undermined the traditional seasonality of the old hunting life. After 1950, hunters were restricted to short seasons and bag limits. Instead of providing a secure economic base for Dene, the Alaska Highway threatened the land, which was the very basis of Dene life. In undermining the culture of the land, the road affected the health of the people. As hunting regulations became more restrictive, and commercial foods more plentiful, people were no longer able to live completely from their traditional foods, which undermined their health. Most significantly, Dene were exposed to unprecedented amounts alcohol. Where alcohol had been relatively scarce before construction of the Alaska Highway, bars became common and alcohol a devastating health problem for Dene communities.

Kenny Thomas Sr. of Tanacross was one of the only Upper Tanana Dene to serve in the military during World War II, and he commented on changes he observed upon returning home to Tanacross in 1946 after a four-year absence:

> One thing I'd like to say, is, after I came back from the army I see lot of changes. . . . A lot of people were still trapping when I got back. But in the summer they always looking for job. When I was kid we didn't even know what work is, but what a change when I got back from the army. People always looking for job. Everybody works in the summertime. So that's a big change for the people. We getting away from the subsistence life.
>
> When I left, most of the people used to live like Native people a long time [the subsistence way of life]. But when I got back from the army there was a lot of changes. They live mostly like the white people, trying to live like the white people. More money, more money for the food, more money for the different things. Lots of people is working on the [air] field, about 50–60 percent working on the field and brings in the money for their family. (Thomas and Mishler 2005: 110–112)

Ivar Skarland from the University of Alaska revisited the upper Tanana region after the highway opened to the public. He wrote about the highway's effect on Dene communities:

> The war brought the Alaska Highway to the valley. I visited the villages this spring (1955) after nearly sixteen years absence. The Healy village has been abandoned as a permanent town, most of the people having scattered or moved to the new settlement at Dot Lake on the highway.
>
> The total number of people is about the same as in 1939 (about 350), but the outlying villages such as Healy Lake, Scottie Creek, Billy Creek and others have been abandoned.
>
> This time I revisited Tanacross and Tetlin, and also visited the settlement near Northway (formerly known as Nabesna Village).
>
> Outwardly, the villages have changed very little, except that in spite of some new houses, they have a more rundown appearance than formerly. Houses are still mostly one-room structures; but few have now separated bedrooms and kitchens (Skarland 1956).

The events of World War II added strength to Northway and Tanacross appeals for a reservation, and the US government sent representatives to assess the situation. Following one assessment in October 1943, the government proposed a 208,000-acre reservation for the people at Northway. Nothing was done. Then, three years later, the government sent Walter Goldschmidt and Theodore Haas to conduct yet another assessment.

In the summer of 1946, Goldschmidt, an anthropologist, and Haas, a government lawyer, conducted interviews with Dene in Tanacross, Tetlin, and Northway. Their report outlines the situation facing upper Tanana Dene as a new world was forced upon them by the opening of the Alaska Highway. Common themes throughout all the interviews were that whites were trespassing on Dene traplines and alcohol was causing serious problems. Goldschmidt writes:

> Native leaders were concerned over the encroachment of whites into their historic domain. They are not hostile to whites as individuals, nor to the now no longer strange ways of the white man. They are, however, concerned with two effects of this encroachment: the depletion of fur animals from which they get a large portion of their livelihood, and the moral effect of the introduction of liquor and other urban delights upon the youth of the community and the resultant destruction of their homogeneity which is so important to their economic welfare of the entire group.
>
> Resources are limited, further encroachment by whites will only reduce those resources and impoverish the local population. Native people have the knowledge and the technology to use the resources to the full extent and have established customary usage or native common law to insure the continued availability of the natural wealth of the area. (Goldschmidt 1948: 17)

Dene had taken jobs during the war, but these were secondary compared to hunting, fishing, and gathering. In 1946 Native people were still producing food for their own use and furs for export. Combined, these created a balance that made the communities self-sufficient. "The modern economy of the natives is not unlike the aboriginal economy, except in that the marketing of fur animals has enabled the natives to purchase the products of civilization, and therefore has integrated their economy with that of American society in general" (Goldschmidt 1948: 7).

Goldschmidt drew several generalizations from his interviews with Dene: All healthy adults engaged regularly in hunting, and most of the food consumed was local. Most of the men trapped. The most important fur animal was the muskrat, but they also trapped mink, fox, lynx, marten, beaver, wolf, wolverine, coyote, and land otter. Whitefish was an important part of the diet, and there are several locations where people fished. Goldschmidt also listed three customs or practices that he thought demonstrated the "foresight and wisdom" of Dene "for without these practices there would be starvation or living on welfare" (Goldschmidt 1948: 7). First, some land, such as fishing sites and berry picking areas, was held in common; second, elders used land and trails closest to the village; and third, traplines were allowed to go fallow.

Jennie Luke of Tanacross testified that berry patches were held in common by everyone in the village.

> I pick berries, low bush cranberries, and strawberries a little this side of the hill toward Mansfield village near the Tanacross trail. I also pick blueberries east of Mansfield and there is another place towards the west and another place between west and south. All of the Native of the village can pick any berries just the same as they can use community halls. (Goldschmidt 1948: 15)

Walter Isaac explained about leaving areas close to the village for the elders:

> We have the old people use the short trap lines around the village. They go around the village with short trap lines because they are not able to walk and climb so far—older men like Titus Isaac, Sam Isaac [Abraham], and Big Albert. We don't want whites trapping in here too close. (Goldschmidt 1948: 15)

Walter told Goldschmidt that when trapping, Dene did not take all of the animals but lately he had been taking every muskrat because white men would take them anyhow.

> We take care of our rats until this spring. We take care that we don't kill them all off.

Figure 10.6. Grandma Jenny Luke. Photo by Terry Haynes.

We let some of them remain so that there will be some of them next year. I know I hurt myself, but this year I cleaned out all the rats. I cleaned them out because the white man will get them anyhow. Then these army people have been killing off the rats. The white people try to clean up all the game. (Goldschmidt 1948: 16)

In 1987, Oscar Isaac (Simeone 1987a), Walter Isaac's son, said certain areas were left for two years so that game could increase. He added that today (at the time of the interview) this would be hard to do, considering how many non-Natives came into the area and how they used machines to get into the backcountry, pushing the game farther away from the roads where many Native people hunted because they could not afford off-road machines or airplanes.

The proximity of the military airbase at Northway made the situation critical. According to Goldschmidt, personnel from the air base hunted, "which resulted in a serious reduction of the wildlife population" (Goldschmidt 1948: 47). The base also polluted the waters that the local people depended on for their drinking water.

Across North America Native people experienced similar effects, but in Northway, Goldschmidt wrote, "the impact has been sudden and recent," and ranged from disruption of the traditional seasonal round to the introduction of infectious diseases and debilitating illnesses. Goldschmidt continued:

> During the recent war an air base was established at Northway with dire results to the village. The men of the post engaged in hunting of game which resulted in a serious reduction of the wildlife population. Natives whose very life depended upon the fur and meat animals were filled with resentment at soldiers who shot for mere pleasure, frequently not even picking up the carcasses of the animals so destroyed. Even more serious was another direct effect of the establishment of the air base. For centuries the natives have used the stream waters as a source of drinking water and for bathing. With literally nobody above them on the stream, there was no danger in this practice. The army post was placed, however, immediately up stream from Northway Village, and the sewage from the barracks allowed to flow into the river. Decimation of the village population was the inevitable result of this practice.
>
> In addition to those influences, the building of the Alcan Highway and the establishment of an army outpost has had a demoralizing effect upon the community itself. Here the weakening influence is that of whiskey. (Goldschmidt 1948: 47)

Walter Northway told Goldschmidt:

> I have tried to learn everything I can. My grandfather told me our way of doing things. He told me how to act. He told me not to use

things to strong. Now the white man had brought us whiskey. Now I am losing all of my own people. I am sorry about this white man business. (Goldschmidt 1948: 47)

In an oral history interview conducted in 2008, longtime Northway resident Lavell Wilson described the discrimination and trauma Dene suffered during and after World War II.

Northway had a big Army contingent there at the airport, so they got subjected to a lot more, a lot quicker then like Tetlin and places like that. Because there was a lot of Army there, a lot of facilities, you know, they weren't always welcomed. There was a lot of animosity in some parts against anybody that wasn't white. Northway got subjected to it a little worse. In some ways it was better for them, I guess, it brought them up quicker, but in some ways it was worse. They got introduced to tobacco and alcohol, and stuff like that, which they weren't prepared for by any means. But I don't know the single biggest impact, that'd be hard to say. You know, probably just the impact on their culture. All of the sudden they're supposed to be integrated into another culture.

That don't take place overnight, you know. Religion, you know, preachers showed up. And not only diseases like diphtheria and smallpox and that, but venereal disease. All them young G.I.'s and all them young Native girls. You know, they were plying them with booze and gifts and everything. It's just the way it happens. All them G.I.'s chasing all them girls, I mean there had to be an impact there. Right away you start getting half-breed kids, and nobody was prepared to handle that particularly. And, of course, as soon as the Army got transferred a lot of the kids were left here. They weren't necessarily taken with them like now.

The military didn't pay much attention to it. The only thing the military did, they wouldn't let the black soldiers go into any of the villages or associate with any of them. In fact they interviewed one of the elders in Mentasta years ago, asking him about the first white men he saw, and he said well he'd heard a few white man had been through down there, but the first white men he really saw were black. (Brewster 2018: 18–19)

Rather than act on Goldschmidt's findings, the secretary of the interior, in July of 1947, withdrew the land that had been set aside for Northway and Tanacross reservations pending further study. Finally, in 1953 and 1954, the Bureau of Indian Affairs (BIA) and the Bureau of Land Management (BLM) recommended the withdrawal of lands for a reservation be revoked altogether (Brown 1984: 72).

STATEHOOD AND THE ALASKA NATIVE CLAIMS SETTLEMENT ACT OF 1971

The question of Native land claims had been raised long before statehood. But neither the federal government nor the new state government addressed the issue when Alaska became a state in January 1959. At the same time, the Alaska Statehood Act allowed the new state to select or choose over 103 million acres of public land but forbade it from selecting lands that were held by Native tribes. As a result, for the next decade, Native groups and the state spent considerable effort arguing over who owned what lands. One of the state's land selections conflicted with Tanacross land claims around George Lake.

The dispute, which was reported in the *Tundra Times* newspaper, was one of many events that led to the Alaska Native Claims Settlement Act. An early headline in the paper began, "Indians of the Tanacross area say the state is trying to auction off their ancestral lands at the New York World's Fair." In 1961 the state offered wilderness estates for sale at the World's Fair even though Tanacross had filed a blanket claim on the land in 1950. In fact, Tanacross Dene had filed claims in 1917, 1934, 1946, and 1950, but both the state and federal agencies denied knowledge of any claim (*Tundra Times* 1969). In 1969, Secretary of the Interior Walter Hickel wrote a letter to Andrew Isaac saying that neither the State Division of Lands nor the federal Bureau of Land Management had any record of a Tanacross claim. Investigations by the *Tundra Times* uncovered several documents relating to the Tanacross claims, including one titled "Petitions for Possessory Rights Hearing and Reservation in the matter of Tanacross" signed by David Paul and dated November 30, 1950, but the BLM did not file the petition on that claim until 1961, when the director of the Bureau of Indian Affairs prepared an appeal and submitted it on behalf of the Dene in Tanacross and Northway. The state arbitrarily denied the claim and closed the land, saying it was unoccupied, even though Native people had applied for Native allotments. After a lot of bad publicity, the state backed downed and took the lots off the market. But as late as 1970, the state continued to turn down Native allotment applications, advising applicants that they were trespassing on state land (*Tundra Times* 1971).

Disputes such as the one between the state and Tanacross forced Alaska Natives to organize and become politically active. In 1966, they formed the Alaska Federation of Natives and began a concerted effort for a comprehensive, statewide land claim settlement. That same year, Secretary of Interior Stewart Udall announced he would refuse to approve any state land selections until the Native claims were settled. Eventually, Secretary Udall made the order permanent with Public Land Order 4582. By this order Udall not only froze all land selections by the state but also blocked the sale of oil leases and construction of the

trans-Alaska oil pipeline. This created a strong incentive for both the state and federal governments to settle the Native Land claims, but the idea of a Native claim remained controversial and progress slow.

Throughout the late 1960s, various land settlements were suggested, and in 1967 Alaska Governor Walter Hickel appointed a thirty-seven-member land claims commission task force to write a bill acceptable to Natives and the state. The commission came back with three recommendations:

1. Forty million acres of land would be conveyed to villages; lands currently used for fishing and hunting would be available for 100 years, and the Native Allotment Act would remain in effect. The Allotment Act was enacted in 1906 and allowed Alaska Natives to acquire title to 160 acres of land.
2. Ten percent of the income produced by the sale of oil leases would be paid to Alaska Natives.
3. The settlement would be carried out by business corporations organized by the villages and regions. (Arnold 1976: 120)

In 1968, Alaska Senator Ernest Gruening introduced a bill based on the land commission's findings, and in February of that year the Senate Interior and Insular Affairs committee held a three-day meeting in Anchorage. Chief Andrew Isaac testified at the hearing:

I saw my first whiteman in 1904. He was a preacher. During the course of the years I saw more white men. In the early 1940s a highway was built near Tanacross and white man have come on to our land and more. . . .

We made our claim in 1963 because the state came in and selected our land—everything, even our village and graveyard. This is not fair. We own the land—the white man does not. (Arnold 1976: 122)

The principal opposition to the commission's recommendations came from the Alaska Sportsmen's Council and the Alaska Miners Association. The Sportsmen's Council objected to giving any land to Native people, but they did not object to monetary payments. The Alaska Miners Association representative said the government had no legal or moral obligation to grant any claim to Alaska Native people (Naske and Slotnick 2014: 201–202).

After more negotiations, the Alaska Native Claims Settlement Act (ANCSA) was signed into law on December 18, 1971. Under ANCSA, Alaska Natives were entitled to forty-four million acres of land and $962.5 million of compensation for further land claims that were extinguished by the settlement. In many ways ANCSA resembled early treaties, with Native people giving up large chunks of territory in exchange for smaller portions of land.

A principal feature of ANCSA was the formation of regional and village business corporations. Regional corporations were formed along the boundaries of twelve regions, each composed of Natives with a common heritage and common interests and represented by a regional Native organization. Upper Tanana Dene became part of the regional corporation Doyon Limited, the largest regional corporation created under ANCSA with land holdings encompassing more than 200,000 square miles.

ANCSA benefits would accrue to Native people through regional and village corporations of which all eligible Native people would become stockholders. Each Native person alive on December 18, 1971, and enrolled in a village corporation received 100 shares of stock; they also received stock in a regional corporation. The amount of land and money villages received was based on the number of people enrolled. Of the forty million acres allotted, twenty-two million were earmarked for selection by each village corporation, which received surface rights to the land (the regional corporations received subsurface rights). Healy

Lake Village Corporation received 69,120 acres; Tanacross 92,160 acres; Northway 115,200 acres; and Dot Lake 69,120 acres. These lands were located near each village and often included lands considered important for subsistence purposes. In lieu of participating in ANCSA, Tetlin opted to retain lands set aside for the Tetlin Indian Reservation and, as a result, secured both surface and subsurface title to a substantially larger land base (743,000 acres) than it would have received as a full participant in ANCSA.

The land allotted to the regional and village corporations was protected from outside interests in a number of ways. Neither the land nor the cash was given to individuals. Both were placed under control of the corporations. ANCSA also contained provisions to protect the land from loss and seizure for the first twenty years, but by the late 1980s it was clear that if the protections were lifted in 1991 as scheduled, all Native land in Alaska would be exposed and vulnerable. Native leaders went to work, and in 1991 Congress passed House Resolution 278, which extended protections for ANCSA land, granting it immunity from bankruptcy, civil judgments, liens, and taxation as long as the land remained undeveloped.

Fifteen years after ANCSA, Dene were concerned about the eventual outcome. Under the original act, Native people who had shares in Native regional corporations could sell those shares beginning in 1991. Also, under the original settlement Native corporations would have to start paying taxes that, if unpaid, would leave them vulnerable to losing land. ANCSA was eventually amended to protect against these possibilities, but at the time of my interviews with Dene elders there was real concern about the future.

Oscar Isaac, who was of the last generation to live from the land, provided his perspective on changes that occurred in Native life and the differences between Natives and non-Natives. He began by declaring that in the old days, his people might have gone to Canada because of starvation, but they came back. He was pointing out that his people had been in this country for their whole lives and had never left. He then said before World War II, Native people "lived by the country, raised by living on animals." Native people now had to work for money, just like white people, but he reiterated Native people were still very attached to the land.

Comparing Natives and non-Natives, Oscar said:

White people's life to make a business, to make a company, and money which they, and give to their grandchildren and children. Whites love money very much, that's the way White people live. Alaska Native people don't live by money; don't know anything about money, not until World War II. Before that we live by the country, raised by living on animals. We get used to that way, so we really love our country. No one comes around to tell us what to do with our game. We love country so much, and we can't stand, after we get use so much that kind of life. We don't want somebody to come around and tell us what to do. That's something that's going really hurt us. My boys will come around and remember and feel like I feel. (Simeone 1987x)

Oscar also pointed out that young people learned through an oral tradition, and like many young people, they might forget what they heard, but as they got older they remembered what they were told. He concluded by saying that Dene have not stopped living from the land, and they don't use the land like White people.

White people, they set up everything through write down. Papers will stay in the office one hundred years. Us Natives, we don't know how to write, we don't write stories for younger generation. We tell stories for how we can liven by. When we get on to that kind of life, [the hunting life] we cannot

get away from it. When we are young we forget but when we get older around 40 years we start to remember that kind of life.

White people think we don't use the land. We don't use the land [like White people do]. We don't work like White people, they have caterpillar tractor equipment, they survey it up which they use the land. (Simeone 1987x)

He compared non-Natives who had lived in the upper Tanana region before World War II and those who had come after the war. The new arrivals, he said, did not know what life was like before the war, and they had no experience with Native people who had lived on the land.

Some old days White people, them guys understand the Native life. First new people [Whites] come up to Alaska cannot stand [it because there are] no store to buy groceries. And Native can help them out with their own food. What they can eat. White people get to know how Native take care of themselves. Then, if these people, probably more than ten, still living in Alaska, these Whites can prove for us for White people. Too bad we don't have those kind of people left in the country. But they so old and cannot remember. That's how the White people can't understand that we use the land, no trail showing there. (Simeone 1987x)

Oscar then talked about issues concerning the original Alaska Native Claims Settlement Act, and his fear that the state would take the land after 1991. He had no ill feelings against white people—in fact, he thought they had treated Dene people all right—but he was afraid of losing the land.

This is why I realize now after 1991. I think it's going to be hard to get along with White people over the land. Because the Native, they cannot let go how they use to live. And probably hard life waiting for us. Right now, we have good care from White people, hospital bill, all that stuff, welfare for people don't want nothing. They really doing pretty good alright.

But for our country, the—that I wish the State before 1991 to settle the land down a little easy for the Native people. If that way we might get along with the State life. I don't mean against White people. So far I think myself their life is just like us, we don't think they are bad people but only for our country. We don't want State come around bother us for our land, especially after 1991.

White people know that stuff so they might do their best to settle down the problems coming from 1991. But one thing what they did, supposed to be twenty years to settle down, that's too fast.

And if they give us more than twenty years I think that will be better. Young people, might be easy for them to change only way to change that life, I can see. People have to work year around to be on White people's life.

Don't like to see Native against White people. Try to get along with them. Because all over the state they do that kind of work, they know something. (Simeone 1987x)

11 CONCLUSION

The significance of this book is the voice of the elders. Taken together, their voices present a chorus that speaks to more than 100 years of events, people, places, values, and changes. On one level, their stories are about everyday life; on another, they reveal a remarkable resilience, often in the face of extremely challenging circumstances. A variety of sources have been used to present the voices of the elders, but this book represents only a slice of Dene culture and history, and it is not the only possible interpretation.

Through the process of colonialism, Dene culture has undergone many changes. Traditions have been lost or assimilated into modern Dene life. But the culture of the land, as described by the elders, continues to be relevant. In their narratives, the elders emphasized taking care of oneself and one another. They emphasized the importance of skill, knowledge, understanding, and, most importantly, the need to pay attention. Traditional Dene culture was, in many respects, all about paying attention. Young people went through rigorous training so they would learn to pay attention. Survival depended on paying attention.

In the Dene tradition, the relationship between humans and animals is based on a covenant in which humans are obligated to respect animals and in turn animals will allow themselves to be killed. This covenant is sustained through injih: knowing what is and is not acceptable. Injih governs every aspect of Dene life. Knowledge of injih is essential for achieving success and survival in an unpredictable world where humans and animals are equal beings (or where nature rules). Achievement is based on maintaining one's "luck," defined not as something arbitrary but as something brought about by intention. Without "luck," a hunter will not find animals. To encounter and kill animals, it is necessary to pay attention and to have the correct intent.

The elders who contributed to this book wanted to pass on their knowledge, values, and sense of identity as a proud people. What comes through is their devotion to the land and to one another. Two themes emerge: the struggle to maintain a distinct identity based on their relationship with the land, and their ability to adapt to an unpredictable world. The narratives emphasize the values and fortitude needed to make a living from the land. They also describe the unique challenges that form the backdrop to recent Dene history: the fur trade, Christian missionaries, and the struggle for sovereignty and the land.

Dene have lived through successive stages of colonialism. They have either resisted or acquiesced to the changes sought by traders, missionaries, and government agents, but at no time have they been passive: Dene have always been actors in their own history. Colonialism, beginning with the fur trade, has been viewed as an inevitable process by which Dene would become assimilated into white North American culture. This was the underlying assumption of anthropologists who conducted "salvage anthropology," recording what was left of traditional Dene culture. There is no

https://doi.org/10.5876/9781646423347.c011

doubt that colonialism changed Dene and their culture, but Dene elders stress that the culture of the land has not become irrelevant.

During the fur trade, Dene became acquainted with the outside world and sought out new goods. But in becoming consumers, Dene did not abandon their culture. Instead, they used the new goods to enhance the culture of the land. Firearms made hunting somewhat easier, but people did not immediately give up the old methods of snaring animals, which in many ways is more efficient than guns. The white Hudson's Bay blanket with its multi-colored stripes is today a symbol of love and respect displayed on grave houses and given only to highly esteemed persons. Dentalium shells remain symbols of not only status but also affection. On occasion trade goods were destroyed to emphasize the importance of relationships over things, as in the story Oscar Isaac told about his father, Walter Isaac, and the chief of Joseph Village. Perhaps most significantly, Dene did not hoard the objects they obtained in the fur trade. Sharing always remained a prime value with multiple effects: one should never refuse to help another person in need, sharing is a way to maintain or restore a tear in the social fabric, and the distribution of gifts in the potlatch is cathartic, releasing grief over the death of a loved one.

The Episcopal missionaries who came to convert upper Tanana Dene believed God's realm of the spirit and man's earthly domain are entirely separate. One was holy and the other profane. Dene, on the other hand, did not separate the material from the spiritual; in the Dene tradition, these domains intersected and were "simultaneously pragmatic and theistic" (Slotkin 1973: 45).

Missionaries like Margaret Graves and E. A. McIntosh came from an agrarian and settled society where, to be useful, the land needed to be cultivated and made productive by growing things.[1] Agrarian life was seasonal, but the seasons were based on cultivation. Civilization meant a settled existence where people did not move around. Those who did move were considered vagrants, untrustworthy, Gypsies; in other words people not under control. For the missionaries civilization meant control, including controlling the environment, as in the domestication of animals (Slotkin 1973). Dene, on the other hand, knew they only had control over themselves, and that to be successful they had to control their behavior and their mind; they could not control the animals (Easton 2008).

While the missionaries appeared sympathetic, and came with good intentions, Dene refused to accept all the changes the missionaries desired. Perhaps most importantly, they refused to give up the potlatch. By rejecting the missionaries' call to abandon the potlatch, Dene restated the fundamental importance of maintaining reciprocal obligations between clans. Unlike the missionaries, who held great store in the accumulation of individual wealth, Dene understood that things had no value except in being given away.

While rejecting some of the changes desired by the missionaries, Dene did not reject Christianity outright. Missionaries had influence for a variety of reasons. They had access to an apparently endless supply of food, and they promised an afterlife where all one's relatives would be together forever. Christianity also offered an alternative to problems presented by alcohol. To understand the influence of the Church, it is necessary to understand how individuals such as the Reverend David Paul came to accept Christianity. When offered alcohol, the Reverend Paul said he saw two men, one urging him to take the whiskey and the "other say[ing] no good." David prayed, he said, and

---

1 Thus, missionaries complained about the Dene only

eating meat and foods such as muskrat candy. When visiting Tetlin, Reverend Drane (1917: 84) complimented the people on their clean cabins but complained their "tastes seem to be about what they were a hundred years ago. Their diet is straight meat, of moose, caribou, or other game, and fish and they drink tea without sugar."

then he felt "something go into my head to say I shouldn't take the whiskey but I should take the Lord. And I get better like before and I trap like before and my wife and I get enough fur to buy groceries for the winter" (Paul 1987a: 8).

Early missionary work on the upper Tanana River should be placed within the context of the gold rush, a period of dramatic and often traumatic change. In the missionaries' view, Dene, when not corrupted by contact with unscrupulous whites, were "fine, true, and childlike" (Rowe 1910–1911: 67). Well aware Dene were being pushed off the land and "their hunting grounds overrun and exhausted by the Whiteman" (Rowe 1910–1911: 67), missionaries like Bishop Rowe advocated gathering Dene into enclaves controlled by the Church, such as envisioned for St. Timothy's mission at Tanacross. The objective was to protect Dene by helping them to assimilate into white middle-class North American culture.

The discovery of gold changed the social and political landscape of Alaska. The Alaska gold rush fit the American ideal of men violently wresting civilization from the wilderness and making their own fortunes. Before 1898, Americans had largely ignored Alaska; the discovery of gold made it "White man's country" (Dillingham 1904) and finally worth something. Control of the land became the fundamental issue, but under the Treaty of Cession, whereby the United States obtained possession of Alaska, most Native people, including most Dene, were classified as uncivilized tribes with no rights except those granted by the government, including the right to own land.

As control of the land became the issue, so did the question of what to do with Alaska Native people. There were few places for Dene people in the new economy, since unlike in Africa or South America, large amounts of labor were not needed in the gold-mining industry. At the same time, Dene had to compete with non-Natives for fur and essential sources of food. Beyond the road system, the upper Tanana region remained isolated and slow to develop—but this did not stop the conflict over land and resources.

World War II and the construction of the Alaska Highway ended the region's isolation. By the end of the war, all upper Tanana Dene were living in permanent villages, spent less time on the land, and looked for seasonal employment. Kenneth Thomas Sr. of Tanacross said after the war Dene were "getting away from the subsistence life" and began to live "mostly like white people, trying to live like white people. More money, more money for the food, more money for different thing" (Thomas and Mishler 2005: 55). The Alaska Highway opened the region to settlement, and Tok Junction became the regional center. The military base at Tanacross was dismantled, but the airport at Northway became a center for the Federal Aviation Administration. In sum, there was now a relatively large number of non-Natives settled in the upper Tanana region. Dene suffered discrimination and trauma. Lavell Wilson of Northway said Dene were not always welcome in the government facilities at Northway and there was "a lot of animosity in some parts against anybody that wasn't white" (Brewster 2018: 19). The biggest impact, according to Lavell, was "all of the sudden they're supposed to be integrated into another culture." The disruption caused by the highway split some communities. Because of problems in the village, some residents of Tanacross established the village of Dot Lake.

Access to and control over the land continued to fester. Under the Alaska Statehood Act, the state began selecting lands, putting them at odds with Native elders, such as Andrew Isaac. In countless interviews, Andrew and others restated the necessity of keeping the land for future of generations. For the elders, the land and the culture of the land is everything. Some of the land issues were resolved by ANCSA, although the amount of land secured in the agreement by upper Tanana villages was

Figure 11.1. Old Paul, Big Frank, Ellen Isaac, and unknown. According to Rev. Drane, Ellen was a "very fine bead worker." Photo by F. B. Drane. Photo by F. B. Drane Photo collection UAF-2000-181-246. Alaska and Polar Regions Department, Elmer E. Rasmuson Library, University of Alaska, Fairbanks.

Figure 11.2. Peter Thomas, his wife Sarah, and children: Lucy on the left, then Lulu, Calvin in front, and Kenneth in back, circa 1930. Photo by E. A. McIntosh, William E. Simeone photo collection.

Figure 11.3. Albert Charles, also known as Big Albert, and his wife Minnie. Big Albert was from Mentasta, Minnie was from Mansfield and reportedly the daughter of Stsêey Netlé also known as Adam (see chapter 6).

significantly less than the total of their traditional territory. The sentiments of the elders may be best expressed by Maggie Isaac of Dot Lake, who said:

We on this land, forever, since I was born. This my really good home. We don't want to be bothered, to be told where to go, we belong to state, we belong to government, government feed us, that's greatest help because we lose our relatives so the government share with us, treat us right. (Simeone 1987o)

Figure 11.4. Old Paul and family. Front row, from left to right, are David Paul, Old Paul holding his son Julius, Julia, Titus, and Salina Joseph holding her son Edward. In the back, from left to right, are Laura holding Celia, Matthew, Mary, and Joe Joseph. Photo by F. B. Drane. Drane photo collection, Alaska and Polar Regions Department, Elmer E. Rasmuson Library, University of Alaska Fairbanks.

Figure 11.5. Sam Abraham and his wife Belle at Mansfield, 1937/38. Sam is making what appear to be arrows for a big game called *k'ä'* in the Tanacross language. Photo by Lucille Wright. William E. Simeone photo collection.

Figure 12.1. Paul and Margaret Kirsteatter and family. Photo by Robert McKennan, McKennan collection UAF-1985-98-804. Alaska and Polar Regions Department, Elmer E. Rasmuson Library, University of Alaska, Fairbanks.

APPENDIX A

Paul Kirsteatter Letters to Robert McKennan and Description of Healy Lake Culture

Paul Kirsteatter was married to Margaret, whose parents were from Healy Lake and Ketchumstuk. After World War II, Paul moved to Healy Lake. He wrote several letters to the anthropologist Robert McKennan that contained long description of some aspects of Healy Lake culture. The letters were transcribed by myself and my wife, Colleen. Kirsteatter wrote in cursive using a pencil. For the most part his writing is quite legible. There were only one or two words that we could not make out, and these have been noted. Kirsteatter was a keen observer and curious. Most of what he learned came from Margaret and from Chief Walter Isaac, who lived at Tanacross. Walter Isaac's father was Chief Isaac, who died about 1912. Kirsteatter says that Chief Isaac was originally from Healy Lake but moved to Ketchumstuk. Chief Isaac's sons were Walter, Titus, and Follet. Walter married Maggie Demit from Ketchumstuk; Titus, the oldest, married Annie Esau from Ketchumstuk; and Follet first married a woman named Ellen, who died, then moved to Northway and married Pauline. Titus Isaac had a son named Andrew, and Walter had a son named Oscar.

March 9, 1964
Dear Bob,

Will try to send along some information pertaining to Healy River people an Ketchumstuk, Lake Mansfield group.

Chief Walter Isaac at the present time is in the Anchorage hospital and I am un-able to find out as much as I would like, but will see when he returns. I was down to Big Delta and had a talk with John H. so will give you what little I can. But I am like John, it is you might say too late to get accurate first hand information.

As you say the Healy people, Ketchumstuk, Mansfield people were closely related.

I was told by Chief Walter that during the time that the Chief that buried on the hill at Sam Lake carried raids into Copper Center an as far as the coastal tribes, that he called every available man and family into the Sam Creek and Healy area where the banded together for a no. of years here at Healy and Same creek for protection against raids for a no. of years. After the death of this chief "Cheen chetal" as he was called the survivors spread out to Mansfield, Ketchumstuk and Healy area. I understand no one lived at Sam Creek, where a no. of people and the chief died of starvation, for a no. of years after that.

Chief Walter informed me that his father was from Healy band and moved to Ketchumstuk area. Margaret's father, Jacob Isaac, was a brother to Chief Walter Isaac. It seems the Ketchumstuk people were or became more closely linked with the bands on the Yukon Eagle area later. I gather that after the death of this chief here at Sam Creek a number of people moved to Mansfield and Ketchumstuk area. Chief Walter says most of the old

https://doi.org/10.5876/9781646423347.c012

people fore fathers came from this area into Ketchumstuk and Mansfield. I gather that the Mansfield people, who came from everywhere, were not as closely related to Northway and Tetlin people in the old days before white mans coming as they are or have been since white influence in recent years. In early times I am informed there was a good deal of friction between these groups although they did band together to raid people toward the coast. I am told a chief from here would buy men to fight from Northway and Tetlin at times to raid people south of the range.

It seems the Northway and Tetlin group became more closely related in later times as a good many people from here an Mansfield married into those villages in later days.

Chief Walter informed me that Healy, Ketchumstuk, Mansfield, Sam Creek called themselves the "caribou people." Tetlin people "muskrat people," Northway "yellow grass people." I will check with him again concerning this.

As far as Goodpaster people from what I gather they were more closely related with groups down river, than Healy. But I have been informed some from there married into Healy group and in later years, after coming of whites most of Goodpaster people moved to Healy, Mansfield, and a far as Northway.

It seems that the Goodpaster people were more close to the people who lived on river close to Birch Lake—Salchaket including Chena. They were some times spoken of by these people here as fish eaters as salmon came up river to Goodpaster in any no. The village at mouth of Goodpaster was a fish camp I gather.

Chief Walter and Margaret informed me that the language of Ketchumstuk and Mansfield and Healy were more alike

sounding than other groups. This may account for the people from here moving into this area, I don't know.

As far as Chief Joseph. I have been convinced that he belonged to neither Healy or Ketchumstuk. People here at Healy were related to him, some that is, I am informed. But everyone says Chief Joe came from the Goodpaster Village, it seems he married Chief Javis's wife after this chief's death. He moved from Goodpaster Village, to Joseph Village on the Middle Fork, and the mouth of Joseph Creek where a small group lived. Chief Joe I am told played an important role in helping show the route for a telegraph line down from Goodpaster. After he left Joe Village he moved here to Healy Lake and had a house on hill at mouth of Healy River then he moved to George Lake where he lived for a number of years. I am informed he was hospitalized at Fort Yukon and died there. Margaret knew Chief Joseph when she was young at the time he lived at Healy and George Lake.

Joe Joseph of Tanacross was closely related to Chief Joe. A far as the village at Joseph I have been informed that people lived there before Chief Joe. But I gather people lived there at certain times for caribou and I am told they had fish traps there. But no salmon came that far as white fish only grayling were caught.

Silas Solomon at Mansfield who is from Ketchumstuk informs me that Ketchumstuk Mansfield moved up to Joe Village at times for caribou. Also I am informed that Healy and Goodpaster people lived there at times for caribou. Also I am told there is another place half way between Joe Village and head of Healy River where people came to camp while hunting caribou. John H. seems to believe that Chief Joe came from Goodpaster Village as I am told by Margaret and others.

John H. [Hajdukovich] informs me that Chief Healy had some white blood and that his name was taken from this man. Chief Healy's background becomes more confusing as one tries to find out more. The natives living now insist that he had no white blood and that his father before him was Indian so if there was white blood it may of come from his mother's side. John H. informs me that a man named Healy from and living in the Eagle area some place along the Yukon was responsible. I am informed that Chief Healy could not speak English nor his father—not John Healy, Chief Healy's son.

Well Bob will try to get this off hope it will do you some good if you can make it out and when I find time I have a good deal to write about these people that differs from the Upper Tanana group. If I can find anything else that you can use let me know.

We are all well and are out trapping beaver every day will no doubt get all our limits that year as the Army did not bother us this year. We have not heard anything from the Army at this time, but will keep you informed.

With Best Wishes and Regards.
Paul and Margaret

[no date]
Dear Bob

Will attempt to put down a few things I have come across here about the Healy people. I am a relatively new comer here an no doubt a good many old timers who lived here before me had a good deal more information about the Healy Band than I but unfortunately not much was recorded. I regret that someone didn't get more history of these people a few years back where there were still old people living here who could have given a wealth of information.

This is hard for me to undertake as I am not a writer and I hope you will excuse the pencil and manner of hand writing, misspelling and arrangement of this material. I have only a few of my notes with me and I have written this by candle light out here on the trap line. I have read your history of the Upper Tanana group and have tried by memory to outline some of the differences. If you care for any more of this scribbling I have many stories of the social life of these people, customs, stories, notes about tools, implements, more on warfare, life and stories or early contact with first whites of the Healy people. But that would make a book. So have only used a few of my notes and am writing as much a time permits now! Hope some of this will useful to your research and if I have not made anything clear do ask concerning anything I have written here. I suppose you will have a good deal of trouble deciphering my writing.

My source of information come from Margaret and her recollections of teaching by her grandfather and grandmother Sam who were Healy People.

Margaret's cousin Andrew Isaac, Chief Walter of Tanacross whose father and grandparents were Healy People. Some accounts by pioneers to this area and traders, prospectors.

Sincerely,
Paul

DESCRIPTION OF HEALY LAKE CULTURE

My information comes from Margaret and her recollections and teaching by her grandfather and grandmother who were Healy people. [Additional information came from] Margret's cousin Andrew Isaac, Chief Walter [Isaac] of Tanacross whose father and grandparents were Healy [Lake] people, [and] some accounts by pioneers to this area, and traders, and prospectors.

BEAR

Bears no doubt gave these people a good deal of trouble as the old people tell of bears raiding food caches attacking people and dogs.

Margaret recalls her grandfather telling that green sticks with dry birch bark wrapped the ends where kept around the camp to be torched when bears raided caches and camps at night. Men used spears and horn clubs to kill bears.

Bear fat was highly prized as food. Bears fat was rendered by hanging close to heat let drip in birch bark containers then mixed with pounded dried meat and berries. Then poured into large intestines of big game animals let cool then stored for winter.

The bone in bear's penis was prized as a toothpick [and] was worn around neck on a thong. Bear was not spoken of by name, if one thought he may meet him or if you intended to hunt him or his den, [i.e., it is injih to speak about bears directly, especially if a hunter intended to hunt them].

On finding an empty den during the summer, would tie a small piece of skin, string near by on a bush. Then ask the den not to reveal to the bear that is den had been discovered.

Later during the winter when the person thought the bear may be inside the den he would announce to his hunting partners that he thought it time to hunt rabbit or something not mentioning bear by name lest bear know your decision that heavy weapons be carried all would know what kind of hunt this was. [As mentioned above, it is injih to refer to a bear directly because the bear might hear you and become offended. Instead, a person should refer to the bear indirectly, using a word such as "rabbit." People would know a hunter intended to hunt bear by the weapon he carried.] Upon reaching the bears den the men carefully blocked his entrance a den with poles then cut hole in roof of den large enough to spear the bear then he was taken out of the entrance of den.

I have been informed that the fat of bears were dried, the flesh was not eaten except the ribs of black bears were eaten only by the men and sometimes old women, never by young girls.

Margaret informs me that it is believed that bears are extremely jealous of people. A female bear was jealous of female people and vice versa. In case of women meeting bear that was male, women usually held up her dress or exposed her privates so bear could tell and usually this was enough to put bear on the run in case the bear was female the woman was sure to be attacked in jealously. [If a woman met a female bear, the bear would attack out of jealousy.]

I have observed while hunting with Margaret's people that whoever first sees a bear never announces bear by bringing bears attention or presence by pantomiming or by calling him something. The person who first spotted the bear is always allowed to first shoot at him. No one else in the party can shoot first lest it bring bad luck to the first one that saw the bear.

Margaret informs that old people during times of hunger during the summer sometimes ate bear dung if it contained undigested berries.

Margaret recalls that her grandfather told her of bear hunts and young boys were brought along after the man had wounded or killed a grizzly bear. The saliva of the bear was rubbed on the young mans face a young man be asked or forced to rub his face against the bears and the bears strength in later life.

THUNDERBIRD

Margaret and her people believed there was a thunderbird. The birds arrived in the spring had nests and high mountains. By mid summer when he had his young he became very cross. During rainstorms he stayed concealed within the clouds when he was angry. He showed his anger by shooting forth streaks of fire from his eyes. Care was taken not to offend this bird. During electrical storms a person may talk to the bird telling him to go away. To war doff the birds fire smudges were made of green tops of a moss. This was supposed to blind this bird and lessen the damage of his fire hitting you. Margaret still practices this. I have observed while out hunting with her people and while in her villages they would put out these smudges of the moss top mentioned during thunderstorms.

RABBITS

Rabbits were important as food clothing. Drives were made entire villages coming together, rabbits were killed this way by clubs, sinew snares were used a lot.

Rabbit robes were made by twisting hides, hair in, then weaving.

To prevent frost bite cheeks and noses in winter when facing cold winds a person stuck a piece on his nose and cheeks with salvia. Skins were used to line boots. Nursing women used them over the breast to protect them from cold.

Rabbit hearts were never eaten by young people less become mild and timid in face of danger.

Rabbits hind foot was carried for napkin, also used to wipe fingers, cooking utensils birch bark pots.

CARIBOU

Of all the big game this was no doubt the most important animal to the Upper Tanana people's way of life. Here at Healy River at groundhog camp corrals and fences still can be seen that were used to catch and hold caribou.

I am informed by Margaret that the first bands of caribou to appear were always allowed to pass and were not molested in their way of travel. The leaders of the band were never killed. This was practiced by all the people on the upper Tanana that I have talked to.

Hides were used to make clothing, robes, babiche, drags. Meat was dried eaten raw and roasted, boiled in birch bark containers with hot stones. Bones were valued for marrow which was eaten raw or roasted inside bones. Bones were cleaned of flesh a score was made on each side of bone, it was placed inside a fire or hot rocks to melt marrow and re-baked. Bone was then, while hot, struck a hard blow breaking bone length wise along the score. Marrow was mixed with powered dried meat and stored for use. Bones were used for tools, skin scrappers, awls, etc. Ends of tendons for sewing awls.

The bones of fall or early winter killed animals were most desired for tools as they claimed the bones were hardest at that time, very soft when killed in spring.

Hides were used of caribou that were late summer or early fall for clothing as the hair was shorter and wore better for clothing, did not shed as bad. The hooves of unborn calves prized as beads, they were polished and strung on garments. Unborn calves were a favorite with old people for food. Young people were not generally allowed to eat this. Fat around the eyeballs was a delicacy. Nose was a favorite also. Contents of caribou stomachs were eaten raw at certain periods.

Caribou horns were shaped and soaked in hot grease by campfire for a very effective club. The fat gave the horn weight and temper I am informed.

The larger arteries of moose and caribou the one from heart to brain were used to stretch when wet over spear handles then let dry to give these handles greater strength.

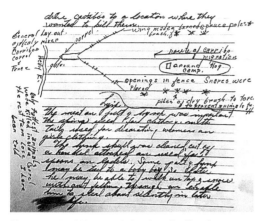

Figure 12.2. Paul Kirsteatter's drawing of caribou fence at K'ąąy Kęę' ("marmot den").

Bones of all big game animals and hooves were cached even after marrow had been taken against the time of famine. Each family had their cache hidden high in the trees known only to themselves at times when no food was available they could recover these bones. They would be boiled then the soup, which has a milky appearance and greasy, was drank. Many old people lived off almost entirely his broth I am informed.

I have hunted with Margaret's people and have observed them call caribou up to shooting range by imitating the grunts of caribou. I have observed them drive caribou to a location where they wanted to kill them.

LYNX

The meat and pelt of lynx was important. The skins used for clothing, mitts, tails used for decorating women's or girls' clothing. The lynx skull was cleaned, cut off, a handle attached and used for spoons and ladles. Same part of lynx may be tied to a baby boy so he may be able to walk in deep snow without falling through and enable him to steal about silently in later life.

Lynx was thought to be people one [time] woman. There is a fable as to how lynx get her appearance. I may add flesh of lynx was not generally eaten except during famine.

WOLF

Wolf was thought to be people, considered cousin to Indian. When one is caught in trap Indian may talk to the wolf telling wolf that he is sorry to find him in this trap he keeps talking to wolf until wolf turns and is not looking before he is shot.

Margaret's people are very good at imitating the different calls of wolves and have witnessed wolves being called up within shooting distance on many occasions.

WOLVERINE

Wolverine was also thought to be a person. He is thought to possess strong medicine, all bad. There are many stories relating to wolverine. One great insult was to be called a wolverine by another person, such a person was a thief, robber, wife stealer, rapist, etc. also a liar.

Wolverine parts were used by medicine men in making medicine against certain people.

FLYING SQUIRREL

Was considered bad luck to catch one in any trap. If person catching a flying squirrel in a set of any kind he at once cut the squirrel up into small pieces and burned it completely. If this was not done this person would have bad luck in catching all animals.

PORCUPINES

These animals were important food animals. They would [illegible text] held by forked stick through leg tendons over fire quills and hair burned off and the hides scraped clean fat stored for later use meat could be dried [illegible text] were eaten by old people. Quills were died and used for woven bead work and on moccasins.

The hip bone was used around camp as a game. A group sat in a circle, taking the bone in one hand extended arms extended straight out sideways from body the person then closed his eyes bring the hand with the bone around horizontally and in front of him at the same time bringing the other hand around to meet the bone finger extended. The object was to place the finger into the socket on the first try. The bone was passed around the circle of players.

FISH

Although the people here caught a good number of whitefish and grayling I gather their dependence was primarily on meat. Fish traps were maintained at Ground Hog Camp on Healy River and at several locations near the outlet of Healy River. As Margaret and others have described the traps I gather they were similar to the ones you have described on the upper Tanana.

No salmon of any importance come this far. Although the Goodpaster people caught a good number.

White fish were stored her in pits I believe Margaret described them to you—also dried. Fish eggs were mixed with snow and eaten raw or boiled and eaten. I am informed that lincod was speared through the ice and gaffed. Cannot find any mention of fish hooks. The liver of the cod was eaten although the flesh was not often used for food the livers are rich and fat which they liked.

THE USE OF KNIVES

I have always observed the people in their use of knives whether in skinning, cutting meat, woodworking, carving, that they always cut towards themselves. This was done by all the old people and many of the young ones today.

I have been informed by Margaret that this was taught to all young people the belief that by cutting towards ones body was assurance animals and material would always be easy to catch or kill that the animals would be more likely to come to the hunters, in case of wood it would always be easily found. [Note on letter—"see back of page."]

I have noticed that the older people almost always used dull knives and when they were sharpened it was only from one side. [diagram]

It has been explained that they preferred this shape blade for skinning and meat cutting. They seldom cut across grain on any meat as individual muscles were separated with fingers and cut off at tendons. In cutting meat to dry the meat is flayed thin with the grain therefore it did not require such sharp knife.

Margaret has said the old people skinned came almost entirely by pulling and parting the hide with the hands. This was so as not to make any cuts an inside of hide which makes skins hard to tan on thin places.

Margaret recalls old people using stone scrapers in scarping hides although steel knives were to be had. Her grandmother refused to use them as she said the steel became hot and spoiled the hides.

I believe that their preference to dull knives and the way they used them came from the use of stone knives used by the before them.

FIRST CAUGHT AND KILLED GAME OF THE SEASON

When trapping upon catching any animal before the animal was taken out of trap or snare a bit of his hair was pulled through the snare or trap. This bit of hair was kept in a skin bag. By this way animals would always come to your snares and trap instead of away.

BIRCH AND POPLAR JUICE

This was a food to be gathered every spring when the sap was rising. First the outer bark was peeled off then the inner bark pulp was scraped off and juice collected in birch bark baskets. This was sometimes boiled and juice allowed to slightly ferment and drank.

BERRIES

Berries were an important part of the diet. After gathering they were kept in birch bark containers hung in high caches and buried in ground sometimes. Some berries were mixed with grease and fat. I have noticed that upon eating large quantities of fat that afterwards the people like to eat berries afterwards and I believe that the acids of the berries is only way that kept the grease down after seeing the amount of fats eaten at one time. The low brush cranberries being the most desired when eating fats. Berries were also cooked with marrow grease and any fats including fish that were fat.

HERBS AND PLANTS USED FOR MEDICINE

I am familiar with a good many but knowing the scientific names will only mention a few. The puff ball fungus found on the ground was used to stop bleeding and in leaky wounds. Fresh pitch from spruce was used for cuts and burns.

Old pitch was used for gum and for cleaning the teeth. Wild rhubarb roots were made into strong tea for heart trouble. There was a plant here used for tea the leaves gathered and dried and used a brew. Popular buds were brewed and used for sore throats.

Bear galls and beaver caster was used for some internal aliments. Of the three types of birch fungus one is burned and the ash used in tobacco and sometimes in tea. The dog nose fungus is used for mosquito smudges. The other kind used to make fire with and given to pups when young as when they became grown dogs they could endure long periods of famine.

Urine of young female person was used for cramps.

Milk from nursing mothers' breast was dabbed on sores to cure them.

Feathers were used to pull through wounds to clean them.

Of any drug or plants used for the purpose of stimulating sexual desire I have not heard of any here used by the Healy Band only of a few medicine men who had certain power over females no doubt through fear or power over mind.

Although it is said that the Scottie Creek people use certain plants to seduce members of the opposite sex against their wish I have heard of different instances and other people of the Upper Tanana groups believe this is true and do not allow their women to mix with this band, if so, not eat or drink anything.

A brew made from pitch was drank for stomach or intestines passing blood or vomiting blood.

DOGS

These people I have observed show great love towards dogs. A dog is sometimes given peoples names and kept inside of the dwelling, eating same food as they themselves. I think this love and respect of the dog comes from way back before contact with whites.

As I have been informed that dogs were taught hunt game for their masters, as well as help drive away bears that raided camps and caches, also used to warn against raiding parties of other bands.

The raising of you dogs as very important only certain food were given the pups. Bear meat was not given to pups lest it make them mean. Certain plants and funguses were given to small pups which I am familiar but not knowing the names of these can not put it down.

While one desired a pup that would grow into a hunting dog for a certain animal or animals such as a dog to trail and hold moose a piece of moose hide with hair on would be tied around the pups neck until it wore out. Later that dog could be easily trained be trained to hunt moose and hold the moose at bay until hunters arrived.

Dogs were allowed to live out their natural lives even carried or pulled on hide drags from one camp to another when it became too old to move on its own.

I have been informed by Margaret that potlatches have been given in honor of dogs. The dog being cremated or buried the same as people. Of all the stories of famines in the past I have not heard of any accounts of people eating dogs and they seemed shocked at the mention of it, as do they do eating any member of the dog family such as the wolf and fox.

A stick or wood giving off a loud popping sound or bang means that that person has lost something from trap or snare, referring to wood cracking while in campfire or stove.

Fur animals were not skinned inside the abode always out from site of camp. The carcass of animals related to man were burned or hung up in the trees out of reach of the dogs or other animals. Bad luck was sure to strike if this was not complied with. Now today this is not practiced.

A person when excreting always went away from camp excrement was placed in bark or moss up in brush away from dogs or people.

Spit or urine were taken from a sick person in bark or moss and taken away from village placed high in tree or bush less someone make contact and bad luck befall him.

There is legend about a cannibal who lived in this area and who wore fish skin clothing but it's said his origin is not known. Several stories have been built up around this person.

WEATHER

I have noted that the older people could forecast the weather with great accuracy. It is said that some people had great influence over the weather. I have seen that during a cold spell someone who has warm weather would be called upon to change the weather. A speech may be made calling for his weather to drive away the cold. A person may select a large spruce tree with many thick branches and set fire to it to bring his kind of weather. This person calling for warm weather is usually born during warm weather.

It is believed the wind are an old man and woman. When it is calm all is well with them. A cold wind is the old man starting a fight with the old woman. The old woman wind will most always win out by blowing warm winds.

Many of the stars had names to them and the positions of stars told them the time, seasons, directions.

The bones on the palms of their hands were red, every line had a meaning as how many times a person would marry or how many wives, how lucky he would be how brave and so on.

CANOES

Canoes were made of birch bark and skin with birch frames as Upper Tanana people. The paddles were the same.

The purpose of the point was to stick in to the bank at ground level at right angles to canoe. The handle of paddle was grasped by both hands along with cross member of canoe to steady canoe while stepping out onto bank and getting into. The handle of paddle was about five and half feet long enabling man to stand up in these canoes an paddle in this manner he could look over high banks while drifting down stream watching game.

I am informed that the old people traveled the length of the Tanana River to Tanana to visit fur trader then walked back maybe taking all summer. The early traders one Mr. Hajdukovich claimed the Healy people were the most skilled at using boats and reading water, and were in demand for hire by the early traders needed help getting freight boats up the Tanana River and many of the Healy people worked these boats.

These people no doubt became skilled as they lived along the roughest stretch of the Tanana to navigate.

In shallow water instead of a paddle to move their canoes two short sticks were used in each hand, one in each hand in each side of canoe to press against bottom and push the canoe along even up riffles and swift waters.

Surprisingly few of the Indian people know how to swim. I know from experience that the canoes used by them which are only wide enough to sit or kneel in are extremely cranky and one cannot fire a gun from right angles from one without being flipped over. Margaret told me that the canoes were used to hunt ducks, beaver, rats. Ducks were shot with blunt wood arrows during the molt of the birds and before the young could fly.

Caribou were also run down in Healy Lake while swimming across. They were killed by a sharp lance back of the skull cutting neck tendons or spearing behind shoulder blade only after the animal expelled its breath so muscles were not taught over ribs allowing spear or lance to penetrate lungs. No doubt these people spent a good deal of the summer hunting from canoes as it was the easiest way of getting about. I am informed that most of the Healy people living on the islands on Healy Lake and islands on Tanana River at mouth of Healy River so this would account for their dependence on canoes also.

SNOW SHOES

Snow shoes here at Healy that I have saw made by Healy people are similar to the ones you have described in upper Tanana. A round point toe used for brush. Sharp turned up pointed toed shoes used for open hard snow.

A snow shoe was considered inferior and cheap unless sinew was used to lace through the wood. Caribou babich was laced through (toe front) this moose hide under foot.

Holes in the wood of shoe frame were not drilled or burned through. A sharp pointed bone awl parted fibers of wood around the inside edge of frame and sinew was run through in this manner no wood fibers were broken or cut making a stronger frame. Moose hide babiche was wrapped around frame and woven foot part. Cross piece under foot was sometimes strengthened sinew rope for wet snow. Men made the frames, selecting the birch with great care. The women filled in lacing.

PAINT

Mr. J. Hajdukovich informed me that paint form a Healy made snowshoe was analyzed and was a form of [cannot make out this word, appears to begin with a V].

There was three colors of paint gathered by the Healy people, bright orange, dark red, and blue.

Many prospectors had looked for the source here on Healy River but from what I gather the Healy people only know the exact location. They use this paint for trade as far away as coastal tribes I am told.

The red I understand was used for dances painting face hands also for war paint. The orange was used for tools and equipment. The people had a pencil although I don't believe they did any writing at all and can find no evidence that it was used to communicate by drawing.

This was a decayed form of birch when under certain conditions becomes partly decomposed and water stained to a deep blue.

I am informed by Margaret that her grandmother used pieces of this wood to mark out patterns on hides to be made into garments.

Also I am told each person had a sign known only to his people. That when travelling that he left his mark in certain places so that his relations could trace him in the event he did not return. This was used by members of any band who were sent to spy on others. Along this route he always left his mark in certain places so if he did not return his people could trace him an bring the people responsible for his disappearance to account.

In the event he did not return this was used by members of any band who were sent to spy on others. Along his route he always left his mark in certain places so if he did not return his people could trace him and bring the people responsible for his disappearance to account.

Feathers of birds were also used to mark the trails taken by people. Also paint markings at several parts of trail were left to mark his way not for his self but for anyone of his own people to follow.

I have been informed by Chief Walter that Mansfield, Healy River, Ketchumstuk, Sam Creek people were called the caribou people. The Tetlin people the muskrat people. There was group downriver called the bear people but their location was vague. These people I have been told wear bearskin clothing use bear hide, coated with pitch and sand shields.

As these people were almost constantly at war or expecting raiding parties they took great care in storing food hidden in places sometimes a good distance from their villages. During my travels I have observed pits in out of the way places that were not prospect pits made by prospectors. I have been informed that each family had these pits secreted and for storage of food known only to each individual family in case they were driven out of their villages in winter they could survive they were described to me to be as built similar to the ones you have mentioned the Upper Tanana people using. Sometimes I have been told storage was made in large crack in bank that had begun to sluff off around lake and river banks. The tops were covered with birch bark, dirt then logs, then rocks brush to prevent animals from digging into them.

WARFARE

I gather by what has been told to me by Margaret and her people that they were almost always at warfare, raiding parties and family feuds.

It seems that the young men were trained in the use of weapons, toughened to endure sever hardships at an early age.

I have been informed that the young men were awakened early in the morning during the winter before sunup and a contest was run as to distance from village and back without hardly any clothing on and in bare footed

through the snow during the coldest weather. They were encouraged to jump over brush so as it wiped their privates in doing so. They were taught the use of weapons at an early age.

I'm told guards were constantly on alert for raiding parties. Scouts were patrolling miles out from villages year around and guard against raiding parties also for lookouts for big game. At night men usually slept fully clothed weapons on hand. Grass blades were placed across all trails leading to and from villages that would be disturbed if any spies had come close to camp. Men were constantly drilled in defense of their villages, attacks were usually to be expected at nights during storms and in winter.

In case of alarm or any danger at night usually old women were sent to investigate. She was not to cry out if she saw danger but pretend to urinate and return to spread the alarm or prearrange signal imitating night birds call.

In case of danger I am told the men rally to the defense of the village. A number were sent out as scouts. In case of attack heavy rawhides of bull moose which were doubled and kept inside the walls of dwellings were cared for by the women. If a man had more than one wife the more protection he may have as women held these moose hide shields in front of her husband and at his back while he could use bow or club the women being crouched down around the men.

From what I gather these raiding parties seldom took prisoners. Women children and men with the exception of some young women were all slain in case of defeat by the attacked village.

Spies were sent out in all directions to watch other bands, counting the people, watching their activities for any sign that they were making preparation for a raid anywhere. It seems that the Healy River people were at warfare with the Copper River and Burwash bands. Have not heard of any raids exchanged down river toward Tanana. These people being closely related may account for this. When a raid was made on any band the raiders were very careful not to harm anyone in the camp who was related to their band. Spies I have been told have given location of any relatives in a camp to be raided before hand so they will not be harmed.

I have been informed that when the chief of one band makes war he sometimes borrows men from friendly bands. But in these raids his men were not to harm the relations of any of the borrowed men, or he was responsible if harm came to these men relatives, he usually paid with his life (pertaining to the chief).

I have been informed by Chief Walter at Tanacross who was raised in Ketchumstuk and Mansfield area but whose father and grandfather were originally Healy River people that the Healy River people were ruled by two powerful chiefs. One made a stand on top of the hill by Sam Lake he had the people of Healy River, Ketchumstuk area, Sam Creek constantly at war with Copper River bands. His village was established on top of the hill called Nose Hill after him [see chapter 6 for more on Ch'inchedl]. This high hilltop afforded good protection from counter raids. It seems his people suffered so many defeats and counter raids that the Healy River people including his others were almost wiped out. Then came a winter of famine wiping out most of them.

It seems this chief has lost a son while the son was away on a spying mission. The chief had a remaining son, a brother to the missing one who everyone feared as he even killed his own people by treachery and the chief was constantly sending spies and raiding party's out. To find and avenge his lost son by his madness he almost lost all his people. As he was also a powerful medicine man everyone feared him. Finally a young girl was offered to him I am told, and his own relation at that, to make up for his lost son. That same winter his village including him died of starvation the remainder of his people moved back to Healy River, Ketchumstuk and Mansfield.

I suppose that the famine was brought about by not keeping enough men at home

long enough to hunt game for the large number of women and children. And no doubt the raiding parties of the Copper River kept them from gathering food for the winter.

Another powerful chief and a medicine man ruled here at Healy Lake who lived with his band on the islands of Healy Lake and island at the mouth of Healy River. It was explained the islands gave protection against raids and raiders as raiders could be spotted before they could approach the islands.

It seems that all the chiefs here at Healy River were powerful medicine men as was later the several generations of Healy chiefs.

I have been informed by Chief Walter that he can trace Healy chiefs back four generations and that old man Healy was a original Healy and all his men before him. Chief Walter says the Healy Chiefs did not come from down river as someone at Tanacross told you. Margaret and others have confirmed this also.

I have been told that the name Healy was given to him by a party of prospectors who were passing through Ground Hog camp enroute from Dawson area. It is said Old Chief looked like a member of their group whom they knew in the Dawson area. They called him Healy and the name stuck.

I gather that Old Chief Healy was a remarkable chief and medicine man, all early white men speak highly of him. It seems he did not learn to speak English and maintained his old ways always impressing on his people that white man ways were bad for his people although he remained friends with all white men and I am told his camp was always welcome to white men. It is said he always gave food and shelter to any white man. His people no doubt have saved many of the early white man lives from accounts told to me by our pioneers.

I am told that his father and father before him were also chiefs as well as his son John who was the last Healy chief who died sometime about 1916. I am told that the Healy chiefs were peaceful and always had plenty.

It seems that the Healy chiefs had great power over not only the people here at Healy River but Joseph Village, Ketchumstuk, Mansfield, Sam Creek, and George Creek villages. I understand that the people in the above mentioned villages were all closely related to the Healy band.

I gather that the medicine men held power and influence over the lives of these people. Some medicine men who were also chiefs used this influence for the good of the people while others had people constantly at war or ruled them by fear and his powers.

I believe that the center of rule has more or less come from Healy River. This area geographically was ideally located for abundance of game, islands for village sites, fish, water animals, waterfowl, moose, close to sheep mountain, squirrels, marmots, and the caribou migration routes. Food of some kind was more apt to be available here.

As the abundance of game during these times would certainly be a factor in location of villages, also the number of village sites around the mainland of Healy Lake. Islands and village sites up river are an indication that there has long been people here compared to single village sites at other locations.

By the artifacts found although I am not an authority but judging from the different makes of tools I believe other peoples have long past from this area.

I have been informed by Chief Walter and memories of Margaret's hearing stories of her grandfather Sam that the Healy people traveled out long distances from here. Accounts of travels to vicinity of Tanana at the mouth of Tanana River to trade and visit. Also to the coast from here, also the Chiefs sent parties from here to trade with people in Eagle, Fort Yukon area. Margaret recalls her grandfather talking of trips taking all summer to trade for tobacco on the Eagle area perhaps this was their first contact with whites in the interior and in the Tanana area.

There is tales told of contact with Russian who were hated by the people here. There is a account of a powerful medicine man from here who made a trip to the Copper River area to meet the Russians and see for himself how strong their medicine was. It seems while there the Russian Priest tried to convert the medicine man from here after telling the medicine man that the white man's god was stronger medicine that his. The medicine man demanded proof where upon he displayed a number of feats challenging the priest to match them. One I am told the man had a long pole smoothed and greased erected within the camp, the medicine man Got up to the top of the pole and stood on the top challenging the priest to follow him. It is said this medicine man also walked across the water challenging the priest to follow. After a number of such feats the medicine man is said to have expressed great disgust to the who had the copper river people so [cannot make out word seems to be spelled "caudeled"—could be coddled?] that every one was almost his slave. This medicine man returned to Healy River. Later I am told he acquired his first muzzle loader gun and while in Mansfield area had an accident shooting his arm nearly off. He called the villagers together to ask that they carry out his instructions where as a hide was placed on the ground which he lay down on, another moose hide, the strongest in the village was placed over him, slits were cut around the edge and heavy stakes driven through securing him tight to the ground. Everyone feared for the medicine man's life as he had lost much blood. After a while a fox ran there out the village barking then all the dogs began howling. At this time it is said a terrific struggle took place under the moose hide and unearthly sounds. The pegs holding down the moose hide over the medicine man began to pull out, the hide tore and split. Up rose the medicine man, his bleeding arm had stopped bleeding and healed quickly but it is said that there after the arm was a good deal shorter that the other.

I have been informed that a Russian party penetrated with area to some where near the mouth of the Tok River where they met a band of Mansfield people on a hunting trip. It seems that a few women were with the hunters, the women were taken captive by the Russians where upon the hunting party of natives sent for help and wiped then out. I was told this by Peter Charles of Dot Lake as told by his grandfather. Others have told stories of this and said it was kept quiet to the early whites who came into this area for fear of retaliation.[1]

---

1   Peter Charles is probably referring to Russian incursions into the upper Copper River that took place at Natnełde, or Batzulnetas, probably in the winter of 1794–1795, and at Stl'aa Caegge, or "Rear River Mouth," at the confluence of the Slana and Copper Rivers in 1848. There is no written evidence Russians made it over the mountains into the upper Tanana drainage, but Gaither Paul told a story to the author about the Russians coming to Lake Mansfield.

APPENDIX B

Traditional Territories and Community Histories

At the end of the nineteenth century, Dene were organized into six local groups, or bands, each with a distinct territory (McKennan 1959: 17–18; 1980: 564, 566; Guédon 1974: 12). The Reverend David Paul of Tanacross provided this succinct description of the region, from the Canadian border to the confluence of the Goodpaster and Tanana Rivers. David said that when Chief Jarvis moved from the village of Goodpaster to the Episcopal mission at Salchaket, he moved out of the upper Tanana region.

> In 1907 Chief Jarvis moved from Goodpaster to Salchag, to mission there. This [Salchag] out of Upper Tanana and do away with village at Goodpaster. My Daddy [Old Paul] and his brother have ch'elaats'eyh'shax (bark house) at Big Delta. They moved to Mansfield. . . . Goodpaster is end of Upper Tanana people and Scotty Creek end of Upper Tanana too. Have no relations there (Scotty Creek). All people at George Creek, Sand Creek, and Healy Lake dead now or moved to Mansfield or Dot Lake. (Pitts 1972: 16)

The maps below show the territories of each band and the place names associated with each area. Place names are from Andrews 1980; Kari 1997; Kari and Thoman n.d.

Territorial boundaries were strictly enforced in the sense that local Dene controlled access to fishing sites and hunting areas, but outsiders could use resources by invoking clan affiliation or rights through marriage with the owners. It was particularly shameful to deny access

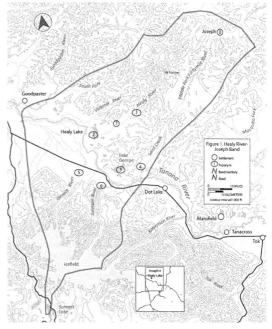

Figure 13.1. Healy River–Joseph territory included the entire drainage of the (1) Healy River (Ts'aadleey Nediig', "least cisco whitefish creek"); (2) Healy Lake (Mendees Cheeg Menh, "shallow lake mouth lake"); (3) George Lake (Nxaal Měnn', "big whitefish lake"), and (4) Sand Lake (Ch'inchedl Měnn', "nose lake"). It also included the drainages of the (5) Big Gerstel (Ts'iitsiiy Ndiig) and (6) Johnson Rivers (Ts'eethaay Ndiig, "gravel creek"). Villages included (7) K'ąąy Kęę' ("marmot den") on the Healy River and (8) Joseph (TehłuugNiindeex Ndiig, "whitefish moves creek") on the Middle Fork of the Fortymile River. Map by Matt O'Leary, adapted from McKennan (1981: 564).

to one's father's clan. A person from Tetlin explains that hunting in another group's territory required permission from the chiefs:

> If Tanacross guy came over here, all right to hunt, if he goes with somebody. You go

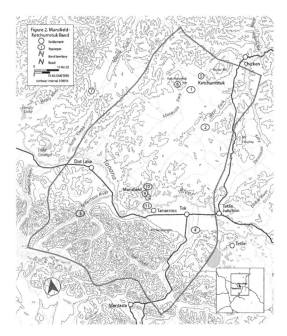

Figure 13.2. Mansfield-Ketchumstuk territory encompassed the entire drainages of the (1) Mosquito (Ch'edzagh Ndiig, "ear creek") and (2) West Forks of the Fortymile River, as well as the lower parts of the (3) Robertson (Njhtsiił Ndiig, "house river") and (4) Tok Rivers (Tth'itiy Ndá, "strong river"). Villages included (5) Ketchumstuk (Saagés cheeg, "sun fork mouth") at the mouth of Ketchumstuk Creek, (6) Mbehts'eh Těyy' ("flint hill"), (7) Boat Bottom or Canoe Bottom (Ts'eyh Keetl'agh) at the head of the Healy River (Ts'aadleey Ndiig, "least cisco whitefish creek"), (8) Mansfield (Ch'enaa Ndedh, "long omen") between (9) Mansfield Lake (Dihthâad Měen', "nearby place lake") and (10) Fish Creek (Taacheeg Ndiig), and (11) the ancient village of Dihthâad ("nearby place") on Fish Creek. Map by Matt O'Leary, adapted from McKennan (1981: 564).

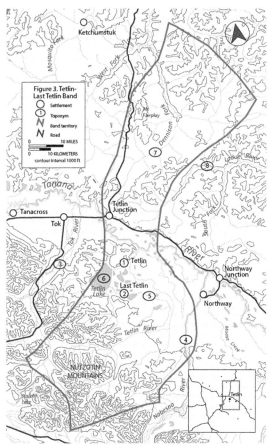

Figure 13.3. The boundaries of (1) Tetlin (Tee łay) and (2) Last Tetlin (Nahk'ädn, "fishing place") territory encompassed the southern slopes of the Nutzotin Mountains between the (3) Tok (Tth'iitiy Ndá, "strong river") and (4) Nabesna (Naambia Niign, "stone river") Rivers, including the (5) Tetlin River (Teełay Niign, "current flows river"), (6) Tetlin Lake (Mänh Choh, "big lake"), (7) the Dennison Fork of the Fortymile River (Mbethts' ayh Niign, "obsidian river"), and (8) the Ladue River (Ch'ign Niig, "cut bank river"). Map by Matt O'Leary, adapted from McKennan (1981: 564).

Last Tetlin, any place, you have to go with them; people ask you to go with them, then it's all right for you to go. You can't go by yourselves. He who wants to go hunting Last Tetlin had to ask Chief Luke, to ask everybody. Ask everybody that's the way. Sometimes, a big bunch of people coming for caribou hunting. They got to ask, to let them know where they are going. (Guédon 1974: 149)

Members of each local group were related by either blood or marriage, with kin ties extending to other regional groups as well as to Dene living outside the area. Today, families in Tetlin can trace their ancestry to Han who live on the upper Yukon River, while families from Tanacross, Dot Lake, Tetlin, and Northway have ancestors among the upper Ahtna. The number of people in a local band varied. When food was scarce, a band disbursed as families went off in separate directions to search for food.

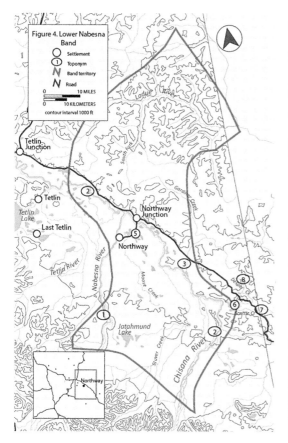

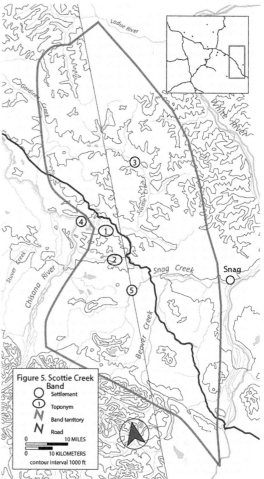

Figure 13.4. Lower Nabesna territory included parts of the lower and middle (1) Nabesna River (Naambia Niign, "stone river"), (2) the lower and middle Chisana River, along the Tanana River to the mouth of (3) Gardiner Creek (Cheejil Niign, "grayling creek") and the lower Ladue River (Ch'ign Niig, "cut bank river"). Villages included (4) K'ehtthîign ("lake outlet") and (5) Tayh Tsäł T'aat ("beneath little hill"), also called High Cache Village, at the confluence of Big Scottie Creek (Ttheek'ädn Keey, "rock weir place") and Desper Creek. Map by Matt O'Leary, adapted from McKennan (1981: 564).

Figure 13.5. Scottie Creek territory encompassed the lower Chisana River basin, including the (1) Scottie Creek (Ttheek'ädn Keey, "rock weir place") and (2) Mirror Creek valleys (Ch'ign Niign, "? creek"). Villages included (3) Niiduu Ts'in-ehdaayh ("we shoot lynx with an arrow") at the head of the Scottie Creek valley, (4) Tahmìil K'èet ("fishnet place") at the confluence of the Chisana River and Scottie Creek, and (5) Taatsaan ("raven" or "crow") on the right bank of Snag Creek where it crosses the international border. Map by Matt O'Leary, adapted from McKennan (1981: 564) and Easton (2021).

When food was plentiful, family units came together. Under certain circumstances, such as the annual caribou migration, many people joined together. For example, Dene from as far away as Northway and Mentasta often joined their relatives at Ketchumstuk to hunt caribou.

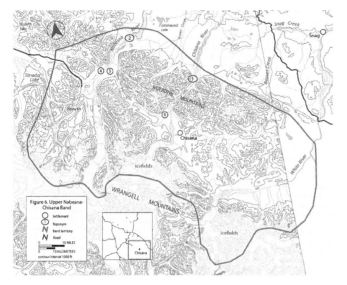

Figure 6. Upper Nabesna-Chisana Band

○ Settlement
N Toponym
N Band territory
N Road

0 ___ 10 MILES
0 ___ 10 KILOMETERS
contour interval 1000 ft

Figure 13.6. Upper Nabesna–Upper Chisana (Ddhał Tot iin, "among the mountain people") territory included the basins of the (1) White, (2) upper Nabesna, and (3) upper Chisana Rivers. Villages included (4) Dit' aan Niig ("falcon creek"), a precolonial village at the mouth of Platinum Creek, (5) Tthiix ąą' Cheeg ("brain mouth") at the mouth of Cooper Creek, and (6) Tsayh Niig ("ochre creek," or Cross Creek) on the east bank of the upper Chisana River just below Red Hill Creek. Map by Matt O'Leary, adapted from McKennan (1981: 564).

"OUR GRANDPA'S FACE": THE GEOGRAPHY OF MEMORY AND HOW TO LIVE

Before settling into permanent villages in the early twentieth century, upper Tanana Dene maintained winter villages, usually on a river or lake. An extensive system of trails linked these places to outlying camps, traplines, stopping places, and lakeside camps. Winter villages (*keey* in both languages) were relatively permanent settlements with one or more large semisubterranean houses. These were often the headquarters of prominent clan leaders, where important ceremonies were held. They were distinguished from camps or stopping places (*haał* [T], *háał* [UT]) by a geographic landmark such as a hill, mountain, or riverbank referred to as "our grandpa" or "our grandpa's face" (Guédon 1974: 147). Rising above the landscape, these landmarks are memorials to the people who came before, paved the way, sustained them, and provided the moral and ethical compass to becoming a complete human being (Basso 1996). The hills, mountains, and riverbanks function as moral and historical lessons about how to conduct oneself in the world as well as one's place in it.

In Dene culture, these landmarks are associated with specific clans. Writing about Tlingit, Frederica de Laguna (quoted in Thornton 2011: 14) said, "It would be possible to show that an individual's sense of history and geography is strongly affected by the dominance of the sib [i.e., clan] which controls the social, political and ceremonial aspects of his or her life." It is the clan, de Laguna wrote, "that provides a sort of unity to geography and history." Place names are important, not only as reference to economic activities, such as fishing, but to understand the social history of the clan. This sense of place is enlivened and enriched by experience on the land. Land is part of the social fabric and expressed in language.

In an interview with the author (Simeone 1987a), Julius Paul of Tanacross talked about how important places, such as Ketchumstuk, Tetlin, and Northway, were designated by these landmarks, whereas camps, such as Paul's Place, Billy Creek, and Sam Lake, were not. According to Julius, Mansfield was the lead village for all the Upper Tanana communities, whereas Ahtna from the Copper River were under a different chief. Ketchumstuk had two associated hills for which Julius names. The people of Mansfield, the ancestral village of many contemporary Tanacross people, are represented by Naadę̨ę̨y Xú' ("marmot tooth" or "frog tooth"), a prominent mountain in the Alaska Range with two peaks resembling two teeth or fangs. They are also represented by Mesiin Tsiits'iig, a smaller hill near the old village of Dihthâad. Using the analogy of the American flag, Julius explained the importance of Naadę̨ę̨y Xú'. In discussing the different places, Julius recited the names of people associated with those places. This is important information because it places individuals in a geographic context. Knowing where people came from provides important clues about clan affiliation, training, and knowledge.

[Naadę̨ę̨y Xú' stands] for Lake Mansfield, like American flag. Then Maseeen siitsii is next, like the Alaska flag, underneath Naxęy Xú' which is more great than Mesiin Tsiits'iig.

Tetlin hill, Northway same way too, Mentasta same way, Healy Lake same way. Paul's Place is just like campground so there is no place like that. Mansfield used to be lead for all those guys. Copper River is different, different chief. Ketchumstuk has two different kind of hill, Wudzih Naa Ddhel' is one but cannot remember name of other one; same as Naadę̨ę̨y Xú'.

Billy Creek, Sam Lake are just like out camps and have no hill or mountain attached to them. George Lake used to have a village but no more; belonged to Chief Joe, David and Alex Joe's grandfather. Logan's (Luke) mother, her uncle was Chief Joe, mother's youngest brother. Jenny Healy and Abraham's [Luke] wife Eva, and Ruth's mother. Chief Joe was their uncle, [he was also Joe from Joseph Village who met the surveyor William Mitchell]. Probably had a mountain there. Chief Joe was Joe Joseph's uncle, mother's cousin so Chief Joe was his uncle and that's how he stayed there. From Joe village, Joe Joseph walk to Saagés cheeg [Ketchumstuk] before he married Salina. Chief Joe told him to look for Ketchumstuk

people who had moved to Mansfield for the late spring and summer. Before missionary that's all we got is to move around.

This is great man, that kind of man, this, who is the good lead man. That's why they call this [Naadę̨ę̨y Xú'], just like lead man, smart man in the village to lead people, use to be that's why they call this, higher than other one [referring to Mesiin Tsiits'iig]. In old days they use to say, Mansfield use to lead all over, Healy Lake, Mentasta, Northway, Tetlin, Ketchumstuk, lead the village, that's why they call this our flag. (Simeone 1987a)

In 1960, the Reverend David Paul, who was Julius's older brother, talked to the anthropologist Frederica de Laguna about Naadę̨ę̨y Xú' and Mansfield.

Let me tell you one more thing about what the Indian think about the village. Mansfield Village—you see this little hill? [points, to Naadę̨ę̨y Xú'] . . . Mansfield Village (has) fish run. We used village just for fish. Last fall I told some white person, see this little hill? 300 years ago, they talk about that hill. It's like somebody put a post there, like Indian headman put a post and seal that nobody could break. Two little hills—(one on each side)—like: [hold up fingers to make a V signifying the twin peaks of Naadę̨ę̨y Xú'].

They talk about that one, just like Copper River talk about Mt. Sanford. Like Tetlin Hill, where there's high place. They talk about it. Sand Creek got (hill) talk about it. And down Mendees (Mentasta) got little hill. Like talk about that little hill. They talk about that mountain. (de Laguna and McClellan 1960b)

Oscar Isaac of Tanacross said each clan had a "top man" and that landmarks such as Naxęy Xú' represent that man and his clan. Oscar said Naadę̨ę̨y Xú' represented the Ałts'i̧ Dendeey clan, while Mesiin Tsiits'iig represented the

Dik'aagyu clan, and a hill near the village of Eagle represented the Naltsiin clan. Oscar went on to add additional details. Naadęęy Xú' represented Old Chief Isaac (Oscar's paternal grandfather) and all of the preceding generations of Ałts'į'Dendeey that stood behind him. According to Oscar, Old Chief Isaac was the last great Ałts'į'Dendeey leader. Oscar said the mantle of "top man" in the Ałts'į'Dendeey clan now belonged to him and his first cousin Andrew Isaac. In the future the honor would go to Kenneth Thomas.

Oscar said he was "under" many different hills because he was related not only to his mother's clan, who was Ałts'į'Dendeey, but to his father's clan, who was Dik'aagyu. Therefore, he was also under the Mentasta Mountain (Mendaes Dzele') because Chief John of Mentasta was a member of the Dik'aagyu clan, just like Oscar's father. Oscar added that Mesiin Tsiits'iig stands for the Dik'aagyu clan and the clan's deceased leader, a man called Stsêey Netlé'. When talking about these landmarks, Oscar compared them to the American flag. He said when the US Army was at Tanacross during World War II, they raised the flag and men would sing. Oscar said the hills and lakes were like the flag, which is "something really great in army life" (Simeone 1987b).

When de Laguna and her student François-Marie Guédon visited Tetlin in 1968, elder Titus David told them that every village had a hill. Titus said:

> Ya, every village [had] a hill. They speak about it [for potlatch]. When people come they make good talk. Hill belong to Tetlin. Same way, old people go to Mentasta, they speak about Mentasta's hill. Mentasta, Tanacross . . . to make people happy.

De Laguna then asked Titus if seeing a hill like was like seeing the face of your grandpa. Titus answered:

> "Ya, same way." Titus then said the Tetlin hill was just like the name "Tetlin," it was

like a "sign" for Tetlin or "just like a flag." The name of the Tetlin hill is Teełay Shyüü' or "current flows—ridge." (de Laguna and Guédon 1968a)

COMMUNITY HISTORIES

Until the beginning of the twentieth century, the ancestors of contemporary Upper Tanana Dene lived in small communities and camps that have since disappeared into the vastness of the land. Unlike modern communities, these older places were strategically located to provide access to crucial resources, especially whitefish. Old-time settlements were more numerous, and smaller, than contemporary villages. Most of the modern communities, in contrast, are located for the convenience of missionaries, government agents, or traders. Tetlin is an exception, but the old village of Tanacross has its origins as mission station for the Episcopal Church while Healy Lake was the site of a trader's store, as was the village of Lower Nabesna. While modern upper Tanana Dene communities are largely the result of colonial processes, the people have not been removed from the land; they continue to inhabit and identify with the land of their ancestors.

HEALY LAKE PEOPLE'S VILLAGES

The ancestors of the contemporary Healy Lake people had several winter villages and numerous fish camps scattered around Healy Lake, George Lake, Sand Lake, the Healy River, and the Middle Fork of the Fortymile River. The name of the lake and the people derives from Chief Healy, who was born in 1849, probably at Joseph Village. Chief Healy took his (English) name from the trader John J. Healy at Fortymile.

Around Healy Lake were a variety of camps, as well as one called K'ąąy Kęę', or "marmot den," up the Healy River about half a mile (1 km) or more from the lake. A secondary village

Figure 13.7. Salchaket Henry at Paul's Place, 1919. Paul's Place, or Paul's Cabin, was located on the Tanana River at the beginning of a trail to Mansfield. It was the camp of Old Paul and Chief Isaac. Photo by F. B Drane, courtesy Episcopal Church Archives, Austin, Texas..

Figure 13.8. Joseph Village. National Archives, Washington, DC.

called Tehłuug Niindeex Ndiig, "whitefish moves creek" (also known as Joseph), was near the tree line, about 15 miles (24 km) up the river where there was a caribou fence about 2 miles (3 km) long (Cook 1989: 114). K'ą̈ay Kę̈ę̈' and TehłuugNiindeex Ndiig are profiled below.

K'Ą̈AY KĘ̈Ę̈' ("MARMOT DEN")

On August 18, 1980, Jimmy Huntington and Elizabeth Andrews (1980) of the Doyon Cemetery and Historic Sites program interviewed Healy Lake elder Margaret Kirsteatter about K'ą̈ay Kę̈ę̈'. Margaret said that Healy Lake people gathered there because of the caribou fence (see appendix A for Paul Kirsteatter's drawing of the caribou fence at K'ą̈ay Kę̈ę̈'). She explained,

> because back in those days they had a caribou fence up there. And they have a fish trap up there. So this village, when time to hunt, all old people go up there. My great grandfather and my grandmother's relations all and all go up there and they got caribou fence up there. Right in front of that old man's cabin. And out in the flat. They get their caribou and stay right there

till everything dry and then go back to the main village down here.

Margaret then recited the names of her family members who had lived on and used the land to survive. In this way, she claimed the land for her family.

> My people [John Healy] that was Chief Healy's family. Chief Healy. Old man, senior, John Healy, Paddy Healy, Paul Healy, and Mary Healy, all those use this Healy River for trapping. All them brothers. And everybody come down to Healy Lake. All, whole family. You know they live there. Oh, for all survive. Fish, dry meat, and everything before they move up there [Healy River]. But when the winter time they all come up all way this way.

She then recited the names of chiefs, or headmen, who lived before Chief Healy and claimed the land as their territory. Beginning with Daathoo, Margaret then mentions Tiich'aghooz and the chief who lived at Ch'inchedl Těyy', "nose hill," whose name she could not remember.

> That Chief Healy son here. His old man's name, his name Daathoo means that chief, he is just like his Dad, two same way— [both have] like a little bit of brown mustache. Before that, back in [when] Indians

Figure 13.9. Chief Joe and his people, upper Fortymile River. In 1902, while conducting a winter survey for the telegraph line between Eagle and Valdez, Lt. William Mitchell encountered a band of thirteen families hunting caribou on the middle fork of the Fortymile River under Chief Joe's direction. McKennan (1969: 103) reports locals told him this was the same group with a summer fish camp at Healy Lake and a caribou fence near the village of Joseph. Jeany Healy collection UAF-2000-181-247. Alaska and Polar Regions Department, Elmer E. Rasmuson Library, University of Alaska, Fairbanks.

Figure 13.10. Healy River people circa 1905. From left: Kataba, his wife (Belle Sam's mother), Kataba's son, Old Chief Healy, another son, Chief Joe, his wife Lucy, and Belle Sam. Jeany Healy collection UAF-2000-181-1. Alaska and Polar Regions Department, Elmer E. Rasmuson Library, University of Alaska, Fairbanks.

use to have a way, you know, there's another Tiich'aghooz used to be on that Twelve Mile Hill, another one used to be up on that Sam lake, the highest hill you see over there Ch'inchedl Těyy'. Those two [chiefs] they make smoke signals and send and when man from somewhere send signal.

See all those places, the oldest places, each point on the lake. Name for all those places. The village, down a little ways from George creek there, oldest one and right there close to the mouth is Ch'inchedl Těyy' "Nose Hill." He's the guy that use to live in there. That's old-time story, I don't know his name. Just that we heard about. (Andrews and Huntington 1980)

TEHŁUUG NIINDEEX NDIIG ("WHITEFISH MOVES CREEK")

Tehłuug Niindeex Ndiig, or Joseph Village, was in the Tanana uplands at the confluence of Joseph Creek and the Middle Fork of the Fortymile River. According to oral history, the village was established sometime in the 1800s

because of the presence of the Fortymile caribou herd and because it was close to American trading posts on the Yukon River (Solomon 1962). One of the earliest descriptions of Joseph comes from Robert J. Farnsworth (1901), who visited the community in 1899 and 1901. Farnsworth wrote:

camped at an Indian village of eight or ten teepees and about thirty people. Each Indian home had its cache for caribou meat which must be placed on stilts high enough so the dogs can't get to it. Each Indian has at least three dogs. Before the advent of rifles, the Indians used to build fences, some of which are still standing to deflect the caribou from their course and herd them toward the place where the hunters were concealed with their bows and arrows.

Silas Solomon of Tanacross told Robert McKennan that people from Sand Lake and Healy Lake moved to Joseph Village to be closer to the trading stations on the Yukon River. There were trails leading from Joseph Village to Healy Lake and Ketchumstuk. Eventually, the people moved back to Sam Lake when the trader Newton established his store at Healy Lake (Solomon 1962).

In an interview with the anthropologist Elizabeth Andrews (1980), Silas Solomon and Margaret Kirsteatter said Joseph Village was not as old as Ketchumstuk. Joseph Village people came from an old village near the mouth of the Goodpaster River. They moved up to Joseph because of the presence of caribou and because there was good fishing for trout, grayling, and whitefish. There was also a moose fence and a caribou fence located between Joseph and Ketchumstuk. As Silas explained to Andrews, as soon as Newton established his store at Healy Lake, the people of Joseph moved back down toward the Tanana River. Silas put it this way: "Instead of pack tea and powder from way down the mouth of Fortymile post, you know, they [got] a little close to Tanana [River] and trading post starts [at] Healy Lake" (Andrews 1980). Margaret said that in 1980 people from Healy Lake continued to go to Joseph to hunt and trap (Andrews 1980).

TEYH CH'ETS'EDZE' (HEALY LAKE VILLAGE)

Old Healy Lake Village was originally located on a bend around Healy Lake, near the mouth of the Healy River. However, epidemics during the 1900s caused surviving community members to evacuate the village. The current community is about a mile from the traditional site of Old Healy Lake Village.

In 1906, John Hajdukovich went to Healy Lake on a prospecting trip; he later became the primary trader on the upper Tanana. A year later, in 1907, William Newton established a trading post at the mouth of the Healy River and ran it until 1925 or 1926, when the post burned. Kathleen Newton Shafer, Newton's daughter, recalled some of the goods that were traded to the local Dene (Cook 1989: 112). Particularly, she remembers the beads. She also said there were no guns other than the common .30-30 and .22 calibers. Blankets were important items, as was cloth for dressmaking.

Construction of the Alaska Highway in the 1940s led to an increase in mortality and sickness in the local Native population. Healy Lake was hit especially hard, and in 1943, probably two-thirds of the Healy Lake people died within

months. Most affected were young children and elders. According to Lee Saylor (Callaway and Miller-Friend 2001: 143–144), the mortality was higher at Healy Lake compared to other communities like Tanacross and Northway because medical treatment was not readily available. By 1946, Healy Lake had disappeared as a year-round village. At the same time the community of Dot Lake came into existence.

TANACROSS PEOPLE'S VILLAGES

Many of the descendants of the current residents of Tanacross came from communities in the highlands between the Yukon and Tanana Rivers in the upper Fortymile River drainage. including places like Flint Hill, Ketchumstuk, and Dihthâad. Today Tanacross people call themselves "the people of Dihthâad."[1]

MBEHTS'EH TĚYY' ("FLINT HILL")

Mbehts'eh Těyy', which is 3.5 miles northeast of Ketchumstuk, derives its name from a stone classified as an opal (BIA 1989: 6). Flint Hill was abandoned sometime before 1900 and is known only from oral accounts. Silas Solomon (1984a) of Tanacross said his father-in-law saw the village and told him that people lived in small houses and hunted ducks and muskrats at a lake near Flint Hill. Silas also said there was a cremation site and a lookout for caribou. According to oral history, a fight took place at Flint Hill between locals and Dene from Canada. There is little information about the fight, and elders were reluctant to talk about it.

Mbehts'eh Těyy' is the site of a corral used to capture caribou. It is the largest corral in the area and constructed in a figure eight with two openings. Silas (1984a) said: "Yeah double corral, that's the biggest one along the line from Camp Lake to right down here, 10 miles. Ketchumstuk is smaller one-way corral."

---

1 According to http://www.tanacrossinc.com, accessed March 21, 2021.

The corral was constructed to intercept caribou coming from the north or the south. The chief at Flint Hill managed the construction and maintenance of the fence as well as the actual hunting. He had assistants who worked to keep the fence up. Maintenance was done in the spring (Solomon 1984a). Different clans cooperated in the construction and maintenance of the caribou fences at Flint Hill. However, according to Solomon, there was a "boss," the Dik'aagyu headman whose name was Stsêey Netłé'. He told people what to do. This headman used to live at Mansfield but was originally from Flint Hill. There is a graveyard at Flint Hill where Stsêey Netłé' is reported to be buried (Solomon 1984a).

SAAGÉS CHEEG ("SUN FORK MOUTH")

The name Saagés Cheeg applies to two sites. The older site is at the confluence of Ketchumstuk Creek and the Mosquito Fork of the Fortymile River, and the newer site is about a mile up Ketchumstuk Creek. The age of the older village is unknown, but it certainly predates Native people's contact with non-Native Americans. Tanacross elder Silas Solomon (1984a) said people moved up the creek sometime in the 1880s because the old village flooded. During the gold rush, both Native and non-Native prospectors

Figure 13.11. Silas Solomon's cabin at Ketchumstuk. Photo courtesy of BIA ANCSA Office.

Figure 13.12. View of Ketchumstuk. Photo courtesy of BIA ANCSA Office.

lived at the newer village, where there was a large corral and drift fence used to capture caribou. Referring to the older village site at the mouth of Ketchumstuk Creek, Solomon said:

> Yeah that's the real Ketchumstuk. There's no other place they can use, cause sometimes no caribou and hardly any moose. Fish, got to depend on fish like I say Mansfield starved out cause they had no fish.

According to Chief Andrew Isaac (1987), two principal clans were represented at Ketchumstuk: the Naltsiin (represented by American eagle and raven) and Tc'a z (represented by seagull). He said members of the Ałts'ı̨'Dendeey, Dik'aagyu, and Ch'echĕelyu clans also lived there, but the Ch'echĕelyu grandfather or clan leader was from Flint Hill.

Both villages became known as Ketchumstuk in the early 1900s, when miners, prospectors, and travelers left their horses on Mosquito Flat to feed in the rich grasses. Solomon (1984a) said, "During stampede days a lot of people left their horses here. They only feel they could turn the horses loose here. They could graze all summer. When I was a kid there were two or three hundred horses here on the flat." In the spring the flat was burned

> for horse feed or caribou feed. They (Dene) burned the dead grass out every spring so the caribou could graze on it. . . .
> Then the grass is so high. Its all bunched up. It hadn't been burned for years. They used to just burn it off every spring, the corral in the fire. It didn't touch the poles (of the corral). Just burned the grass inside you know. (Solomon 1984a)

In the summer of 1889, newspaper reporter E. Hazard Wells visited the older village of Ketchumstuk, which he said was deserted as all of the people had gone to Mansfield to fish. Wells writes the village was "nestled in a wooded gulch a short distance from the Fortymile" and "consisted merely of a few bark houses, several tent frames and few log caches

Figure 13.13. "Ketchumstuk Saul, Hootnah, and Julius" at Ketchumstuk, circa 1919. Photo by F. B. Drane, Drane photo collection, Alaska and Polar Regions Department, Elmer E. Rasmuson Library, University of Alaska Fairbanks.

Figure 13.14. Sam Abraham and Family. Sam Abraham was born about 1873 at Ketchumstuk and his wife Belle was born at Mansfield about 1893. Jeany Healy photo collection UAF-2000-181-2. Alaska and Polar Regions Department, Elmer E. Rasmuson Library, University of Alaska Fairbanks.

elevated upon posts" (Wells 1974: 210). In 1899, Basil Austin (1968), a prospector on his way to the Klondike, visited the new village farther up Ketchumstuk Creek. Austin counted thirty cabins at the new site, some built with squared logs. There were piles of caribou horns and enough caribou hair to start a "mattress plant." The village was deserted as everyone was out hunting caribou.

Visiting the newer village in 1902 during a survey for the Valdez–Eagle telegraph line, Lt. William Mitchell (1982: 50) described Ketchumstuk as "quite a respectable cabin community." On a hill nearby were the graves, with each body encased in a coffin that was surrounded by long poles and enclosed by fences that were strung with pots and pans that had belonged to the dead man. The poles were hung with streamers of various kinds to keep away the evil spirits.

In the early 1900s, Ketchumstuk was hit by a tuberculosis epidemic. Sometime between 1910 and 1920, the disease took the lives of at least nine people. Archdeacon Frederick Drane wrote:

> At Ketchumstuk was the pitiful sight of a dying village. Even in the eight years of my acquaintance with the Indians of this place about half have died of tuberculosis, and the doom of the remaining four families was written in the scrofulous sores, the sunken cheeks and the prominent eyes. (Drane n.d.b: 185)

Chief Andrew Isaac said many residents of Ketchumstuk died of flu, referring to the 1918 influenza epidemic. Even before he was born, Andrew said, "people out in the country died," that is, away from the village in isolated camps. David Tega, who was a nephew of Chief Peter of Tetlin, lived at Ketchumstuk, and moved to Tanacross before he died. His wife, who was Silas Solomon's sister, was one of the last to leave. Ketchumstuk was completely abandoned by 1947. Chief Sam Abraham was the last to leave (Isaac 1987).

Silas Solomon (1984a) was born at the new Ketchumstuk in 1902. He thought about 200 people lived in the community at the time. There were people in Ketchumstuk from all over "Northway, Tetlin, Mentasta, Healy Lake." They came for the food. "Place to eat, lots of

Figure 13.15. Ketchumstuk graveyard, circa 1915. National Archives, Washington, DC.

food here you know." He also said tuberculosis killed a lot of people. Silas's mother died of tuberculosis in 1918, as did other relatives. When Charlie Demit's and Elijah Demit's wives and children died, the men moved to Northway, where they remarried. At the time Sam Abraham was chief at Ketchumstuk (Solomon 1984a).

In 1980 Elizabeth Andrews (1980a), who was working for the Alaska Native Corporation Doyon Ltd, interviewed Chief Andrew Isaac and Silas Solomon about the time they lived at Ketchumstuk in the early 1900s. Both Chief Isaac and Solomon emphasized the Dene claim to the land by attaching individuals to a specific place. Chief Andrew explained that when anticipating the caribou migration, families spread out across the land, and he named specific places where people camped. For his part, Solomon named the specific people who lived in Ketchumstuk.

ANDREW ISAAC: We raised up Ketchumstuk. We know [when] caribou heading across [the country] in Long Cabin, Wolf Creek, and Mosquito Fork, and Indian Creek, so many family they move in. Like just what I try to explain. Certain families, they go in one area. And [in] another [area], three families. They stop in one place. And so many miles beyond that another three, four families, two families. They spread it out and line up all the way to Ketchumstuk. And that's why that trail I always [try to] explain, me use land across country and according to the people, they get their winter supplies in there. And right now, in August, we should be up there.

SILAS SOLOMON: My father was raised at Ketchumstuk, too. They got place up there, you know. They originally build that place. My grandfather [started that place]. They're [my father's] parents. My grandfather. Down the mouth of the creek, where village is now. We made that caribou fence you know. Caribou corral. That used to be caribou going through there.

    Ketchumstuk village at the mouth [of Ketchumstuk Creek]. That's for fishing you know. There's no other way. Fishing and snare moose.

ANDREWS: When did you move up to Ketchumstuk?

SILAS SOLOMON: When they ran out of fish at Mansfield. Caribou was around too at Ketchumstuk. We had fence there. Corral for caribou. And fishing . . . you go down to the mouth of the creek, there's good fishing. People moved up there in September.

ANDREWS: What kind of fish?

SILAS SOLOMON: Grayling mostly. Round whitefish. When they moved up there [his parents] they continued staying. After they got organized. White people came up the Fortymile River too, you know. Discovered the mines [referring to gold strikes on the upper Fortymile River in the 1880s]. That was 17 or 18 years before Dawson-Klondike strike. [They had the] opportunity to get things down at the Yukon, you know [at the town of Fortymile]. That's why they just stayed over there. Over here [Tanana River] nothing [no stores]. We had that fence. The caribou must have run through quite awhile back.

ANDREWS: Other people who built cabins at Ketchumstuk were?

SILAS SOLOMON: My father's oldest brother is Bob. Then Ben, then Albert. This one is David . . . the only other one was Saul, my mother's cousin. And Sam Abraham. Sam Abraham he was from Eagle.

Silas also talked about the last potlatch at Ketchumstuk in 1919:

The last potlatch held at Ketchumstuk was in 1919 [held for Silas's mother Annie Solomon and Sam Abraham's son]. People came From Eagle and Fortymile. There was a village down the Fortymile. Mouth of the Fortymile. Some from Salchaket, Tetlin, Mansfield, Moosehide—Chief Silas [from Moosehide]. Sam Abraham, Silas's father, Saul and Elijah Demit made potlatch.

Me and Jimmy Bob, David [Tega] and Elijah built a potlatch house. It was the biggest house ever built. Whipsaw lumber. Me, Jimmy Bob, David and Elijah. Just the four of us, sawing. I was young. Hard work. Cut all the lumber, log everything. Use axe, no chainsaw, just axe. It was 30 by 40 feet.

DIHTHÂAD ("NEARBY PLACE")

Contemporary Tanacross people call themselves "people of Dihthâad." The village was on Fish Creek, locally known as Mansfield Creek, about half a mile from Mansfield Lake. It was home to important clan leaders. This is confirmed by the presence of the hill Mesiin Tsiits'iig, which stands for the Dik'aagyu clan. It is one of the few precolonial Dene villages on the upper Tanana River to be excavated by archaeologists. In 1936 and 1937 Froelich Rainey excavated there, as did John Cook and Robert McKennan in 1971. Using different dating techniques, the site has been estimated to be more than 2,000 years old. The site was eventually abandoned, and by 1910 all the people had settled in the nearby village of Mansfield.

At Dihthâad, Rainey found nine house pits, eleven tent rings, and a number of storage pits. Excavations by Rainey and later John Cook and Robert McKennan produced 759 artifacts of copper, bone, antler, and stone. Copper artifacts included awls, arrowheads, and knife blades; artifacts made from bone or antler included a barbed arrowhead and a bone drinking tube. There were also glass trade beads, some iron artifacts, and pieces of birch bark. All the artifacts are housed in the Museum of the North at the University of Alaska in Fairbanks (Shinkwin 1979: 90).

Based on information collected by Rainey, Cook, and McKennan, archaeologist Anne Shinkwin (1979: 89) thinks Dihthâad was a "semi-permanent summer village" where people gathered to fish for whitefish. The area is rich in food resources. Besides the seasonal runs of whitefish, there are northern pike, ducks and geese, beaver, muskrat, and moose, and just a few miles north are caribou.

The first non-Native to visit Dihthâad was Lt. Henry Allen (1887: 79) in the summer of 1885.[2] Allen named the village after Ketl'aad Tá', who was chief at the time.[3] After leaving the village of Tetlin in June 1885, Allen and his party floated down the Tanana River. At 6:30 in the evening, the party stopped at some cache houses at the point where the trail from Mentasta Lake reaches the Tanana River. This may have been the eventual site of St. Timothy's Mission and the village of Tanana Crossing. Here, Allen's Native guides, who had accompanied the expedition from Tetlin, returned home while Allen and his party continued downstream for another four miles before stopping for the night on the north bank of the Tanana

Figure 13.16. Left to right: Arthur John, Oscar Isaac, Julius Paul, and Silas Solomon were employed by McKennan to help excavate Dihthâad. Photo by Robert McKennan, Robert McKennan collection UAF-1988-98-77. Alaska and Polar Regions Department, Elmer E. Rasmuson Library, University of Alaska, Fairbanks.

River. Allen (1887: 79) writes that this camp was half a mile above a "tributary 30 yards wide with muddy water similar to the Tanana." This was the Little Tanana Slough, or Tth'iitú' Gaay ("little straight water"). About an hour later three runners arrived from Ketl'aad Tá'. Allen writes:

> At 11 p.m. Fickett and myself started for Kheeltat's, having been carried to the right bank of the tributary in the canoes, and having the youngest of the three natives for a guide. At 1:30 a.m., June 16, after a forced march over country showing no signs of a trail, we walked into the miserable looking house of Kheeltat very much fatigued. (1887: 79–80).

Allen said little about the village and the people, except that there were twenty-six men and four women, "all attired in their best." Allen did learn from Ketl'aad Tá' about a trail from Dihthâad to Fetutlin (a Han village) on the Yukon River, and before leaving, Ketl'aad Tá' promised to meet Allen there in July (Allen 1887: 79–80).

Dene oral histories associate Dihthâad with starvation and renewal. Tanacross elder Kenneth Thomas says that before the people lived at Dihthâad, they lived at a place called

---

2   In his dissertation, "Among the Dene: Allen's 1885 Trans-Alaska Expedition" (2022), Russ Vanderlugt writes that it was more than likely Allen did not make to Dihthâad, which was too far away, but met Ketl'aad Tá' at his fish camp Taahcheeg, located at the confluence of Fish Creek and the Little Tanana Slough.

3   According to Kenneth Thomas Sr. of Tanacross (2005: 218), Ketl'aad Tá' translates to "the father of someone who has been over that route before."

Taxelts'ih Keyh, "Thirty-mile Hill," up the Tanana River from Old Tanacross and were led by the two headmen Ketl'aad Tá' and Stsêey Netlé.

In his version of the story, Thomas refers to several lakes located north of present-day Tanacross. From Taxelts'ih Keyh, Thomas said, the people traveled first to Ch'aghadh Mĕnn' ("ducks gather lake") and then on to Fish Lake (Luug Mĕnn'). From there they went to Uljaadh Menn' ("pike lake") and finally to Dihthâad Mĕen' (Mansfield Lake) before settling at Dihthâad (Thomas and Mishler 2005: 220).

When she was interviewed by Elizabeth Andrews in 1980, Maggie Isaac (Andrews 1980) of Dot Lake told her version of how Dihthâad was settled. Dene discovered Lake Mansfield when they were living at Łuug Mĕen' and starving. They were saved when a young man caught a big northern pike using a fire-harden wooden hook and squirrel as bait. After regaining their strength, the people began traveling. Isaac says an old man climbed a hill and saw a "big lake," which was Lake Mansfield, and then they walked "downriver" (following Fish Creek to Dihthâad) and found a place where they could catch lots of fish (referring to whitefish in Fish Creek).

> They [were staying] way up Fish Lake. Way behind it. Fish Lake in the brush. All the people just about starving. No food, wintertime. And one, his boy, young boy, he check around the lake and you know where is water, bubbles come out. Lots of bubbles in the lake and he tell his dad, "Lots of bubbles on the lake. You cut chop hole where it [ice] will split." Okay, he does it. And he say, "You cut that burned tree [fire harden wood makes a strong hook]. Make hook. Get squirrel [for bait] and put on and put that hook on that water." That night he caught that one pike. That big. Big. He never tell nobody and he bring it in his house and he tell his dad. He say, "I got big pike. Don't tell nobody." Threw it in the fire, clean out all the scale. And that scale put it in the fire

and burned up. "You bring that rocks and fix and place for them." They cook that fish. Just little piece like that. They make soup. And later, they cut little piece. Just one, few [because they were starving].

> Okay. They give little soup. And finally, all that people one week, they all get up and start moving. And springtime. Grandpa finally make climb way on hill. He said he saw big lake on that side. "I going. We come back tonight. Late night." "Okay."

> That grandpa that find Lake Mansfield. And they went downriver [i.e., down Mansfield Creek] and they find lots of fish down creek . . . they make fish trap like this. Later on, they get back home. They told people get ready and move down on real good fishing place he said. So they all move in the village and they fix fish camp. And they fix real home. Early days ago they build moss house and they fix. And that hill just thick, just same grass grow and nice place. So they all went down there. And all from there they beginning. Some his nephew, some his grandson, some great aunt. Some all that his grandfather. Whosoever come and marriage each place. (Andrews 1980)

Tanacross elders Silas Solomon and the Reverend David Paul told Andrews (1980) how, at one time, all of the people at Dihthâad died of starvation except for one young woman, who left and then returned to revive the community. Solomon began by declaring that people at Dihthâad "starved out one time." The only survivors were a man, his wife, and daughter. They left Dihthâad and started out for Tetlin, but the man died at Thirty-mile Hill. The women went first to Midway Lake, but the people were starving there too, so they went on to Tetlin, where the wife died. Later, the daughter and people from Tetlin went over to Suslota, on the Copper River, to fish for salmon. The daughter and a young man, whom Solomon characterized as "young and lazy. Not good looking!," returned to Dihthâad and "that's the renewal of Dihthâad village."

SILAS: This Mansfield [Dihthâad] starved one time, you know. Long ago. Before my mother. And she come back. And they left there. And her father died up there. Thirty-mile Hill. Starved to death.

ELIZABETH: Who's this?

SILAS: My father's ancestors. There were only two. Her father and mother. Must be the chief. They live till the last one, all the rest died. They start out going to Tetlin, [but] they can't get up there. They got to "Thirty-mile Hill."

ELIZABETH: Where is Thirty-mile Hill?

SILAS: The second hill from this "Twelve-Mile Hill," up the river, Tanana River. That far he make it. He [the father] died there. Her mother was pretty weak too. [They walk] Mile a day in the spring too. Took a long time to get to Midway Lake. Our people there. They find out they were starving to death too. Nobody, just one woman. They couldn't go anywhere. Eating people, starving. So she left. She leave it. Took her mother back. Went down the lake. Went down the river. And she find canoe this side of river. [at] The mouth of Tetlin Creek. Took her further up to Tetlin Village. Her mother told her, "Watch them. See what they eat. Don't go out in the open. Watch them go by." She lay down. She see someone carrying rabbits and carrying rabbits and ducks. She told her mother, "It looks like they're eating human food." Her mother told her, "All right, go in." She went in. And her mother's down there laying down. She feed her up carefully. When you starve, when a person doesn't eat a long time, [if] they eat, they going to die. That's what happened to her mother. Eat just soup, broth. She told them, "My mother down there, laying down." They got up, pretty healthy. They got up and went down there and they

brought her in and feed her. She got too much [they fed her too much food]. She die. Later on, in the summer about June . . . They had the fish run over at Suslota. She [the girl] went over there with them [Tetlin people], you know. She camped over there.

That's the only way they can make it, find food. She went over there. She got over there. She started working and fish. She had no people over here you know. She start fish. She [the girl became attached] got a young man. Not a worker. Young and lazy. Not good looking. She does all the work, but he was helping her put the rack [up]. She was cutting the fish. All he does is hanging up. Evidently, they make it. Putting up the fish. All kinds of fish. So they come over to Mansfield—Dihthâad, not Mansfield, but below it. This time come all by themselves. Good woman. Young woman. Young girl. He comes with her. Comes over [to] Dihthâad. Just nothing left. Not even berries, not very much of anything.

ELIZABETH: Do you remember what the man's name was?

SILAS: [Man's name]—"little father." That's the beginning of Dihthâad village. He start learning pretty good. They start having children. They got fish coming. He build a fish dam. That time she told him how to do it. How they catch fish in a trap. They catch whitefish. They don't have to go back to Copper River. (Andrews 1980)

In his book *According to Papa*, the Reverend David Paul (1957b: 10–11) tells a similar story in which all of the people die except for a mother and a daughter. This daughter is David's great-great grandmother. At the time she was twelve or fourteen years old. The mother and daughter make their way first to an unnamed village and then to Tetlin, where they find the people starving as well. David says:

They can just crawl to Northway village where they are saved. Later word comes "lots of salmon by Copper River. Everyone go there and this girl work hard, catch fish and hang them on rack to dry." The girl wants to return and find where her father died so she and a young man go.

There where the Tanana go back under a steep hill and cliffs hang out over water, they see on this hill a moose-skin bag for carrying arrows. And she knows this is her father's and she go there and carry his bones back to her old home and burn them. And these two people marry and get three children that I know. My great grandfather and his brother and his sister. And these five people stay in Mansfield and a whole new village grown around them and there is a village there even now.

CH'EENAA NDEDH ("LONG OMEN")

Ch'eenaa Ndedh, or Mansfield, is on a hill above Fish Creek close to Mansfield Lake. Like Dihthâad, Mansfield was an important place where important people lived. The community is represented by the mountain in the Alaska Range called Naadęęy Xú' (marmot tooth or frog tooth), which can be seen from the village.

Possibly the first mention of Mansfield Village in the written record was made by E. Hazard Wells (1974: 42) in 1889, when he mentioned seeing Chief John's house at the outlet of Lake Mansfield. Nine years after Well's visit, in 1898, the US Army topographer, C. E. Griffiths described a village located on a small stream called Fish Creek, which he said was at the outlet of Lake Mansfield (Griffiths 1900: 731). That same summer Quartermaster Clerk John Rice (1900) counted fifty "Ketchumstuk Indians" at Mansfield. He wrote that the Dene spent their summer hunting and fishing in Mansfield, and in the fall they returned to their winter homes at Ketchumstuk. Rice counted sixty-five people. The men came out to meet Rice and wanted to purchase tobacco before anything else. They had plenty of money and all the young men spoke good English. Rice commented

Figure 13.17. Mansfield, circa 1920. Photo by Olas Murie B21643P. National Archives, Washington, DC.

Figure 13.18. At Mansfield. Left to right: John Healy, Walter Isaac, Paddy Healy, Peter Charles, Jimmy Walter, Pete Charlie from Copper River, and Andrew Isaac, circa 1920. Jeany Healy Photo collection UAF-2000-181-2. Alaska and Polar Regions Department, Elmer E. Rasmuson Library, University of Alaska Fairbanks.

on people's healthy appearance, but he was told many people had died from an epidemic and that the chief had died. Rice and his crew camped on Mansfield Creek, which he noted was filled with whitefish weighing between 0.75 and 2.5 pounds, and they saw a pike that weighed eight pounds (Rice 1900: 786).

Silas Solomon told Elizabeth Andrews the reason people moved from Dihthâad to Mansfield was because they expected to be attacked (Andrews 1980: 40). Solomon described Dihthâad as a trap.

Trap place. The war. They expect war. At Mansfield they got a chance. It's a long hill up there you know. On each side. They can watch the lake on that side, creek on that side. They expect war. It never did happen.

Solomon said old Chief Isaac was chief at the time of the move. He added that the people began to build log cabins at Mansfield after 1898. Today, Mansfield is the site of the Tanacross culture camp, and many Tanacross residents have summer houses at Mansfield and continue to fish in Fish Creek and Mansfield Lake.

TETLIN PEOPLE'S VILLAGES

Nahk' ät ("fishing place"), or Last Tetlin, and Tee łay ("current flows"), or Tetlin, are two separate communities. According to Chief Peter and Chief Luke, Last Tetlin was the older of the two (Rainey 1939). Last Tetlin is at the foot of the Alaska Range, and archaeological evidence suggests it has been inhabited for a millennium. Tetlin is on the Tetlin River. According to anthropologist François-Marie Guédon (1974: 12), the communities had very close ties. She writes:

> It is sometimes difficult to ascertain the ties between the two camps if one cannot take the feeling of the people themselves into account. . . . There is a strong relationship between Last Tetlin and Tetlin and the two settlements are not too far from one another, yet for all that they form distinct units.

NAHK' ÄT ("FISHING PLACE"), OR LAST TETLIN

Lt. Allen arrived at Last Tetlin, which he called Nandell's, after the village chief, on June 10, 1885, at 3 a.m. There were forty men, twenty-eight women, and eighteen children living in the village. The village was composed of four houses situated on a small clearwater stream. The houses were large, constructed without the use of bark, and had no attached steambath like those found on the Copper River (Allen

Figure 13.19. Last Tetlin with fish weirs. Photo by F. B. Drane UAF-1991-46-674. Drane photo collection Alaska and Polar Regions Department, Elmer E. Rasmuson Library, University of Alaska Fairbanks.

1887: 75–76). Firewood was scarce, indicating that the village had been inhabited for years. Trails surrounding the village showed continued and heavy use. There were two trails from Last Tetlin to Fort Reliance, which is on the Yukon River. One was entirely a foot trail and the other included a portage to a tributary of the White River, and then down the White and Yukon Rivers in a skin boat (Allen 1887: 76). When Allen arrived, the residents were fishing for whitefish, northern pike, and grayling using a dipnet. Allen reported there were several "medicine men" in Last Tetlin, and one of them accompanied him to Tetlin. Allen noted that Native people had burned much of the surrounding country to kill mosquitos (and probably to increase moose browse).

Allen and his party arrived in Tetlin in the afternoon and immediately began to bargain for the construction of a boat that would take them down the Tanana River (Allen 1887: 77). At Tetlin were six men who had been at Last Tetlin, four women, and seven children living in two houses on the bank of a stream.

In 1937, archaeologist Froelich Rainey (1939) visited Last Tetlin and reported fifteen adults and thirty children living there. The river was cutting away the bank, exposing house pits and refuse pits that Rainey thought indicated a once-large population. In his diary Rainey wrote that people were busy fishing with dipnets in Tetlin Creek, and people from Tanacross, Mentasta, and Nabesna were staying there. He also met Little John, who remembered Lt. Allen, the first iron axe, and using bone and copper arrowheads. Little John also recalled that people gathered to fish in summer and lived in bark and log houses; during the winter, they spread out to hunt, living in movable caribou skin tents.

Figure 13.20. "Tetlin Village May 15th, 1919." Drane was attending the funeral of Chief David. Photo by F. B. Drane, Drane photo collection Alaska and Polar Regions Department, Elmer E. Rasmuson Library, University of Alaska Fairbanks.

TEE ŁAY ("CURRENT FLOWS") OR TETLIN

Tee łay, or Tetlin, is approximately ten miles from the Alaska Highway. Until 1981 there was no road to the village, which could only be reached by boat or airplane. Descendants of people from Last Tetlin now live primarily in Tetlin. During the summer, residents hold a culture and wellness camp at their ancestral village.

Figure 13.21. Tetlin in the 1980s. Photo by Terry Haynes.

In 1912, a trader named Flannigan established the first trading post at Tetlin at the mouth of the Kalukna River, locally referred to as Old Store Creek, or Xaal Niign ("least cisco river"). Later John Hajdukovitch set up a store. The stores drew people from the surrounding area, and by 1929 there was a school (started by Jack Singleton), and people were living more or less full-time at Tetlin. In 1930, under provisions of the Vocational and Educational Reserves Act (Public Law N. 468, 68th Congress) President Herbert Hoover signed an executive order that established the 768,000-acre Tetlin Reserve. Tetlin residents credit the creation of the reserve to Chief Peter (Halpin 1987: 10). A post office opened in Tetlin in 1932, and an airstrip was constructed in 1946. Chief Peter told Rainey that the village of Tetlin was relatively recent. When Rainey visited in 1937, the population had grown because families had come in from surrounding camps so their children could attend school (Rainey 1939).

In the winter of 1929–1930, Earl J. Beck, superintendent of education for the central district of Alaska, visited Tetlin. Beck said Tetlin was one of the most isolated communities in Alaska and that the people had had little contact with non-Natives. He counted seventeen houses. According to Beck, the Office of Education had maintained a school at Tetlin since 1925, but there was no building—the teacher taught in people's homes. Instead of waiting for the government to build a school, the people were in the process of building one themselves when Beck visited. Chief Peter gave a speech on Beck's arrival in which he said the people "were getting along fine, before the white man came, but that they were getting along much better since the white man came." Chief Peter went on to say, "They didn't ask the government for any help, they had plenty to eat and plenty to wear and that the only thing they wanted was a good school house" (Beck 1930: 34). Beck noted there were no medical services

Figure 13.23. Chief Peter and Walter David at Tetlin. Photo by Robert McKennan UAF-1985-98-480. Alaska and Polar Regions Department, Elmer E. Rasmuson Library, University of Alaska, Fairbanks.

Figure 13.22. Charlie David Sr. Photo by Terry Haynes.

Figure 13.24. Jessie and Joe John. Jo John was born in 1888 to John and Jessie Tega. Jessie was born in 1892 to Little John. Photo by Terry Haynes.

Figure 13.26. Emma Titus and her children, 1950. Photo by C. Heller, Anchorage Museum of History and Art.

Figure 13.25. Jimmy Joe. Photo by Terry Haynes.

Figure 13.27. Jessie Mark. Photo by Terry Haynes.

Figure 13.28. Fred Demit, Photo by William E. Simeone.

Figure 13.30. Kitty David. Photo by Terry Haynes.

Figure 13.29. Helen David, Photo by Terry Haynes.

Figure 13.31. Patrick Joe. Photo by Terry Haynes.

Figure 13.32. Tabesa Gene. Photo by Terry Haynes.

Figure 13.33. Moose Creek caches, 1930. Photo by Robert McKennan, courtesy William Workman.

available, and many people were afflicted with tuberculosis.

NORTHWAY PEOPLE'S VILLAGES

In a 1984 interview with Yvonne Yarber and Curt Madison, Chief Walter Northway said, "Young people should know that my dad came a long way back. It would be nice if they remembered that their great-grandfather came from Canada" (Yarber and Madison 1987: 22). Chief Walter mentioned thirteen locations, beginning with a place called Xaaguu, where his father's people started from and which is now in Canada. Chief Walter's maternal relatives came from Shya' Naaltaał, six miles from Burwash Landing. Eventually they stopped at Ttheek'ädn Keey, where they discovered a lot of fish in the creek. The men made a fish weir from rocks and pulled roots to make a fish net. They also made camps at Ts'oo Got Gaaiy, or Little Scottie Creek ("little spruce knee"), and Ts'oo Got Choh, or Big

Scottie Creek ("big spruce knee") (Yarber and Madison 1987: 29–31). The Scottie Creek people never established a contemporary community, and many members and their descendants now reside in Whitehorse, Beaver Creek, and Northway.

In this narrative recorded and translated by Jim Kari, Mary Tyone (1996: 5–8) tells how her mother's family moved out of the mountains and lived at several places along the US–Canada border before settling at Scottie Creek, where Mary was born. Eventually, Mary moved her parents to K'ehtthîign (Northway Fishcamp village or Old Northway), where they died. She begins by telling where her father was born.

Shta' shta' du' Northway Sheh Nia k'it mi-hoołiin nt'eh, my Dad.
My father [Bell John] was born at Northway at Sheh Nia [ridge near Northway Junction of the Alaska Highway].

My mom, nign' Naat'aayät, Naat'aayät Tth'aal' shyit ch'eah shnąą ihoołiin.

My mom [Laura John] was born upland
there at Naat'aayät's cradle [Mt. Natazhat
on the upper White River].

Daanii nign' Chidahłeen hinay danh ch'a
shnąą k'I'nthädn
My mother grew up way upriver at the
place they call Chidahleeh "fish channeled into weir lake" [Tchawsahmon Lake
on the Canadian side of the border west
of the upper White River].

Ishyetts'ähn wunąą chitin eh Snage tthän'
ts'eeneełhįhdeeł Haltäl Cheegn hinay
dänh ishyit hukeey hoołi.'
From there, after her mother died, they
moved in a group down below to Snag [in
about 1901], and their village was where
they call Haltäl Cheegn [the mouth of
Snag Creek].

Ishyitts' änh noo' Nįį'įį xogn įį'eh tah nee-
neelhihteldik ts'ä'.
From there they moved again in a group
over to "Lookout" [also called Sour-
dough].

Ts'oo Got Gaay hinih danh hiihdeltth' iiy eh
They then lived at "little spruce knee" [Little
Scottie Creek], and

naanohts'ąy hihdeltth'iiy eh tl'uuł huts'eed-
aał niihio ts'ą' tthän Haltäl Cheegn ts'ä'
k'aa nahtitdäl.
they were living across there [across the border on the Alaska side] when they made
the boundary [in about 1901], and they did
not return to the mouth of Snag Creek.

Ts'ä' Ttheek'ädn hinih dänh keey hihultsįį
ts'ä'.
And then they lived in the village called
"rock weir" [the mouth of Big Scottie
Creek near the Tanana River].

LOWER NABESNA

Before the 1930s, Dene living on the lower
Nabesna and Chisana Rivers had a fish camp
at K'ehtthîign ("lake outlet"), now known as old
Northway Village (Yarber and Madison 1987).
Beginning in the late 1920s, non-Native traders established stores on the lower Nabesna
and Chisana Rivers. According to Chief Walter
Northway (Yarber and Madison 1987), Herman
Kessler built the first store at Stover Creek up
the Chisana River, and John Hajdukovich built
a second store on the Nabesna River. Almost
as soon as the stores were established, people
began to build cabins which they used periodically. Northway elder Ada Gallon (2008)
remembered the traders who established stores
at Nabesna.

ADA: When we grow up, there's no store, no
nothing. After we had some people who
start store there across the river in the old
village. One German built a big store over
there. He used to make a good Christmas
for us. He would put a big tree in community hall, they put lots of goodies under
there. He was from Germany.
INTERVIEWER: What's his name?
ADA: There was another one across the way, he
got store, he buy wood and gave people groceries and those things. They buy for two.
INTERVIEWER: The store keeper-his name?
ADA: Herman Kessler and Milo Hajdukovich
all live in Northway. They go back and forth.
They go to Tetlin and Tanacross. They have
a big boat to bring groceries. That's how
they went to Dawson; No road, no nothing;
just Indian trail. Three months it took them
to bring those things. Clothes, groceries,
100-pound rice they pack. And dogs, blankets and clothes for kids. I was 11 years old,
I don't even own shoes. I have moccasins.
INTERVIEWER: Do you think the highway
helped change that?
ADA: You got shoes, you got . . . Yea, we got a
new house.

Figure 13.34. Chief Sam, Walter Northway, and his parents at Lower Nabesna, 1919. Photo by F. B. Drane. Drane Photo collection Alaska and Polar Regions Department, Elmer E. Rasmuson Library, University of Alaska Fairbanks.

INTERVIEWER: Who owned the first car in the village?

ADA: I think Oscar Albert.

INTERVIEWER: Did you go for a ride?

ADA: We go all over! We just jump in. He had a big pickup too. Kids hide under the car and everything. Herman Kessler, after old village, move down here by river and he start store again. That's where he died. He's buried over there in Northway.

When Robert McKennan arrived at Lower Nabesna in early February 1930, he found a single row of cabins strung out along the bank of the Nabesna River. Most of the people were awaiting the arrival of the trader in order to secure "grub" before going out on the traplines (Mishler and Simeone 2006: 90). Earl J. Beck of the Office of Education also visited Nabesna in 1930. He wrote that the people wanted a school, but because they were away from the village for such long periods, Beck did not think building a school was justified. He urged the people to move to Tetlin so their children could attend school (Beck 1930: 43). When Froelich Rainey arrived in June 1936, the whole village was temporarily abandoned, and the people were camped at the old site (K'ehtthîign) for the

summer's catch (Rainey 1939: 362–372). Rainey wrote that Lower Nabesna was built around a trading post seven miles above the mouth of the Nabesna River, but an older fishing village was on a lake (K'ehtthîign) some five miles distant.

According to anthropologists Martha Case (1986), in the early 1930s a Tetlin school teacher held classes in a tent at K'ehtthîign during the summer. In 1939–1940, a Bureau of Indian Affairs school was built at Lower Nabesna on the west bank of the Nabesna River. An Episcopal church was established there but later replaced by a Pentecostal Holiness church and Roman Catholic church (Case 1986: 16).

Walter Northway (Yarber and Madison 1987) said Chief Sam was the first to build a house at lower Nabesna River. Later on, Walter Northway, Bill Northway, Danny Northway, and Peter Albert built houses, as did Frank Sam. After Elijah and Bertha Demit got married, they moved and Big Mark built a house (Yarber and Madison 1987: 44). When flu swept through the community, many older people died. Chief Northway said:

> It was a beautiful village. In the wintertime the smoke would go straight up the stovepipe, like steamboats. So Beautiful, and we finally had to move because the river spoiled the village by digging into the banks. (Yarber and Madison 1987: 45)

To avoid periodic flooding, people moved to the other side of the Nabesna River. Chief Northway said:

> In 1940, I think it was Peter Charlie who first built on this side of the river. They had a flood in the village across the river. It flooded out everybody, so they moved to this side for security because it was a higher bank than other side. So I guess it was in the forties when everybody decided to move over to this side to prevent a flood from washing out everything again. The airport was just barely started when people decided to move. (Yarber and Madison 1987: 23)

Figure 13.35. Andy Frank. Photo by Terry Haynes.

Figure 13.37. Bertha Demit was married to Elisha Demit, originally from Ketchumstuk. Photo by Terry Haynes.

Figure 13.36. Annie Sam was married to Frank Sam. She was born in Tetlin to Jessie Tega and Big John. Photo by Terry Haynes.

Figure 13.38. Liza John Northway was married to Bill Northway. Her parents were Big John and Jessie Tega of Tetlin. Photo by Terry Haynes.

Figure 13.39. Martha Sam is the daughter of Walter and Lilly Northway. She is married to Andrew Sam. Photo by Terry Haynes.

By 1946 everyone had moved across the river, and Chief Northway said he named the community Northway after his father. A post office was established at the new site in 1941, and the community's name was changed to Northway the following year. In 1942, the Alaska Highway was completed, and a road was built to connect the highway to the village and airport.

NACH'ETAY CHEEG AND TTHIIXAA' ("BRAIN MOUTH")

Dene occupying the upper Chisana and upper Nabesna Rivers were known as Ddhał Tot iin, or "Among the Mountain People." They had semipermanent villages at the mouth of Cross Creek (Nach'etay Cheeg) and the mouth of Cooper Creek, or Tthiixaa' ("brain mouth"), where families spent the winter (Kari 1986). This group never established a modern village. Many members of the band and their descendants now live in Northway, Mentasta, and Chistochina. In the winter of 1929–1930, Robert McKennan stayed at Tthiixaa', where the families of Chisana Joe, Nabesna John, Scottie Creek Titus, and Andy Toby lived. Joe and John were brothers, and their sister Corinne was married to Titus. Andy Toby's deceased father was their maternal uncle. Along with several children, there was "old Mama," the mother of Joe, John, and Corinne (McKennan 1959: 121). These families are the ancestors of the Albert and Frank families of Northwa, and the Sanford and Justin families of Nabesna Bar, Chistochina, and Mentasta (Reckord 1983: 230).

Figure 13.40. Joe Demit. Photo by Terry Haynes.

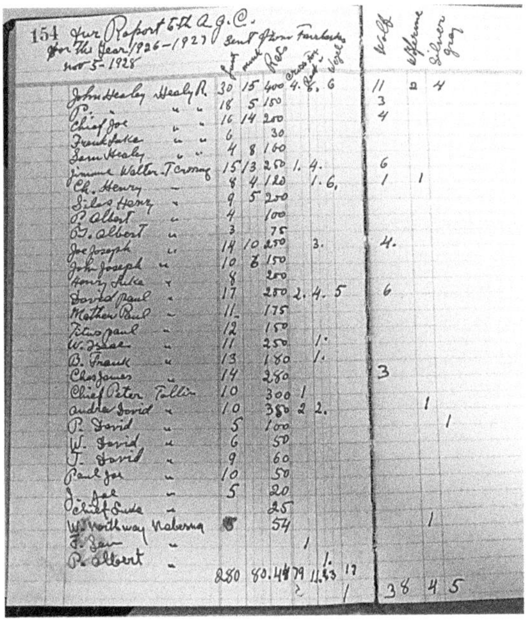

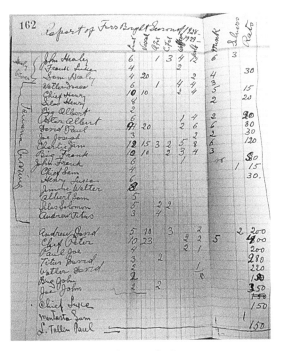

Figure 14.1. Fur Report to the A.G.C. for the year 1926–27 [dated] Nov. 5–1928. Dene listed by name from Healy Lake, Tanana Crossing, Tetlin, and Nabesna. Furs listed: lynx, mink, rats, cross fox, red fox, weasel, wolf, and silver and gray fox. Total number of furs for each species listed. Source: Hajdukovich collection. Source: Hajdukovich collection. Journals and Ledgers, 1922–1948 Accounts Hajdukovich ledgers Box 3 Tanana Crossing 1931–32, 1937, 1929–31, 1932 and 1939. Box 5 Accounts 1927–1930. Alaska and Polar Regions Department, Elmer E. Rasmuson Library, University of Alaska Fairbanks.

Figure 14.2. Fur Report to the A.G.C. for the year 1928–29 for the communities of Tanana Crossing and Tetlin. Source: Hajdukovich collection. Journals and Ledgers, 1922–1948 Accounts Hajdukovich ledgers Box 3 Tanana Crossing 1931–32, 1937, 1929–31, 1932 and 1939. Box 5 Accounts 1927–1930. Alaska and Polar Regions Department, Elmer E. Rasmuson Library, University of Alaska Fairbanks.

APPENDIX C

Fur Trade Documents

The John Hajdukovich collection of correspondence and papers at the University of Alaska Fairbanks Archives contains many documents related to the fur trade in the upper Tanana region. Hajdukovich's ledgers show different transactions: some record the number of furs received from different trappers; others record the purchase and sale of blankets, the amount of credit due to the traders, and food bought by Dene.

AMOUNT AND TYPES OF FURS

Fur trade ledger entries have yearly fur reports including the names of people who trapped and the kinds of furs. Muskrats provide the bulk of the trade. For the year 1926–27 Hajdukovich bought 4,479 "rats," 280 lynx, 80 mink, 11 cross fox, 23 red fox, 17 weasel, 38 wolf pelts, 4 wolverine, and 5 silver/gray foxes.

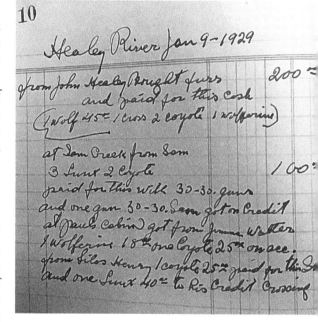

Figure 14.3. Note about furs bought from John Healy and Sam at Sam Creek dated January 9, 1929. Sam paid $100 for 3 lynx and 2 coyote and received a .30-30. Sam also got a gun on credit at Paul's cabin from Jimmie Walter. Source: Hajdukovich collection. Journals and Ledgers, 1922–1948 Accounts Hajdukovich ledgers Box 3 Tanana Crossing 1931–32, 1937, 1929–31, 1932 and 1939. Box 5 Accounts 1927–1930. Alaska and Polar Regions Department, Elmer E. Rasmuson Library, University of Alaska Fairbanks Archives.

https://doi.org/10.5876/9781646423347.c014

Figure 14.4. Ledger showing transactions from December 1928 to January 15, 1929. The entry begins with 5 lynx and 1 coyote from Charley Jim, then credits John Healy for 15 blankets, furs received from Jimmie Walter; from Chief Henry, Chief Peter, Paddy Healy, Andrew David, and Joe John. Source: Hajdukovich collection Journals and Ledgers, 1922–1948 Accounts Hajdukovich ledgers Box 3 Tanana Crossing 1931–32, 1937, 1929–31, 1932 and 1939. Box 5 Accounts 1927–1930. Alaska and Polar Regions Department, Elmer E. Rasmuson Library, University of Alaska Fairbanks Archives

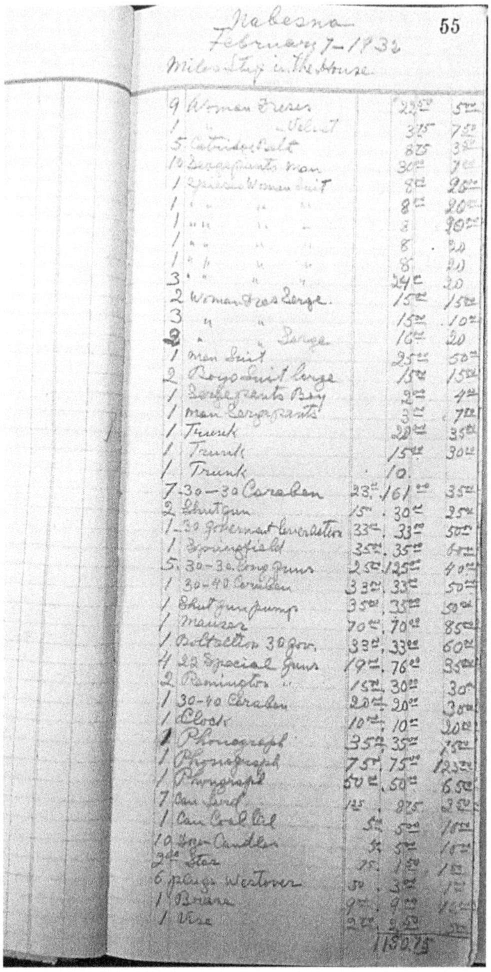

Figure 14.5. Goods and prices for the store at Nabesna dated February 7, 1936. Source: Hajdukovich collection Journals and Ledgers, 1922–1948 Accounts Hajdukovich ledgers Box 3 Tanana Crossing 1931–32, 1937, 1929–31, 1932 and 1939. Box 5 Accounts 1927–1930. Alaska and Polar Regions Department, Elmer E. Rasmuson Library, University of Alaska Fairbanks Archives.

TYPES OF TRADE GOODS

Traders supplied a wide variety of goods, including guns and ammunition, women's dresses, men's suits, packing trunks, phonographs, candles, and a vise.

BLANKETS

Upper Tanana Dene measured wealth in blankets. In the 1880s, Upper Tanana Dene traded for Hudson's Bay blankets at the towns of Fortymile and Dawson or from Tutchone and Tlingit. Elders talked about getting a "pair of blankets" because two blankets came stitched together. The narrow black lines on the blankets indicated the size of the blanket. John

Pendleton Woolen Mills
Portland, Oregon

Date	5-16-27
Inv. No.	6634
Your No.	
Dept.	
Salesman	CAS
Via	BOAT W-3571

Sold to
JOHN HAJDUKOVITCH
C/O ROY LUND
FAIRBANKS, ALASKA.

TERMS: 2% 30 DAYS, NET 60 F.O.B.

MAKE ALL REMITTANCES TO PORTLAND, OREGON

Quan.	Item	Price	Total
350	66X80 YELLOWSTONES	7 50	2625 00
	MAR INS		18 04
			2643 04

PENDLETON WOOLEN MILLS

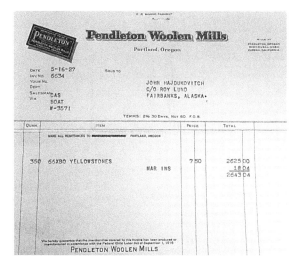

Figure 14.6. Invoice from Pendleton Woolen Mills dated 5.16.1927 for 350 Yellowstone blankets at $7.50 a piece. Source: Hajdukovich collection Bills and Receipts, 1919–1963 General Transportation Co.—Fortymile Roadhouse Subject File Accounts-Map Box 3. Alaska and Polar Regions Department, Elmer E. Rasmuson Library, University of Alaska Fairbanks Archives.

Northway Blankets
May 1946

S.N	400	550 00
B	300	230 00
M	150	75 00
B2	100	50 00
W	200	250 00
P	40	40 00
FJ	300	200 00
JM.	200	250 00
	1690	1645 00

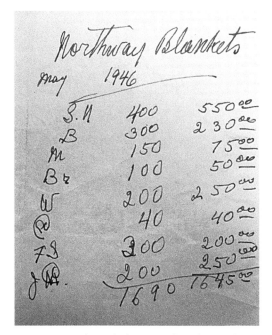

Figure 14.7. "Northway Blankets." List of people's initials and what looks like the number of blankest purchased and the amount, dated May 1946. Source: Hajdukovich collection Bills and Receipts, 1919–1963 General Transportation Co.—Fortymile Roadhouse Subject File Accounts-Map Box 3. Alaska and Polar Regions Department, Elmer E. Rasmuson Library, University of Alaska Fairbanks Archives.

Hajdukovich did not trade in Hudson's Bay blankets; instead, he bought blankets from the Pendleton Woolen Mills in Oregon.

CREDIT ACCUMULATED BY INDIVIDUAL DENE

Traders operated primarily on credit. No one had money to buy things, so they used their furs to build up credit and became indebted to the traders year after year.

119

Credit Due to Milo at Nebesna

Ketch Charley	294.00
Chief Sam	200.00
Bessie "	28.00
Gisha	270.00
[illegible] Northway	52.00
Scottie Ollie	62 50
Sarah Solomon	26 00
Elsie Peter Albert	77 00
Chief Sam Girl	15 00
Bill Northway	116.50
Frank + Annie Sam	284.50
Bill Kie	172 00
Walter Northway wife	20 00
Polly Follett	16 50
Big Mark	58 00
Peter Albert	156 25
Steve Northway	4.00
Old Lady Northway	66 50
Lee Northway	150 00
Jack Janich	96 00
Follett	169 00
Walter Northway	279 50
Martha Gisha	2 50
Maggie Northway	1 50
Jake Charley	237 00
Joe Mark	54 00
Esau Charley	16 50
	2923 75
	2924 75

Credit Due to John From Nabesna People

Frank Sam	62 25
Annie Sam	19 75
Follette Isaac	74 00
Peter Albert	14 25
Kelshim Charley	77 50
Esay Charley	24 50
Martha Sisha	22 50
Lee Northway	11 75
Emma Northway	4 50
Laura Charley	12 50
Joe Charley	87 75
Maggie Northway	8 50
Big Mark	29 50
Polly Follette	3 25
Joe Mark	31 25
Old Sam Wife	4 00
Celia Mark	5 25
Bill Northway	150 25
Steve Northway	68 00
Chief Sam	1 75
Peter Albert wife	3 00
Laura Northway	1 50
Sarah Northway	5 50
Bertha John	3 50
Old lady Northway	4 00
Oskar Peter	1 00
Old Anna	1 50
	733 00

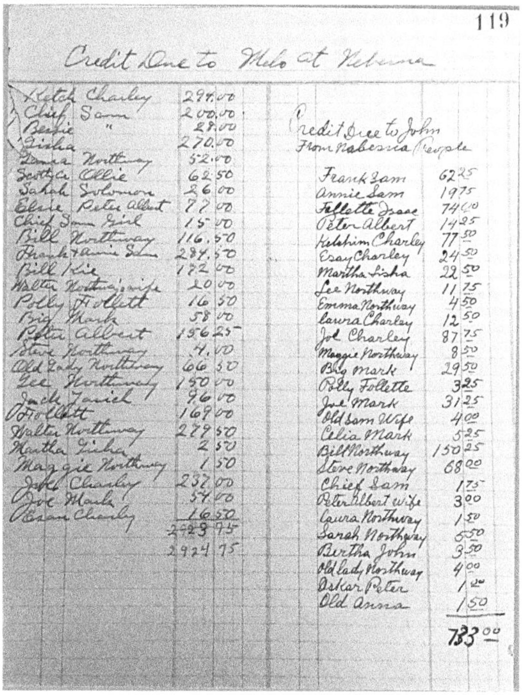

Figure 14.8. Page of a ledger showing the credit due to Milo and John Hajdukovich, no date. This is a list of names of Nabesna people and the amount owed. Milo was owed a total of $2,924.75, John was owed $733. Source: Hajdukovich collection Subject File, 1923–1961 Medical Trading Post Photographs 1985-002-01 through 16 Box 4. Alaska and Polar Regions Department, Elmer E. Rasmuson Library, University of Alaska Fairbanks Archives.

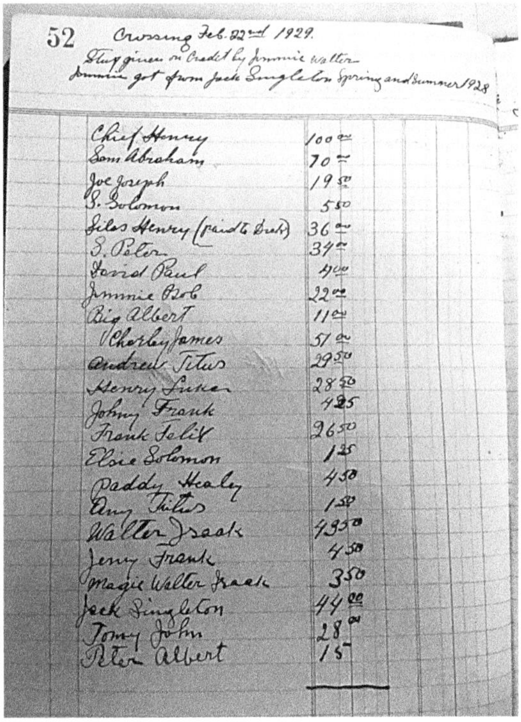

52 Crossing Feb. 22nd 1929.
Stuff given on Credit by Jimmie Walter
Jimmie got from Jack Singleton Spring and Summer 1928

Chief Henry	100.00
Sam Abraham	70.00
Joe Joseph	19.50
S. Solomon	5.50
Silas Henry (paid to Dick)	36.00
S. Peter	34.00
David Paul	4.00
Jimmie Bob	22.00
Big Albert	11.00
Charley James	51.00
Andrew Titus	29.50
Henry Luke	28.50
Johny Frank	4.25
Frank Felix	26.50
Elsie Solomon	1.25
Paddy Healy	4.50
Amy Titus	1.50
Walter Isaak	43.50
Jeny Frank	4.50
Magie Walter Isaak	3.50
Jack Singleton	44.00
Tomy John	28.00
Peter Albert	15

Figure 14.9. List of Tanacross creditors dated 2.22.1929 and list of people and amount owed. Source: Hajdukovich collection Journals and Ledgers, 1922–1948 Accounts Hajdukovich ledgers Box 3 Tanana Crossing 1931–32, 1937, 1929–31, 1932 and 1939. Box 5 Accounts 1927–1930. Alaska and Polar Regions Department, Elmer E. Rasmuson Library, University of Alaska Fairbanks Archives.

PURCHASE OF FOOD AND GOODS

What the elders called "groceries" came to be an important supplement, adding variety to people's diet and tiding them over when wild foods were in short supply. These two receipts show the type and amount of food Dene purchased. The food for both was paid by December's Pension Check.

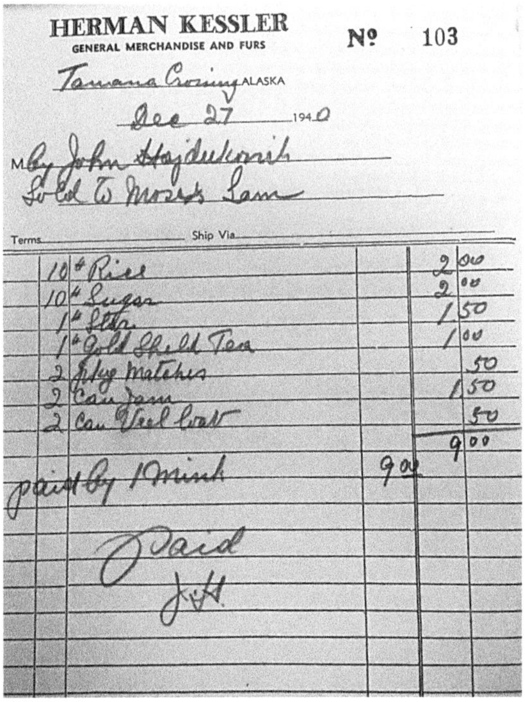

HERMAN KESSLER
GENERAL MERCHANDISE AND FURS
Nº 103
Tanana Crossing ALASKA
Dec 27 1940
M By John Hajdukovich
Sold to Moses Sam
Terms Ship Via

10# Rice	2.00
10# Sugar	2.00
1# Star	1.50
1# Gold Shield Tea	1.00
2 Pkg Matches	.50
2 Can Jam	1.50
2 Can Veal Loaf	.50
	9.00

paid by 1 Mink 9.00
Paid
J.H.

Figure 14.10. Receipt issued by Herman Kessler at Tanacross dated 12.27.1940 to Moses Sam for food: 10 pounds of rice and sugar, 1 pound of star chewing tobacco, 1 pound of Gold Leaf Tea, 2 packages of matches, 2 cans of jam, and two cans of (illegible). Source. Hajdukovich collection. Journals and Ledgers, 1922–1948 Accounts Hajdukovich ledgers Box 3 Tanana Crossing 1931–32, 1937, 1929–31, 1932 and 1939. Alaska and Polar Regions Department, Elmer E. Rasmuson Library, University of Alaska Fairbanks Archives.

HERMAN KESSLER
GENERAL MERCHANDISE AND FURS
№ 102

Tanana Crossing ALASKA
Dec 27 1940

M. By John Hajdukovich
Sold to Bessie Sam

Terms Cash Ship Via

25	# Flour		4.00
10	# Sugar		2.00
1	pkg Macaroni		1.50
1	# Gold Shield Tea		1.00
1	# Star Tobacco		1.50
2	pkg Dry Peaches		1.50
10	# Corn meal		1.50
1	Can Lard		
			15.00

Paid by Dec pension Check 15.00

Paid
JH

Inter-State Press, 2214 Venice Blvd., Los Angeles

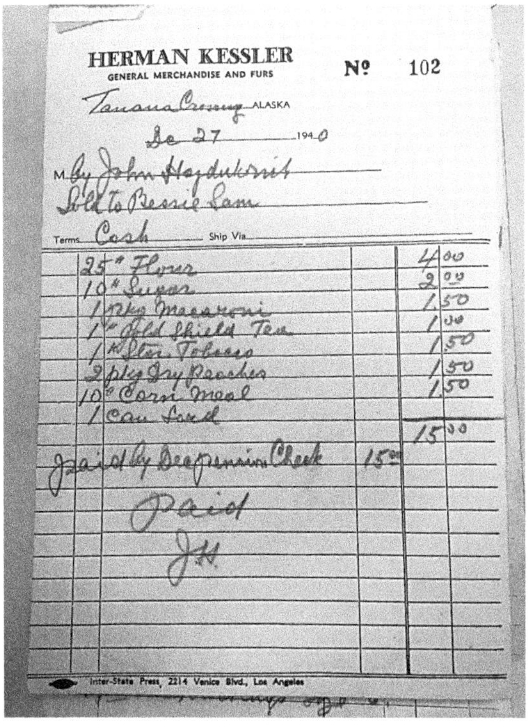

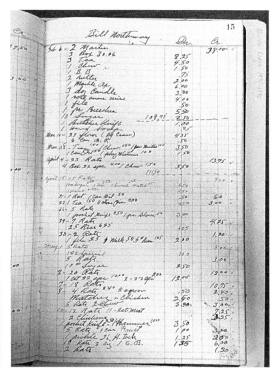

Figure 14.11. Receipt issued by Herman Kessler at Tanacross dated 12.27.1940 to Bessie Sam. 25 pounds of flour, 10 pounds of sugar, 1 package of macaroni, 1 pound of gold shield tea, 1 pound of star tobacco, 2 packages of dried peaches, 10 pounds of corn meal, and 1 can of lard. Source: Hajdukovich collection. Journals and Ledgers, 1922–1948 Accounts Hajdukovich ledgers Box 3 Tanana Crossing 1931–32, 1937, 1929–31, 1932 and 1939. Alaska and Polar Regions Department, Elmer E. Rasmuson Library, University of Alaska Fairbanks Archives.

15

Bill Northway

Dr. Cr.

Feb 6 – 2 Marten 38.00
3 Box 30.06 8.25
3 Tea 4.50
1 Chew 1.50
1 B. B .75
2 Butter 2.00
1 Marble Ax 6.00
3 doz Candle 3.00
1 roll snare wire 4.00
1 file .50
1 pr Breeches 5.50
10 Sugar 2.50
1 Butcher Knife 1.00
1 Hand Soap .25

Figure 14.12. Ledger showing what Bill Northway bought in February, March, April, and May. In February Northway paid with 2 marten skins; later he traded muskrat skins for things as diverse as candles, snare wire, butcher knife, chewing tobacco, and rice. Source: Hajdukovich collection. Journals and Ledgers, 1932–1938 Tetlin-Nabesna Box7. Alaska and Polar Regions Department, Elmer E. Rasmuson Library, University of Alaska Fairbanks Archives.

.

APPENDIX D

Census Records for Healy Lake, Ketchumstuk, Mansfield/ Tanacross, Tetlin / Last Tetlin, and Northway/Nabesna

An analysis of census data illustrates Robert McKennan's (1969) point that Dene bands on the upper Tanana River formed an interlocking social unit rather than discrete entities. For example, the data graphically illustrate the close connection, created by blood and marriage, between upper Tanana, Tanacross, and upper Copper River people. The data also illustrate the movement between bands precipitated by the fur trade and mining development, disease, and the wish to stay mobile. The data also show how the bands eventually coalesced at points along the Alaska Highway, abandoning outlying points such as Ketchumstuk, the upper Chisana River, and Healy Lake.

Ketchumstuk is a case in point. In 1910, the population of Ketchumstuk was fifty-two people, including six non-Native miners and one trapper. In 1920, twenty-three people were counted at Ketchumstuk. All these people appeared on the 1910 census. There were nine men, eight women, and seven children under the age of twelve. Sometime between 1910 and 1920, tuberculosis took the lives of at least nine people at Ketchumstuk. After 1920, there are no figures for Ketchumstuk, which for all intent and purposes was abandoned.

The earliest census records come from explorers attached to the US Military. Lt. Henry Allen (1887) was the first to provide demographic information on the Dene in east-central Alaska. When Allen arrived in Last Tetlin, he found forty men, twenty-eight women, and eighteen children. At Tetlin he counted six men, whom he had seen previously at Last Tetlin, four

women, and seven children. At Dihthâad he counted twenty-eight men, eighteen women, and six children. Fourteen years later, in July 1899, quartermaster John Rice counted fifty "Ketchemstak" Indians at Mansfield. He called Ketchumstuk the Mansfield people's winter quarters (Rice 1900: 786). Griffith, a topographer with the US Army, encountered sixty-five "Indians" at Mansfield in August 1899. Dene told Griffith "a great tale of woe of how many Indians had died from which we understood that some epidemic had afflicted them" (Griffith 1890: 726). They might have been referring to the smallpox epidemic of 1838–1839 that possibly reached the upper Tanana, two scarlet fever epidemics, and an apparent diphtheria epidemic that occurred in 1882 along the Yukon (McKennan 1969: 106; Osgood 1971: 32).

The use of census records is not with problems. People moved around, and especially during the late winter and early spring, people were spread out living in camps and not in main villages. Most of the local population probably spoke little English, so communication was a problem. Early on, people were not using English surnames but only single names they had adopted to facilitate their relationship with the few traders and miners living in their country. For these reasons, it is difficult to be certain of the population and to figure out who is who and how they are connected to later censuses. Later censuses, taken after 1930, are more accurate because they were taken by enumerators who were familiar with the people,

https://doi.org/10.5876/9781646423347.c015

and people were more concentrated in regional centers rather than out in camps. The local people spoke more English, and they used surnames that are recognizable today.

Table 15.1. Thirteenth Census (1910) Healy River
Enumerated January 10 and February 4, 1910

Name	Relation	Birthdate	Mother	Father	Birthplace	Notes
Sam, Little White man, Kat'ba	Head	1864		Tsek (Red Paint)		Little Sam's older brother, married to Belle Sam's mom
Carotuck (?)	Lodger	1891				Sam's mother
Linas	Daughter	1897				
Pilot	Son	1893				
Healy, Indian	Head	1849		Geti Theeg (Tall Old Man)		Chief Healy
Josie	Wife	1864		Tsek (Red Paint)		2nd wife of Chief Healy, Sam's sister, Chaaz
Paul	Son	1896				
Soutel	Son	1905				
Johhny	Son	1899				
Chief Joseph	Head	1874			Salcha (?)	Chief "Joe," brother of Belle Sam
Lucy	Wife	1879				
Eva	Daughter	1900				
Martha	Daughter	1904				
Jessie	Daughter	1907				
Billican, Jimmy	Lodger	1899				
Sam, Little	Head	1859		Tsek (Red Paint)		
Belle	Wife	1864				
Maggie	Daughter	1891				John Healy's first wife
Billy	Son	1902				
Jeany	Daughter	1904				
Lucy	Daughter	1905				
Luke	Son	1908				
Jacob, Guss	Head	1877				Solomon's brother
Agnes	Wife	1889	Belle Sam		Ketchumstuk	
Esaw	Son	1909				
Fred	Head	1864				
Annie	Wife	1879				
David	Son	1901				
Charlie	Son	1903				

Table 15.2. Fourteenth Census (1920) Healy River
Enumerated March 21, 1920

Name	Relation	Age
Newton, William	Head	47
Jane	Wife	42
Madge	Daughter	9
Kathleen	Daughter	7
Harold	Son	7
Ray, George	Head	49
Healy, Chief	Head	61
Josie	Wife	54
Satelle	Son	13
Paul	Son	9
Julius	Adpt. Son	11
Chief, Joseph, Joe	Head	41
Agnes	Wife	39
Alex	Son	3
Walter	Son	2
Healy, John	Head	34
Jennie	Wife	19
Arthur	Son	1
Healy, Patrick	Head	
Agnes	Wife	27
Alice	Daughter	6
Margarite	Daughter	4
Little Whiteman	Head	64?
Ellen	Adpt. Daughter	11
Blind Jimmy	Head	49
Salina	Wife	52
Frank	Son	7
Fred, Annie	Head	38
Eva	Daughter	12
Martha	Daughter	7
Sam	Head	52
(Belle) Mary	Wife	54
Lucy	Daughter	15
Eva	Daughter	8
Emma	Daughter	6

Note: Birthplaces and the names of the parents are unknown.

Table 15.3. 1937 Healy Lake Population counted 55 persons, this includes Sand Creek
Enumerated by L. R. Wright, Govt. Nurse

Name	Relation	Birthdate	Mother	Father	Birthplace	Notes
Healy, Josie	Head	1868		Conchathtah	Healy Lake	Widow of Chief Healy
Healy, Paul	Son	1910				
Martha	Daughter-in-law		Annie	Fred		Deceased
Healy, John	Head	1890	*Kwhoish*	Chief Healy	Healy River	John is son of Chief Healy's 1st wife
Jennie	Wife	1904	Belle	Chief Sam	Healy River	
Arthur	Son	1918			Healy Lake	
Bessie	Daughter	1923			Healy Lake	
Laura	Daughter	1929			Healy Lake	
Sarah	Daughter	1931			Healy Lake	
Stella	Daughter	1933			Healy Lake	Married Lee Saylor
Louie	Son	1936			Healy Lake	
Marilyn	Daughter	1938			Healy Lake	
Healy, Arthur	Head	1918	Jennie Sam	John Healy	Healy River	
Laura	Wife	1912	Maggie Demit	Walter Isaac	Mansfield	On the census father is "chief Isaac"
Healy, Blind Jimmy	Head	1868		Joseph Healy	Healy Lake	Brother of Chief Healy
Old Saline	Wife	1871	Conaguntha	Charlie	Healy Lake	
Little Old Whiteman	Head	90 to 100		Conchathatah	Sand Creek	
Charlie, Mary	Head	1898	*Kwhoish*	Chief Healy	Healy Lake	Widow of John Charlie (*Hootnah*)
Joseph, John	Head	1897/1883	Haxtala	Joseph	Salchaket	Brother of Joe Joseph
Emma Charlie	Wife	1917	Mary Healy	John Charlie	Healy Lake	
Susie Tommy	Wife					1st wife
Nancy	Daughter	1931				
Walter	Son	1934				
Matthew	Son	1935				
Jessie	Daughter	1936				
Susie	Daughter	1937				Died, 1940
Laura (?)	Daughter	1939				
Felix, Frank	Head	1915	Bod'la	Felix	Healy Lake	
Ellen	Wife	1917	Eva David	Julius	Chena	Now Ellen Demit
Mary	Daughter	1934				
Agnes	Daughter	1936				
Alfred	Son	1938				
Enid	Daughter	1939				

Table 15.4. Twelfth (1900) US Census
Ketchumstuk, Alaska
Enumerated February 2, 1900

Name	Relation	Birthdate	Age
Isaac	Head	1836	63
Martha	Daughter	1873	26
Maggie	Daughter	1883	16
Walter	Son	1876	23
Titus	Son	1880	19
Saul	Head	1861	38
Sarah/Uda (?)	Wife	1863	36
Solomon	Head	1864	35
John	Son	1893	6
Frank	Head	1859	40
Charlie	Head	1834	62
Albert	Partner	1871	28
Paul	Head	1859	40
Lucy (?)	Wife	1869	30
Samual	Head	1875	24
Benjiman	Partner	1877	22
Robert	Head	1864	35
Sarah Bob	Wife	1869	30
Fred	Son	1893	6
Maggie	Daughter	1895	4
Albert	Son	1897	2

Table 15.5. *Census at Ketchumstuk, 1903*

Enumerated by the Episcopal Church April 7, 1903

"Most of the people in the 1903 census were considered baptized but not confirmed or had communion as opposed to those people at Eagle."

Chief Isaac	Selina (d)
Wife (no name given)	Fred (s)
Walter (s)	Arthur (s)
Phillip (s)	Dick (s)
Titus Isaac	Jimmie (s)
Annie	Little boy Mark
Silas (s)	Edna
Albert	Maria
Maggie (w)	Joe (s)
Elisha	Jennie (d)
Wife	Caroline (d)
little boy	Ginnis (s)
Charlie	Kir
Wife	Jessie (d)
Martha (d)	Saul
Jane (d)	Eva (d)
Sam	Solomon
Belle (w)	Annie (w)
Little boy	Silas (s)
Bob	Louisa
Sarah (w)	Jeannie (d)

Source: Eagle Historical Society AE 87-21-1 Box 48 File 18

Table 15.6. Census at Ketchumstuk, 1905
Enumerated by Episcopal Church April 7, 1905

Name	Baptism status
Crooked Tom	Not baptized
Mary	Not baptized
James	Not baptized
little girl	Not baptized
Frank	Not baptized
wife	Not baptized
Billie	Not baptized
Little Frank	Not baptized
Arthur	Not baptized
Ellen	Not baptized
Sarah	Baptized
Little girl	Baptized
Kit (nephew)	Baptized
Laura	Unknown
Harry	Baptized
Maggie	Baptized
Laura	Baptized
Sallie	Unknown
(old man) Charlie	Baptized
Jeannie (w)	Baptized

Source: Eagle Historical Society AE 87-21-1 Box 48 File 18

Table 15.7. Thirteenth (1910) US Census from Ketchumstuk
Enumerated February 18, 20, 21, 1910

Name	Relation	Birthdate	Age	Name	Relation	Birthdate	Age
Matchalt, John	Head	1854	55	Chechaga	Daughter	1905	4
K. Thomas J.	Head	1857	52	Bob, Pedro	Head	1864	45
Unclear, Frank E.	Partner	1865	44	Sarah	Wife	1871	38
Sumer, Henry	Head	1857	52	Cannot Make Out	Son	1895	14
Carlson, Augustine	Partner	1861	48	Jimmie	Son	1903	6
Mitchell, Richard C.	Head	1864	45	Edna	Daughter	1908	2
Sol (Saul)	Head	1879/61	30	Isaac, Walter	Head	1884	25
Esau, Eva	Cousin	1869/1863	40	Maggie	Wife	1879	36
Unclear	Daughter	1881	18		Daughter	1908	1
David (Unclear)	Nephew	1882	17	Demit, Elisha	Head	1874	35
Solomon	Head	1883	26	Ella (married 6 years)	Wife	1885	24
Annie James	Wife	1885	24	Jessie	Niece	1895	14
Silas	Son	1904	5	Demit, Charlie	Head	1879	37
Archie	Son	1906	3	Mary (married 14 years)	Wife	1881	28
Mary	Daughter	1908	1	Jimmy	Son	1901	8
Elsie	Daughter	1909		Henry	Son	1908	1
Sam, Stephen	Head	1879	30	Susan (?)	M/in Law	1849	68
Bella	Wife	1884	25	Chutaki (?) Felix	Head	1872	37
Walter	Son	1903	6	Bedal (married 10 years)	Wife	1884	25
Eva	Daughter	1907	2				
John, Jim	Head	1858	51	Elsie	Daughter	1901	8
Laura.	Wife	1864	45	Rodney	Son	1905	4
Charles	Son	1895	14	Joseph	Son	1909	1
Oltama	Daughter	1898	11	Little David	Head	1886	23
Bean, Pedro	Head	1884	25	Salina	Wife	1896	19
Lucy	Wife	1890	19	Norvel, Benjamin	Head	1866	43
Chuchocom	Head	1869	40				

continued in next column

Table 15.8. Fourteenth (1920) US Census Ketchumstuk
Enumerated March 13, 1920

Name	Relation	Age
Robert, Peter	Head	48
Sarah	Wife	43
James	Son	21
?	Daughter	11
Tega, David	Dead	29
Selina	Wife	27
Mary	Daughter	7
Archie	Son	1.5
Felix	Head	51
Mary	Daughter	16
Frank	Son	7
Abraham, Sam	Head	45
Belle	Wife	36
Bessie	Daughter	9
Peter	Head	48
Solomon, Peter	Head	47
Silas	Son	14
Elsie	Daughter	11
Saul	Head	48
Mary	Wife	35
?	Daughter	6.5
Abraham, Eva	Head	54
Jennie	Daughter	27

Note: Birthplaces are unknown.

Table 15.9. Mansfield Lake, Mansfield April 7, 1905
Enumerated by the Episcopal Church, April 7, 1905

Name
Chief Sam
Bessie (w)
Albert (w)
Billie (w)
Joseph (s)
Timothy (s)
Peter
Susan (w)
Peter's sister Jeannie
Moses
Jacob
John
Albert
Minnie (w)
Peter (s)
Mark (s)
Big Mark
Agnes (w)
Grace (d)
Emma (d)
Philip
Cardin (w)
little girl
Tom
Lillie (w)
Dorothy (d)

Source: Eagle Historical Society AE 87-21-1 Box 48 File 18

Table 15.10. Thirteenth US Census (1910) Lake Mansfield
Enumerated February 22, 25 and 26, 1910

Name	Relation	Birthdate	Age	Name	Relation	Birthdate	Age
Charley	Head	1849	60	Albert, Big	Head	1874	35
Jennie	Wife	1884	25	Minnie (married 14 yrs)	Wife	1888	28
Dewey	Son	1904	5	Mike	Son	1895	14
Charlicleck (?)	M/in law	1854	55	Jumbo	Son	1904	5
Peter	Head	1877	32	Walter	Son	1893	16
Sarah (married 10 yrs)	Wife	1886	23	Cligatah (?) Old Walter (?)	Head	1849	60
Walter	Son	1906	3	Bessie (married 20 yrs)	Wife	1876	33
Sam	Head	1869	40	Jimmie	Son	1891	18
Mabel (married 15 yrs)	Wife	1879	30	Ella	Daughter	1909	6 months
Moses	Son	1899	10	Paul (Old Paul)	Head	1864	45
Walter	Son	1901	8	Alice (married 18 yrs.)	Wife	1874	35
Annie	Daughter	1904	5	Paul	Son	1892	17
Joseph	Son	1905	4	Salina	Daughter	1894	15
Albert	Son	1894	15	No Name	Daughter	1907	2
Jennie	Sister	1894	15	Follet	Head	1886	23
Albert Moses	Head	1884	25	Ellen (married 1 yr)	Wife	1888	21
Mark, Big	Head	1879	30	Thomas	Head	1879	30
Agnes (married 12 yrs)	Wife	1882	27	Maggie (married 9 months)	Wife	1892	17
Eva	Daughter	1899	10	Gus (Jacob)	Head	1881	28
Joseph	Son	1906	4	Agnes (married 1 year)	Wife	1889	20
Betsy	Daughter	1909	6 months	John	Son	1909	3 months
Titus Isaac	Head	1880/1878	29	Hamilton (Widower)	Head	1854	55
Annie Esau (married 8 yrs)	Wife	1885	24	Harry	Son	1889	20
William	Son	1903	7	Julia	Daughter	1897	12
Barney	Son	1904	5	Grace	Daughter	1901	8
Laura (?)	Daughter	1909	6 months	Martin, John (prospectors)	Head	1859	50
Galuch (?) (Female, Widow)	Head	1867	48	Struck (?), Julius	Head	1869	40
Alfred	Son	1892	17	Hogan, Thomas	Head	1873	36
Sarah	Daughter	1891	19	Britton, Frank	Head	1870	39
Emma	Daughter	1895	14				
Isaac, Chief	Head	1849	60				
Edna (married 10 yrs)	Wife	1881	28				

continued in next column

Table 15.11. Fourteenth US Census (1920) Tanana Crossing
Enumerated April 26, 1920

Name	Relation	Age	Name	Relation	Age
McConnel, David	Head		Edna	Daughter	9
Kessler			David	Son	8
Strelic			Celia	Daughter	5
Olie Frederickson			Old Walter	Head	56
Charles, Albert	Head	46	Bessie	Wife	44
Minnie	Wife	42	Jimmy	Son	27
Mark	Son	25	Maggie	Daughter	12
Peter	Son	12	Thomas, Sam	Head	57
Louise	Daughter	9	Bessie	Wife	
Charlie	Head	72	Albert	Son	
Albert, Walter	Head	27	Moses	Son	
Eva	Wife	21	Annie	Daughter	
Lillie	Daughter		Thomas, Peter	Head	
	Daughter		Sarah	Wife	
Isaac, Walter	Head	41	Silas	Son	
Maggie	Wife		Lena	Daughter	
Jessie	Daughter	11	Jim, Minnie	Sister-in-law	
	Daughter		Jim, Charlie	Brother-in-law	
Oscar	Son		Old Gert	Mother	
Elisha Steve	Brother-in-law	42	Petersend, John	Head	
Jessie Joseph	Niece	28	Henry, Silas	Head	
Big Mark	Head	42	Charlotte	Wife	
Agnes	Wife	34	Arthur	Son	
Joe	Son	11			

Note: Birthplaces are unknown.

continued in next column

Table 15.12. 1937–1938 Tanacross Census*
Enumerated by L. R. Wright, Govt. Nurse, on November 23, 1937

Name	Relation	Birthdate	Father	Mother	Birthplace
Abraham, Sam	Head	1872			Ketchumstuk
Belle	Wife	1893	Peter	Lilly	Mansfield
Agnes	Daughter	1923			Ketchumstuk
Nissie	Daughter	1928			Tanacross
Charles, Albert	Head	1871	Old Charlie, Mentasta		Mentasta
Minnie	Wife		Adam, Tsiint-le' (?)		Mansfield
Lilly	Gr. Child	1917	Little Albert	Eva Mark	Paul's Place
McConnell	Gr. Child	1923			Tanacross
Charles, Peter	Head	1905	Albert Charles	Minnie	Tanacross
Doris	Wife	1910/07	Batzulnetas Billy		Batzulnetas
Charles, Walter	Son	1927			Mansfield
Theodore	Son	1928			Tanacross
Carl	Son	1930			Tanacross
Stella	Daughter	1932			Tanacross
Dorothy	Daughter	1934			Tanacross
Banford	Son	1937			Tanacross
Fleischmann	Son	1939			Tanacross
Charles, Nellie	Head	1911	Charlie Singleye	Jessie	Mentasta
Alice	Daughter	1931			Mentasta
Delia	Daughter	1935			Mentasta
Earl	Son	1938			Tanacross
Charlie, Sandford	Head	1905	Sanford Charlie	Jessie	Copper River
Jennie	Wife	1894	Chief John	Lucy	
Sandford, Bentley R.	Son	1935			Tanacross
Denny, Thomas	Head	1900			Seattle
Annie	Wife	1907	Sam Thomas	Bessie	Tanacross
Alice	Daughter	1927			Last Tetlin
Martha	Daughter	1929			Tanacross
Archie	Son	1930			Tanacross
Marjorie	Daughter	1933			Tanacross
Nellie	Daughter	1935			Tanacross
Robert	Son	1937			Tanacross
Sally	Daughter	1939			Tanacross
Esau, Eva	Head	1863			Ketchumstuk
Frank, Big	Head	1863	Frank		Minto
Jessie	Wife	1880	Chief John		Mentasta
Charlie, Nellie	daughter		Charlie Singleye	Jessie	

continued on next page

Table 15.12.—*continued*

Name	Relation	Birthdate	Father	Mother	Birthplace
Charlie, Pete	Son				
John, Tommy	Head	1883	John		Salchaket
Annie	Wife	1873			Good Paster
John, Abbie	Daughter				
Esther	Daughter				
Jonathan, Gert	Head	1885			Mansfield
Jonathan, John Frank	Head		Frank Jonathan	Jennie	Mansfield
Emma	Wife	1915	John Moses (Albert?)	Annie Steve	Mansfield
Virginia	Daughter	1936			Tanacross
Helen	Daughter	1938			Tanacross
Jonathan, Timothy	Head	1912	Frank Jonathan	Jennie	Mansfield
Mary (Isaac)	Wife	1919	Walter Isaac	Maggie Demit	Tanacross
Olive	Daughter	1937			Tanacross
Dan	Son	1938			
Robert	Son	1939			
Joseph, Joe	Head	1885	Joseph	Haxtala	Salchaket
Saline	Wife	1895	Old Paul	Julia	Mansfield
Joseph	Son	1925			Tanacross
Ellen	Daughter	1930			Tanacross
Betty Jean	Daughter	1933			Tanacross
Fannie	Daughter	1936			Tanacross
Nancy	Daughter	1938			
Martha (Isaac)	Daughter				
Luke, Henry	Head	1880	Luke		Mansfield
Jennie (Thomas)	Wife	1890	Thomas		Mansfield
Elsie	Daughter	1918			Mansfield
Stella (Solomon)	Daughter	1918			Tokio Camp
Richard	Son	1923			Tanacross
Moses	Son	1927			Mansfield
Paddy Herbert	Son	1938			Tanacross
Solomen, Ambrose		1937	Solomon	Stella	Mansfield
Solomon, Irene		1939			Tanacross
Paul, Julius	Head	1913	Old Paul	Julia	Mansfield
Celia (1st wife)	Wife	1915	Big Mark	Agnes	Chicken
Robert Franklin	Son	1936			Tanacross
Reka (2nd Wife)	Wife	1928			
Paul, Old	Head	1859	Paul		Wood River

continued on next page

Table 15.12.—*continued*

Name	Relation	Birthdate	Father	Mother	Birthplace
Julia	Wife	1861	Thomas		Mansfield
David	Son				
Julius	Son				
Saline	Daughter				
Henry, Silas	Head	1882	Henry	Laura	Mansfield
Lizzie (2nd wife)	Wife	1880	John	Lucy	Mansfield
Drane	Son	1918		Charlotte Luke (1st)	Mansfield
Mark	Son	1925		Charlotte Luke (1st)	Paul's Place
Paul	Son	1926			Mansfield
Rica	Daughter	1928			Mansfield
William	Son	1923			Paul's Place
Isaac, Andrew	Head	1904	Titus	Annie Esau	Mansfield
Maggie	Wife		Old Walter	Bessie Thomas	Mansfield
Louise	Daughter	1932			Paul's Place
Madeline Faith	Daughter	1934			Mansfield
Kathaleen Virgie	Daughter	1938			Mansfield
Isaac, Oscar	Head	1914	Walter	Maggie Demit	Tanacross
Martha	Wife	1918	Joe	Saline	Mansfield
Mary Jean	Daughter	1936			Tanacross
Edward	Son	1937			Tanacross
Marie	Daughter	1937			Tanacross
Isaac, Titus	Head	1878	Old Isaac		Sam Creek
Annie	Wife	Easu	Eva		
Abraham	Son	1917			Mansfield
Isabel	Daughter	1922			Ketchumstuk
Isaac, Isaac	Son	1924			Mansfield
Laura	Daughter	1928			Mansfield
Isaac, Walter	Head	1883	Old Isaac		Mansfield
Maggie (Demit)	Wife	1881	Jack Demit		Ketchumstuk
Jacob	Son	1924			Ketchumstuk
James, Charlie	Head	1889	Old Jim (Batzulnetas)	Laura/Salina (Suslota)	Batzulnetas
Eliza (Saul)	Wife	1905	Saul	Uda	Ketchumstuk
Frances	Daughter	1923			Tanacross
Arthur	Son	1925			Copper River

continued on next page

Table 15.12.—*continued*

Name	Relation	Birthdate	Father	Mother	Birthplace
Myra	Daughter	1933			Tanacross
Harvey	Son	1935			Tanacross
Clarence	Son	1938			Tanacross
John, Lucy	Head	1862			Mentasta
John, Henry—Chief	Head	1872	John	Julia	Good Paster
Laura	Wife	1872/1866	Adam		Mansfield
Married Children					
Jennie Sanford					
Sam, Moses			Old Sam	Bessie Sam	
Paul, David	Head	1887	Old Paul	Julia	Mansfield
Laura Luke (1st wife)	Wife				
Ina (2nd Wife)	Wife	1912	Titus Isaac	Annie Esau	Mansfield
Dora	Daughter	1921	David	Laura	Tanacross
Gaither	Son	1923		Laura	Tanacross
Baily	Son	1925		Laura	Tanacross
Eldred	Son	1935		Ina	Tanacross
Gilbert	Son	1937		Ina	Tanacross
Winferd	Son	1938		Ina	Tanacross
Paul, Mathew	Head	1907	Old Paul	Julia	Mansfield
Edna (Roberts)	Wife		Robert	Sarah	Ketchumstuk
Rainey	Son	1937		Edna Roberts	
Roberts, Sarah	Head	1871	Mentasta	Last Tetlin	
Alice		1928	Jimmy Roberts	Mary Paul	Mansfield
Solomon, Silas	Head	1904	Solomon	Annie James	Ketchumstuk
Tega, David	Head	1881	Tega	Batzulnetas	
Elsie	Wife	1909	Solomon	Annie James	Ketchumstuk
Edbert	Son	1934			Tanacross
Ada Marie	Daughter	1937			Tanacross
Charlie	Son	1942			Tanacross
Thomas, Sam	Head	1862 or 59	Thomas		Mansfield
Bessie	Wife	1872 or 75	Old Charlie, Mentasta		Copper River
Moses	Son	1903			Fish Creek
Thomas, Peter	Head	1875	Thomas		Mansfield
Sarah	Wife	1890	Old Jim		(Mentasta?)
Silas	Son				Mansfield
Kenneth	Son	1922			Tanacross
Lena	Daughter	1917			Tanacross

continued on next page

Table 15.12.—*continued*

Name	Relation	Birthdate	Father	Mother	Birthplace
Lula	Daughter	1927			Tanacross
Calvin	Son	1931			Tanacross
Henry, Gene	Head	1913	Batzulnetas Billy	Jessie	Batzulnetas
Susie	Wife	1917	Walter Isaac	Maggie Demit	Mansfield
Henry, John	Head	1915	Batzulnetas Billy	Jessie	Copper River
Esther	Wife		Tommy John		Mansfield
Mildred	Daughter	1939			Tanacross
Walters, Bessie	Head	1871	Adam, Tsiint-le' (?)		Mansfield
Jimmy	Son	1893	Old Walter	Bessie	Tanacross

* Spring 1937 population includes Lake Mansfield.

Table 15.13. Sixteenth Census (1940) Tanacross
Enumerated December 1939 by E. A. McIntosh

Name	Relation	Age	Name	Relation	Age
Dasch, Carl James	Head	43	Lizzie	Wife	59
Isaac, Walter	Head	56	Mark	Son	14
Maggie	Wife		Reka	Daughter	11
Jacob	Son		Paul, Matthew	Head	31
Henry, Gene	Son-in-law	26	Edna Roberts	Wife	29
Henry, Susie (Isaac)	Daughter	23	Rainey	Son	2
Fred Howard	Son	5 months	Paul, Old	Head	82
Walter, Jimmie	Head		Julia	Wife	69
Bessie	Mother		Roberts, Alice	Granddaughter	11
Isaac, Andrew	Brother-in-law	37	Julius	Son	29
Walter, Maggie	Sister	32	Robert Franklin	Grandson	3
Louise	Niece	7	Jonathan, John Frank	Head	29
Madaline Faith	Niece	5	Emma Thomas	Wife	25
Kathaleen Virgie	Niece	1	Virginia	Daughter	3
Charles, Big Albert	Head	67	Helen	Daughter	1
Lilly W.	Granddaughter	22	Denny, David Thomas	Head	41
Joseph, Joe	Head	54	Annie	Wife	32
Salina	Wife	45	Alice	Daughter	12
Joseph	Son	14	Martha	Daughter	10
Ellen	Daughter	10	Archie	Son	8
Betty Jean	Daughter	6	Margie	Daughter	6
Fanny	Daughter	3	Nellie	Daughter	4
Nancy	Daughter	11 months	Robert	Son	2
Thomas, Old Sam	Head	85	Clara Sally	Daughter	
Bessie	Wife	65	Charles, Peter Albert	Head	35
Isaac, Oscar	Head	23	Doris	Wife	32
Martha	Wife	21	Walter	Son	12
Mary Jean	Daughter	3	Theodore	Son	11
Edward Durance	Son	2	Carl	Son	9
Paul, David	Head	42	Stella	Daughter	7
Ena	Wife	27	Dorothy	Daughter	4
Gaither	Son	16	Banford	Son	2
Bailey	Son	14	Fleischman	Son	5 months
Eldred	Son	4	Jonathan, Timothy Frank	Head	27
Gilbert	Son	2			
Winfred	Son	1	Mary Isaac	Wife	20
Henry, Silas	Head	58	Dan Muller	Son	1

continued in next column

continued in next column

Table 15.13.—*continued*

Name	Relation	Age	Name	Relation	Age
Alec Frank	Brother	12	Arthur	Son	14
Thomas, Moses Sam	Head	43	Misa	Daughter	6
Luke, Henry	Head	53	Harvey	Son	4
Jennie	Wife	50	Clarence	Son	1
Elsie	Daughter	26	Frank, Big	Head	76
Moses	Son	12	Jessie	Wife	60
Paddy	Son	4	Charlie, Nellie	Stepdaughter	28
Abraham, Sam	Head	68	Charlie, Alice	Stepgrand-daughter	8
Belle	Wife	46			
Agnes	Daughter	14	Charlie, Delia	Stepgrand-daughter	4
illegible	Daughter	11			
James, Charlie	Head	47	Charlie, Earl	Stepgrandson	1
Eliza	Wife	35	Jonathan, Gert	Head	84
Francis	Stepdaughter	15	Roberts, Sara		68

continued in next column

Table 15.14. Thirteenth US Census (1910) from Tetlin
Enumerated March 1 and 2, 1910

Name	Relation	Birthdate	Age	Name	Relation	Birthdate	Age
Northway, James A.	Head	1851	58	Paul	Head	1883	26
Blythe, Arthur R. W.	Head	1870	39	Ruth (married 4 years)	Wife	1887	22
Woodruff, Han	Head	1858	51	Esther	Daughter	1906	3
David, Chief	Head	1849	60	Peter	Head	1881	28
Sarah (married 10 yrs)	Wife	1879	30	Julia (married 5 yrs)	Wife	1886	23
John	Son	1905	4	Steve	Head	1885	24
George	Son	1907	2	Leah (married 3 yrs)	Wife	1889	20
Charlie	Son	1888	21	Johnny, Little	Head	1881	28
Antoine (Andrew)	Son	1893	16	Bella (married 7 yrs)	Wife	1884	25
Joseph, Old	Head	1854	55	Jim	Son	1905	4
Mary (married 30 yrs)	Wife	1859	58	Jacob	Son	1908	1
Olio	Son	1897	12	John, Little	Head	1859	50
Johnny Big Tetlin	Head	1874	35	Rachel	Daughter	1901	8
Maggie (married 16 yrs)	Wife	1877	32	Links	Head	1888	21
Bessie	Daughter	1894	15	Rebbeca (married 1 yrs)	Wife	1891	18
Alex	Son	1897	15	Silas	Head	1869	40
Martha	Daughter	1906	3	Elizabeth (married 20 yrs)	Wife	1874	35
Dudley	Son	1908	1	Eva	Daughter	1891	18
Albert	Head	1874	35	Chief John	Head	1859	58
Minnie	Wife	1878	31	Deliah (married 19 yrs)	Wife	1864	45
Nellie	Daughter	1894	15	Jaur (?)	Daughter	1897	12
Daisy	Daughter	1906	3	Amandy	Daughter	1906	3
Annie	Mother-in-law	1837	70	Sampson	Head	1879	30
Old John	Head	1857	51	Irma (married 3 yrs)	Wife	1889	20
Joe, Indian	Head	1879	30	Old Charlie	Head	1844	65
Mabel (married 3 yrs)	Wife	1889	20	Annie	Daughter	1884	25
Joshua	Son	1908	1				

continued in next column

Table 15.15. 14th US Census (1920) Tetlin

Enumerated May 7, 1920

Name	Relation	Age
David, Andrew	Head	33
Maggie	Wife	25
Rachel	Daughter	4
David, Charlie	Head	38
Ada	Wife	37
Adalaida		9
William, William	Adopted son	11
David, Peter	Head	26
Kitty	Wife	17
Martha	Daughter	28
Walter	Son	13
Titus	Son	11
Joseph	Head	49
Mary	Wife	34
David	Son	12
Agnes	Daughter	9
Edna	Daughter	?
Alice	Daughter	5
Joe, Peter	Head	38
Eva	Wife	34
Jennie	Sister	51
Annie	Adopted daughter	12
David, Joe	Head	62
Joseph, Joe	Head	61
Jimmy	Son	25
Big John	Head	48
Jessie	Wife	43
Joe	Son	21
Annie	Daughter	14
Lucy	Daughter	9
Linda	Daughter	7
Alfred	Son	5.5
Tabessa	Daughter	2

Note: Birthplaces are unknown.

Table 15.16. Tetlin 1930 Census

Name	Age	Attend School	Read/ Write	Name	Age	Attend School	Read/ Write
Joe, Peter	50	yes	yes	Alfred	14	yes	yes
Eva	42	yes	yes	Tabessa	12	yes	yes
Daivd, Stanley	8	yes	yes	John, Joe	33	yes	yes
Joseph, Senior	66	no	no	Jessie	25	no	no
Agnes	17	yes	yes	Stephen	8	yes	yes
Edna	15	yes	yes	Edward	4 months	blank	
Alice	13	yes	yes	David, Kitty	23	yes	yes
Bella	6	yes	yes	Jonas	4	blank	
Joe, Jimmy	28	yes	yes	Singelton, Theodore	13	yes	yes
Jenny	33	yes	yes	Luke, Chief	56	no	no
Clara	5	yes	yes	Helen	48	no	no
Luke, Jessie	17	yes	yes	Adams, Alfred	30	no	yes
David, Martha	40	no	no	Lucy	27	no	yes
Titus	20	yes	yes	Mary	7	yes	yes
Joe, Lilly	13	yes	yes	Anna	4	no	no
David, Walter	23	yes	yes	Ruth	7 months		
Lena	17	yes	yes	Tom, Paul	47	no	no
Earl	1			Ellen	32	no	no
David, Andrew	38	blank	yes	Martha	10	no	no
Lucy	20	yes	yes	Jimmy	7	no	no
Rachael	12	yes	yes	Maggie	4		
Myra	4	blank		Susie	2		
Carle	1	blank		Son	1 month		
Joe, Paul	45	no	no	Ada, Paul	60	no	no
Annie	20	no	no	John, Old	70	no	no
Mary	4	blank		Albert, Old	71	no	no
Stella	6 months	blank		Gert	65	no	no
John, Big	63	no	no				
Jessie	55	no	no				

continued in next column

Source: Special Cases John Hajdukovich, Information on Upper Tanana Indians 1930–32. National Archives BIA Records, Box 217

Table 15.17. Tetlin (1938 census)
Enumerated by L. R. Wright, Govt. Nurse

Name	Relation	Birthdate	Mother	Father	Birthplace
David, Kitty	Head		Gert Tega		Last Tetlin
Stanely	Son	1922			
Jonas	Son	1925			
Preston	Son	1936			
David, Ada (Albert?)	Head				
Charlie					
David, Helen		1925	Susie	Paul David	Chena
David, Patrick (Patrick Joe?)		1932	Susie	Paul David	Chena
John, Big	Head	1865		John	Tetlin
Jessie (Tega)	Wife	1869		Tega	Chisana R.
Eliza Northway	Daughter				
Annie Sam	Daughter				
Lucy David	Daughter				
Joe John	Son				
Alfred	Son	1915			
Tabesa	Daughter	1918			
Joe, Chief Peter	Head	1876?			Copper River
1st Wife Eva	Wife			Chief David	Copper River
Paul Joe	Son	1890			Scotty Creek
Lilly	Daughter	1915			Tetlin
2nd Wife Annie	Wife	1906		Al Hunter	
Mary	Daughter	1927			Tetlin
Unclear		1928			Tetlin
Rica (?)	Daughter	1930			Last Tetlin
Nancy	Daughter	1932			Last Tetlin
Alexander	Son				Tetlin
Fred					Tetlin
Joe, Jimmy				Chief Joe	Tetlin
Jenny	Wife			Chief David	Tetlin
Clara	Daughter	1924			Nabesna
Donald	Son	1930			Tetlin
Joseph, Old	Head	1962			Last Tetlin
Mary	Wife				
Agnes Paul	Daughter				
Bella	Daughter	1923			Tetlin
Mark, David	Head	1912			Mansfield

continued on next page

Table 15.17.—*continued*

Name	Relation	Birthdate	Mother	Father	Birthplace
Jessie	Wife	1902 (?)	Lucy	Dawson Luke	Last Tetlin
Harry	Son	1934			Nabesna
Ginger	Daughter	1936			
Paul, Titus	Head	1911	Julia	Old Paul	Mansfield
Agnes Joseph	Wife	1915			
Joe, Paul	Head	1890		Chief Peter (?)	
Annie	Wife	1906			
David, Martha	Head	1983			Tetlin
David, Titus	Head	1909		Chief David	Tetlin
Jessie	Wife	1909	Maggie Demit	Walter Isaac	Ketchumstuk
Katherine	Daughter	1932			Tanacross
Adam	Son	1935			Tanacross
Roy Howard	Son	1937			Tetlin
David, Andrew	Head			Chief David	Tetlin
Lucy	Wife	1896	Jessie Tega	Big John	Tetlin
Myra	Daughter	1926			Tetlin
Isabel	Daughter	1933			Tetlin
Amos Whitney	Son	1936			Tetlin
Berthlyn Jean	Daughter	1938			Tetlin
Rachael	Daughter	1917	Maggie Luke	Andrrew David	Tetlin
David, Lena	Head	1913	Jessie Tega	Big John	Tetlin
Nelson	Son	1931			Tetlin
Ida Marilyn	Daughter	1938			Tetlin

Note: Total of 81 includes Last Tetlin.

Table 15.18. Last Tetlin, 1938

Name	Relation	Birthdate	Mother	Father	Birthplace
Adams, Alfred	Head	1895	Anna	Charlie Adams	Tetlin
Lucy	Wife	1902	Helen	Chief Luke	Last Tetlin
Mary	Daughter	1922			Tetlin
Amos	Son	1926			Last Tetlin
Ruth	Daughter	1929			Last Tetlin
Herbert	Son	1931			Last Tetlin
Elsie	Son	1933			Last Tetlin
Helen	Daughter	1935			Last Tetlin
Franklin	Son	1938			Last Tetlin
John, Little	Head	1854			Last Tetlin
Jessie	Daughter				
Luke, Chief	Head	1867		Luke	Mentasta
Helen	Wife	1882	Elia		Last Tetlin
Paul, Little	Head	1919			Tetlin
Ellen	Wife	1922	Ada (Sutah)	Paul	Last Tetlin
Martha	Daughter	1926		Paul	Last Tetlin
James	Son	1927			Last Tetlin
Maggie	Son	1929			Last Tetlin
Susie	Daughter	1931			Last Tetlin
Frank	Son	1936			Last Tetlin
Jimmie	Son				Last Tetlin
Minnie	Daughter				Last Tetlin
Paul, Ada	Head	1861			Mentasta
Albert, Old	Head	1861	Lega		Tetlin
Gert (Tega)	Wife	1867			Chisana R.

Table 15.19. Thirteenth US Census (1910) Nabesna River
Enumerated March 3, 1910

Name	Relation	Birthdate	Birthplace
Nachant, John	Head	1883	Germany
Rasmusson, Hans	Partner	1874	Denmark
Hams, Martin	Head	1849	Virginia
Sargeant, Bud	Head	1864	North Dakota
Shushana, Sam	Head	1869	
Sarah	Wife	1869	
Cora	Daughter	1901	
Samson	Son	1904	
Frank	Son	1894	
Bill	Head	1861	
Young	Son	1883	
Peter	Head	1879	
Lucy	Wife	1887	
Jimmie	Head	1884	
John	Head	1869	
Nancy (married 15 yrs)	Wife	1874	
Archie	Head	1873	
Maggie	Wife	1877	
Bob	Son	1899	
Susie	Daughter	1904	
Godfrey	Head	1874	
Laura (married 13 yrs)	Wife	1879	
Ellen	Daughter	1897	

Table 15.20. Thirteenth US Census (1910) Shushana River
Enumerated March 5, 1910

Name	Relation	Birthdate
Felix	Head	1857
Rachel (married 15 yrs)	Wife	1863
Jumbo	Son	1886
Alice	Daughter	1890
Edna	Daughter	1895
Solomon	Head	1871
Annie (married 17 yrs)	Wife	1875
Skookum	Son	1894
Isaac	Son	1897
Benjamin	Son	1904
?	Daughter	1907
Jacob	Head	1888
Lizzie	Wife	1891
Daisy	Daughter	1908
Esau	Head	1844
Jonathan	Head	1884
Moses	Son	1905

Table 15.21. Nabesna 1930 Census

Name	Relation	Age	Attend School	Read/Write	Speak English
Sam, Chief	Head	65	no	no	no
Bessie	Wife (?)	30	no	no	no
Fred	Son (?)	23	yes	yes	yes
Helen		8	no	bo	no
Mary		6	no	no	no
Andrew		6 months			
Ketchumstuk, Charely		70	no	no	yes
Esau		18	yes	yes	yes
Emma		14	yes	yes	yes
Sam		12	blank	blank	yes
Martha		8	yes	yes	yes
Joe		21	yes	yes	yes
Laura		18	yes	yes	yes
Louise		10 months			
Sam, Frank		40	yes	yes	yes
Annie		24	yes	yes	yes
David		6	no	no	
Susie		3			
Julius		3 months			
Isaac, Follet		37	no	no	yes
Polly		18	no	yes	yes
Albert, Peter		50	no	yes	yes
Elsie		40	no	no	yes
Oscar		11	yes	yes	yes
Northway		9	no	no	no
Ada		7	no	no	no
Danny		6	no	no	no
Abraham		3	no	no	no
Alice		1 month			
Northway, Walter		43	no	yes	yes
Lilly		30	no	no	yes
Eva		11	yes	yes	yes
Celia		7	no	no	no
Harry		2			
Northway, Anna		75	no	no	no
Lea		26	yes	yes	yes
Maggie		15	yes	yes	yes
Northway, Stephen		25	yes	yes	yes

continued on next page

Table 15.21.—*continued*

Name	Relation	Age	Attend School	Read/Write	Speak English
Edna		18	blank	yes	yes
Arthur		3	no	no	no
Alfred		1.5	no	no	no
Elisha Demit, Jack		55	no	yes	yes
Bertha Demit		27	no	no	yes
Fred		6	no	no	yes
Tom		3	no	no	no
Jessie		1			
Johnny, Annie		70	no	no	no
Martha		24	yes	yes	yes
David, Ada		53	no	no	yes
Charley		5	no	no	yes
Northway, William		50	no	no	yes
Eliza		40	no	no	no
Sarah		15	yes	yes	yes

Source: National Archives BIA Records, Box 217, "Special Cases John Hajdukovich, Information on Upper Tanana Indians 1930–32

Table 15.22. 1937–1938 Nabesna Census
Enumerated by L. R. Wright, Govt. Nurse

Name	Relation	Birthdate	Mother	Father	Birthplace
Albert, Peter	Head	1887		Albert	Nabesna
Elsie	Wife		Anna Northway	Old Northway	
Pauline	Daughter	1911			
Northway	Son	1920			
Ada	Daughter	1923			
Daniel	Son	25			
Abraham	Son	1926			
Alice	Daughter	1927			
Jennie	Daughter	1933			
Roger	Daughter	1937			
Albert, Oscar	Head	1918		Old Albert	Nabesna
Mary	Wife	1919	Lucy	Dawson Luke	Last Tetlin
Mary	Daughter	1937			Nabesna
Demit, Elisha	Head	1867		Jack Demit	Ketchumstuk
Bertha	Wife	1897	Ann John	John	Scotty Creek
Fred John	Son	1924			Nabesna
Jessie	Daughter	1928			
Palace	Son	1931			
Herbert Allen	Son	1935			Nabesna
Davis	Son	1936			
Demit, Easu	Head	1912	Mary Sam	Charlie Demit	Nabesna
Demit, Joe Charlie	Head	1910	Mary Sam	Charlie Demit	Nabesna
Laura (Eliza)	Wife	1910	Anna Northway	Old Northway	Last Tetlin
Louie	Son	1928			Last Tetlin
James	Son	1930			
Carl	Son	1932			Gardner Creek
Carrie	Daughter	1935			Nabesna
Eula	Daughter	1937			
Joslyn	Daughter	1938			
Isaac, Follet	Head			Chief Isaac	Mansfield
Pauline	Wife	1911	Elsie Northway	Peter Albert	Nabesna
John, Ann	Head	1862		John	Scotty Creek
Bertha Demit	Daughter				
Martha Demit	Daughter				
Pauline	Daughter				
Kye, Andrew	Head		Laura	Bill	Scotty Creek
Laura (Eliza)	Wife	1910	Anna Northway	Old Northway	Last Tetlin

continued on next page

Table 15.22.—*continued*

Name	Relation	Birthdate	Mother	Father	Birthplace
Louie	Son	1928		Last Tetlin	
James	Son	1930			
Carl	Son	1932		Gardner Creek	
Carrie	Daughter	1935		Nabesna	
Eula	Daughter	1937			
Joslyn	Daughter	1938			
Isaac, Follet	Head		Chief Isaac	Mansfield	
Pauline	Wife	1911	Elsie Northway	Peter Albert	Nabesna
John, Ann	Head	1862	John	Scotty Creek	
Bertha Demit	Daughter				
Martha Demit	Daughter				
Pauline	Daughter				
Kye, Andrew	Head		Laura	Bill	Scotty Creek
Maggie	Wife	1913		Nabesna	
Dora	Daughter	1938			
Mark, Joe	Head		Agnes J.	Big Mark	Mansfield
Martha	Wife		Annie	John	Scotty Creek
Agnes	Daughter	1933		Chisana River	
John	Son	1936		Nabesna	
Joe, Paul, Flushman	Son	1938		Nabesna	
Northway, Anna	Head	1867	Scotty Creek	Tsuul Ta'	Scotty Creek
Northway, William	Head	1884	Anna	Old Northway	Nabesna
Laura Eliza	Wife	1887	Jessie Tega	Big John	Tetlin
Sarah	Daughter				
Northway, Walter	Head	1885	Annie	Old Northway	Nabesna
Lilly	Wife		John	Scotty Creek	
Eva	Daughter	1919		Nabesna	
Celia	Daughter	1923		Nabesna	
Ena	Daughter	1925		Nabesna	
Harry	Son	1927		Nabesna	
Martha	Daughter	1931		Nabesna	
Selina	Daughter	1933		Ladue Creek	
Theodore	Son	1935		Nabesna	
Northway, Stephen	Head	1906	Anna	Old Northway	Nabesna
Edna	Wife		Agnes	Big Mark	Mansfield (?)
Arthur	Son	1928		Nabesna	
Alfred	Son	1930		Ladue River	
Avis	Son	1931		Ladue River	
Esther	Daughter	1933		Tanacross	

continued on next page

Table 15.22.—*continued*

Name	Relation	Birthdate	Mother	Father	Birthplace
Aubrey	Daughter	1935		Nabesna	
Harold, Hurly	Son	1937		Nabesna	
Titus, Frank	Head	1914	Titus	Scotty Creek	
Emma	Wife	1914	Mary Sam	Charlie Demit	Nabesna
Bernice Pauline	Daughter	1936		Nabesna	
Kathleen					
John, Titus	Head	1880 (?)	Titus	Scotty Creek	
Lucy	Wife	1884	Albert	Nabesna	
Frank	Son				
Lena	Daughter				
Titus (?)	Son (?)			Scotty Creek	
Albert	Son (?)			Scotty Creek	
Luarana				Scotty Creek	
Sam, Chief	Head	1865		Nabesna	
1st Wife Lou Frank	Wife				
2nd Wife Bessie	Wife	1897		Scotty Creek	
Helen	Daughter	1918		Nabesna	
Mary	Daughter	1921		Nabesna	
Andrew	Son	1928		Nabesna	
Silas	Son	1931		Nabesna	
Sam, Frank	Head	1885	Bessie	Chief Sam	Nabesna
Annie	Wife	1907	Jessie Tega	Big John	Tetlin
David	Son	1925			Nabesna
Susie	Daughter	1927			Nabesna
Julius	Son	1928			Gardner Creek
Samuel	Son	1930			Nabesna
Roy	Son	1934			Nabesna
Adam	Son	1936			Nabesna
Harry	Son	1939			Nabesna
Charlie, Peter	Head			Mentasta Charlie	Mentasta
Mary	Wife	1920	Annie Sam	Frank Sam	
Alice Marie	Daughter	1938			Nabesna
Jackson, Elisha	Head				
Johnnie, Bertha	Wife				
Jessie	Daughter	1928			
Palace	Daughter	1931			
Herbert Allen	Son	1935			
Fred Johnnie	Son	1923			
Davis	Son	1936			

Table 15.23. 1937–1938 Scotty Creek / Nabesna
Enumerated by L. R. Wright Government Nurse

Name	Relation	Birthdate	Mother	Father	Birthplace
Austin, Bill (Chisana)	Head	?	?	?	Scotty Creek
Maggie	Wife				Scotty Creek
Frank, Andy	Widower	?	?	?	Scotty Creek
Celia	Daughter	1934			
Alfred	Son	1936			
Kye, Bill	Head	1895			Scotty Creek
Laura	Wife	1898			Scotty Creek
Andrew	Son	1918			
Percy	Son	1932			
Mary	Daughter	1936			
Eliza	Wife	1910			Snake Creek
John Little	Head	1885		John	Scotty Creek
Old Lucy	Wife			Enoch John	
Celia	Daughter	1914			
Joe	Son	1916			
Bessie	Daughter	1927			
John	Son	1937			

REFERENCES

Alaska Division of Community and Regional Affairs (Alaska DCRA). 2019. Alaska Department of Commerce, Community and Economic Development. dcra-cdo-dcced.opendata, arcgis .com Accessed October 18, 2022.

Allen, H. T. 1887. *Report on an Expedition to the Copper, Tanana, and Koyukuk Rivers in the Territory of Alaska, 1885*. Senate Executive Document No. 125, 49th Congress, 2nd Session. Washington, DC: US Government Printing Office.

Andersen, David B., and Gretchen Jennings. 2001. *The 2000 Harvest of Migratory Birds in Seven Upper Tanana River Communities, Alaska*. Final Report No. 2 to US Fish and Wildlife Service under Cooperative Agreement No. 701810J252. Fairbanks and Anchorage: Division of Subsistence, Alaska Department of Fish and Game.

Anderson, L. D. 1956. *According to Mama, as Told to Audrey Loftus*. Fairbanks: St. Matthew's Episcopal Guild.

Andrews, Elizabeth F. 1975. "Salcha: An Athapaskan Band of the Tanana River and Its Culture." Unpublished MA thesis, University of Alaska Fairbanks.

Andrews, Elizabeth. 1980. *Native and Historic Accounts of Some Historic Sites in the Tanacross-Ketchumstuk Area*. Compiled for Doyon Cemetery and Historic Sites Committee, Doyon Limited, Fairbanks, Alaska.

Andrews, Elizabeth, and Jimmy Huntington. 1980. *Progress Report of Tanacross Pilot Program to Record Information on Cemetery and Historic Sites—Healy Lake Area*. Prepared for the Doyon Cemetery and Historic Site Committee, Doyon Limited, Fairbanks, Alaska.

Arnold, Robert D., Janet Archibald, Margie Bauman, Nancy Yaw Davis, Ribert A. Frederick, Paul Gaskin, John Havelock, Gary Holthaus, Chris McNeil, Thomas Richards Jr., Howard Rock, and Rosita Worl. 1976. *Alaska Native Land Claims*. Anchorage: The Alaska Native Foundation.

Attla, Catherine. 1990. *K'etelaal Kaanee: The One Who Paddled among the People and the Animals*. Yukon Koyukon School District and the Alaska Native Language Center, University of Alaska Fairbanks.

Austin, B. 1968. *The Diary of a Ninety-Eighter*. Mt. Pleasant, MI: John Cumming.

Baggen, Merttie. n.d.a. Field notes, Mertie Baggen Papers 1964–1967. Alaska and Polar Regions Department, Elmer E. Rasmuson Library, University of Alaska Fairbanks Archives.

Baggen, Merttie. n.d.b. Interview with Mrs. Arthur Wright. Mertie Baggen Papers 1964–1967, box 1 typed field notes, folder 15. Alaska and Polar Regions Department, Elmer E. Rasmuson Library, University of Alaska Fairbanks Archives.

Bales, L. L. 1904. "The Caribou Fences of Alaska." *Pacific Coast Sportsman* 1 (5): 264–265.

Basso, Keith, 1996. *Wisdom Sits in Places: Landscape and Language among the Western Apache*. Albuquerque: University of New Mexico Press.

Beck, E. J. 1930. *Report of Official Visit to Upper Tanana and Copper River Valleys, Dec. 29, 1929, to Feb. 14, 1930. Anchorage. Office of Superintendent of Central District, Alaska US Department of the Interior, Office of Education, Chief of the Alaska Division, Anchorage.* National Archives, Record Group No. 75, Alaska Division: General Correspondence Files: Special Cases—John Hajdukovich, Information on Upper Tanana Indians, 1930–32. Washington, DC.

Betticher, Charles. 1913. "By Trail and Poling Boat." *Alaskan Churchman* 7 (3): 75–77.

Blaser, Mario. 2018. "Doing and Undoing Caribou/ Atiku: Diffractive and Divergent Multiplicities and Their Cosmopolitical Orientations." *Tapuya: Latin American Science, Technology and Society* 1 (1): 47–64. https://doi.org/10.1080/25729861.2018.1501241.

Bowen, Richard J. n.d. "Incidents in the Life of the Reverend Richard John Bowen among the Natives, Trappers, Prospectors, and Gold Miners in the Yukon Territory before and after the Gold Rush

https://doi.org/10.5876/9781646423347.c016

of the Year 1898." Unpublished manuscript in the National Archives of Canada, Ottawa.

Brewster, Karen, 2018. *For the Love of Freedom: Miners Trapper, Hunting Guides, and Homesteaders: An Ethnographic Overview and Assessment Wrangell–St. Elias National Park and Preserve National Park Service*. National Park Service. https://www.nps.gov/wrst/learn/historyculture/upload/For-the-Love-of-Freedom-508-compliant.pdf.

Brown, C. Michael. 1979. Navigable and Non-Navigable Water Bodies in the Northway Area, Eastern Alaska BLM. (Letter from Seattle Fur exchange acknowledging the receipt of 1,000 rat skins from Hajdukovich.)

Brown, C. Michael. 1984. *Indians, Traders, and Bureaucrats in the Upper Tanana District: A History of the Tetlin Reserve*. Anchorage: Bureau of Land Management State Office.

BIA (Bureau of Indian Affairs). 1987. Report of Investigation for Ketchumstuk Village and Caribou Fence. BLM F-22731. Report on file at the Bureau of Indian Affairs, Anchorage, Alaska.

BIA (Bureau of Indian Affairs). 1989. Report of Investigation for Flint Hill and Cemetery, Doyon Ltd. BLM 22477. Report on file at the Bureau of Indian Affairs, Anchorage, Alaska.

Callaway, D. G., and C. A. Miller-Friend. 2001. *Mendees Cheeg Naltsiin Keyh': An Oral History of the People of Healy Lake Village*. Report prepared with a grant from the Alaska Humanities Forum and with support from the Healy Lake Traditional Council, Tetlin National Wildlife Refuge, National Park Service, and the Alaska Native Language Center at the University of Alaska Fairbanks.

Cannon, Chris M., Wilson Justin, Paul Herbert, Charles Hubbard, and Charlie Neyelle. 2020. "Northern Dene Constellations as World View Projections with Case Studies from the Ahtna, Gwich'in and Sahtúot'įnę." *Arctic Anthropology* 56 (2): 1–26.

Capps, S. R. 1914. "Mineral Resources of the Chisana-White River District." In *Mineral Resources of Alaska: Report on Progress of Investigations in 1914*. US Geological Survey Bulletin 622: 189–228.

Capps, Stephen R. 1916. "The Chisana-White River District, Alaska." *US Geological Survey Bulletin* 630: 1–130.

Case, David S. 1984. *Alaska Natives and American Laws*. Rev. ed. Fairbanks: University of Alaska Press.

Case, David, and David Voluck. 2012. *Alaska Natives and American Laws*. 3rd ed. Fairbanks: University of Alaska Press.

Case, Martha F. 1986. *Wild Resource Use in Northway, Alaska*. Alaska Department of Fish and Game, Division of Subsistence Technical Paper No. 132. Fairbanks.

Clark, Donald W. 1995. *Fort Reliance, Yukon: An Archaeological Assessment*. Mercury Series Archaeological Survey of Canada Paper 150, Canadian Museum of Civilization.

Cole, Terrence M. 1979. *Historic Uses of the Chisana and Nabesna Rivers, Alaska*. Alaska Department of Natural Resources, Division of Lands, Anchorage.

Comaroff, Joan L., and J. Comaroff. 1991. *Of Revelation and Revolution: Christianity, Colonialism and Consciousness in South Africa*. Chicago: University of Chicago Press.

Cook, John P. 1989. "Historic Archaeology and Ethnohistory at Healy Lake, Alaska." *Arctic* 42 (2): 109–118.

Cruikshank, Julie. 1990. *Life Lived Like a Story*. Lincoln: University of Nebraska Press.

David, Cora. 2017. *Teedlay t'iin naholndak niign: Stories by the Tetlin People*. Edited by Olga Lovick. Fairbanks: Alaska Native Language Center.

de Laguna, Frederica, and Catharine McClellan. 1960a. Field notes, Dot Lake and Tanacross. Typescript on file at the Alaska Native Language Center, University of Alaska Fairbanks.

de Laguna, Frederica, and Catharine McClellan. 1960b. Oral history interview with David Paul, 19 July 1960; Tanacross, Alaska. Transcript on file at the Alaska Native Language Center, University of Alaska Fairbanks.

de Laguna, Frederica, and Catharine McClellan. 1960c. Oral history interview with Maggie Isaac, 18 July 1960; Dot Lake, Alaska. Transcript on file at the Alaska Native Language Center, University of Alaska Fairbanks.

de Laguna, Frederica, and Marie-Françoise Guédon. 1968a. Oral history interview with Titus David, 26 July 1968; Tetlin, Alaska. Transcript on file at the Alaska Native Language Center, University of Alaska Fairbanks.

de Laguna, Frederica, and Marie-Françoise Guédon. 1968b. Field notes recorded 23 July 1968; Tetlin Oral History. Transcript on file at the Alaska Native Language Center, University of Alaska Fairbanks.

de Laguna, F Frederica, and Marie-Françoise Guédon. 1968c. Oral history interview with Jessie David, 23 July 1968; Tetlin, Alaska. Transcript on file at the Alaska Native Language Center, University of Alaska Fairbanks.

de Laguna, Frederica, and Marie-Françoise Guédon. 1968d. Oral history interview with Titus David,

25 July 1968; Tetlin, Alaska. Transcript on file at the Alaska Native Language Center, University of Alaska Fairbanks.

Dillingham, W. P. 1904. *United States Congress, Senate, Committee on Territories 1904 Conditions in Alaska. Report of Subcommittee of Committee on Territories Appointed to Investigate Conditions in Alaska*. 58th Congress, Report No. 282, Part 2. Washington: Government Printing Office.

Drane, Frederick B. 1915. Letter addressed to the Woman's Auxiliary St. Paul's Church, Edenton, North Carolina, dated November 4, 1915. F. B. Drane Collection Acc # 20072–023 Box 1. Alaska and Polar Regions Archives, Rasmuson Library, University of Alaska Fairbanks.

Drane, Frederick B. 1917. "Camp and Trail among Tetlin Indians." *Alaskan Churchman* (May 11, 1917): 83–88.

Drane, Frederick B. n.d.a. Frederick B. Drane Collection, 1915–1925. Elmer E. Rasmson: Alaska and Polar Regions Collections and Archives, Elmer E. Rasmuson Library, University of Alaska Fairbanks.

Drane, Frederick B. n.d.b. "A Circuit Rider on the Yukon or Life among the Sourdoughs and Indians, Subarctic Alaska. A Narrative of Ten Years Experience and Travel by Frederick Drane Missionary of the Protestant Episcopal Church in the Interior of Alaska from 1915 to 1925. Archdeacon of the Yukon from 1921 to 1925." With an introduction by Rt. Rev. Peter T. Rowe, DD. Bishop of Alaska. Unpublished manuscript, Elmer E. Rasmson: Alaska and Polar Regions Collections and Archives, Elmer E. Rasmuson Library, University of Alaska Fairbanks.

Ducker, J. H. 1983. *Alaska's Upper Yukon Region: A History*. Anchorage: Bureau of Land Management.

Easton, Norman. 2001. "Intergenerational Differences in Ethnic Identification in an Athapaskan Community." *The American Review of Canadian Studies* 31 (1–2): 105–119.

Easton, Norman. 2008. "It's Hard Enough to Control Yourself; It's Ridiculous to Think You Can Control Animals: Competing Views of the Bush in Cotemporary Yukon." *The Northern Review* 29 (Fall): 21–38.

Easton, Norman. 2021. *An Ethnohistory of the Chisana River Basin*. Northern Research Institute, Yukon College, Whitehorse, Yukon Territory. Report prepared under contract to the Wrangell–St. Elias National Park and Preserve, Copper Center, Alaska.

Executive Order No. 5365. June 10, 1930.

Farnsworth, Robert J. 1901. Letter to William C. Boyd dated May 9, 1901. Farnsworth collection. Alaska and Polar Regions Archives, Rasmuson Library, University of Alaska Fairbanks.

Ferguson, Judy. 2009. *Bridges to Statehood: The Alaska-Yugoslav Connection*. Big Delta: Voice of Alaska Press.

Ferguson, Judy. 2012. *Windows to the Land*, Vol. 1: *From Southeast to the Arctic*. Big Delta: Voice of Alaska Press.

Gallon, Ada. 2008. Project Jukebox UAF # H-2009-07-01 interviewed by Stacey Carkhuff.

Godduhn, Anna R., and Marylynn L. Kostick. 2016. *Harvest and Use of Wild Resources in Northway, Alaska, 2014, with Special Attention to Nonsalmon Fish*. Alaska Department of Fish and Game Division of Subsistence, Technical Paper No. 421, Fairbanks.

Goldschmidt, Walter R. 1948. "Delimitation of Possessory Rights of the Athapascan Indian Natives of the Villages of Northway, Tanacross, and Tetlin in the Interior of Alaska." Unpublished report submitted to the Commissioner of Indian Affairs, US Office of Indian Affairs, Washington, DC.

Grant, John Webster. 1984. *Moon of Wintertime: Missionaries and the Indians of Canada in Encounter since 1534*. Toronto: University of Toronto Press.

Graves, Margaret C. 1913. "Saint Timothy's." *Alaskan Churchman* 7 (3): 72–74.

Greene, Robert. 1957. "St. Timothy's, Tanacross, Looks to Past and Future." *Alaskan Churchman* 52 (2): 2–4.

Griffiths, C. E. 1900. "From Knik Station to Eagle City." In *Explorations in and about Cook's Inlet*, edited by E. F. Glenn, 724–733. Washington, DC: Government Printing Office.

Guédon, Marie-Françoise. 1974. *People of Tetlin, Why Are You Singing?* Mercury Series Paper No. 9. National Museum of Man, Ethnology Division, Ottawa, Ontario.

Guédon, Marie-Françoise. 2005. *Le rêve et la forêt: Histoires de chamanes nabesne*. Québec City: Les Presses de l'Université Laval.

Hajdukovich, John. 1927. Letter to Alaska Game Commission. John Hajdukovich Papers, 1904–1958. Correspondence file, 1927–1963, Agnew–Public Welfare Dept. Photograph 1985-002-17, Box 1. Elmer E. Rasmson: Alaska and Polar Regions Collections and Archives, Elmer E. Rasmuson Library, University of Alaska Fairbanks.

Hajdukovich, John. 1932. "Some Information about Upper Tanana Indians." Unpublished manuscript. Big Delta, Alaska. National Archives, Record Group No. 75, Alaska Division: General

Correspondence Files: Special Cases, John Hajdukovich, Information on Upper Tanana Indians, 1930–1932. Washington, DC.

Hallowell, Alfred I. 1960. "Ojibwa Ontology, Behavior and World View." In *Culture in History: Essays in Honor of Paul Radin*, edited by Stanley Diamond, 19–52. New York: Columbia University Press.

Halpin, Libby. 1987. *Living Off the Land: Contemporary Subsistence in Tetlin, Alaska*. Alaska Department of Fish and Game, Division of Subsistence Technical Paper No. 149, Fairbanks.

Heinrich, Albert. 1957. "Sib and Social Structure on the Upper Tanana." In *Proceedings of the Alaska Science Conference*, edited by Albert W. Johnson, 10–22. Anchorage: Alaska Division, American Association for the Advancement of Science.

Holton, Gary. 2002. Unpublished notes on Tanacross clans. Alaska Native Language Center archives.

Isaac, Andrew. 1984a. Taped interview. A. J. Lynch, Ron Kent, Mike Elder, and Ray DePuydt interviewers; A. J. Lynch and William Simeone transcriber, 14 September 1984; Tanacross, Alaska. Tapes 84ARC007 and 84ARC008. Bureau of Indian Affairs, ANCSA.

Isaac, Andrew. 1984b. Taped interview. A. J. Lynch interviewer; A. J. Lynch and William Simeone transcriber, 20 September 1984; Tanacross, Alaska. Tape 84ARC009. Bureau of Indian Affairs, ANCSA.

Isaac, Andrew. 1987. Taped interview. Dennis Griffin and Peter Mills interviewers; William Simeone transcriber, 21 July 1987; Tanacross, Alaska. Tape 87T001. Bureau of Indian Affairs, ANCSA.

Isaac, Jerry. 1974. *Theata* (2): 50–53.

Isaac, Oscar. 1971. "Tanacross Presents Its Reasons Why Village Needs Relocation." *Tundra Times* 8, no. 25 (March 31, 1971).

Isaac, Walter. 1915. Letter to Governor J. F. A. Strong, September 1915. Governors' Papers, Roll 29, frames 212–19. Alaska State Archives, Juneau.

Ives, John W. 2003. "Alberta, Athapaskans, and Apachean Origins." In *Archaeology in Alberta: A View from the New Millennium*, edited by J. W. Brink and J. F. Dormaar, 256–289. Medicine Hat: Archaeological Society of Alberta.

Jarvis, David H. 1904. *United States Congress, Senate, Committee on Territories 1904 Conditions in Alaska. Report of Subcommittee of Committee on Territories Appointed to Investigate Conditions in Alaska. Hearings Report of Subcommittee of Committee on Territories appointed to investigate conditions in Alaska*. 58th Congress, Report No. 282, Part 2. Washington, DC: Government Printing Office.

Jimerson, Shirley. 1976. *Tetlin as I Knew It*. Anchorage: Alaska Bilingual Education Board.

John, Peter. 1996. *The Gospel According to Peter John*. Fairbanks: Alaska Native Knowledge Network.

Kari, James, ed. 1986. *Tatl'ahwt'aenn Nenn', The Headwaters People's Country: Narratives of the Upper Ahtna Athabaskans*. Fairbanks: Alaska Native Language Center.

Kari, James. 1997. "Upper Tanana Place Names Lists and Maps." Final report for the project "Upper Tanana Athabaskan Place Names in the vicinity of Wrangell–St. Elias National Park," sponsored by Wrangell–St. Elias National Park, Cooperative Agreement: CA 9700-5-9023.

Kari, James. n.d. *Upper Tanana Stem List*. Alaska Native Language Center archives.

Kari, James, and Rick Thoman. n.d. Tanacross Place Names list. Alaska Native Language Center archives.

Kessler, Herman. 1940. Letter to John Hajdukovich, dated March 27, 1940. John Hajdukovich Papers, 1904–1958. Correspondence file, 1927–1963, Agnew–Public Welfare Dept. Photograph 1985-002-17, Box 1. Alaska and Polar Regions Collections, Elmer E. Rasmuson Library, University of Alaska Fairbanks.

Ketz, James A. 1983. *Paxson Lake: Two Nineteenth-Century Ahtna Sites in the Copper River Basin, Alaska*. Anthropology and Historic Preservation Cooperative Park Studies Unit, Occasional paper no. 33. Fairbanks.

Kirsteatter, Paul. 1964. Letter to Robert McKennan dated March 9, 1964. Robert A. McKennan papers, series 1 research files 1928–1980, folder labeled Correspondence Healy Lake Paul Kirsteatter 1962–65.

Knapp, E. J. 1904. *United States Congress, Senate, Committee on Territories 1904 Conditions in Alaska. Report of Subcommittee of Committee on Territories Appointed to Investigate Conditions in Alaska*. 58th Congress, Report No. 282, Part 2. Washington: Government Printing Office.

Koskey, Michael. 2006. *Subsistence Resource Use in the Upper Tanana 2004–2005*. Report prepared for the Alaska Department of Natural Resources. Fairbanks: Division of Subsistence, Alaska Department of Fish and Game.

Koskey, Michael. 2007. *Subsistence Resource Use among Ten Tanana River Valley Communities: 2004–2005*. Draft technical paper. Fairbanks: Division of Subsistence, Alaska Department of Fish and Game.

Krupa, David. 1999. "Finding the Feather: Peter John and the Reverse Anthropology of the Whiteman

Way." Unpublished PhD dissertation, University of Wisconsin.

Larson, Christian L. 1918. Letter dated June 25, 1918, to H. F. Moore, acting Commissioner of Fisheries in Washington. Record Group 22: Records of the US Fish and Wildlife Service, 1868–2008. Records Concerning Fox Farming and Protection of Fur-Bearing Animals, 1911–1928. National Archives, Washington, DC.

LeResche, Robert E., and Richard H. Bishop. 1974. "Distribution and Habitats of Moose in Alaska." In *Alces: Moose Ecology*, edited by J. Bedard. Proceedings of the International Symposium on Moose Ecology, 26–28 March 1973, Québec City, Canada. *Naturaliste Canadien* 101 (1–2): 143–178.

Lovick, Olga. 2016. "Iįih and Request for Formation in Upper Tanana: Evidence from Narrative Texts." *Anthropological Linguistics* 3 (58): 258–298.

Lovick, Olga. 2020. *A Grammar of Upper Tanana*. Volume 1: *Phonology, Lexical Classes, Morphology*. Lincoln: University of Nebraska Press.

Lowell, Theodore. 1979. Interview by Richard Stern and Terrence Cole conducted February 20 and 21, 1979, in *Historic Use of the Chisana and Nabesna Rivers, Alaska*. State of Alaska, Department of Natural Resource Division of Forest, Land and Water Management.

Manville, Julie, and R. Maller. 2009. "The Influence of Christian Missionaries on Alaskan Indigenous Peoples." *Interdisciplinary Journal of Research on Religion* 5: 3–26. Centre for Mathematics and Its Applications, and School of Finance and Applied Statistics, Australian National University Canberra, Australia.

Marcotte, James R. 1989. *Use of the Wrangell–St. Elias National Park and Preserve by Residents of Northway*. Preliminary Report. Fairbanks: Division of Subsistence, Alaska Department of Fish and Game.

Marcotte, James R., Polly Wheeler, and Clarence Alexander. 1992. *Fish and Game Use by Residents of Five Upper Tanana Communities, 1987–1988*. Technical Paper No. 168. Fairbanks: Division of Subsistence, Alaska Department of Fish and Game.

Martin, G. 1983. *Use of Natural Resources by Residents of Dot Lake, Alaska*. Technical Paper 19. Fairbanks: Division of Subsistence, Alaska Department of Fish and Game.

McClellan, Catharine. 1975. *My Old People Say: An Ethnographic Survey of Southern Yukon Territory*. National Museum of Man Publications in Ethnology, No. 6. National Museums of Canada.

McConnell, David L. 1920. "Settling at a New Mission." *Alaskan Churchman* 14 (2): 71–74.

McDowell, C. B. 1904. *Alaska Prospector*, January 21, 1904.

McIntosh, E. A. 1917. Letter to Wood dated March 5, 1917. R.G 62-42 Folder 1, Episcopal Church Archives, Austin, Texas.

McIntosh, Elvrage A. 1918. "A Big Feast at Tanana Crossing." *Alaskan Churchman* 12 (2): 47–49.

McIntosh, Elvrage A. 1941. "St. Timothy's Mission, Tanacross." *Alaskan Churchman* (August): 3–12.

McIntosh Elvrage A. n.d. "St. Timothy's Mission, Tanacross, Alaska." Unpublished manuscript. Elmer E. Rasmson: Alaska and Polar Regions Collections and Archives, Elmer E. Rasmuson Library, University of Alaska Fairbanks.

McKennan, Robert A. 1959. *The Upper Tanana Indians*. Yale University Publications in Anthropology, No. 55. New Haven, CT: Yale University.

McKennan, Robert A. 1962. McKennan Box 15 Ass # 85-098. Tanana 1962 Duplicate Field Notes. Robert Addison McKennan papers, 1929–1980. Alaska and Polar Regions Collections, Rasmuson Library, University of Alaska Fairbanks.

McKennan, Robert A. 1969. "Athapaskan Groupings and Social Organization in Central Alaska." Anthropological Series 84. *National Museum of Canada Bulletin* 228: 93–115.

McKennan, Robert A. 1981. "Tanana." In *Handbook of North American Indians*, Vol. 6: *Subarctic*, edited by June Helm, 562–577. Washington, DC: Smithsonian Institution Press.

McKennan, Robert A. n.d. Unpublished field notes. Robert Addison McKennan papers, 1929–1980. Alaska and Polar Regions Collections, Rasmuson Library, University of Alaska Fairbanks.

Mercier, François X. 1986. *Recollections of the Yukon*. Translated, edited, and annotated by Linda Finn Yarborough. Alaska Historical Commission Studies in History No. 188. Anchorage: Alaska Historical Society.

Mishler, Craig. 1986. *Born with the River: An Ethnographic History of Alaska's Goodpaster and Big Delta Indians*. Alaska Department of Natural Resources, Division of Geological and Geophysical Surveys, Report of Investigations 86-14, Fairbanks.

Mishler, Craig, and W. E. Simeone. 2004. *Han, People of the River: Hän Hwëch'in: An Ethnography and Ethnohistory*. Fairbanks: University of Alaska Press.

Mishler, Craig, and W. E. Simeone, eds. 2006. *Tanana and Chandalar: The Alaska Field Journals of Robert A. McKennan*. Fairbanks: University of Alaska Press.

Mitchell, William. 1982. *The Opening of Alaska*. Ed. Lyman L. Woodman. Anchorage: Cook Inlet Historical Society.

Murie, Olas J. 1921a. Fish and Wildlife Service Field Reports 1860 (1887–1961) Series 1 Box #10, Folder 13; Box 11, Folder 6.

Murie, Olas J. 1921b. Letter from Murie to Dr. E. W. Nelson, Bureau of Biological Survey dated May 21, 1921. MS 51, Box 5 1-40. Alaska State Library, Juneau.

Murie, Olas J. 1935. *Alaska-Yukon Caribou*. US Department of Agriculture, Bureau of Biological Survey, North American Fauna No. 54. Washington, DC.

Naske, Claus M., and Herman Slotnick. 2014. *Alaska: A History*. Norman: University of Oklahoma Press.

Nelson, Richard. 1983. *Make Prayers to the Raven: A Koyukon View of the Northern Forest*. Chicago: University of Chicago Press.

Newton, W. H. 1931. Letter to Robert McKennan dated August 26, 1931. McKennan Collection Series 1 Box 3 Folder 39. Alaska and Polar Regions Collections, Elmer E. Rasmuson Library, University of Alaska Fairbanks.

Northway, Walter. 1979. Letter from Walter Northway. Historic Use of the Chisana and Nabesna Rivers, Alaska. State of Alaska, Department of Natural Resource Division of Forest, Land and Water Management, Fairbanks.

Northway, Walter. 1987. Alaska Native Language Center archives.

Osgood, Cornelius. 1971. *The Han Indians*. Yale University Publications in Anthropology, No. 74. New Haven, CT: Yale University.

Paul, Bella. 1987a. Oral history interview with Isabel John, 10 August 1987; Tanacross, Alaska. Transcribed by William E. Simeone. Transcript on file with the author.

Paul, Bella. 1987b. Oral history interview with Laura Sanford, 4 November 1987; Tanacross, Alaska. Transcribed by William E. Simeone. Transcript on file with the author.

Paul, David. 1957a. "When Jesus Came to Tanacross." *Alaskan Churchman* 52 (2): 6–9.

Paul, David. 1957b. *According to Papa*. Fairbanks: St. Matthew's Episcopal Guild.

Paul, Gaither. 1980. *Stories for My Grandchildren*. Transcribed and edited by Ron Scollon. Fairbanks: Alaska Native Language Center.

Pitts, Roger S. 1972. "The Changing Settlement Patterns and Housing Types of the Upper Tanana Indians." Unpublished MA thesis, University of Alaska Fairbanks.

Potter, Benjamin A., C. E. Holmes, and D. R. Yesner. 2013. "Technology and Economy among the Earliest Prehistoric Foragers in Interior Eastern Beringia." In *Paleoamerican Odyssey*, edited by K. E. Graf, C. V. Ketron, and M. R. Waters, 81–103. College Station: Texas A&M University Press.

Prevost, Jules L. 1893. Letter from St. Michael dated July 3, 1893. Record Group 62-45, Correspondence of the Episcopal Church Folder 3 1893–1899. Episcopal Church Archives, Austin, Texas.

Purcha, Francis P. 1975. "Report of the Board of Indian Commissioners: November 23, 1869." In *Documents of United States Policy*, edited by F. P. Prucha, 131–134. Lincoln: University of Nebraska Press.

Rainey, Froelich. 1939. *Archaeology in Central Alaska*. Anthropological Papers of the American Museum of Natural History Vol. 34, Part IV.

Rainey, Froelich. n.d. Froelich Rainey Papers, 1931–1947. Alaska and Polar Regions Collections, Elmer E. Rasmuson Library, University of Alaska Fairbanks.

Reckord, Holly. 1983. *Where Raven Stood: Cultural Resources of the Ahtna Region*. Anthropology and Historic Preservation, Cooperative Park Studies Unit, Occasional Papers no. 35. Fairbanks: University of Alaska Fairbanks.

Rice, J. F. 1900. "From Valdez to Eagle City." In *Yukon River Exploring Expedition, Alaska 1899*, by Captain W. P. Richardson, 784–789. Compilation of narratives of explorations in Alaska, US Congress, Senate Committee on Military Affairs. Washington, DC: Government Printing Office.

Rollins, A. M. 1978. *Census Alaska: Numbers of Inhabitants, 1792–1970*. Anchorage: University of Alaska Anchorage Library.

Rowe, Peter T. 1910–1911. "Report of the Bishop of Alaska." In *Annual Report of the Board of Missions of the Protestant Episcopal Church in the United States of America 1910–11*. Copy on file at the Episcopal Church Archives, Austin, Texas.

Safina, Carl. 2015. *Beyond Words: What Animals Think and Feel*. New York: Henry Holt and Co.

Sam, Avis, Sherry Demit-Barnes, and Darlene Northway. 2021. *Ts'exeey iin Naabia Niign xah nahiholnegn, Women Tell Stories about Northway*. Transcribed and translated by Caleb Brucks and Olga Lovick, with the help of the storytellers as well as Roy Sam and Rosa Brewer. Edited by Caleb Brucks and Olga Lovick. Fairbanks: Alaska Native Language Center.

Schneider, William. 2018. *The Tanana Chiefs: Native Rights and Western Law*. Fairbanks: University of Alaska Press.

Schwatka, Fredrick. 1900. "A Report of a Military Reconnaissance in Alaska Made in 1883." In

Compilation of Narratives, 283–364. Washington, DC: Government Printing Office.

Seattle Fur Exchange. 1933. Letter to John Hajdukovich from Seattle Fur Exchange dated June 9, 1933. John Hajdukovich Papers, 1904–1958. Correspondence file, 1927–1963, Agnew–Public Welfare Dept. Photograph 1985-002-17, Box 1. Alaska and Polar Regions Collections, Elmer E. Rasmuson Library, University of Alaska Fairbanks.

Shinkwin, Ann. D. 1979. *Dakah Denin's Village and the Dixthada Site: A Contribution to Northern Athapaskan Prehistory*. National Museum of Man Mercury Series, Archaeological Survey of Canada Paper No. 91. National Museums of Canada, Ottawa.

Simeone, William E. 1980a. Oral history interview with Titus David, 4 July 1980; Tanacross, Alaska. Transcribed by William E. Simeone. Transcript on file with the author.

Simeone, William E. 1980b. Oral history interview with Oscar Isaac, 4 July 1980; Tanacross, Alaska. Transcribed by William E. Simeone. Transcript on file with the author.

Simeone, William E. 1980c. Oral history interview with Titus David, 29 May 1980; Tanacross, Alaska. Transcribed by William E. Simeone. Transcript on file with the author.

Simeone, William E. 1985a. Oral history interview with Tommy John, 10 November 1985; Whitehorse, Yukon Territory. Transcribed by William E. Simeone. Transcript on file with the author.

Simeone, William E. 1985b. Oral history interview with Bessie John, 11 November 1985; Whitehorse, Yukon Territory. Transcribed by William E. Simeone. Transcript on file with the author.

Simeone, William E. 1986a. Oral history interview with Gaither Paul, 17 November 1986; Anchorage, Alaska. Transcribed by William E. Simeone. Transcript on file with the author.

Simeone, William E. 1986b. Oral history interview with Larry Jonathan, 29 December 1986; Tanacross, Alaska. Transcribed by William E. Simeone. Transcript on file with the author.

Simeone, William E. 1986c. Oral history interview with Andrew Isaac and Oscar Isaac, 30 December 1987; Dot Lake, Alaska. Transcribed by William E. Simeone. Transcript on file with the author.

Simeone, William E. 1986d. Oral history interview with Martha Isaac, 8 December 1986; Tanacross, Alaska. Transcribed by William E. Simeone. Transcript on file with the author.

Simeone, William E. 1987a. Oral history interview with Julius Paul, 21 May 1987; Tanacross, Alaska.

Transcribed by William E. Simeone. Transcript on file with the author.

Simeone, William E. 1987b. Oral history interview with Oscar Isaac, 11 December 1987; Tanacross, Alaska. Transcribed by William E. Simeone. Transcript on file with the author.

Simeone, William E. 1987c. Oral history interview with Gaither Paul, 14 September 1987; Tanacross, Alaska. Transcribed by William E. Simeone. Transcript on file with the author.

Simeone, William E. 1987d. Oral history interview with Silas Solomon, 18 May 1987; Tanacross, Alaska. Transcribed by William E. Simeone. Transcript on file with the author.

Simeone, William E. 1987e. Oral history interview with Oscar Isaac, 2 December 1987; Tanacross, Alaska. Transcribed by William E. Simeone. Transcript on file with the author.

Simeone, William E. 1987f. Oral history interview with Oscar Isaac, 28 September 1987; Tanacross, Alaska. Transcribed by William E. Simeone. Transcript on file with the author.

Simeone, William E. 1987g. Oral history interview with Oscar Isaac, 25 February 1987; Tanacross, Alaska. Transcribed by William E. Simeone. Transcript on file with the author.

Simeone, William E. 1987h. Oral history interview with Andrew Isaac, 3 February 1987; Dot Lake, Alaska. Transcribed by William E. Simeone. Transcript on file with the author.

Simeone, William E. 1987i. Oral history interview with Larry Jonathan, 22 February 1987; Tetlin, Alaska. Transcribed by William E. Simeone. Transcript on file with the author.

Simeone, William E. 1987j. Oral history interview with Oscar Isaac, 9 March 1987; Tanacross, Alaska. Transcribed by William E. Simeone. Transcript on file with the author.

Simeone, William E. 1987k. Oral history interview with Oscar Isaac, 26 February 1987; Tanacross, Alaska. Transcribed by William E. Simeone. Transcript on file with the author.

Simeone, William E. 1987l. Oral history interview with Martha Isaac, 10 February 1987; Tanacross, Alaska. Transcribed by William E. Simeone. Transcript on file with the author.

Simeone, William E. 1987m. Oral history interview with Oscar Isaac, 29 January 1987; Tanacross, Alaska. Transcribed by William E. Simeone. Transcript on file with the author.

Simeone, William E. 1987n. Oral history interview with Jerry Isaac, 13 October 1987; Tanacross,

Alaska. Transcribed by William E. Simeone. Transcript on file with the author.

Simeone, William E. 1987o. Oral history interview with Maggie Isaac 16 October 1987; Dot Lake, Alaska. Transcribed by William E. Simeone. Transcript on file with the author.

Simeone, William E. 1987p. Oral history interview with Oscar Isaac, 16 January 1987; Tanacross, Alaska. Transcribed by William E. Simeone. Transcript on file with the author.

Simeone, William E. 1987q. Oral history interview with Maggie Isaac, 3 February 1987; Dot Lake, Alaska. Transcribed by William E. Simeone. Transcript on file with the author.

Simeone, William E. 1987r. Oral history interview with Oscar Isaac, 1 January 1987; Tanacross, Alaska. Transcribed by William E. Simeone. Transcript on file with the author.

Simeone, William E. 1987s. Oral history interview with Oscar Isaac, 3 October 1987; Tanacross, Alaska. Transcribed by William E. Simeone. Transcript on file with the author.

Simeone, William E. 1987t. Oral history interview with Gaither Paul, 15 September 1987; Tanacross, Alaska. Transcribed by William E. Simeone. Transcript on file with the author.

Simeone, William E. 1987u. Oral history interview with Gaither Paul, 11 October 1987; Tanacross, Alaska. Transcribed by William E. Simeone. Transcript on file with the author.

Simeone, William E. 1987v. Oral history interview with Gaither Paul, 5 December 1987; Tanacross, Alaska. Transcribed by William E. Simeone. Transcript on file with the author.

Simeone, William E. 1987w. Oral history interview with Oscar Isaac, 6 December 1987; Tanacross, Alaska. Transcribed by William E. Simeone. Transcript on file with the author.

Simeone, William E. 1987x. Oral history interview with Oscar Isaac, 6 December 1987; Tanacross, Alaska. Transcribed by William E. Simeone. Transcript on file with the author.

Simeone, William E. 1995. *Rifles, Blankets, and Beads: Identity, History, and the Northern Athabaskan Potlatch*. Norman: University of Oklahoma Press.

Skarland, Ivar. 1956. "Upper Tanana Revisited." In *Science in Alaska: Proceedings of the 6th Science Conference, 1955*, 152–153. College, Alaska.

Skoog, Ronald. 1956. "Range, Movements, Population, and Food Habits of the Steese Fortymile Caribou Herd." Unpublished master's thesis, University of Alaska.

Slotkin, Richard. 1973. *Regeneration through Violence: The Mythology of the American Frontier 1600–1860*. Norman: University of Oklahoma Press.

Solomon, Silas. 1934. Letter to the Governor of Alaska dated December 15, 1934. RG 101 Series 79-35 Box 461-4 1933–36. Alaska State Archives, Juneau.

Solomon, Silas. 1962. Robert McKennan Collection Box 15, Ass # 85-098. Tanana 1962 Duplicate Field Notes. Alaska and Polar Regions Archives, Rasmuson Library, University of Alaska Fairbanks.

Solomon, Silas. 1984a. Taped interviews. A. J. Lynch and Ron Kent, Mike Elder, and Ray DePuydt, interviewers; A. J. Lynch and William Simeone transcriber, 19 and 21 September 1984; Tanacross, Alaska. Tapes 84ARC007 and 84ARC008. Bureau of Indian Affairs, ANCSA.

Solomon, Silas. 1984b. Taped interviews. A. J. Lynch interviewers; A. J. Lynch and William Simeone transcriber, 24 September 1984; Tanacross, Alaska. Tapes 84ARC0011. Bureau of Indian Affairs, ANCSA.

Solomon, Silas, and Andrew Isaac. 1987. Taped interviews. Dennis Griffen and Peter Mills interviewers; William Simeone interpreter, 18 July 1987; Tanacross, Alaska. Tapes 87TOKOO1; Bureau of Indian Affairs, ANCSA.

Smith, Gerad, M. 2022. *The Gift of the Middle Tanana: Dene Pre-Colonial History in the Alaskan Interior*. Lanham, MD: Lexington Books.

Stern, Richard O. 1979. Nabesna/Chisana Rivers—Interviews with Ted Lowell. File memo, Division of Forest, Land, and Water Management, Alaska Department of Natural Resources, Anchorage.

Strong, B. Stephen. 1973. "An Economic History of the Athapascan Indians of the Upper Copper River, Alaska, with Special Reference to the Village of Mentasta Lake." Unpublished PhD dissertation, McGill University.

Stuck, Hudson. [1914] 1988. *Ten Thousand Miles with a Dog Sled: A Narrative of Winter Travel in Interior Alaska*. New York: Charles Scribner's Sons.

Swinford, A. P. 1887. H.R. Exec. Doc. No. 1, 50th Cong., 1st Sess. (1887). https://digitalcommons.law.ou.edu/cgi/viewcontent.cgi?article=6774&context=indianserialset.

Thomas, Sr., Kenneth, and Craig Mishler. 2005. *Crow Is My Boss: The Oral Life History of a Tanacross Athabaskan Elder*. Norman: University of Oklahoma Press.

Thornton, Thomas. 2008. *Being and Place among the Tlingit*. Seattle: University of Washington Press.

Tsing, Anna L. 2015. *The Mushroom at the End of the World: On the Possibility of Life in Capitalist Ruins.* Princeton, NJ: Princeton University Press.

Tundra Times. 1969. "First Tanacross Claim 1917." 7 July 1969, vol. 6, no. 184.

Tundra Times. 1971. "Tanacross Asks In on Claims." 24 March 1971, vol. 8, no. 24.

Tyone, Mary. 1996. *Ttheek'ädn Ut'iin Yaaniida' Oonign': Old-Time Stories of the Scottie Creek People.* Transcribed and edited by James Kari. Alaska Native Language Center, University of Alaska Fairbanks.

US Government. 1924. Office of the Secretary, Press Service. Press Release No. 1217-24: "Alaska Game Law Now under Department of Agriculture." Released June 28, 1924.

United States Fish and Wildlife Service. 2011. *Historic Use of the Chisana Caribou Herd by Residents of Northway Village.* Tetlin National Wildlife Refuge, Tok, Alaska.

Urquhart, D., and R. Farnell. 1986. *The Fortymile Herd: On the Comeback trial to the Yukon.* Yukon Renewable Resources.

Valkenburg, Patrick, D. G. Kellyhouse, J. L. Davis, and J. M. Hoef. 1994. "Case History of the Fortymile Caribou Herd, 1920–1990." *Rangifer* 14 (1): 11–22.

Vanderlugt, Russell. 2022. "Among the Dene: Allen's 1885 Trans-Alaska Expedition." Unpublished PhD dissertation, University of Alaska.

Vitt, Ramon B. 1971. "Hunting Practices of the Upper Tanana Athapaskans." Unpublished MA thesis, University of Alaska Fairbanks.

Walter, Maggie. 1966. *Tundra Times* (4) 46.

Wells, E. Hazard. 1974. "Down the Yukon and up the Fortymile." *Alaska Journal* 4 (4): 205–213.

Wilson, Lavell. 1995. "Northway and Tanacross: Airports for the War Effort." *Alaska Geographic* (4) 22: 72–76.

Woldstad, Kenneth J. 2011. "A Comparative Analysis of Fish and Wildlife Enforcement in Alaska from the Passage of the 1902 Alaska Game Law to 2011." Unpublished master's thesis, University of Alaska Fairbanks.

Wrangell, Ferdinand P. [1839] 1980. *Russian America: Statistical and Ethnographic Information.* Translated from the 1839 edition by Mary Sadouski and edited by Richard A. Pierce. Materials in the Study of Alaska no. 15. Kingston: Limestone Press.

Wright, Arthur. 1926. "The Potlatch—What Is It?" *Alaskan Churchman* 20 (1): 18–22.

Wright, Arthur R. 1977. *The First Medicine Man: The Tale of Yobaghu-Talyonunh.* Anchorage: O.W. Frost.

Whymper, Frederick. [1868] 1966. *Travel and Adventure in Alaska.* Readex Microprint.

Yarber, Yvonne, and Curt Madison, eds. 1987. *Walter Northway.* Alaska Native Language Center, University of Alaska Fairbanks.

Yarber, Yvonne, and Curt Madison. 1988. *Andrew Isaac.* Alaska Native Language Center, University of Alaska Fairbanks.

INDEX

bears, 22, 32, 204

beavers, 142, 147f, 203, 210, 228

Beck, Earl J., 170, 234, 239

beliefs of Dene: on animals, 13, 15–17, 204, 205; on class system, 99; compared with Christianity, 172, 196; about food, 23–25; about hunting, 22–23; integration with Christianity, 160; about potlatches, 130; on reciprocity with animals, 17–22; on weather, 209

Belle Isle, 144

berries: blue, 33; children learning about, 92; common patches of, 188; eaten with fat, 208; eaten with fish oil, 32; gathering, 38f, 42; picking in September, 46; storing for winter, 30; when to gather, 32

Betticher, Charles, 162, 163f, 168

Big Albert, 179f, 180f, 198f

Big Delta, 149f, 153, 169, 215

Big Frank, 139, 172–73, 198f

Big John, 145–46, 172–73

Big Mark, 239

Big Nose Village, 107

Billy Creek (Dendeyh Ndiig), 75, 151, 187, 219

Birch Creek, 176

Birch Lake, 59, 202

birch trees: bark, 42, 44f, 72, 73; juice of, 207; for paint, 210

birthing, 50, 85–86, 90

black scoters, 92

blankets, 112, 123f, 124, 133, 134, 139, 142f, 149f

boats: missionaries using, 162, 162f, 163f; for muskrat hunting, 151; trade, 149, 149f, 150, 154, 155

Bob, Jimmy, 227

boiling food, 30–31. *See also* food

bones, 30, 35, 55, 62–63, 205, 206

boss (xáxkeh (T) xakkee' (UT)), 97

Bouville, Daniel, 178, 179

Bowen, Robert J., 144–45

boys, 83, 85, 86

bridge, 167f, 168

broad whitefish, 67, 75

brothers-in-law, 81

burbot fish, 67, 70–71

Bureau of Biological Survey, 181

Bureau of Education, 182

Bureau of Indian Affairs, 161, 170, 182, 190

Bureau of Land Management, 190, 191

Burge, Moses, 182

buttons, 141

caches: of animals, 17–18, 52*n*8; fish, 32, 47, 51–52, 72, 73; images, 237f; meat, 26, 30, 33, 62, 65, 101, 204, 206, 222; for potlatches, 125, 132; for trade, 143, 160, 225

calico, 133, 137, 149

Callaway, Don, 32, 39–40

Camp Lake, 40, 41

canoes and canoeing, 46f, 93, 146, 151, 154, 179f, 209–210

canvas, 144

Capps, Stephen R., 178

Captain Northway, 153

caribou: changes in populations of, 45, 176; coming back in spring, 46; cooking of, 33, 35; Dene uses for, 205–206; as dry meat, 31f, 129; feet, 26, 34, 181; fence drawing, 206f; Fortymile herd population, 56–57; hunting, 57, 156, 181, 210; lookout station, 58f; mating and birthing rhythms of, 55–57; migration, 62; processing the bodies, 58; roles in hunting, 62; skins for drums, 121; skins for potlatch gifts, 123; story about baby, 23–25; trade of hides, 142; training babies and, 84. *See also* fences

"caribou people," 202, 211

Carmacks, George, 176

Carmacks, Kate, 176

Case, Martha, 239

Catsah, Chief, 144

ceremonies, greeting, 143. *See also* potlatches

Ch'aadh Che'et'aandiidz (main person for the Ch'âadz clan), 106

Cha Dan Esha (first person to obtain a gun), 142

Ch'aghadh Mĕnn' (Ducks Gather Lake), 229

changes to Dene life and culture: from airport construction, 185–86, 189; brought by fur trade, 157; from gold rush and highway, 173, 175, 176–81, 187, 197; to injih understanding, 130; in potlatches, 128, 131–32, 133–35; resisting from Christianity, 172. *See also* colonialism; colonization; white people

Charles, Albert, 198f

Charles, Doris, 44f, 134f

Charles, Minnie, 198f

Charles, Peter (Peter Charley), 75, 143, 164f, 165f, 214, 231f

Charlie, Dawson, 176

Charlie, Helen David, 83, 97, 100, 115

Charlie, Pete, 231f, 239

Charlie, Sam, 163f

Ch'echĕelyu clan, 225

Ch'eenaa Ndedh (Long Omen), 231–32

ch'elxĕ (T) (drum), 121

Chena, 160

Chena River, 162f

Ch' ichelyuh (clan), 79

Chicken, 177, 178, 180, 185

Chicken Creek, 145, 154, 186

Chidahleeh ("fish channeled into weir lake" [Tchawsahmon Lake]), 238

Chief Creek (Tthee Xaaddh'), 98f, 143

marrow, 7, 30, 35, 47, 205, 206, 208. *See also* bones; fat; food

marten furs, 142, 148

Martin, John, 147

matrilineal descent, 77, 80–81, 80*f*, 82*f*

Mayo, Alfred, 176

Mbehts'eh Těyy' (Flint Hill), 59, 61, 100, 223–24

McCarty, 148, 162

McClellan, Catharine, 85

McConnell (son of Big Albert), 179*f*

McConnell, David, 168

McDowell, C.B., 177

McIntosh, E. A., 108, 161, 166, 168, 170, 172, 185

McKennan, Robert: attending curing ceremonies, 170; excavations of, 227, 228; on Healy Lake potlatch, 127; on history of Chief Sam, 98, 99*f*; on Joseph Village, 222; letter from Newton to, 147; at Lower Nabesna, 239; on Northern pike fishing, 71; Paul Kirsteatter's letters to, 106, 201–203; on trade, 141

McQuesten, Jack, 153, 176

measles, 186. *See also* illness

meat, drying, 42, 47*f*

meat caches, 30, 33

medicine, 23, 134, 169, 208

medicine men and women, 169, 206, 212, 213, 232

memorial potlatches, 111, 112, 115, 124, 132, 137*f*, 139. *See also* death; potlatches

men: dancing, 120, 136, 137*f*; keeping away from menstrating women, 90–91; rich men, 97–107; serving food at potlatches, 115; tasks of while traveling, 37; training for, 85–86

Mendaes Dzele' (Mentasta Mountain), 220

menstruation, 20–21, 84, 85, 90–91, 130

Mentasta, 102*f*, 106

Mentasta caribou herd, 55

Mentasta Lake, 160

Mercier, Francois, 144

Mesiin Tsiits'iig, 219, 227

Metcalf, Hamilton, and Kansas City Bridge Company, 185, 186

mice, 17–18

Midway Lake, 77, 146, 153

military presence, 185

Miller-Friend, Connie, 32, 39–40

mind, power of, 21

mining camps, 108, 176, 177, 179–81, 186

mink furs, 148

missionaries: Celia Wright and Margaret Graves as, 163*f*; concerned about other settler influences, 108–109; fascinated by potlatch, 172; first encounters with, 159; goal to undermine potlatch, 172–73; goal to undermine shamans, 169; Mable Pick and Margaret Graves as, 166*f*; Reverend Vincent

Sims, 159*f*; traveling by boat, 162*f*, 163*f*. *See also* Episcopal Church

Mission Creek, 176

missions, 159–71. *See also* St. Timothy's Mission

Mitchell, William, 59–61, 226

mittens, 113

moieties, 77–81, 78*f*, 95. *See also* clans; matrilineal descent

money, 23, 86–87, 113, 175, 187, 193

Moore, H.F., 179

moose: cooking, 32; decline of around mining camps, 176; eating feet of, 26–27; hides of, 63–64; hunting, 22, 41, 64–65, 156, 181; hunting for potlatch, 115; injih in hunting, 21; introduction to importance of, 55; populations of, 63; skin for drums, 121; skin making hood, 83; skinning and preparing, 33–34, 45; tracking, 94; trade of hides, 142; uses for stomach of, 31–32, 33, 34; which parts to eat when, 25

Moose Creek, 68*f*, 70

Moosehide, 122

Moses, Annie, 72*f*, 164*f*

Mosquito Flats, 59, 225

Mosquito Fork, 57, 58, 69, 74, 224

Mount Fairplay, 59

mourning process, 112, 120, 124, 127. *See also* funerals; grief

Mt. Sanford, 219

murder, 106, 211

Murie, Olaus, 57, 59, 61, 63–64, 181

Museum of the North at University of Alaska in Fairbanks, 228

mushrooms, 42

"muskrat people," 202, 211

muskrats: candy, 52, 156; furs of, 150–51; hunting, 42, 210; respect for, 17–18; trapping for, 183, 188–89

Naadęęy Xú (marmot tooth), 219, 220, 231

Nabesna: Chief Sam at, 99*f*; drying meat at, 47*f*; fish camp at, 72*f*; goods cached at, 147; as Northway, 150; residents of, 160*f*; stores at, 238–39. *See also* Northway

Nabesna, Lower, 238–41

Nabesna band, 47

Nabesna River, 47, 70, 75, 147

Nahk' ät (Fishing Place) (Last Tetlin), 232–33

Naltsiin clan, 61, 78, 134, 220, 225

Natełde ("Roasted Salmon Place") / Batzulnetas, 81, 82, 214*n*1

Na'thee dek, 107, 232

Native businesses, 192

Native land claims, 109*f*, 190–92

Naxey Xú ("marmot teeth" or "thunder teeth"), 219

Nelchina caribou herd, 4, 55. *See also* caribou

Nelson Chief, E.W., 181

potlatches: Ahtna lined up for, 114*f*; article about, 136–38; blankets at, 149*f*; childrens' behavior at, 89; distribution of gifts at, 123–25; elements, 111–13; establishing prestige through hosting, 98; expected after moose hunt, 63, 86; feasting at, 115–17; Frederic Drane's account of, 139; Gaither Paul's memories of, 132–33; in honor of dogs, 209; Jerry Isaac's memories of, 135–38; Jessie David's memories of, 133–35; last in Ketchumstuk, 227; Margaret Kirsteatter's memories of, 127–28; Martha Isaac's memories of, 131–32; missionaries set on abolishing, 163, 168*f*, 172–73; Oscar Isaac's memories of, 128–31; "potlatch men," 99; refusing to give up, 196; reservations offering control over, 183; restrictions of, 125–27, 134–35; singing and dancing at, 118–23; speeches at, 104, 115; trade influence on, 157; words to sing after, 23

power, 13, 22–23, 105, 169, 213

prestige, 104

Prevost, Jules, 159, 172

prices in fur trade, 142, 150, 151, 154, 157

prices of goods in potlatches, 173, 183

Prince William Sound, 141

puberty, 83–85, 86, 90, 125

Public Land Order 4582, 191

punishment, 106

rabbits, 21, 31, 205

racism, 190

rafts, wooden, 164*f*

raids, 211–12

Rainey, Froelich, 227–28, 232–33, 234, 239

Raven, 13–15

raven clan, 77

receiving lines, 114*f*

reciprocation, 125

red fox furs, 142, 148

regalia, 101*f*. *See also* clothing

relations and friends, 81–83, 86, 87–88, 102, 103, 131, 173

religious beliefs of Dene. *See* beliefs of Dene

reservations, 183–85, 187, 190

respect: based on lineage, 105; blankets as symbols of, 124, 134*f*, 196; for Elders, 45, 84, 109; sharing as a sign of, 7; showing for animals, 15, 17–18, 20, 21, 195, 208

restrictions on potlatches, 125

Retano, Roger, 118*f*

Rice, John, 231

Richardson Highway, 148, 169

rich men: characteristics of, 97–98; Chief Sam as, 99*f*; clothing of, 100; introduction, 97; old-time, 97–107; organizing trading expeditions, 100; as work organizers, 99

rifles, 124, 142, 149, 151, 154

road development, 177

roadhouses, 149, 150

roasting meat, 30

Robertson River, 143

roles within communities, 99

Roman Catholic church, 239

roots, 26, 32

rose hips, 33

round whitefish, 67, 74, 227

Rowe, Peter Trimble, 159–61

Russia, 142

Russian American Company, 141

Russians, 213, 214

Saagés cheeg (Sun Fork Mouth) (Ketchumstuk), 219, 224–27, 224*f*. *See also* Ketchumstuk

Salcha, 104*f*

Salchaket, 105, 160

salmon, 67

Salt Creek, 142

Sam, Agnes, 39

Sam, Annie, 119*f*, 240*f*

Sam, Avis, 26, 47–54, 77

Sam, Belle, 222*f*, 225*f*

Sam, Chief, 83, 98, 99*f*, 147, 239, 239*f*

Sam, Frank: with fish weir, 68*f*; fish weir of, 70*f*; loaning a tent, 129; married to Annie, 240*f*; potlatch song of, 121; son of Chief Sam, 83

Sam, John, 163*f*

Sam, Martha, 241*f*

Sam, Roy, 26, 77, 79

Sam Creek, 41

Sam Lake, 106, 219

"Sampson Landing," 147

Sand Creek, 143, 215

Sand Lake, 41, 106, 107

Sanford, A., 119*f*

Sanford, Huston, 118*f*, 120*f*

Sanford, Laura: arranging gifts, 121*f*; on catching Northern pike, 71; on fermented fish, 73; house in Tanacross, 131; at Tanacross potlatch, 120*f*; at Tetlin potlatch, 118*f*

Saylor, Lee, 107, 223

scarves: as gifts at potlatches, 113

school: Dene wanting children in, 170, 234; Isabel John recounting going to, 42; in Lower Nabesna, 239; started by missionaries, 161, 163–64, 166, 168

Schwatka, Ada, 176

Schwatka, Frederic, 144

Scottie Creek: Bessie John from, 142, 154; changes to, 187; descendants of people from, 237; descendents of people from, 102; fishing in, 67; Mary Tyone from, 83; territory, 217*f*; trading at, 147, 155, 156

twenty-first century life structures, 95
Tyone, Mary, 67–69, 83, 237–38
Tzi Tzi bird, 70–71

Udall, Stewart, 191
udzih. *See* caribou
Uljaadh Mĕnn' (Pike Lake), 229
uncles, 82–83
United States, 175, 177
University of Alaska Fairbanks, 135, 187, 228, 243
Upper Tanana Indians, The (McKennan), 98, 141–42
US Board of Indian Commissioners, 159
US marshals, 108
US Post Office, 150–51

Valdez, 144, 160, 176
Valdez-Eagle telegraph line, 226
Valdez-Eagle Trail, 186
village councils, 169
Vocational and Educational Reserves Act, 234
von Wrangell, Ferdinand, 141

Wade, Jack, 108
Wallen, Rika, 150
Walter, Bessie, 30, 44f
Walter, Jimmy, 231f
Walters, Jimmie, 75
wampum, 97, 100
warfare, 210–14
warmth: strategies for, 48, 50–51
Washington–Alaska Military Cable and Telegraph System (WAMCATS), 160
waste, avoiding, 13, 26, 30, 34, 62–63, 89, 163, 181
water, 49, 84, 189
wealth, 97–98, 100, 123, 125, 145, 196
wealth song, 120
weapons, 107, 211
weather, 209
weirs, fishing, 46, 68–69, 68f, 70f, 71f, 74f, 232f, 237. *See also* fish and fishing
Wells, E. H., 106, 225, 231
Wells, E. Hazard, 59
Western Fur and Trading Company, 144
Wheeler-Howard Act, 183
whiskey, 171
whitefish, 67–70, 72f
"white man way," 173
white people: concept of civilization of, 175; contact with, 8–9, 108–109; Dene youth living like, 8, 86, 88, 91, 187; lifestyle of, 193–94; negative influence of, 160, 161; overhunting of, 177, 182, 189. *See also* changes to Dene life and culture; colonialism; colonization

White River, 141
Whitham, Carl, 183
Whymper, Frederick, 142–43
Wien, Noel, 185
willows, 58, 70, 92
Wilson, Lavell, 190, 197
winter: eating fermented fish, 51–53, 66, 67–70; famine in, 26, 89, 212, 229; food in, 28, 29–30, 41, 42, 46–47, 53, 204; moose in, 64; preventing frostbite in, 205; stories told in, 15; trade in, 142, 148; traveling, 37–39, 48, 50; villages in, 211, 218, 220, 221, 231, 241, 249
wives, multiple, 97, 98
wolverines, 22, 206
wolves, 22, 23, 42, 150, 206
women: activities of throughout seasons, 26, 27, 35, 37, 40, 42–45, 46–47, 145; changes in young, 86–87; fish processing of, 72; gathering food, 52–53; meeting bears, 204; not on trade trips, 142; preparing food for potlatches, 115; tasks of while traveling, 37; warfare and, 211; wearing lynx furs, 206; work on snowshoes, 210; young not attending potlatches, 125, 130
wood, chopping, 153, 157
work: on airfield, 185, 186; building a mission house, 168; for Herman Kessler, 155, 156; rich men as organizers of, 99–100; for wages, 157, 186, 187, 197
worldviews. *See* beliefs of Dene; injih
World War II, 1939-1945, 185–90, 197
Wrangell, Ferdinand von. *See* von Wrangell, Ferdinand
wrestling, 143
Wright, Arthur, 162, 166, 168f, 168–69, 170, 172
Wright, Celia, 162, 163f, 167f, 168
Wright, Myrtle, 168, 169, 170
Wudzih Naa Ddhel', 219

Xaaguu, 237
Xaal Niign ("least cisco river"), 234
xáxkeh (T) ("rich man"), 97
xtíitl (T) (potlatch), 111

Yamaagh Teeshyay (UT) / Yamaagh Telch'eegh (T), 13–17
Yamaagn Teeshyay, 15
Yarber, Yvonne, 237
"yellow grass people," 202
youth, 83–86
Yukon River: American traders on, 141, 144; caribou herds near, 55; first missionary encounters trading on, 159; Fort Reliance on, 232; gold on, 145; mineral exploration on, 144; rifles from, 142; Tanacross people on, 107f